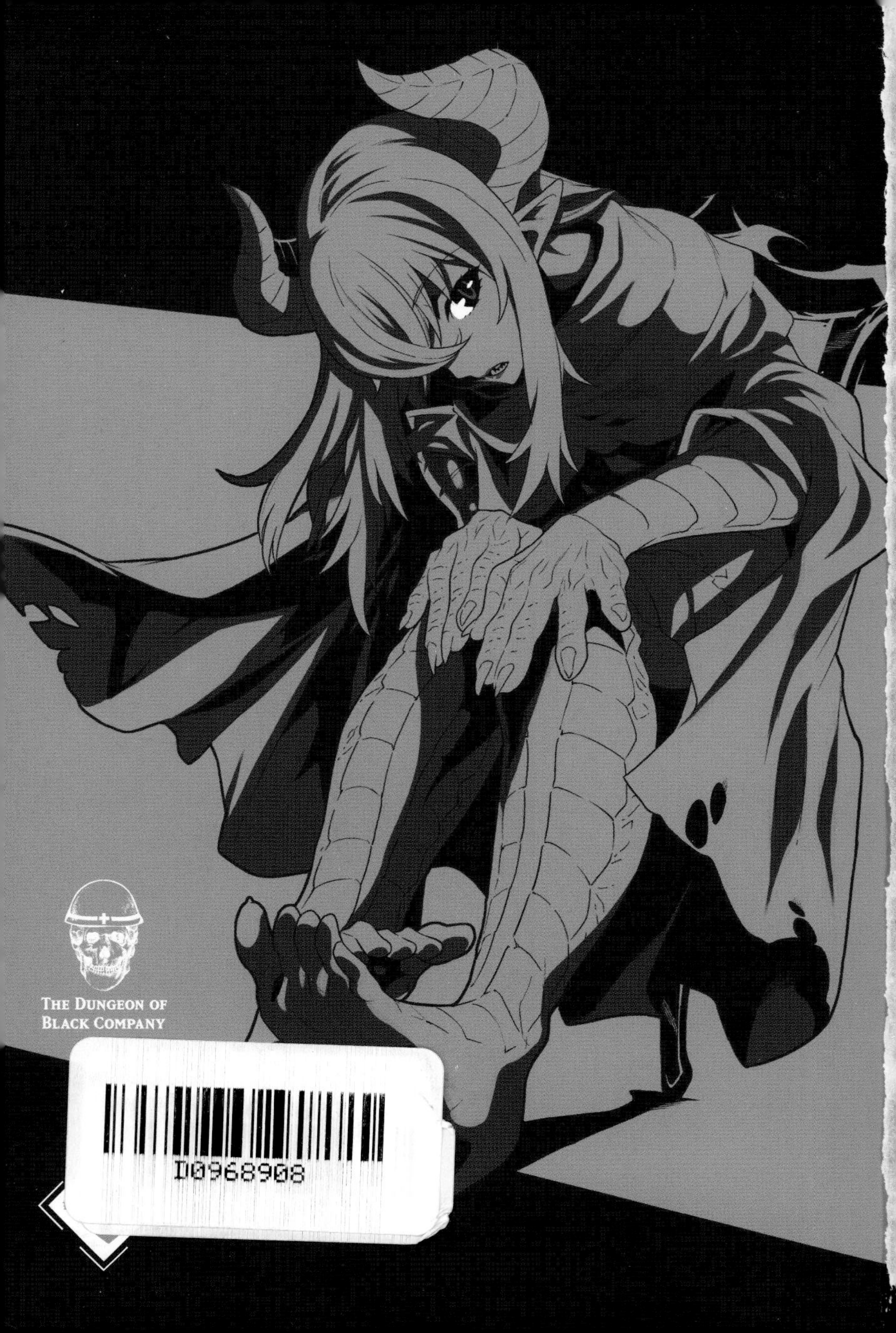
THE DUNGEON OF
BLACK COMPANY

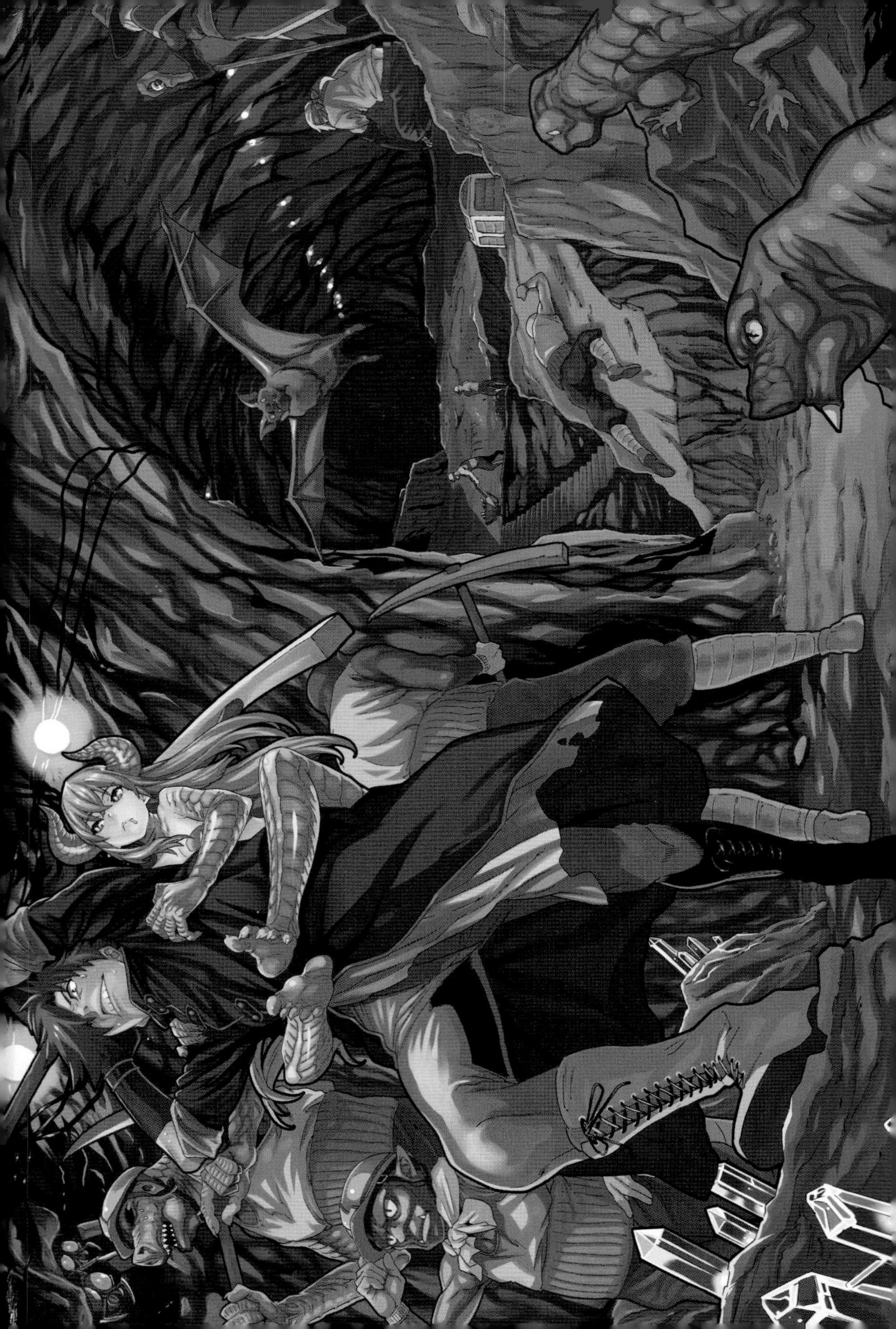

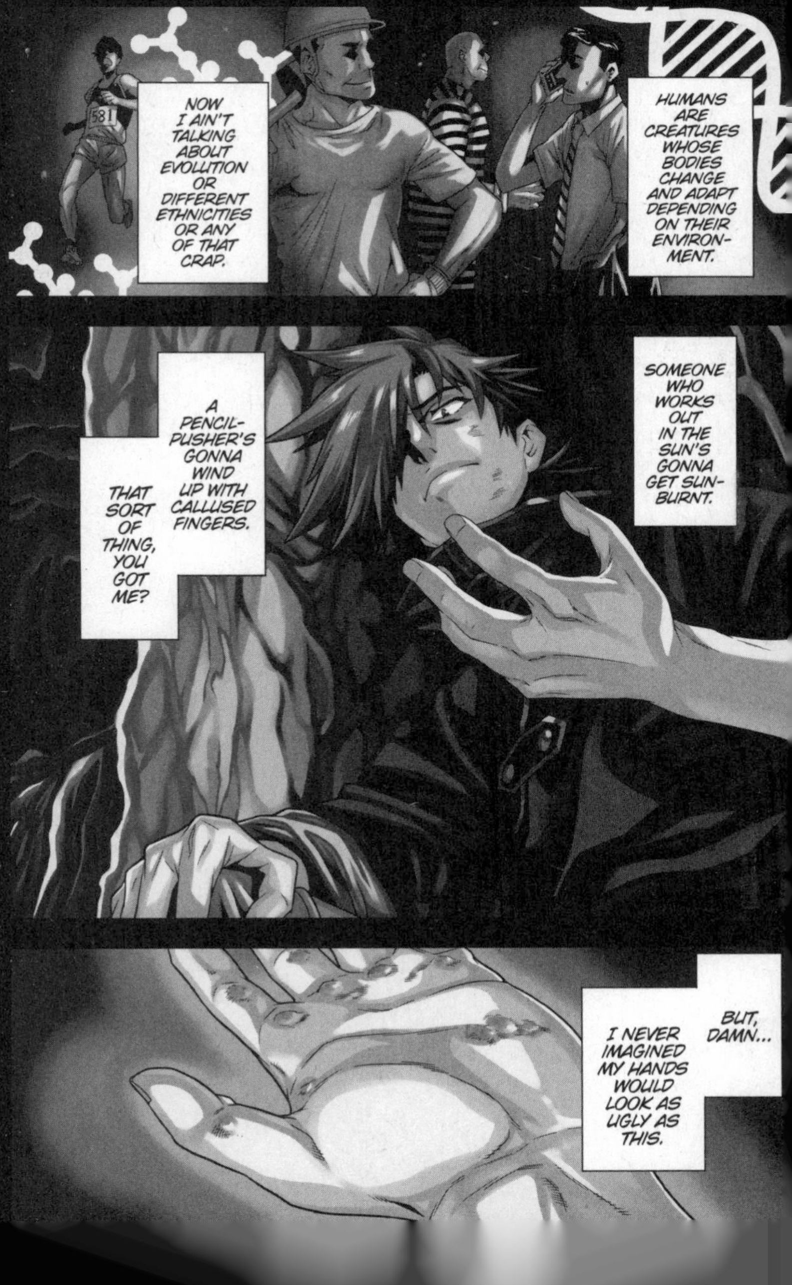
HUMANS ARE CREATURES WHOSE BODIES CHANGE AND ADAPT DEPENDING ON THEIR ENVIRON-MENT.
NOW I AIN'T TALKING ABOUT EVOLUTION OR DIFFERENT ETHNICITIES OR ANY OF THAT CRAP.
581
SOMEONE WHO WORKS OUT IN THE SUN'S GONNA GET SUN-BURNT.
A PENCIL-PUSHER'S GONNA WIND UP WITH CALLUSED FINGERS.
THAT SORT OF THING, YOU GOT ME?
BUT, DAMN...
I NEVER IMAGINED MY HANDS WOULD LOOK AS UGLY AS THIS.

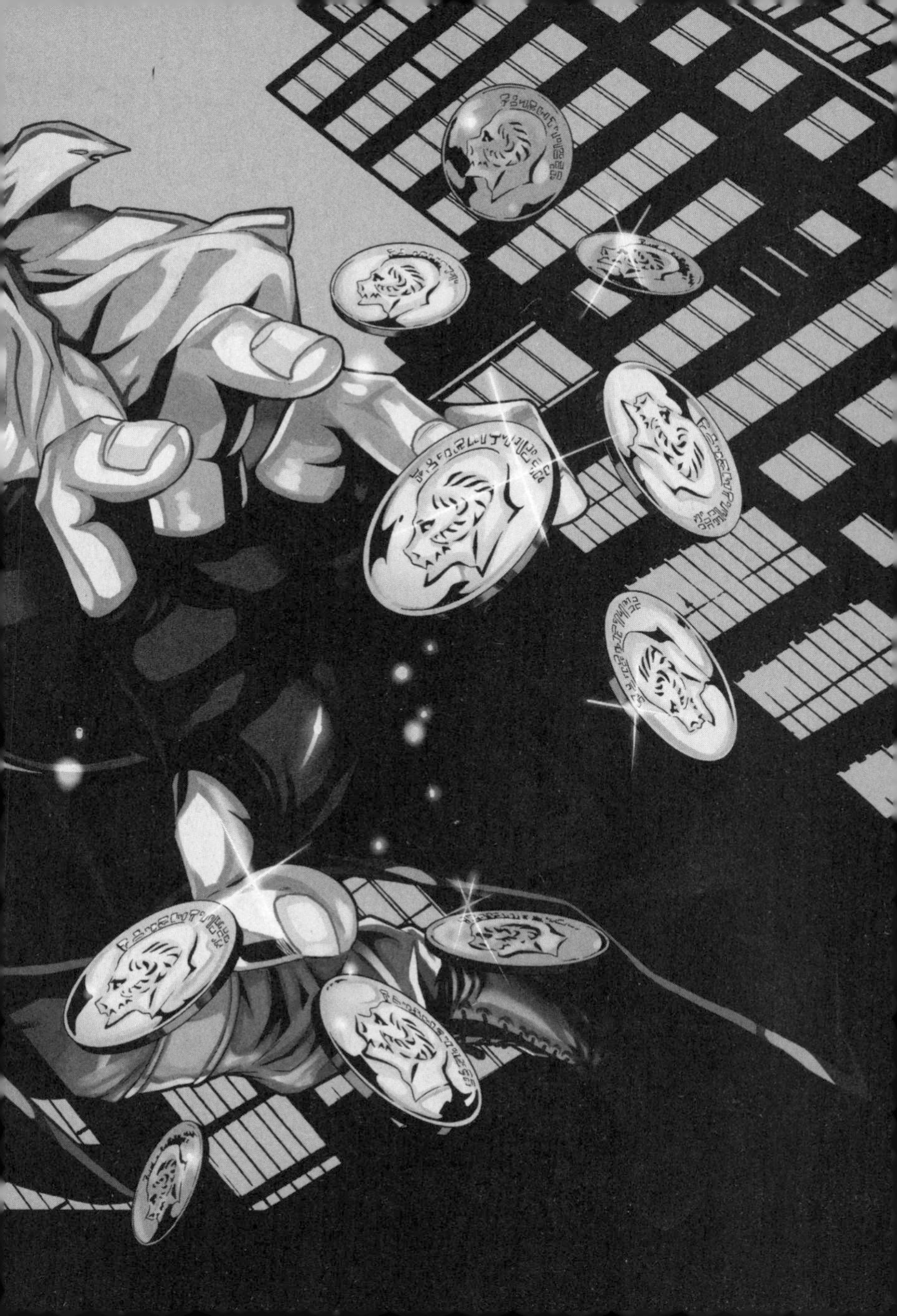

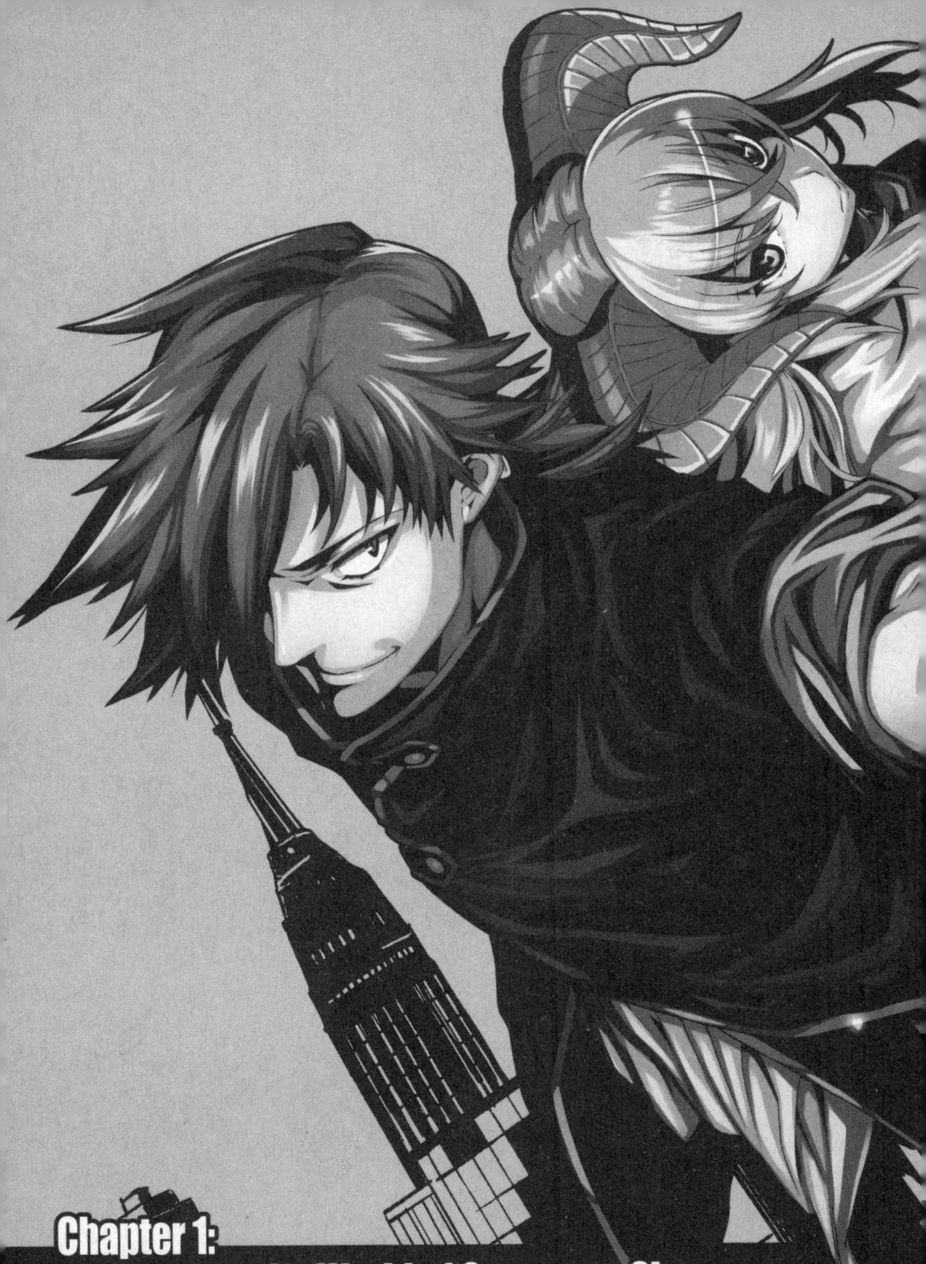

Chapter 1: Welcome to the World of Corporate Slavery

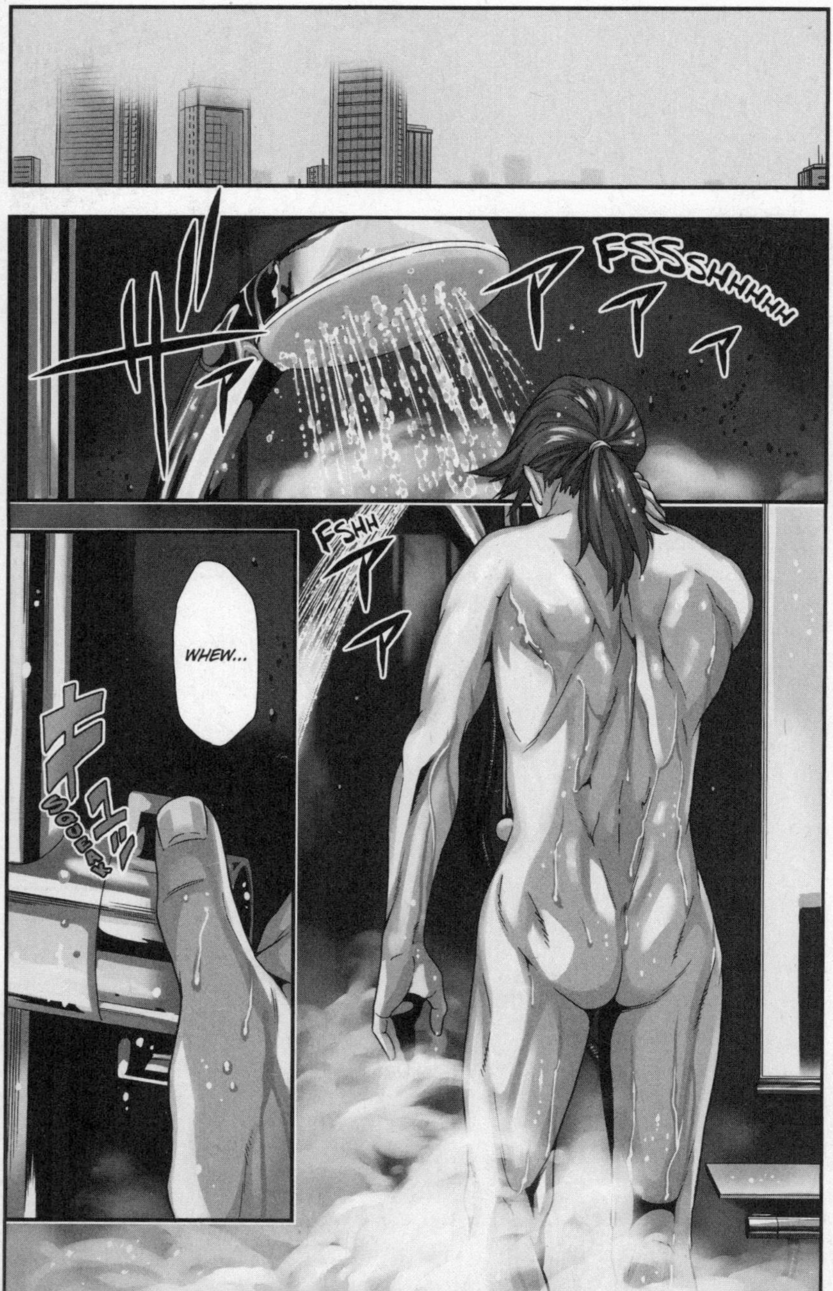
FSSSHHHHHH
FSHH
WHEW...
SQUEAK

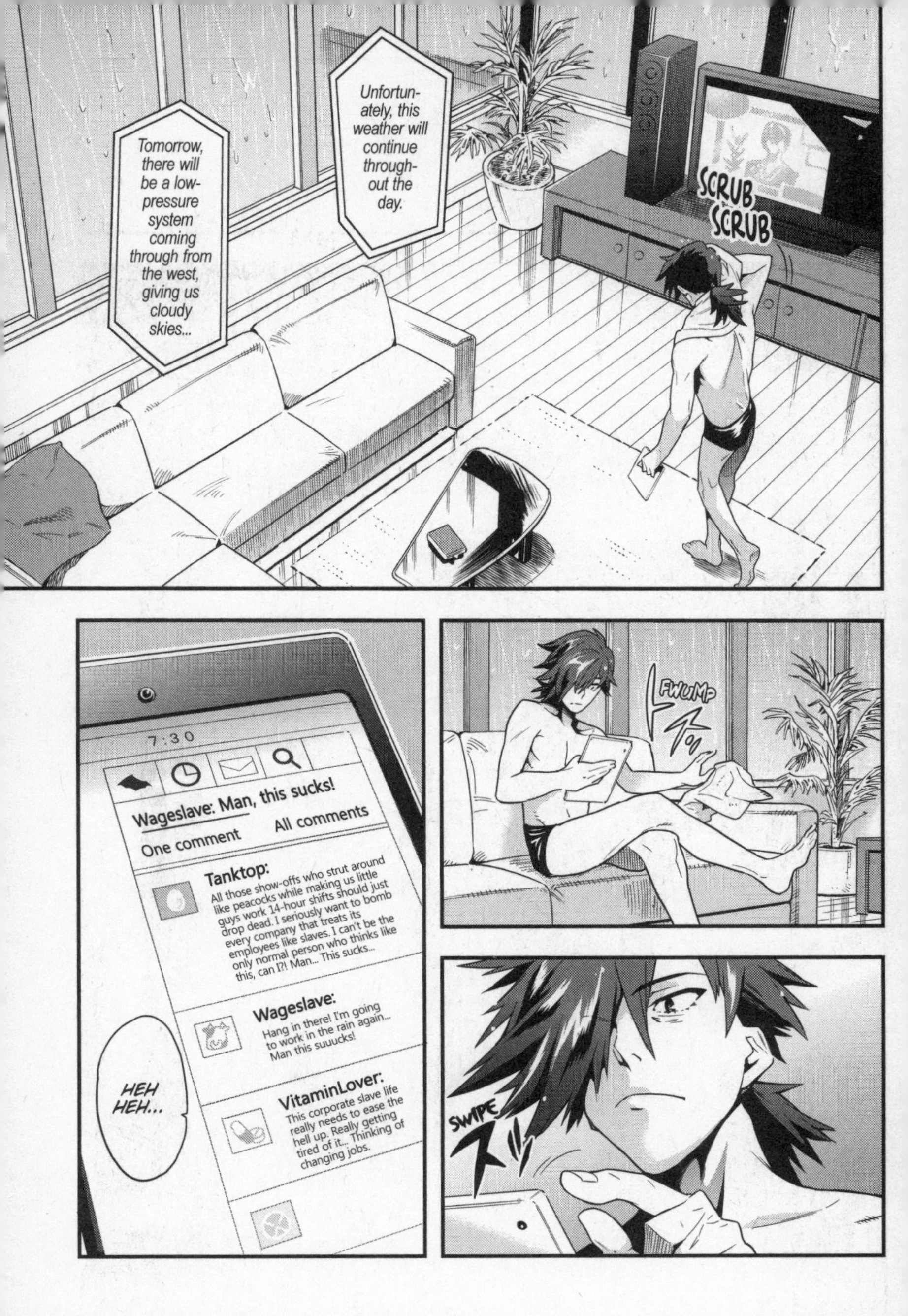
SCRUB SCRUB
Unfortunately, this weather will continue throughout the day.
Tomorrow, there will be a low-pressure system coming through from the west, giving us cloudy skies...
FWUMP
SWIPE
7:30
Wageslave: Man, this sucks!
One comment
All comments
Tanktop:
All those show-offs who strut around like peacocks while making us little guys work 14-hour shifts should just drop dead. I seriously want to bomb every company that treats its employees like slaves. I can't be the only normal person who thinks like this, can I?! Man... This sucks...
Wageslave:
Hang in there! I'm going to work in the rain again... Man this suuucks!
VitaminLover:
This corporate slave life really needs to ease the hell up. Really getting tired of it... Thinking of changing jobs.
HEH HEH...

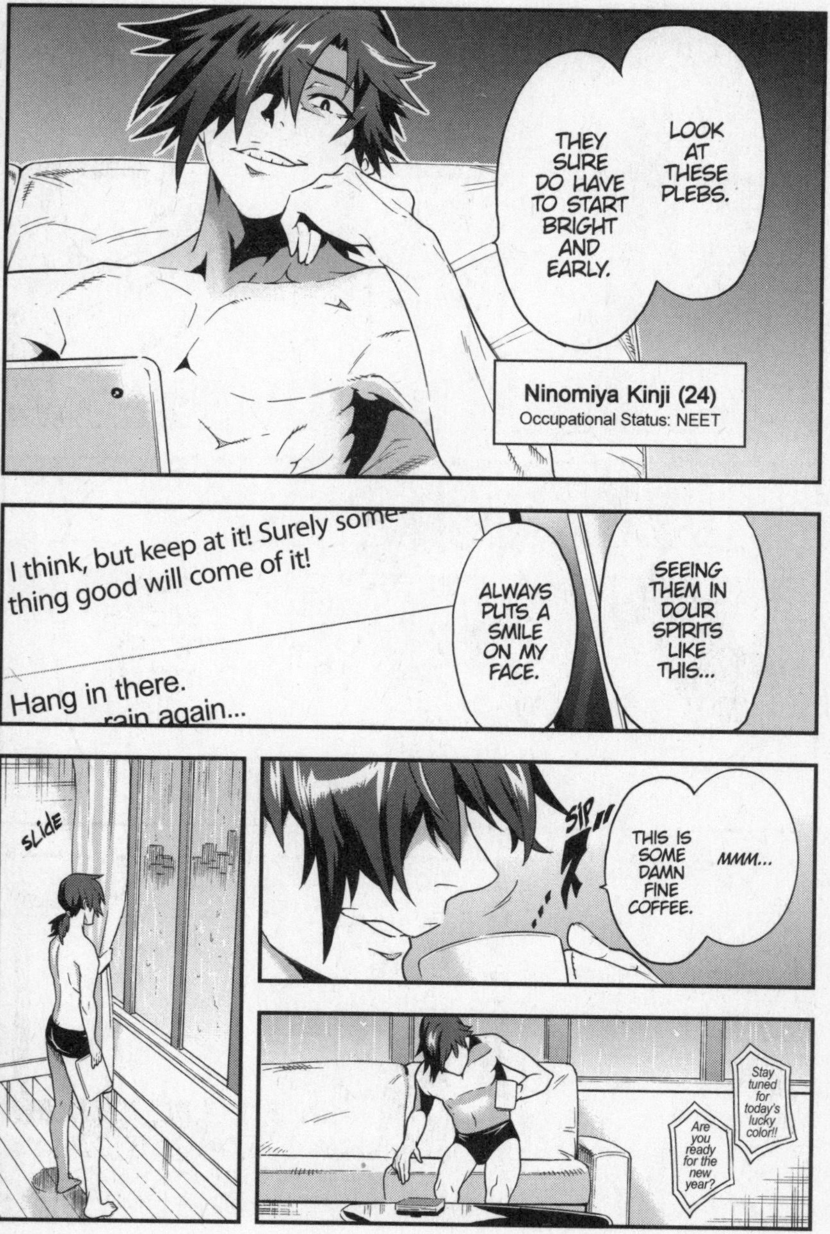
LOOK AT THESE PLEBS.
THEY SURE DO HAVE TO START BRIGHT AND EARLY.
Ninomiya Kinji (24)
Occupational Status: NEET
SEEING THEM IN DOUR SPIRITS LIKE THIS...
ALWAYS PUTS A SMILE ON MY FACE.
I think, but keep at it! Surely some-thing good will come of it!
Hang in there.
rain again...
MMM...
THIS IS SOME DAMN FINE COFFEE.
SIP
SLIDE
Stay tuned for today's lucky color!!
Are you ready for the new year?

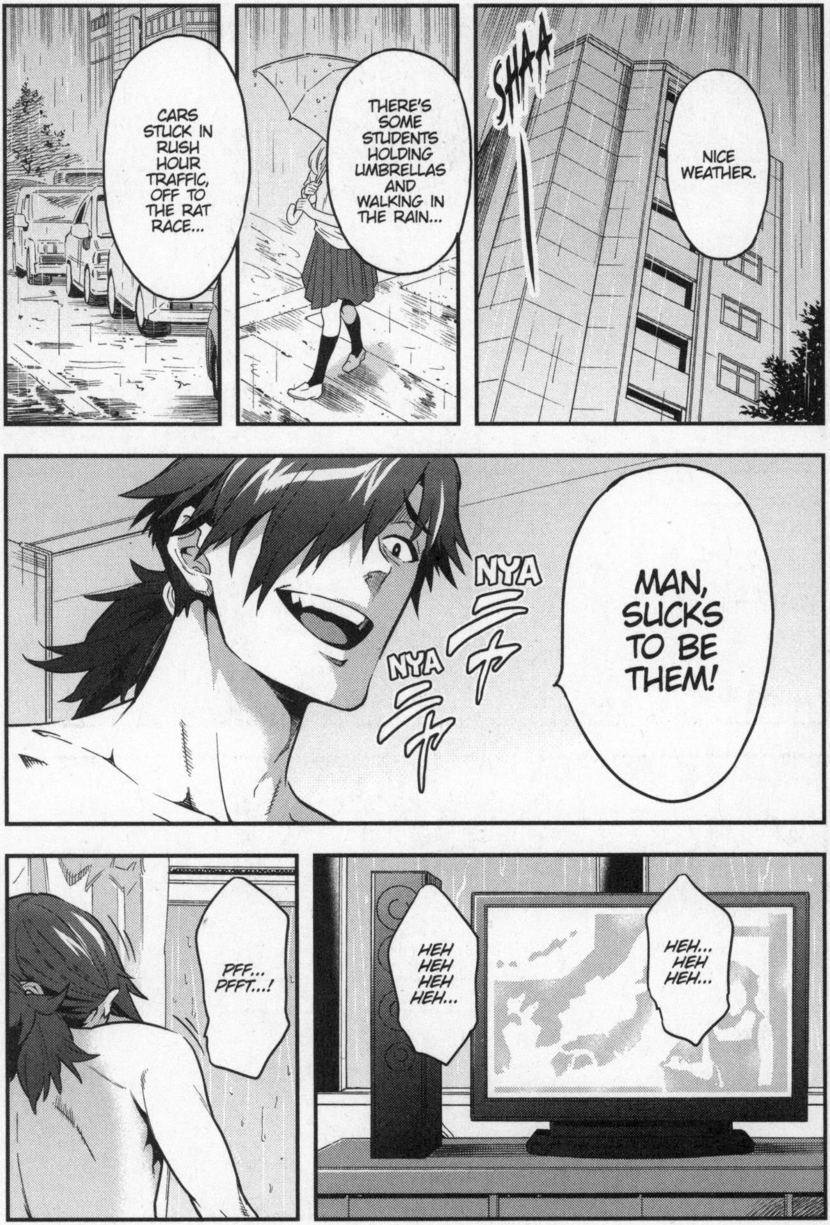
SHAA
NICE WEATHER.
THERE'S SOME STUDENTS HOLDING UMBRELLAS AND WALKING IN THE RAIN...
CARS STUCK IN RUSH HOUR TRAFFIC, OFF TO THE RAT RACE...
MAN, SUCKS TO BE THEM!
NYA
NYA
HEH... HEH HEH...
HEH HEH HEH HEH...
PFF... PFFT...!

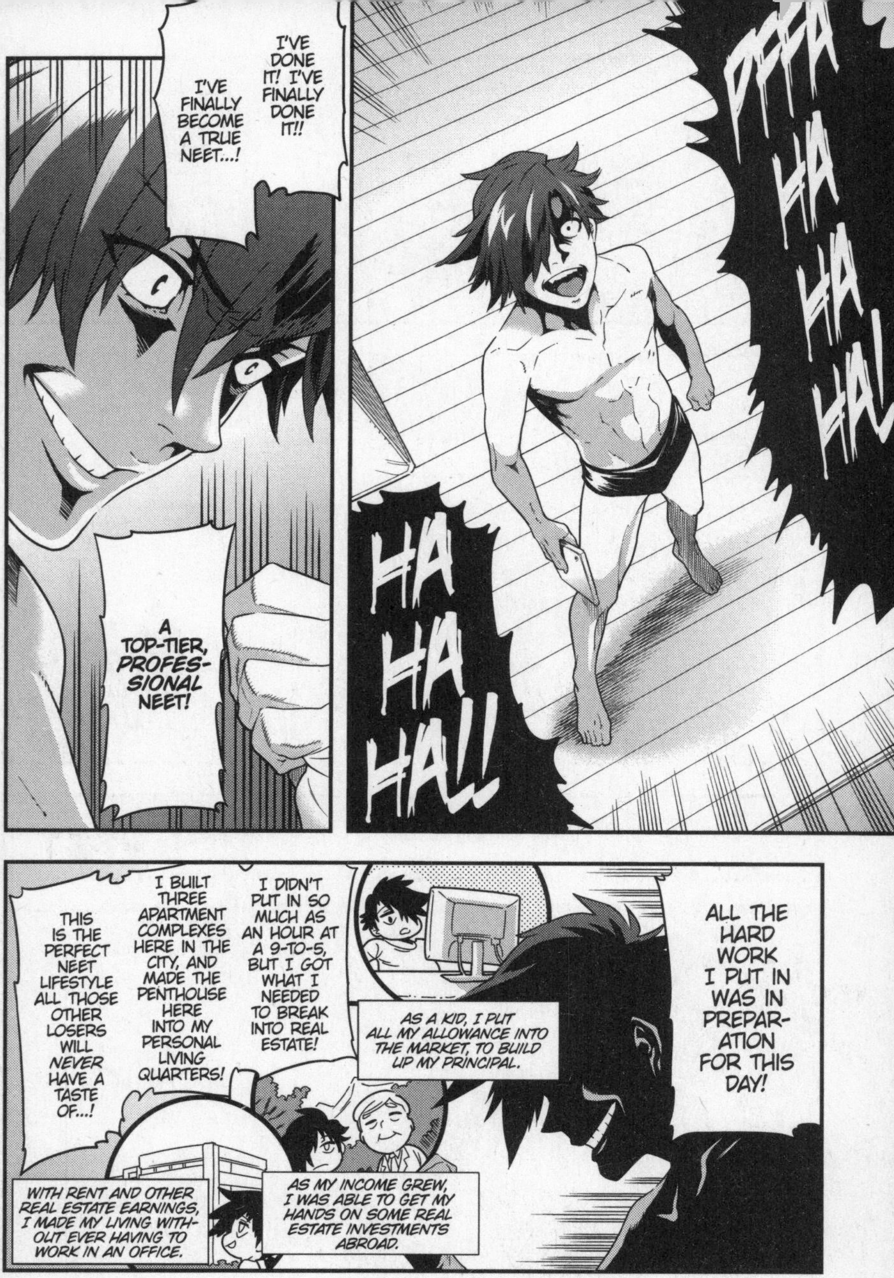
PFFA HA HA HA HA!
HA HA HA!!
I'VE DONE IT! I'VE FINALLY DONE IT!!
I'VE FINALLY BECOME A TRUE NEET...!
A TOP-TIER, *PROFESSIONAL* NEET!
ALL THE HARD WORK I PUT IN WAS IN PREPARATION FOR THIS DAY!
AS A KID, I PUT ALL MY ALLOWANCE INTO THE MARKET, TO BUILD UP MY PRINCIPAL.
I DIDN'T PUT IN SO MUCH AS AN HOUR AT A 9-TO-5, BUT I GOT WHAT I NEEDED TO BREAK INTO REAL ESTATE!
I BUILT THREE APARTMENT COMPLEXES HERE IN THE CITY, AND MADE THE PENTHOUSE HERE INTO MY PERSONAL LIVING QUARTERS!
THIS IS THE PERFECT NEET LIFESTYLE ALL THOSE OTHER LOSERS WILL *NEVER* HAVE A TASTE OF...!
AS MY INCOME GREW, I WAS ABLE TO GET MY HANDS ON SOME REAL ESTATE INVESTMENTS ABROAD.
WITH RENT AND OTHER REAL ESTATE EARNINGS, I MADE MY LIVING WITHOUT EVER HAVING TO WORK IN AN OFFICE.

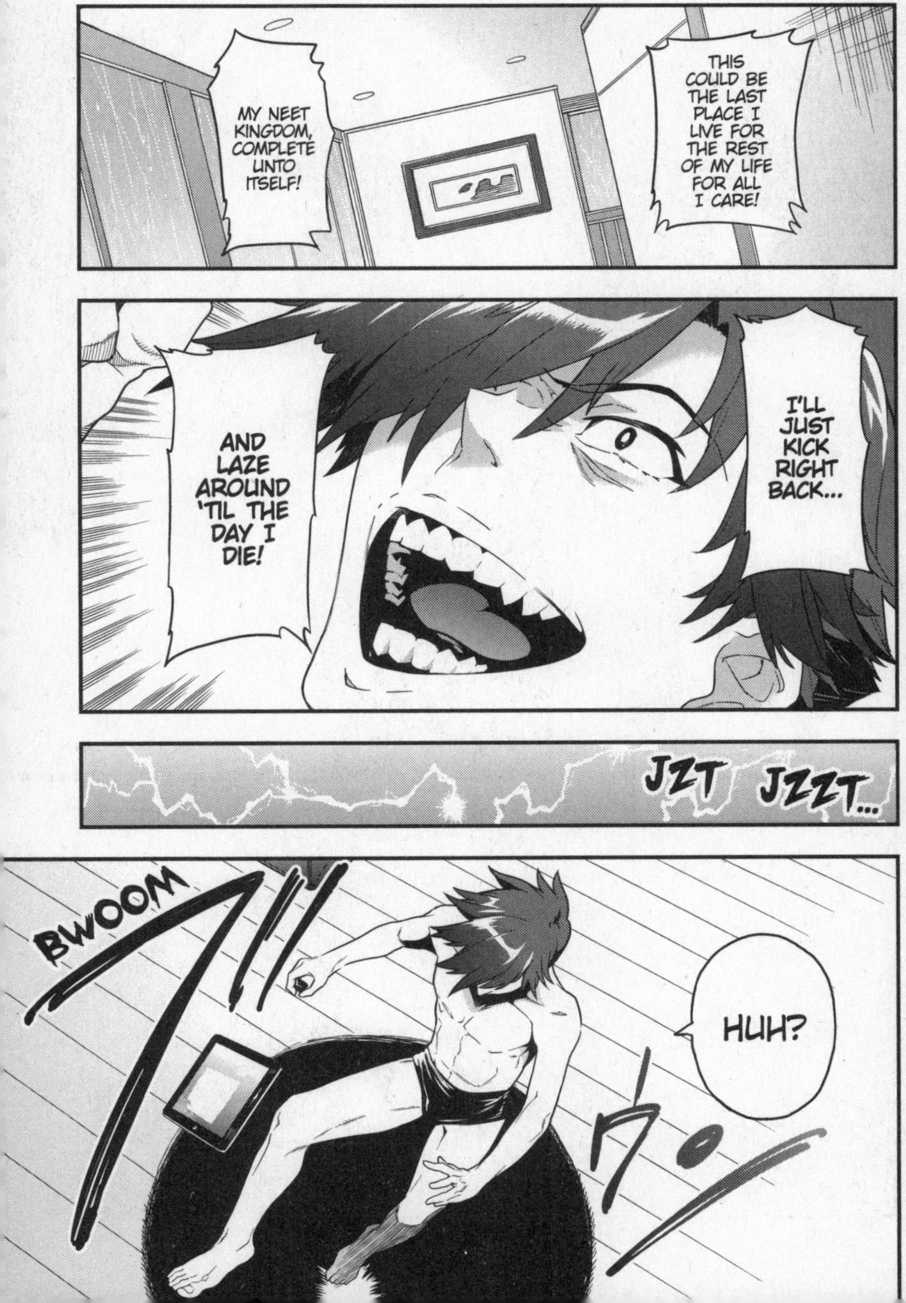
THIS COULD BE THE LAST PLACE I LIVE FOR THE REST OF MY LIFE FOR ALL I CARE!
MY NEET KINGDOM, COMPLETE UNTO ITSELF!
I'LL JUST KICK RIGHT BACK...
AND LAZE AROUND 'TIL THE DAY I DIE!
JZT JZZZT...
HUH?
BWOOM

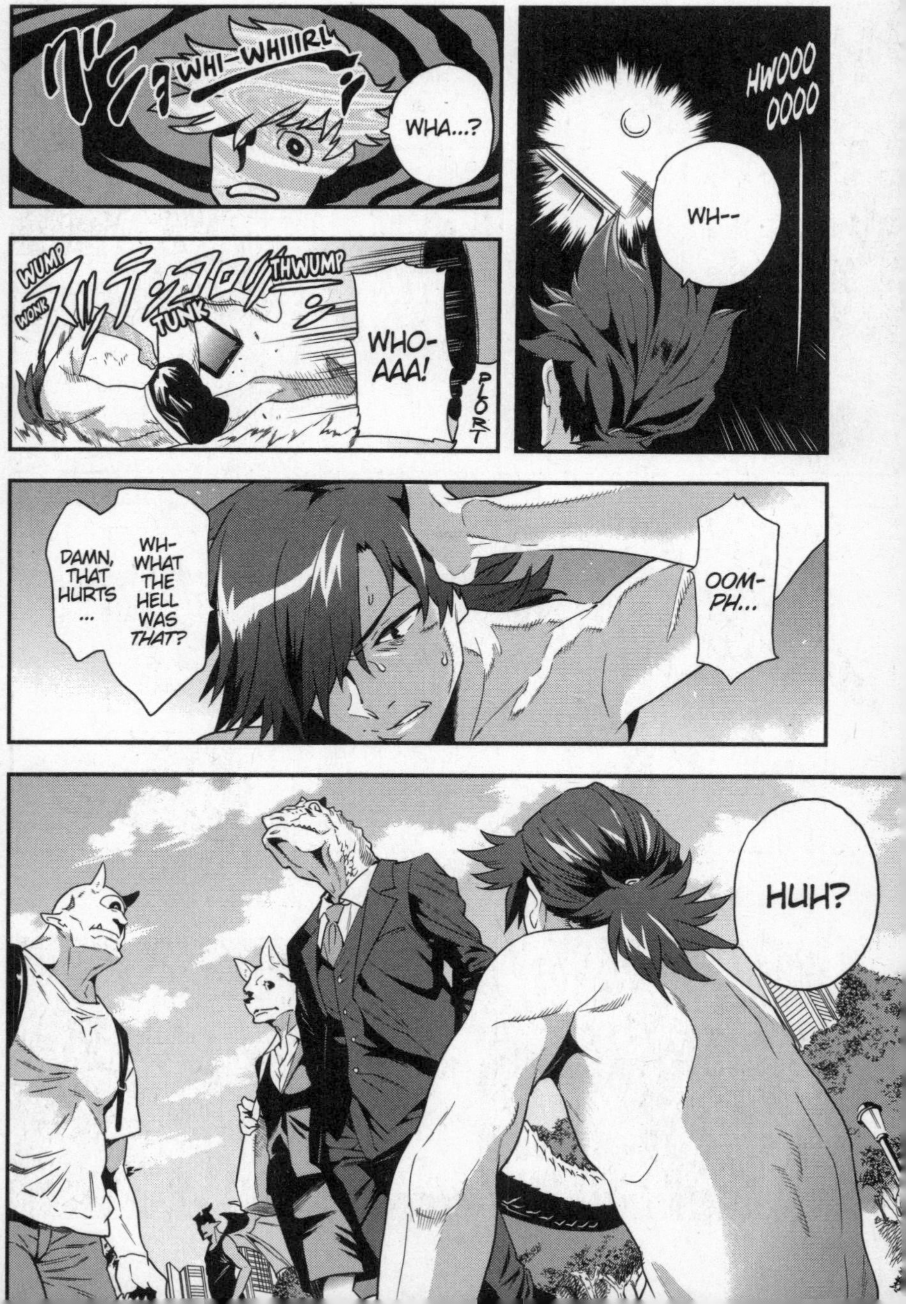
HWOOO OOOO
WH--
WHI-WHIIIRL
WHA...?
WHO-AAA!
PLORT
THWUMP
TUNK
WUMP
WONK
OOMPH...
WH-WHAT THE HELL WAS THAT?
DAMN, THAT HURTS...
HUH?

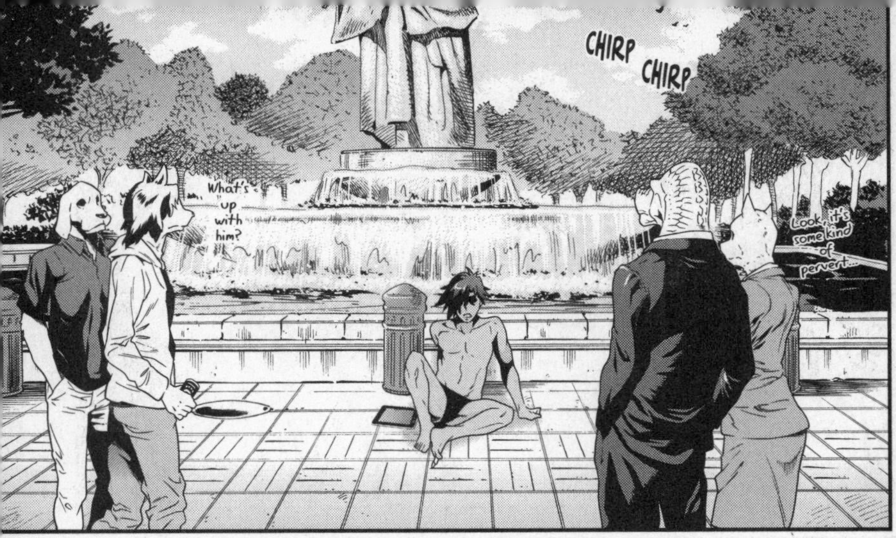
CHIRP CHIRP
Look, it's some kind of pervert...
What's up with him?
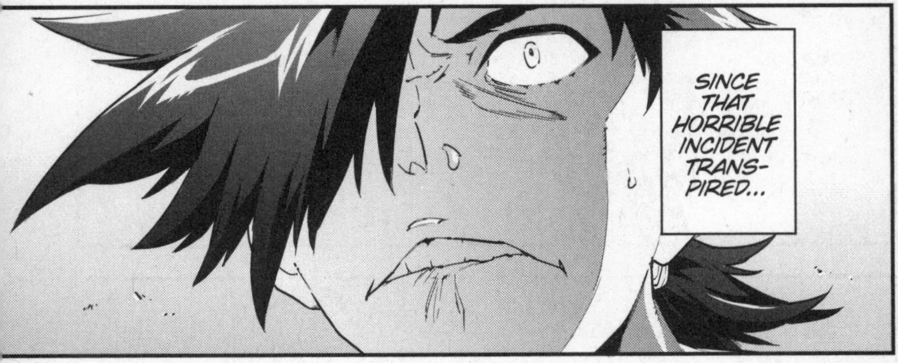
SINCE THAT HORRIBLE INCIDENT TRANSPIRED...
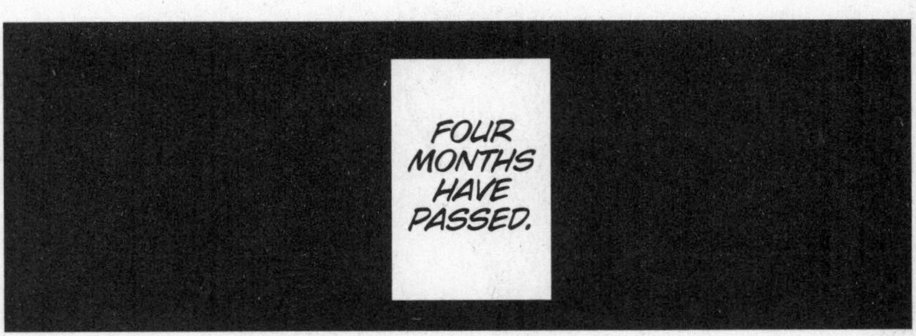
FOUR MONTHS HAVE PASSED.

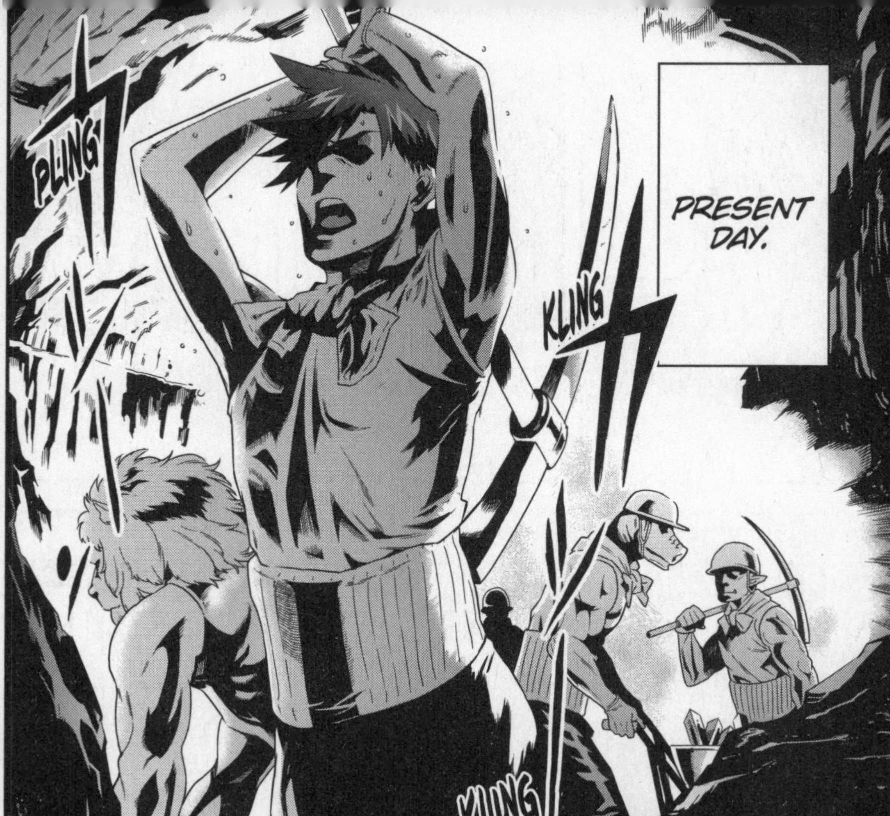
PRESENT DAY.
KLING
KLING
PLING

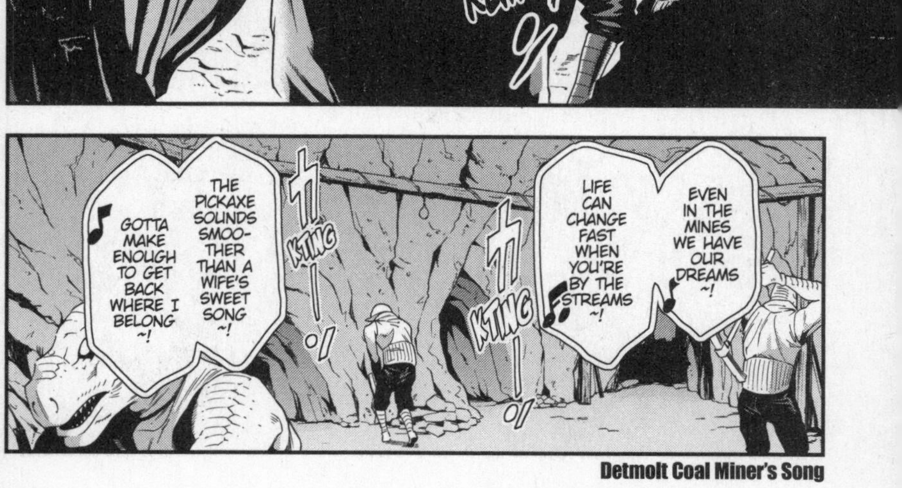
EVEN IN THE MINES WE HAVE OUR DREAMS ~!
LIFE CAN CHANGE FAST WHEN YOU'RE BY THE STREAMS ~!
KTING
KTING
THE PICKAXE SOUNDS SMOO-THER THAN A WIFE'S SWEET SONG ~!
GOTTA MAKE ENOUGH TO GET BACK WHERE I BELONG ~!

Detmolt Coal Miner's Song

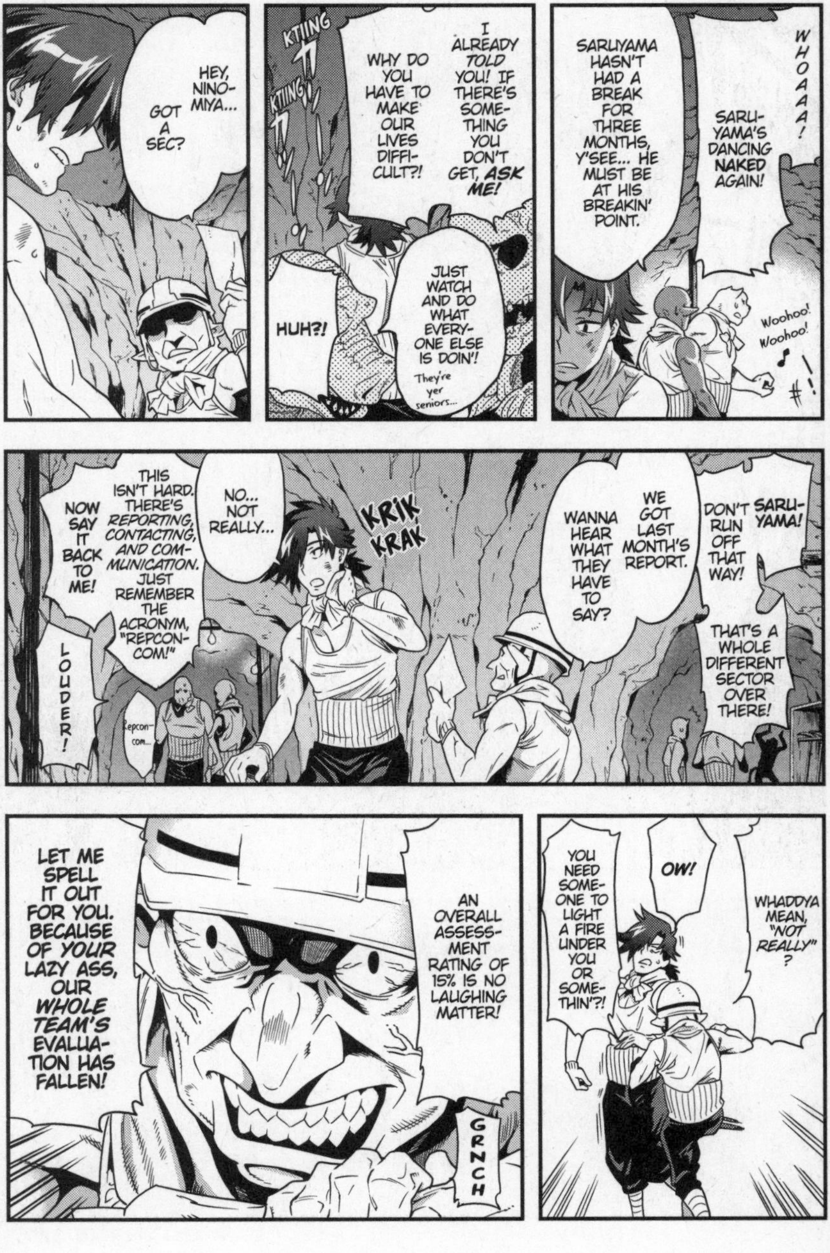
WHOAAAA!
SARUYAMA'S DANCING NAKED AGAIN!
SARUYAMA HASN'T HAD A BREAK FOR THREE MONTHS, Y'SEE... HE MUST BE AT HIS BREAKIN' POINT.
Woohoo! Woohoo!
I ALREADY TOLD YOU! IF THERE'S SOMETHING YOU DON'T GET, ASK ME!
WHY DO YOU HAVE TO MAKE OUR LIVES DIFFICULT?!
KTIING
KTIING
JUST WATCH AND DO WHAT EVERYONE ELSE IS DOIN'!
They're yer seniors...
HUH?!
HEY, NINOMIYA...
GOT A SEC?
SARUYAMA!
DON'T RUN OFF THAT WAY!
THAT'S A WHOLE DIFFERENT SECTOR OVER THERE!
WE GOT LAST MONTH'S REPORT.
WANNA HEAR WHAT THEY HAVE TO SAY?
KRIK KRAK
NO... NOT REALLY...
THIS ISN'T HARD. THERE'S REPORTING, CONTACTING, AND COMMUNICATION. JUST REMEMBER THE ACRONYM, "REPCON-COM!"
NOW SAY IT BACK TO ME!
LOUDER!
Repcon-com...
WHADDYA MEAN, "NOT REALLY"?
OW!
YOU NEED SOMEONE TO LIGHT A FIRE UNDER YOU OR SOMETHIN'?!
AN OVERALL ASSESSMENT RATING OF 15% IS NO LAUGHING MATTER!
LET ME SPELL IT OUT FOR YOU. BECAUSE OF YOUR LAZY ASS, OUR WHOLE TEAM'S EVALUATION HAS FALLEN!
GRNCH

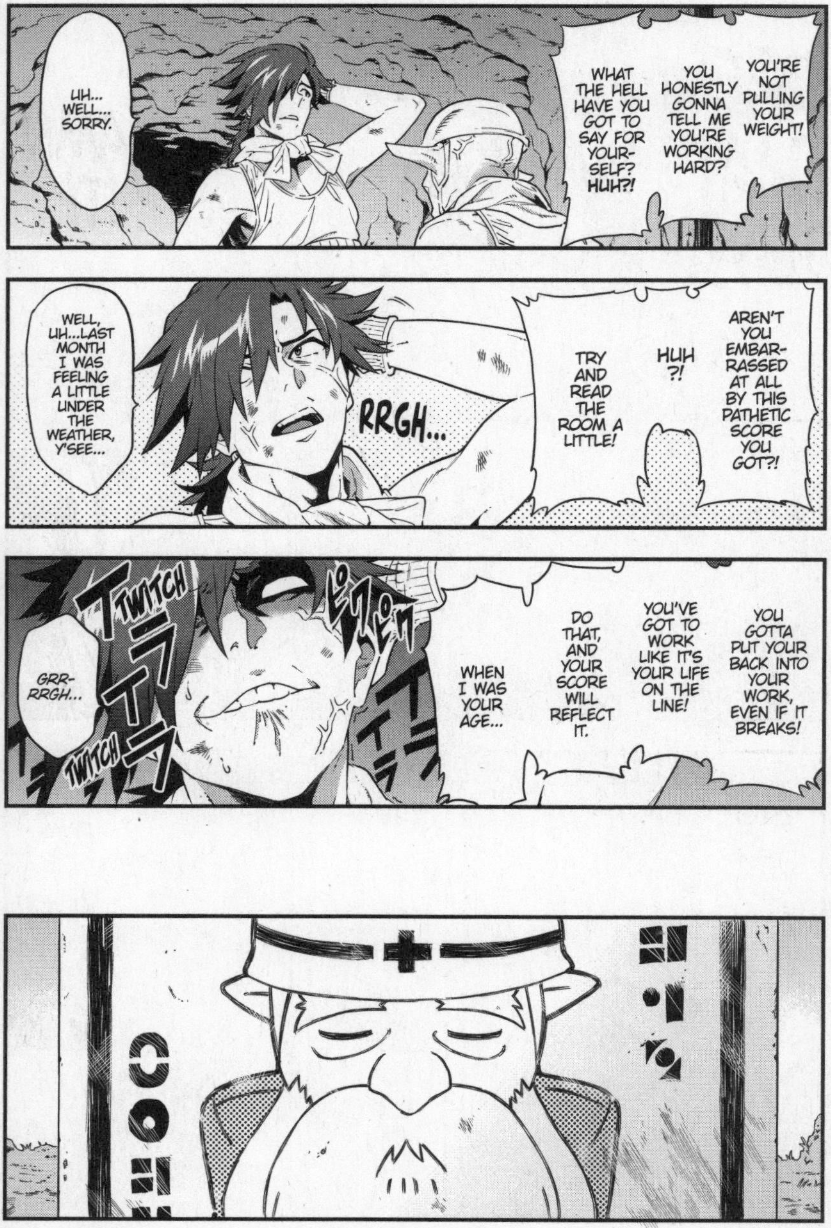
YOU'RE NOT PULLING YOUR WEIGHT!
YOU HONESTLY GONNA TELL ME YOU'RE WORKING HARD?
WHAT THE HELL HAVE YOU GOT TO SAY FOR YOUR-SELF? HUH?!
UH... WELL... SORRY.
AREN'T YOU EMBAR-RASSED AT ALL BY THIS PATHETIC SCORE YOU GOT?!
HUH?!
TRY AND READ THE ROOM A LITTLE!
RRGH...
WELL, UH...LAST MONTH I WAS FEELING A LITTLE UNDER THE WEATHER, Y'SEE...
YOU GOTTA PUT YOUR BACK INTO YOUR WORK, EVEN IF IT BREAKS!
YOU'VE GOT TO WORK LIKE IT'S YOUR LIFE ON THE LINE!
DO THAT, AND YOUR SCORE WILL REFLECT IT.
WHEN I WAS YOUR AGE...
TWITCH
TWITCH
GRR-RRGH...

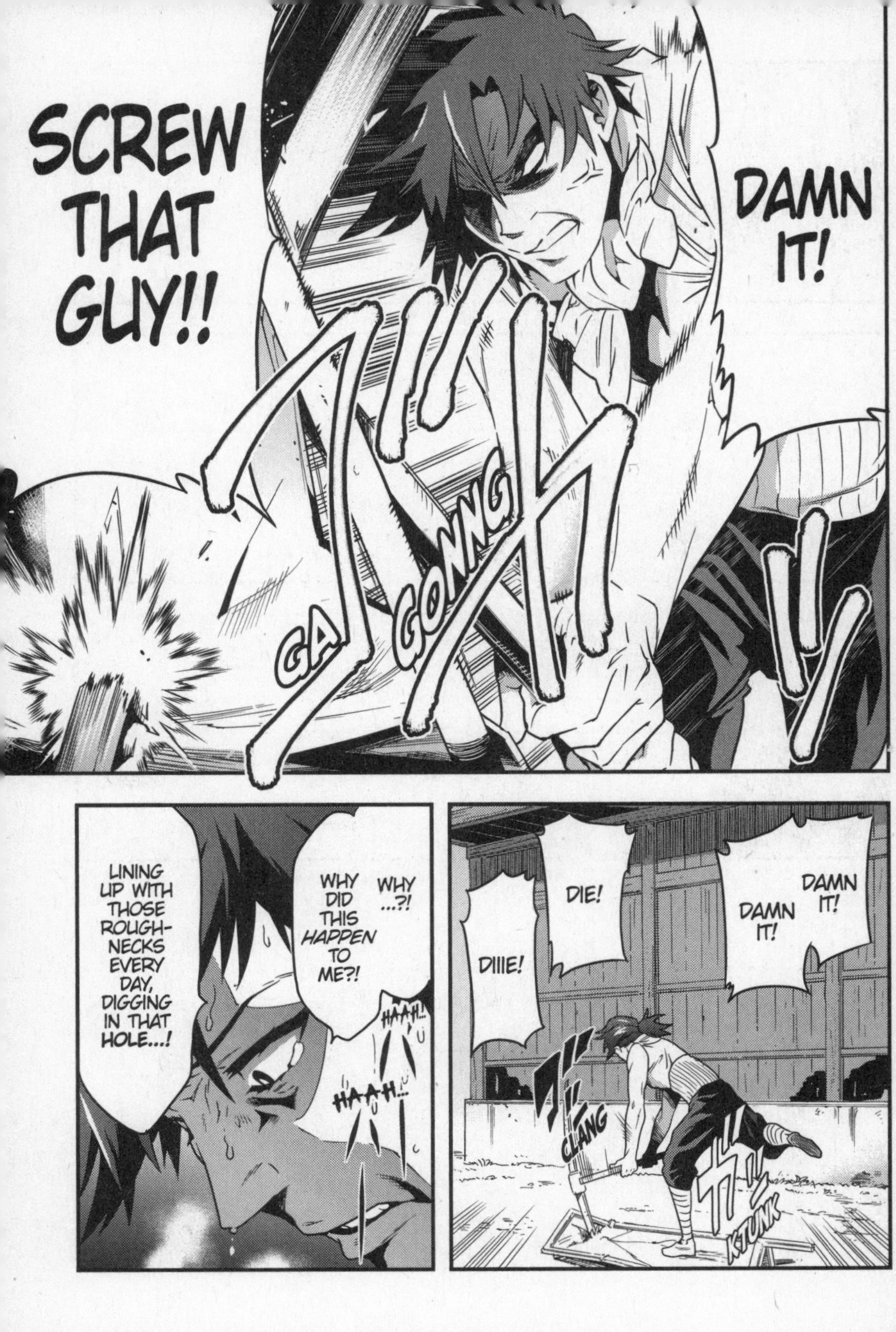
DAMN IT!
SCREW THAT GUY!!
GA GONG
DAMN IT!
DAMN IT!
DIE!
DIIIE!
CLANG
KTUNK
WHY ...?!
WHY DID THIS HAPPEN TO ME?!
LINING UP WITH THOSE ROUGH-NECKS EVERY DAY, DIGGING IN THAT HOLE...!
HAAH...
HA-AH...

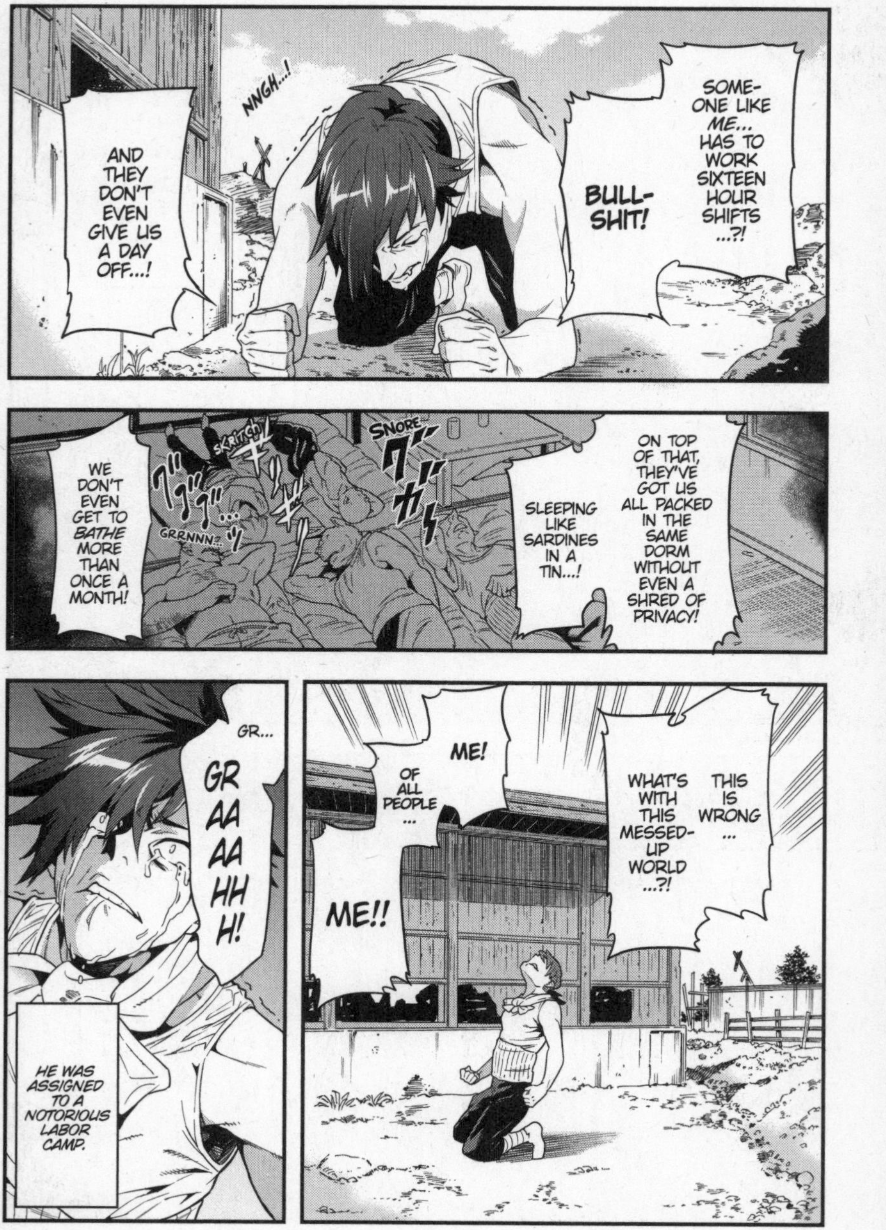
SOME-ONE LIKE ME... HAS TO WORK SIXTEEN HOUR SHIFTS ...?!
BULL-SHIT!
NNGH...!
AND THEY DON'T EVEN GIVE US A DAY OFF...!
ON TOP OF THAT, THEY'VE GOT US ALL PACKED IN THE SAME DORM WITHOUT EVEN A SHRED OF PRIVACY!
SLEEPING LIKE SARDINES IN A TIN...!
SNORE
SKRITCH
GRRNNN...
WE DON'T EVEN GET TO BATHE MORE THAN ONCE A MONTH!
THIS IS WRONG ...
WHAT'S WITH THIS MESSED-UP WORLD ...?!
ME!
OF ALL PEOPLE ...
ME!!
GR...
GRAAAAAHHHH!
HE WAS ASSIGNED TO A NOTORIOUS LABOR CAMP.

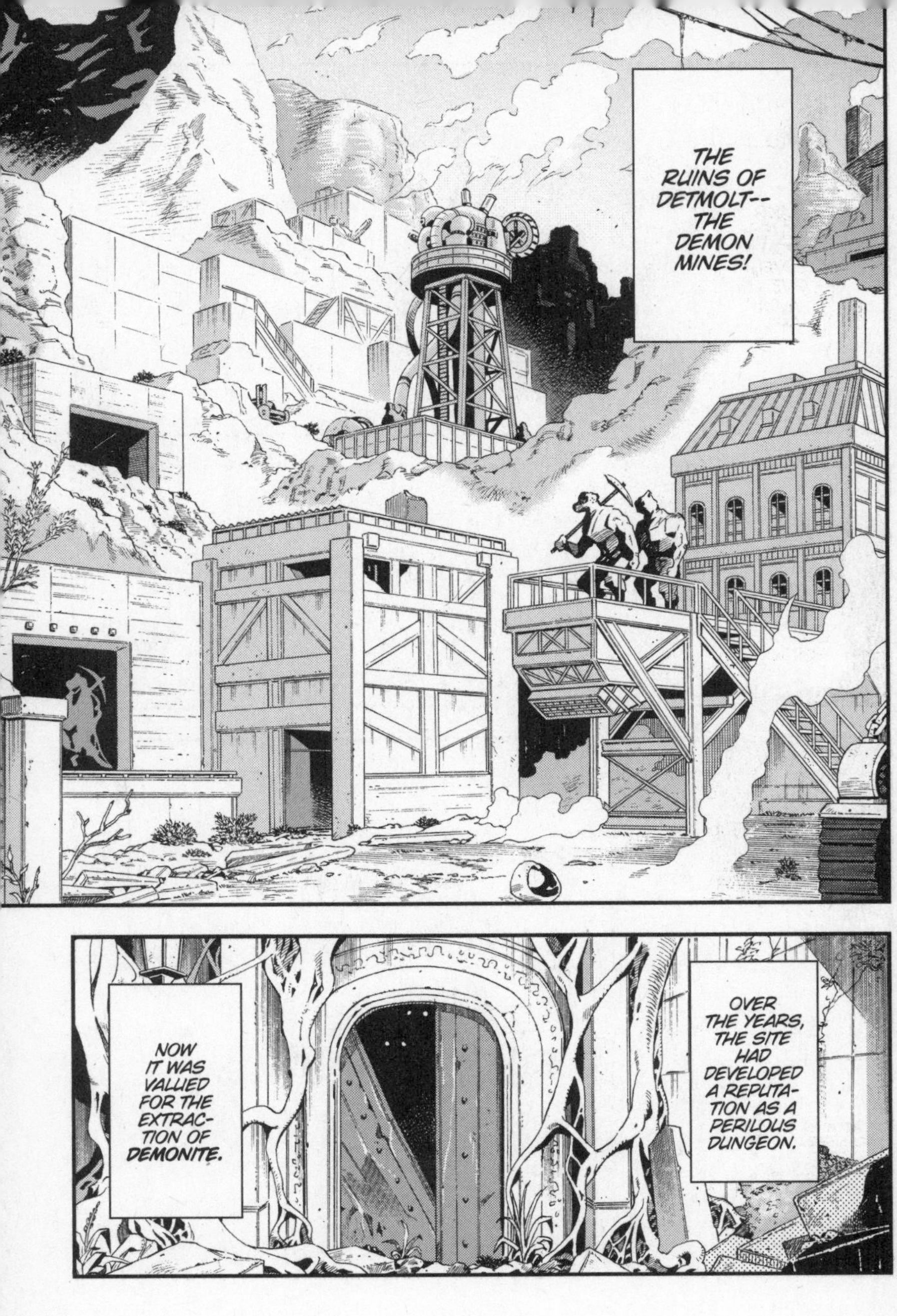
THE RUINS OF DETMOLT-- THE DEMON MINES!
OVER THE YEARS, THE SITE HAD DEVELOPED A REPUTATION AS A PERILOUS DUNGEON.
NOW IT WAS VALUED FOR THE EXTRACTION OF DEMONITE.

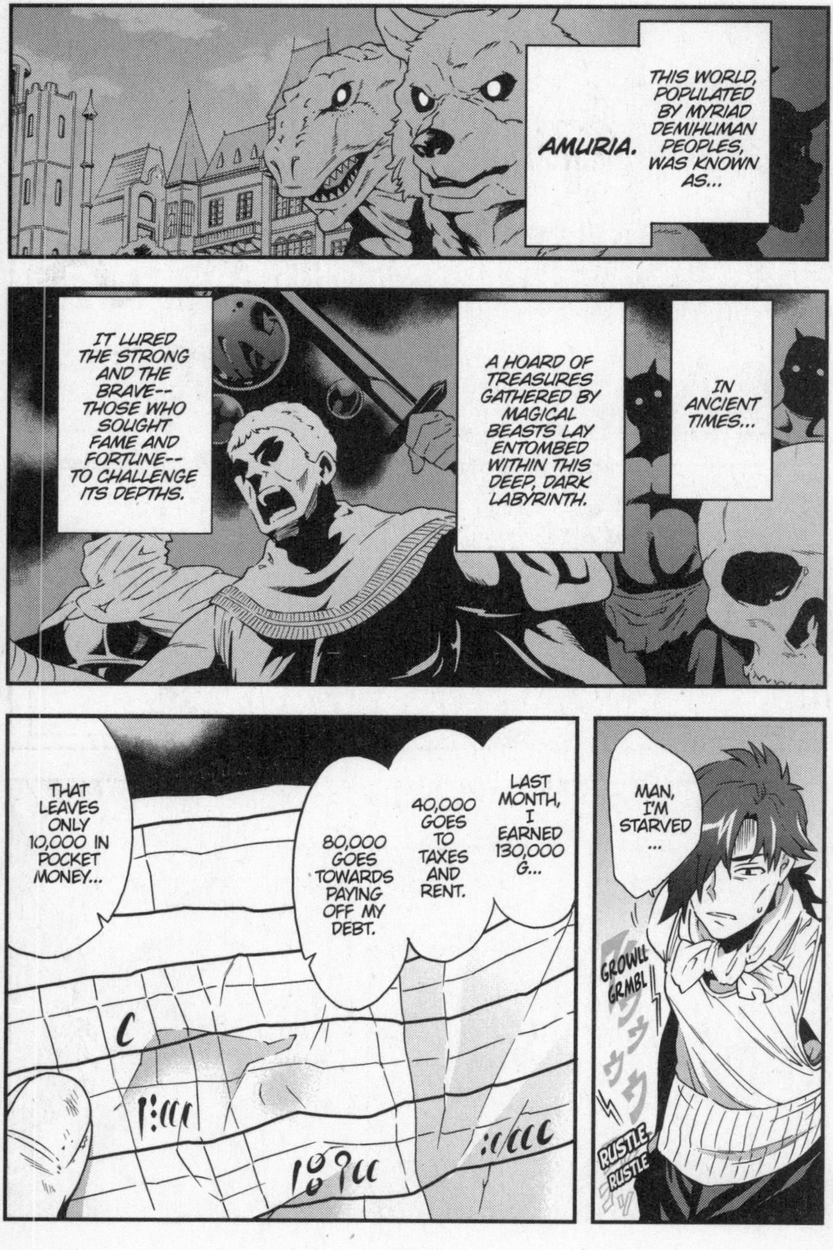
THIS WORLD, POPULATED BY MYRIAD DEMIHUMAN PEOPLES, WAS KNOWN AS...
AMURIA.
IN ANCIENT TIMES...
A HOARD OF TREASURES GATHERED BY MAGICAL BEASTS LAY ENTOMBED WITHIN THIS DEEP, DARK LABYRINTH.
IT LURED THE STRONG AND THE BRAVE-- THOSE WHO SOUGHT FAME AND FORTUNE-- TO CHALLENGE ITS DEPTHS.
MAN, I'M STARVED ...
GROWLL GRMBL
RUSTLE RUSTLE
LAST MONTH, I EARNED 130,000 G...
40,000 GOES TO TAXES AND RENT.
80,000 GOES TOWARDS PAYING OFF MY DEBT.
THAT LEAVES ONLY 10,000 IN POCKET MONEY...

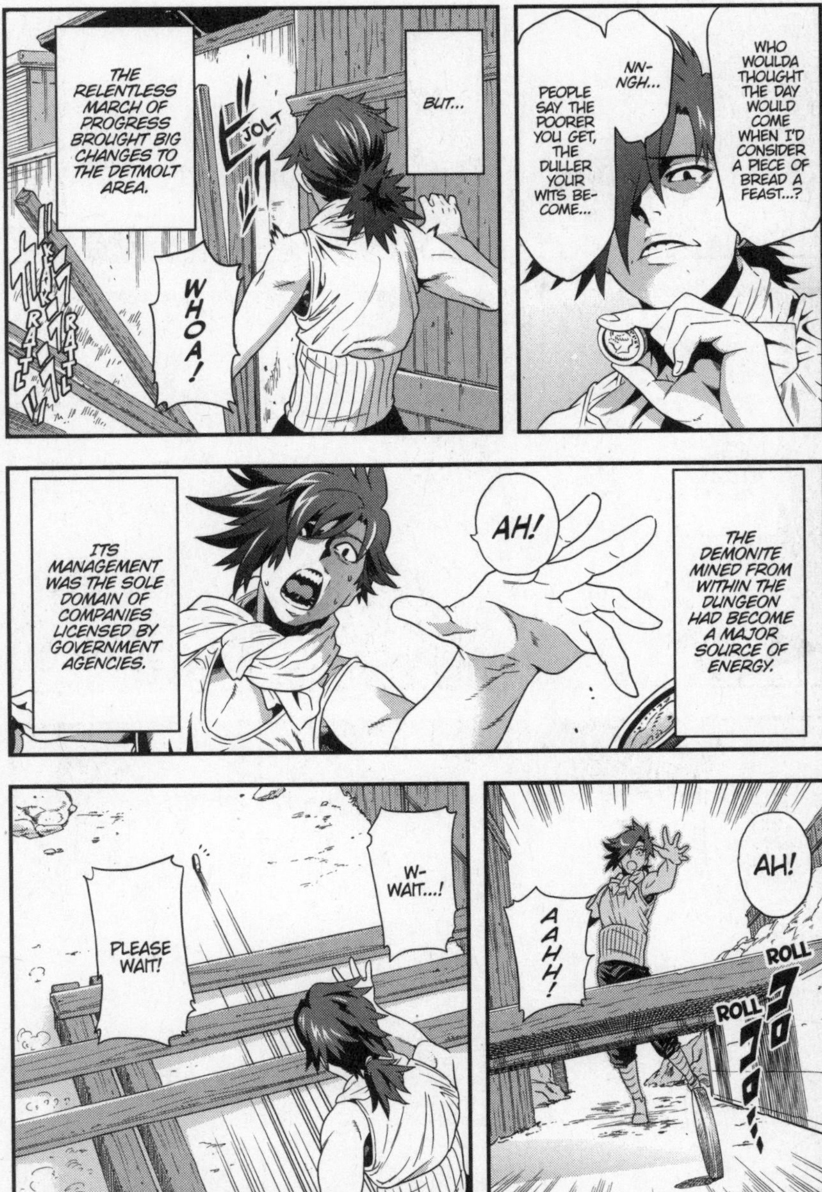
WHO WOULDA THOUGHT THE DAY WOULD COME WHEN I'D CONSIDER A PIECE OF BREAD A FEAST...?
NN-NGH...
PEOPLE SAY THE POORER YOU GET, THE DULLER YOUR WITS BE-COME...
BUT...
JOLT
THE RELENTLESS MARCH OF PROGRESS BROUGHT BIG CHANGES TO THE DETMOLT AREA.
WHOA!
RATTL
RATTL
THE DEMONITE MINED FROM WITHIN THE DUNGEON HAD BECOME A MAJOR SOURCE OF ENERGY.
AH!
ITS MANAGEMENT WAS THE SOLE DOMAIN OF COMPANIES LICENSED BY GOVERNMENT AGENCIES.
AH!
AAHH!
ROLL
ROLL
W-WAIT...!
PLEASE WAIT!

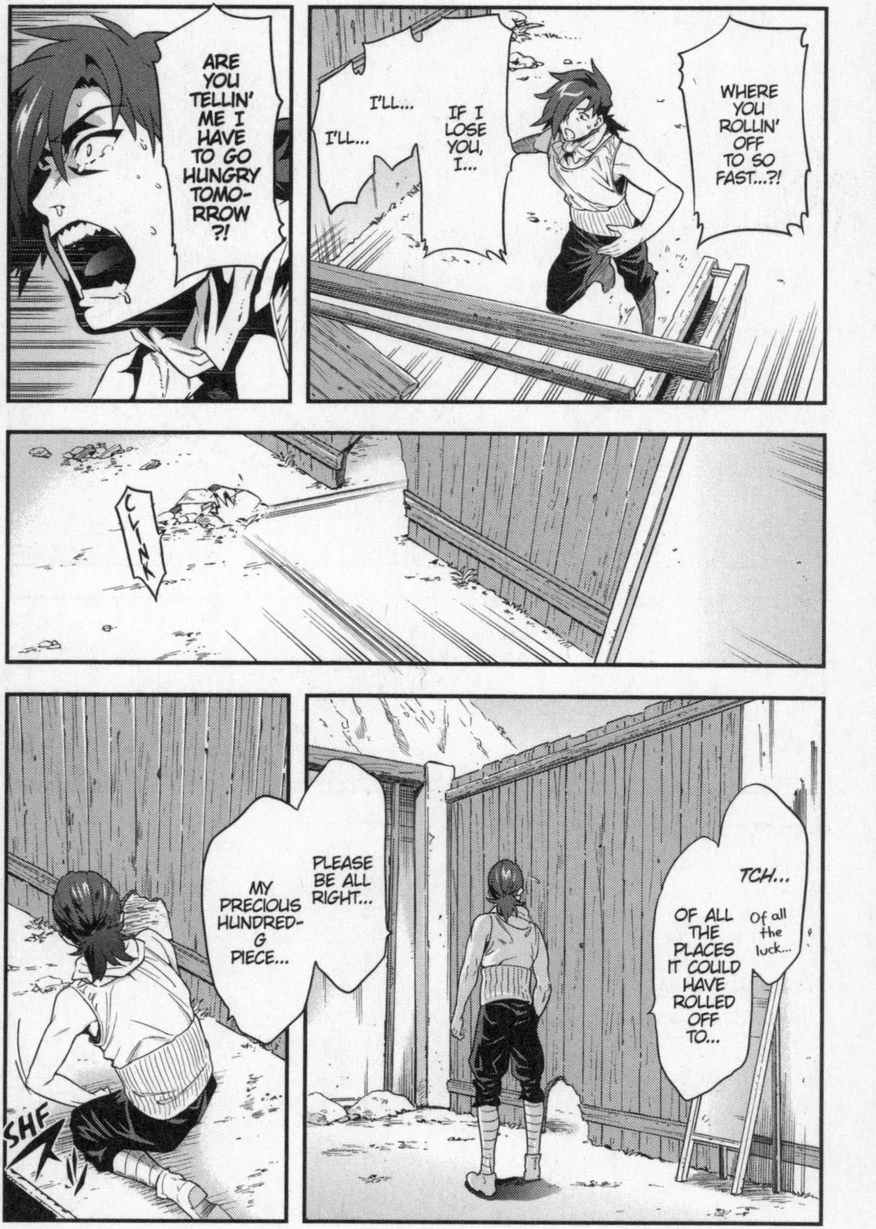
WHERE YOU ROLLIN' OFF TO SO FAST...?!
IF I LOSE YOU, I...
I'LL...
I'LL...
ARE YOU TELLIN' ME I HAVE TO GO HUNGRY TOMORROW?!
CLINK
TCH...
OF ALL THE PLACES IT COULD HAVE ROLLED OFF TO...
Of all the luck...
PLEASE BE ALL RIGHT...
MY PRECIOUS HUNDRED-G PIECE...
SHF

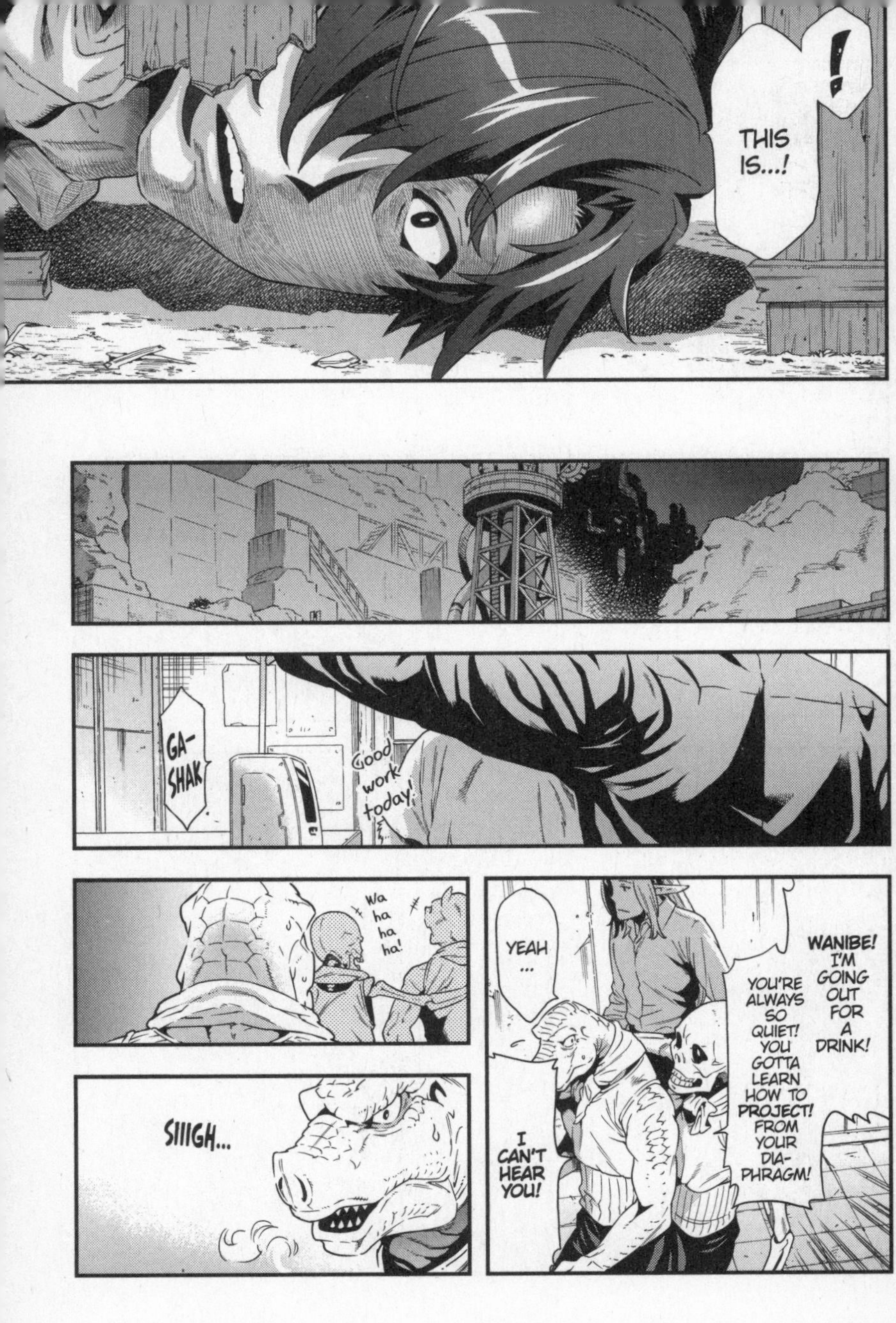
!
THIS IS...!
Good work today!
GA-SHAK
WANIBE! I'M GOING OUT FOR A DRINK!
YOU'RE ALWAYS SO QUIET! YOU GOTTA LEARN HOW TO PROJECT! FROM YOUR DIA-PHRAGM!
YEAH ...
I CAN'T HEAR YOU!
Wa ha ha ha!
SIIIGH...

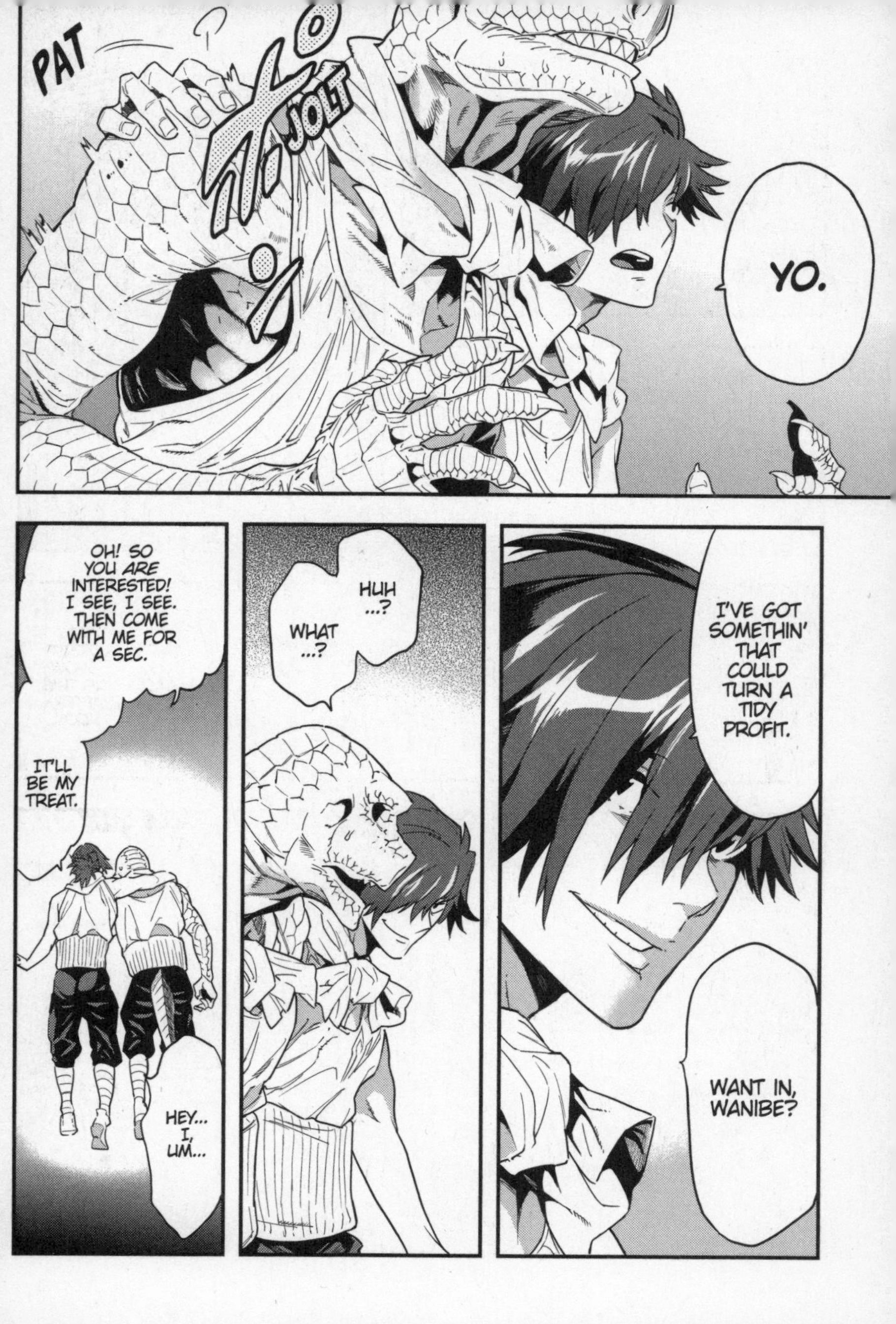
YO.
JOLT
PAT
I'VE GOT SOMETHIN' THAT COULD TURN A TIDY PROFIT.
WANT IN, WANIBE?
HUH ...?
WHAT ...?
OH! SO YOU *ARE* INTERESTED! I SEE, I SEE. THEN COME WITH ME FOR A SEC.
IT'LL BE MY TREAT.
HEY... I, UM...

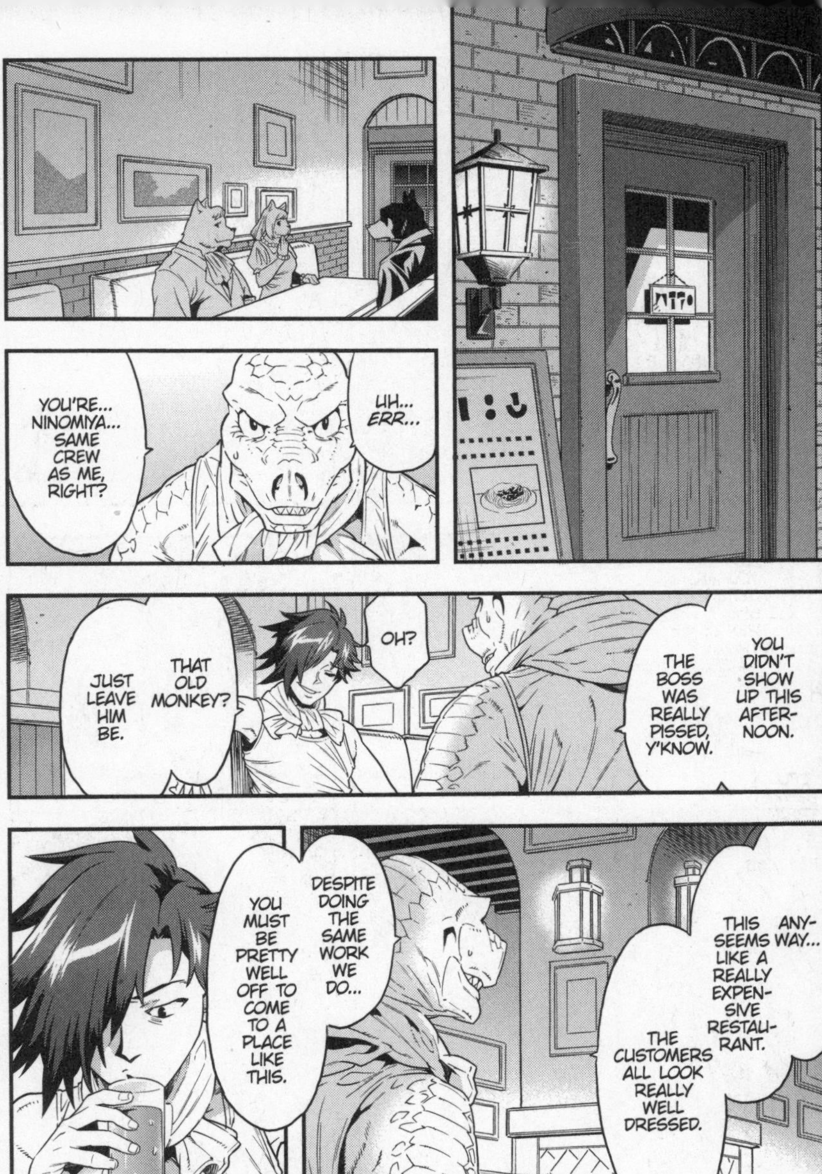
UH... ERR...
YOU'RE... NINOMIYA... SAME CREW AS ME, RIGHT?
YOU DIDN'T SHOW UP THIS AFTERNOON.
THE BOSS WAS REALLY PISSED, Y'KNOW.
OH?
THAT OLD MONKEY?
JUST LEAVE HIM BE.
ANYWAY... THIS SEEMS LIKE A REALLY EXPENSIVE RESTAURANT.
THE CUSTOMERS ALL LOOK REALLY WELL DRESSED.
DESPITE DOING THE SAME WORK WE DO...
YOU MUST BE PRETTY WELL OFF TO COME TO A PLACE LIKE THIS.

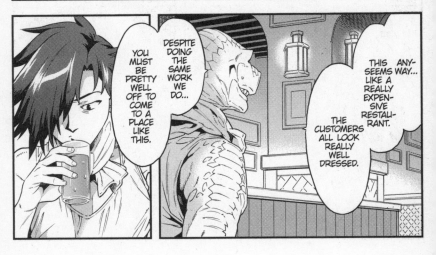

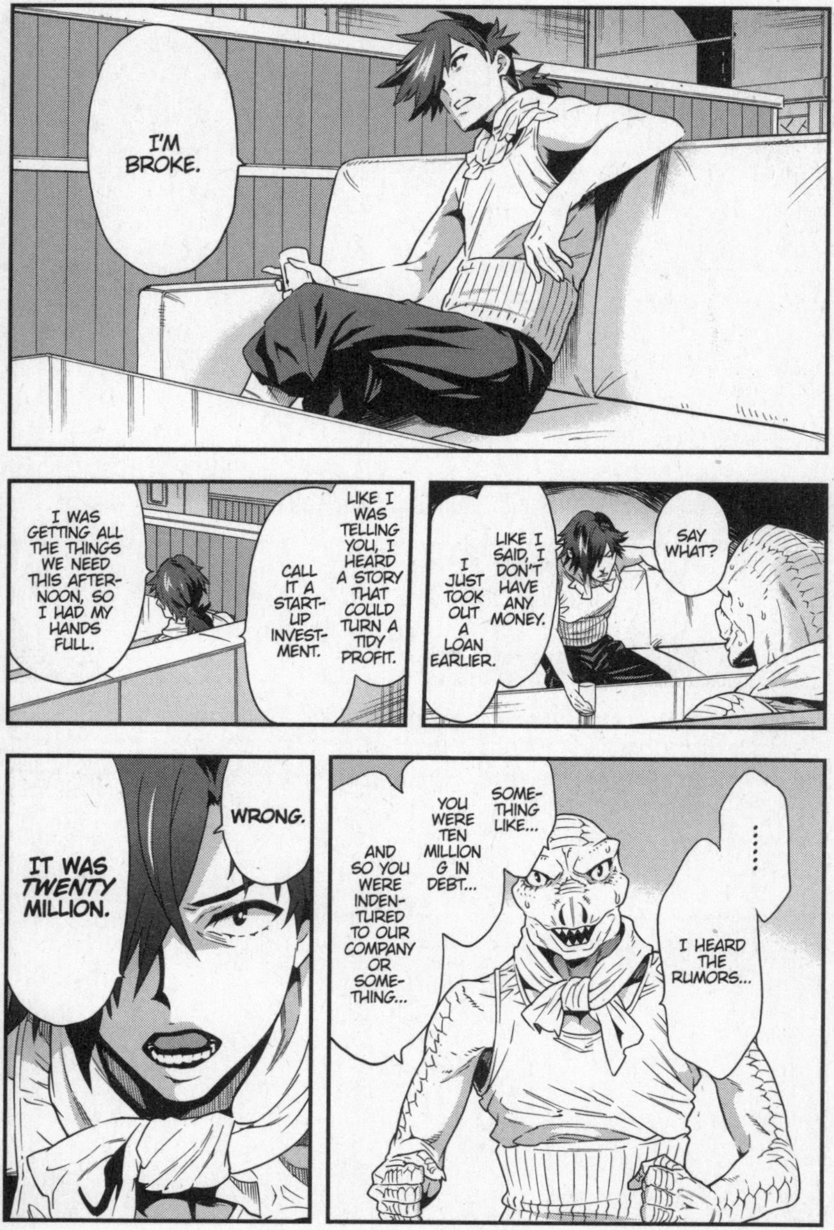
I'M BROKE.
SAY WHAT?
LIKE I SAID, I DON'T HAVE ANY MONEY.
I JUST TOOK OUT A LOAN EARLIER.
LIKE I WAS TELLING YOU, I HEARD A STORY THAT COULD TURN A TIDY PROFIT.
CALL IT A START-UP INVESTMENT.
I WAS GETTING ALL THE THINGS WE NEED THIS AFTERNOON, SO I HAD MY HANDS FULL.
......
I HEARD THE RUMORS...
SOMETHING LIKE...
YOU WERE TEN MILLION G IN DEBT...
AND SO YOU WERE INDENTURED TO OUR COMPANY OR SOMETHING...
WRONG.
IT WAS *TWENTY* MILLION.

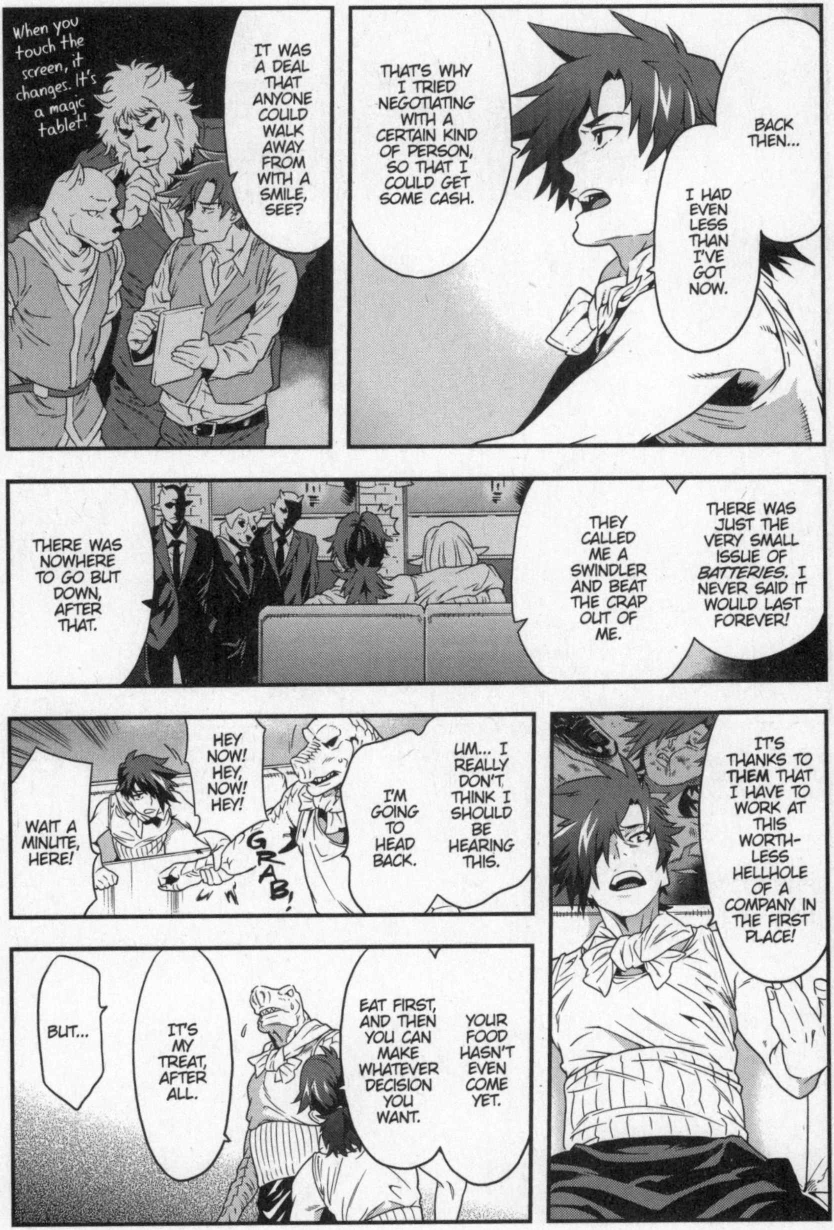
BACK THEN...
I HAD EVEN LESS THAN I'VE GOT NOW.
THAT'S WHY I TRIED NEGOTIATING WITH A CERTAIN KIND OF PERSON, SO THAT I COULD GET SOME CASH.
IT WAS A DEAL THAT ANYONE COULD WALK AWAY FROM WITH A SMILE, SEE?
When you touch the screen, it changes. It's a magic tablet!
THERE WAS JUST THE VERY SMALL ISSUE OF *BATTERIES*. I NEVER SAID IT WOULD LAST FOREVER!
THEY CALLED ME A SWINDLER AND BEAT THE CRAP OUT OF ME.
THERE WAS NOWHERE TO GO BUT DOWN, AFTER THAT.
IT'S THANKS TO THEM THAT I HAVE TO WORK AT THIS WORTH-LESS HELLHOLE OF A COMPANY IN THE FIRST PLACE!
UM... I REALLY DON'T THINK I SHOULD BE HEARING THIS.
I'M GOING TO HEAD BACK.
HEY NOW! HEY, NOW! HEY!
GRAB!
WAIT A MINUTE, HERE!
YOUR FOOD HASN'T EVEN COME YET.
EAT FIRST, AND THEN YOU CAN MAKE WHATEVER DECISION YOU WANT.
IT'S MY TREAT, AFTER ALL.
BUT...

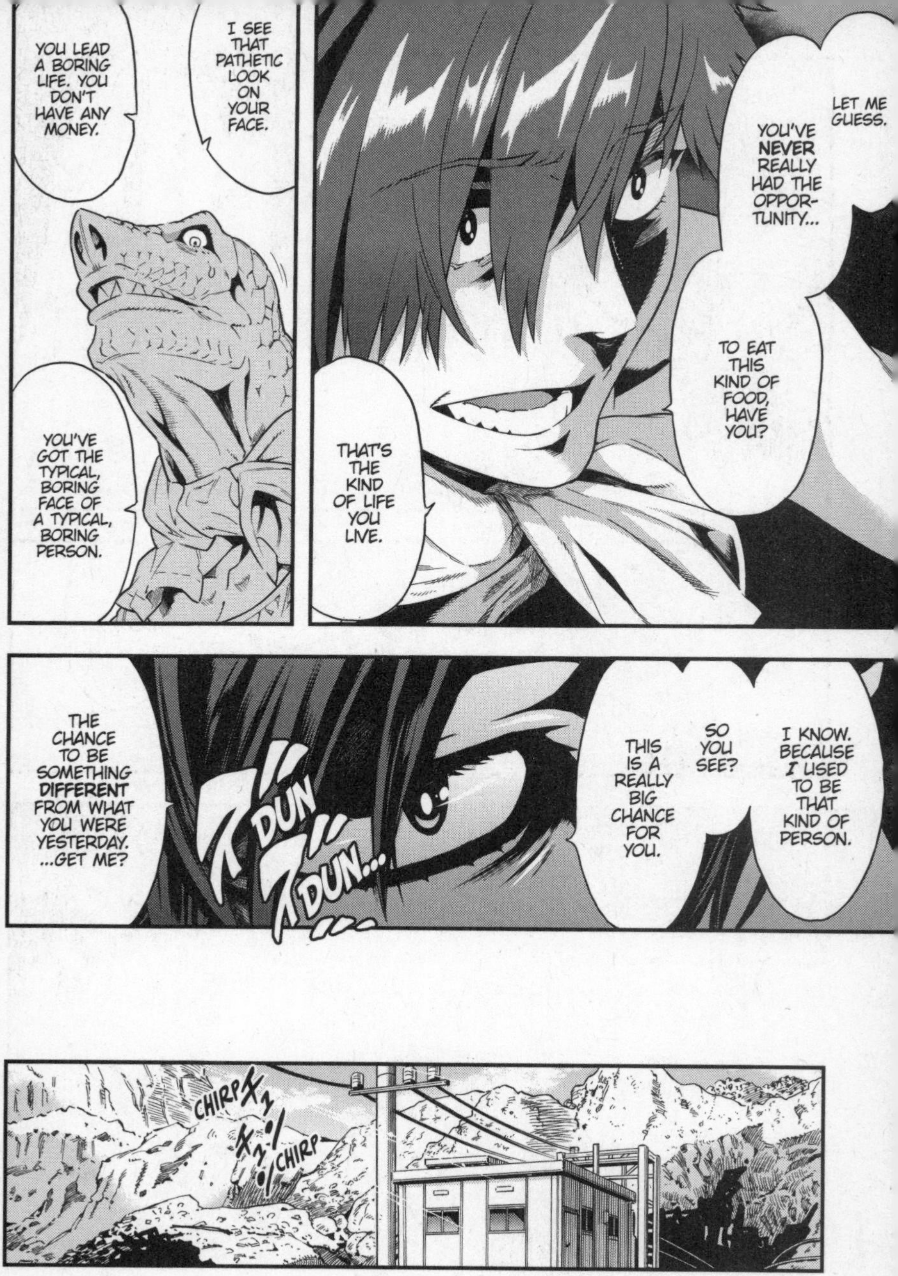
LET ME GUESS.
YOU'VE NEVER REALLY HAD THE OPPORTUNITY...
TO EAT THIS KIND OF FOOD, HAVE YOU?
THAT'S THE KIND OF LIFE YOU LIVE.
I SEE THAT PATHETIC LOOK ON YOUR FACE.
YOU LEAD A BORING LIFE. YOU DON'T HAVE ANY MONEY.
YOU'VE GOT THE TYPICAL, BORING FACE OF A TYPICAL, BORING PERSON.
I KNOW. BECAUSE I USED TO BE THAT KIND OF PERSON.
SO YOU SEE?
THIS IS A REALLY BIG CHANCE FOR YOU.
DUN DUN...
THE CHANCE TO BE SOMETHING DIFFERENT FROM WHAT YOU WERE YESTERDAY. ...GET ME?
CHIRP
CHIRP

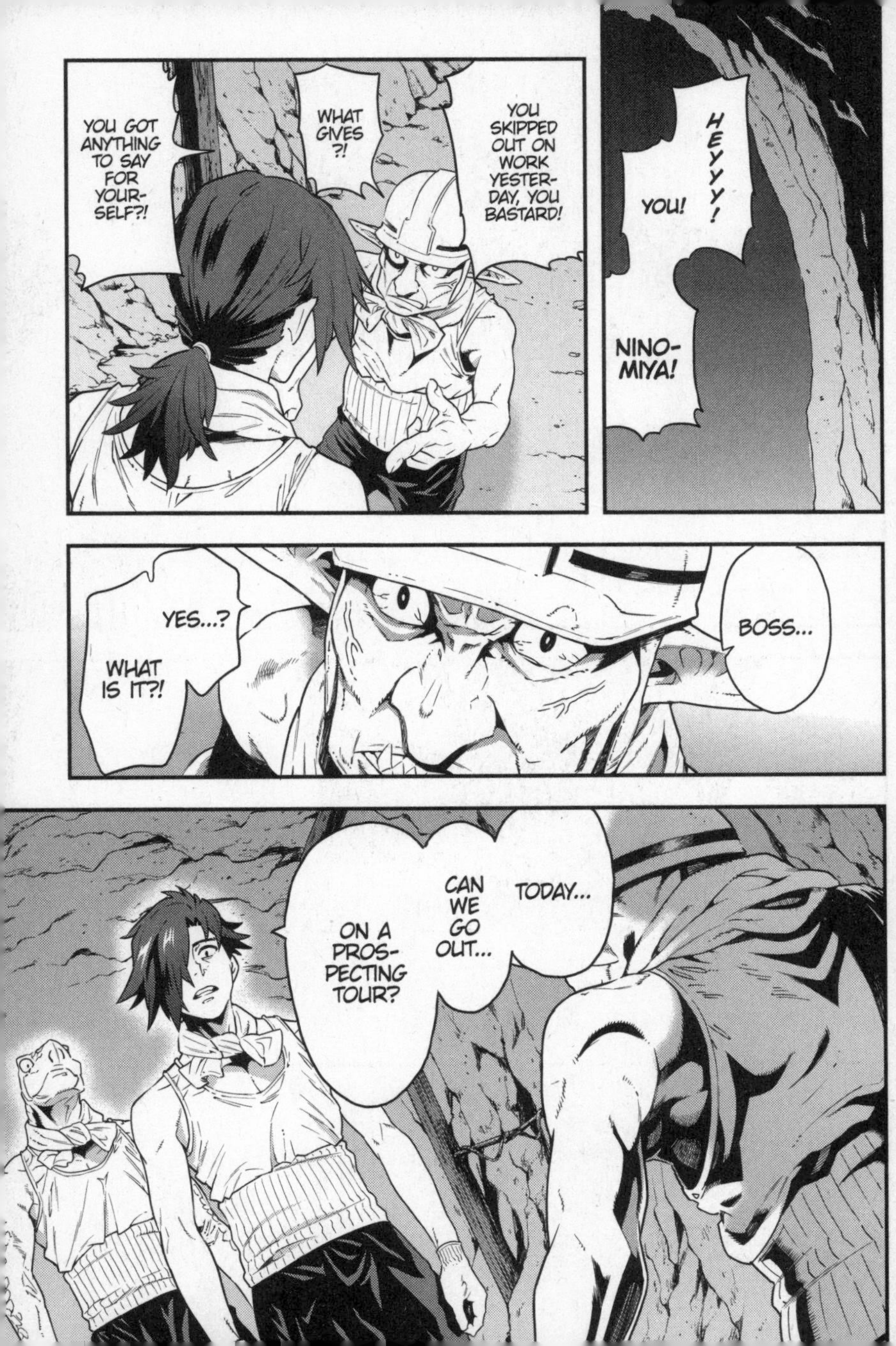
HEYYY!
YOU!
NINO-MIYA!
YOU SKIPPED OUT ON WORK YESTER-DAY, YOU BASTARD!
WHAT GIVES?!
YOU GOT ANYTHING TO SAY FOR YOUR-SELF?!
BOSS...
YES...?
WHAT IS IT?!
TODAY...
CAN WE GO OUT...
ON A PROS-PECTING TOUR?

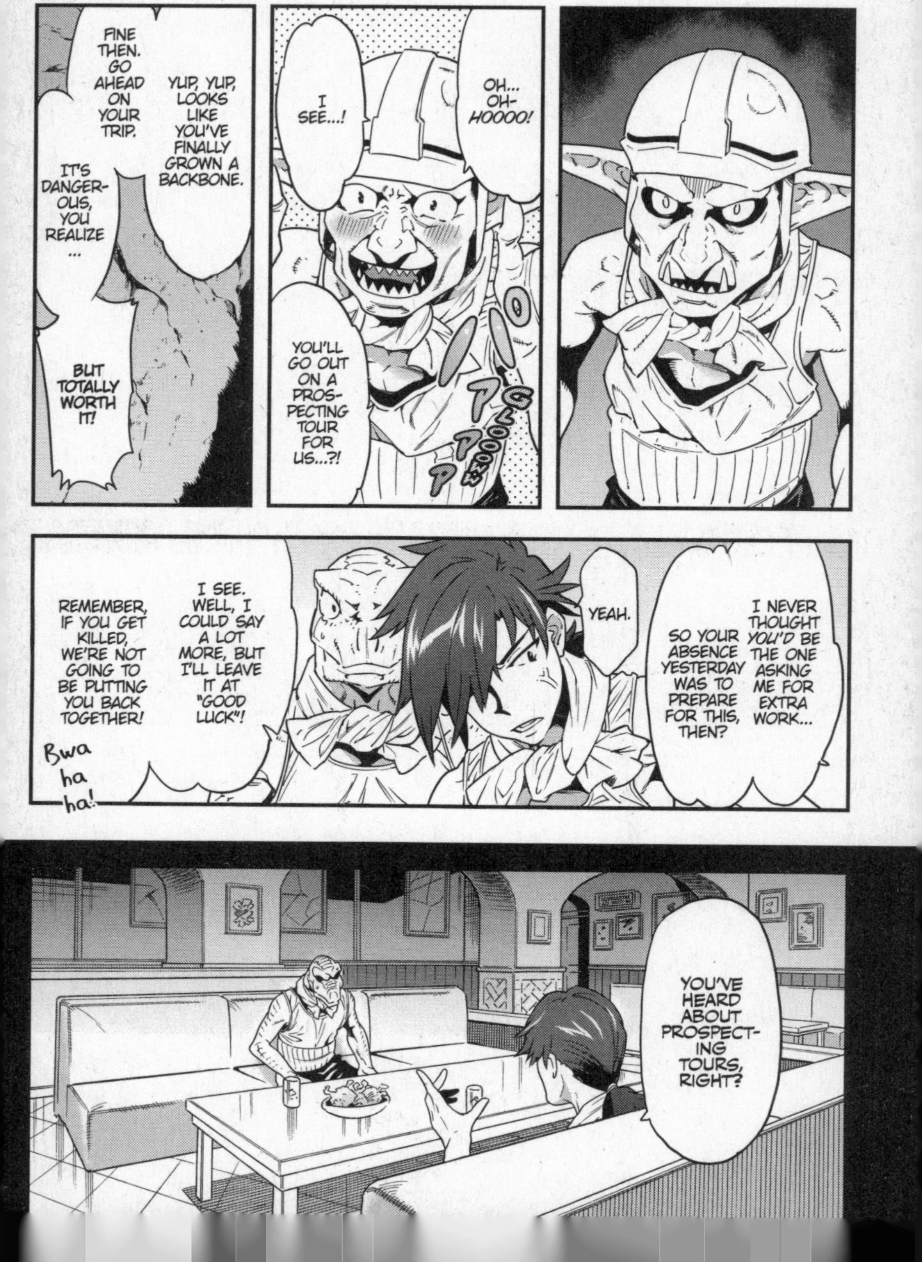
OH... OH-HOOOO!
I SEE...!
YOU'LL GO OUT ON A PROSPECTING TOUR FOR US...?!
GLOOOM
YUP, YUP, LOOKS LIKE YOU'VE FINALLY GROWN A BACKBONE.
FINE THEN. GO AHEAD ON YOUR TRIP.
IT'S DANGEROUS, YOU REALIZE...
BUT TOTALLY WORTH IT!
I NEVER THOUGHT *YOU'D* BE THE ONE ASKING ME FOR EXTRA WORK...
SO YOUR ABSENCE YESTERDAY WAS TO PREPARE FOR THIS, THEN?
YEAH.
I SEE. WELL, I COULD SAY A LOT MORE, BUT I'LL LEAVE IT AT "GOOD LUCK"!
REMEMBER, IF YOU GET KILLED, WE'RE NOT GOING TO BE PUTTING YOU BACK TOGETHER!
Bwa ha ha!
YOU'VE HEARD ABOUT PROSPECTING TOURS, RIGHT?

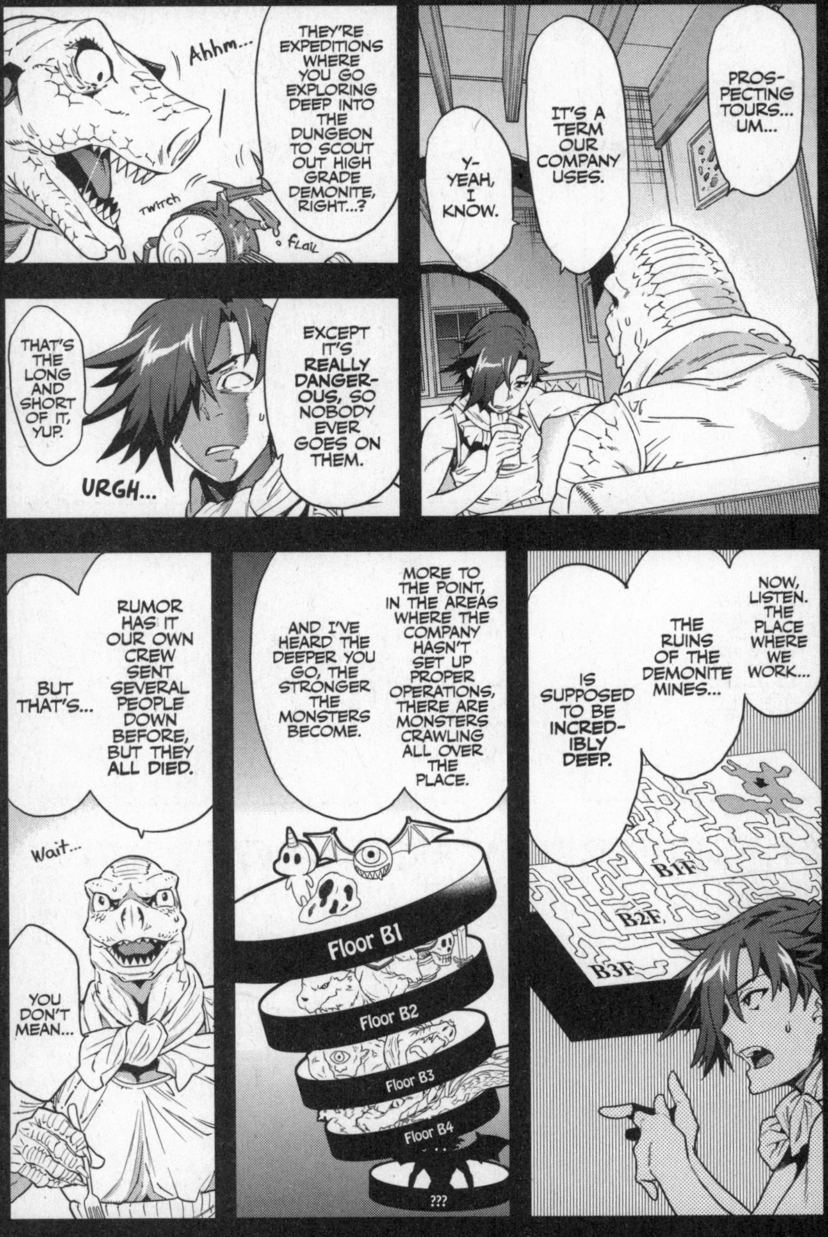
PROSPECTING TOURS... UM...
IT'S A TERM OUR COMPANY USES.
Y-YEAH, I KNOW.
THEY'RE EXPEDITIONS WHERE YOU GO EXPLORING DEEP INTO THE DUNGEON TO SCOUT OUT HIGH GRADE DEMONITE, RIGHT...?
Ahhm...
Twitch
Flail
EXCEPT IT'S REALLY DANGEROUS, SO NOBODY EVER GOES ON THEM.
THAT'S THE LONG AND SHORT OF IT, YUP.
URGH...
NOW, LISTEN. THE PLACE WHERE WE WORK...
THE RUINS OF THE DEMONITE MINES...
IS SUPPOSED TO BE INCREDIBLY DEEP.
B1F
B2F
B3F
MORE TO THE POINT, IN THE AREAS WHERE THE COMPANY HASN'T SET UP PROPER OPERATIONS, THERE ARE MONSTERS CRAWLING ALL OVER THE PLACE.
AND I'VE HEARD THE DEEPER YOU GO, THE STRONGER THE MONSTERS BECOME.
Floor B1
Floor B2
Floor B3
Floor B4
???
RUMOR HAS IT OUR OWN CREW SENT SEVERAL PEOPLE DOWN BEFORE, BUT THEY ALL DIED.
BUT THAT'S...
Wait...
YOU DON'T MEAN...

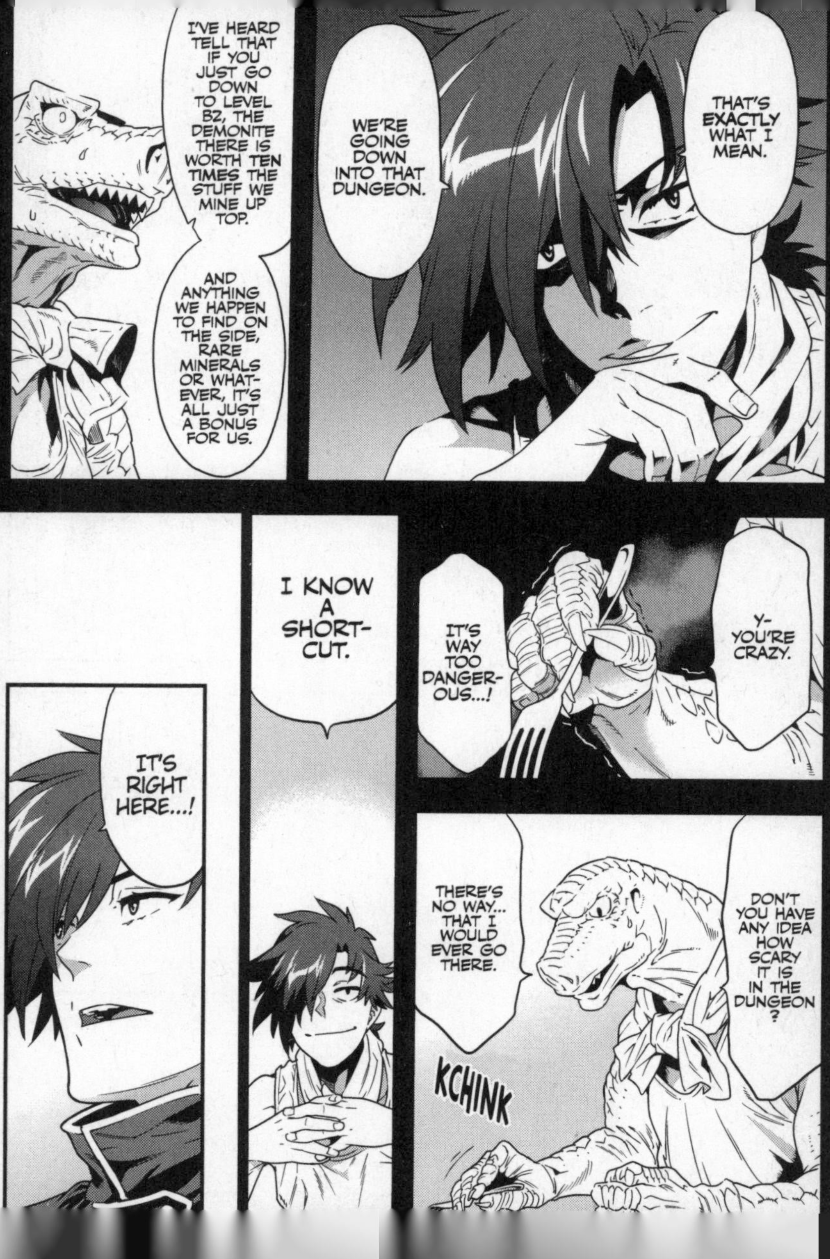
THAT'S EXACTLY WHAT I MEAN.
WE'RE GOING DOWN INTO THAT DUNGEON.
I'VE HEARD TELL THAT IF YOU JUST GO DOWN TO LEVEL B2, THE DEMONITE THERE IS WORTH TEN TIMES THE STUFF WE MINE UP TOP.
AND ANYTHING WE HAPPEN TO FIND ON THE SIDE, RARE MINERALS OR WHAT-EVER, IT'S ALL JUST A BONUS FOR US.
Y-YOU'RE CRAZY.
IT'S WAY TOO DANGER-OUS...!
DON'T YOU HAVE ANY IDEA HOW SCARY IT IS IN THE DUNGEON?
THERE'S NO WAY... THAT I WOULD EVER GO THERE.
KCHINK
I KNOW A SHORT-CUT.
IT'S RIGHT HERE...!

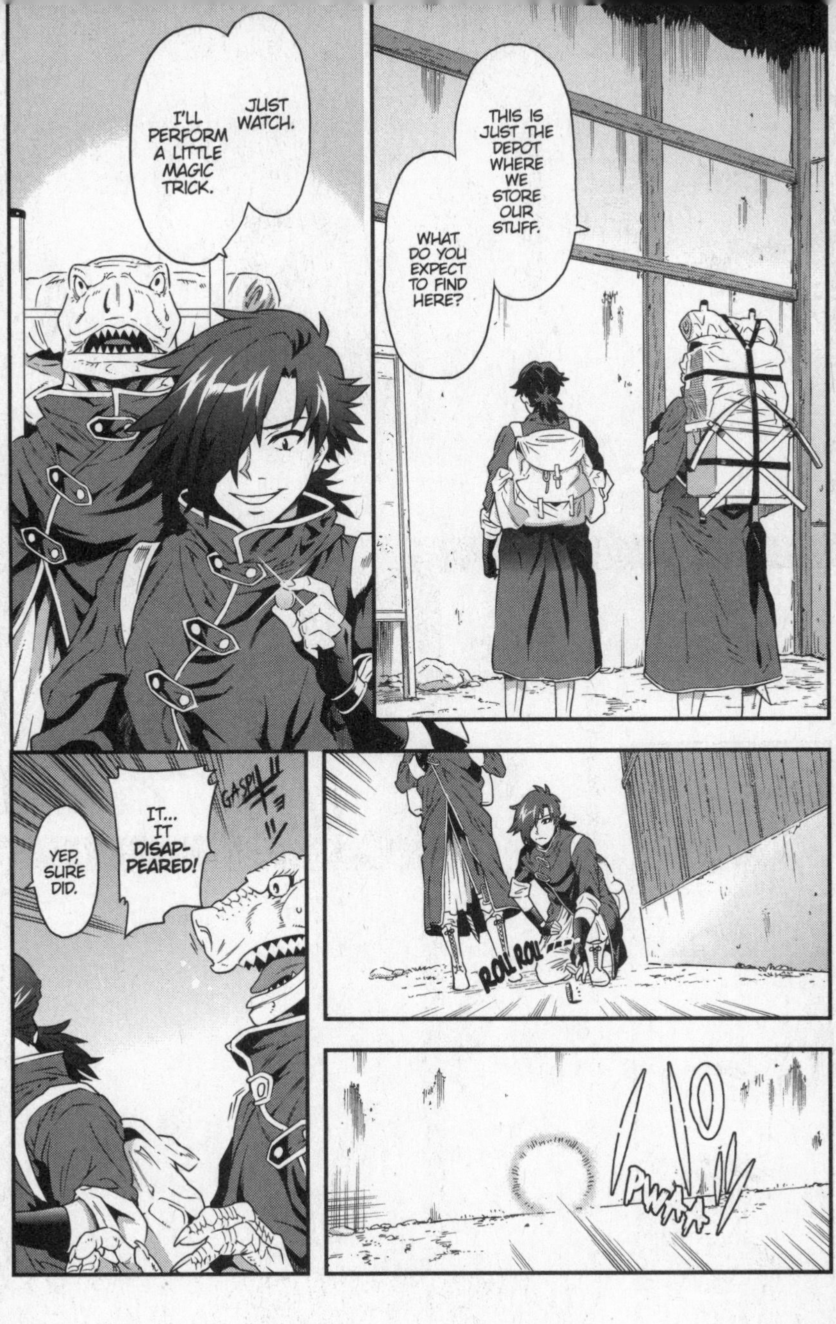
THIS IS JUST THE DEPOT WHERE WE STORE OUR STUFF.
WHAT DO YOU EXPECT TO FIND HERE?
JUST WATCH.
I'LL PERFORM A LITTLE MAGIC TRICK.
ROL ROL...
PWAAA
GASP!!
IT... IT DISAPPEARED!
YEP, SURE DID.

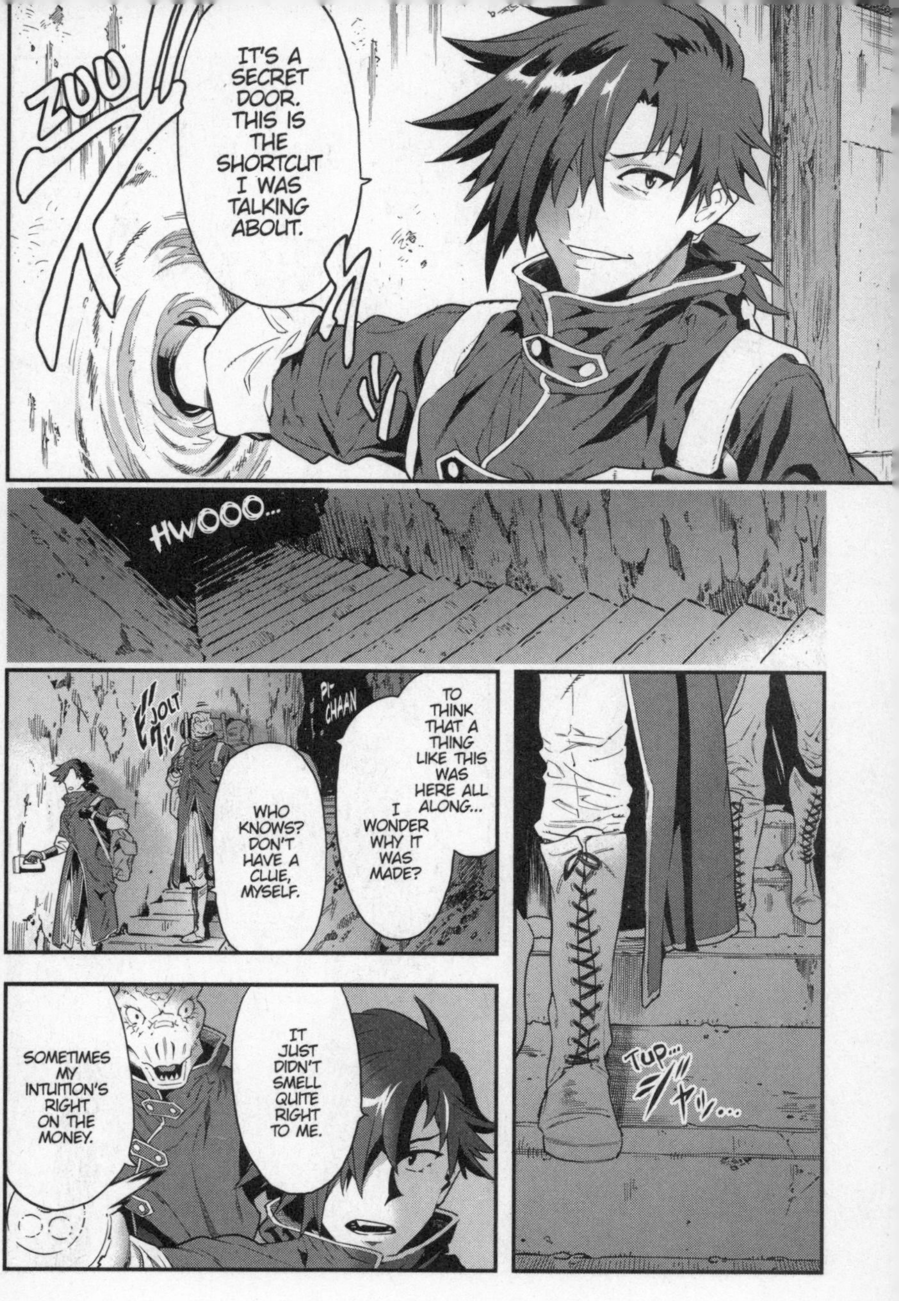
ZUU
IT'S A SECRET DOOR. THIS IS THE SHORTCUT I WAS TALKING ABOUT.
HWOOO...
TUP...
PI-CHAAN
JOLT
TO THINK THAT A THING LIKE THIS WAS HERE ALL ALONG... I WONDER WHY IT WAS MADE?
WHO KNOWS? DON'T HAVE A CLUE, MYSELF.
IT JUST DIDN'T SMELL QUITE RIGHT TO ME.
SOMETIMES MY INTUITION'S RIGHT ON THE MONEY.

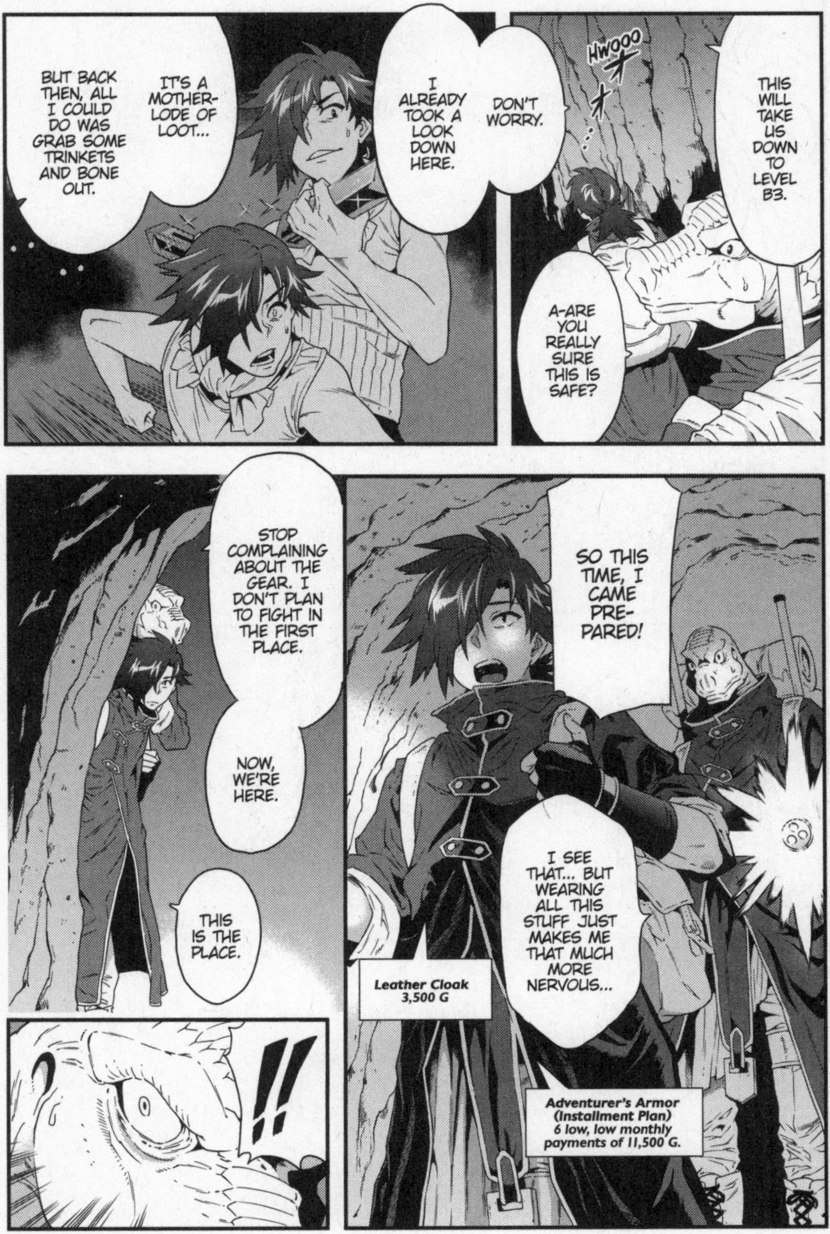
THIS WILL TAKE US DOWN TO LEVEL B3.
HWOOO
A-ARE YOU REALLY SURE THIS IS SAFE?
DON'T WORRY.
I ALREADY TOOK A LOOK DOWN HERE.
IT'S A MOTHER-LODE OF LOOT...
BUT BACK THEN, ALL I COULD DO WAS GRAB SOME TRINKETS AND BONE OUT.
SO THIS TIME, I CAME PRE-PARED!
I SEE THAT... BUT WEARING ALL THIS STUFF JUST MAKES ME THAT MUCH MORE NERVOUS...
Leather Cloak 3,500 G
Adventurer's Armor (Installment Plan) 6 low, low monthly payments of 11,500 G.
STOP COMPLAINING ABOUT THE GEAR. I DON'T PLAN TO FIGHT IN THE FIRST PLACE.
NOW, WE'RE HERE.
THIS IS THE PLACE.
!!

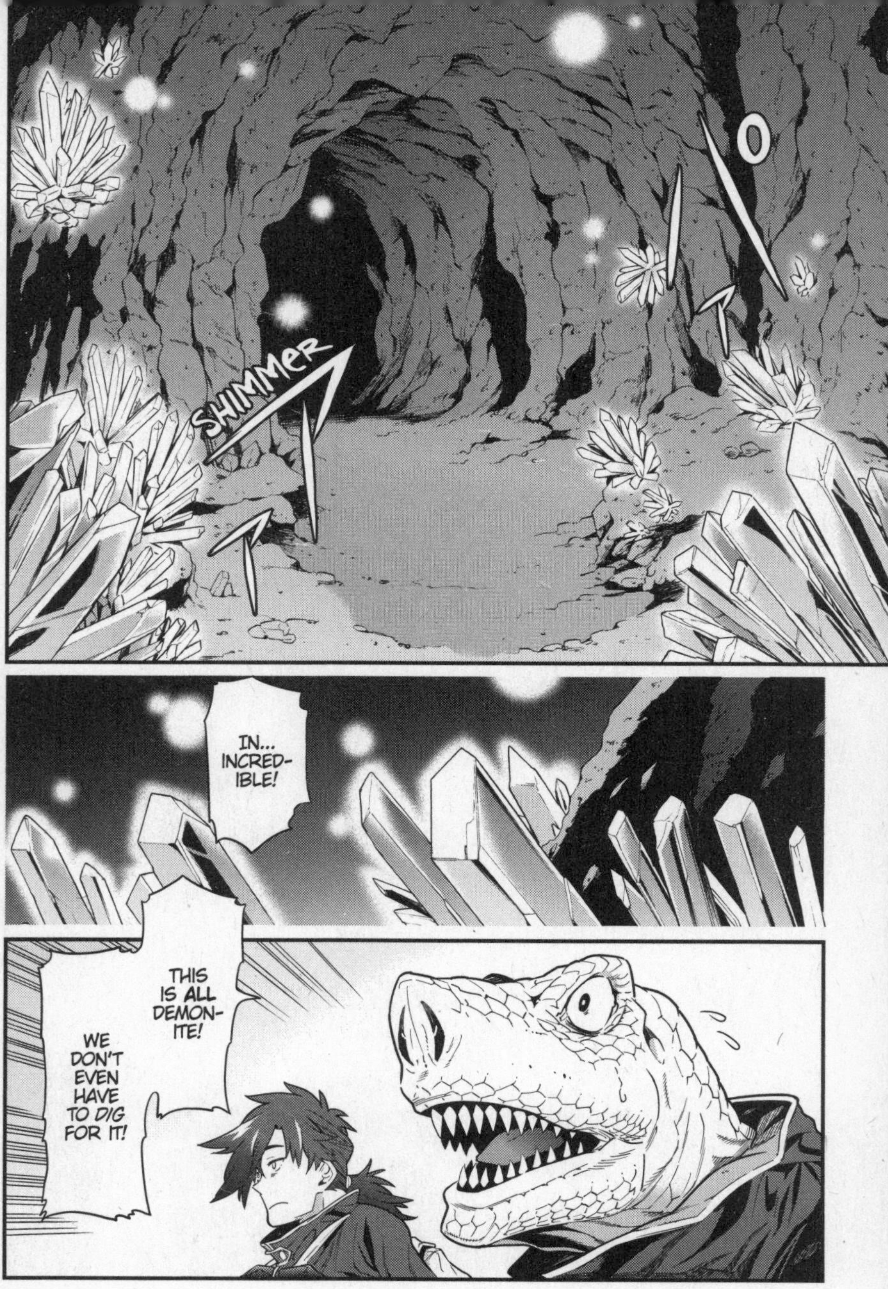
SHIMMER
IN... INCRED-IBLE!
THIS IS ALL DEMON-ITE!
WE DON'T EVEN HAVE TO DIG FOR IT!

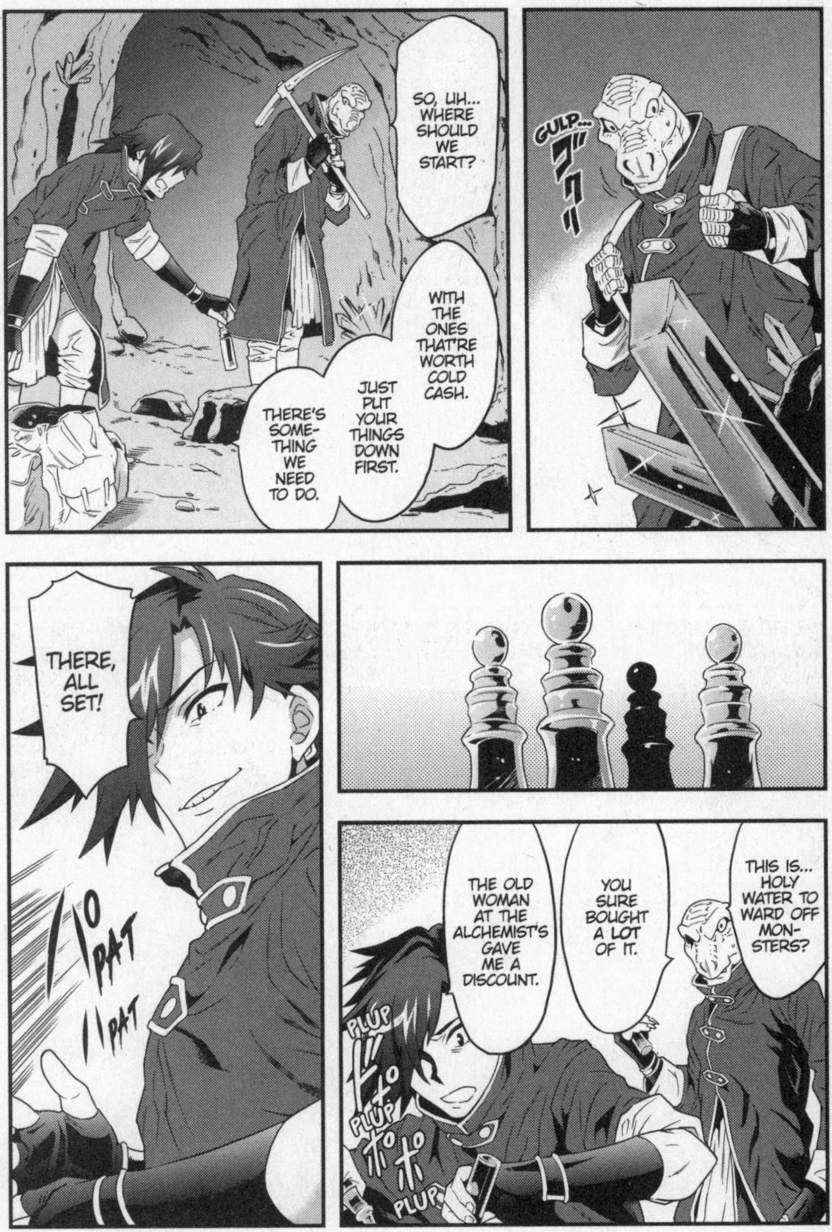
GULP...
SO, UH... WHERE SHOULD WE START?
WITH THE ONES THAT'RE WORTH COLD CASH.
JUST PUT YOUR THINGS DOWN FIRST.
THERE'S SOME-THING WE NEED TO DO.
THIS IS... HOLY WATER TO WARD OFF MON-STERS?
YOU SURE BOUGHT A LOT OF IT.
THE OLD WOMAN AT THE ALCHEMIST'S GAVE ME A DISCOUNT.
PLUP
PLUP
PLUP
THERE, ALL SET!
PAT
PAT

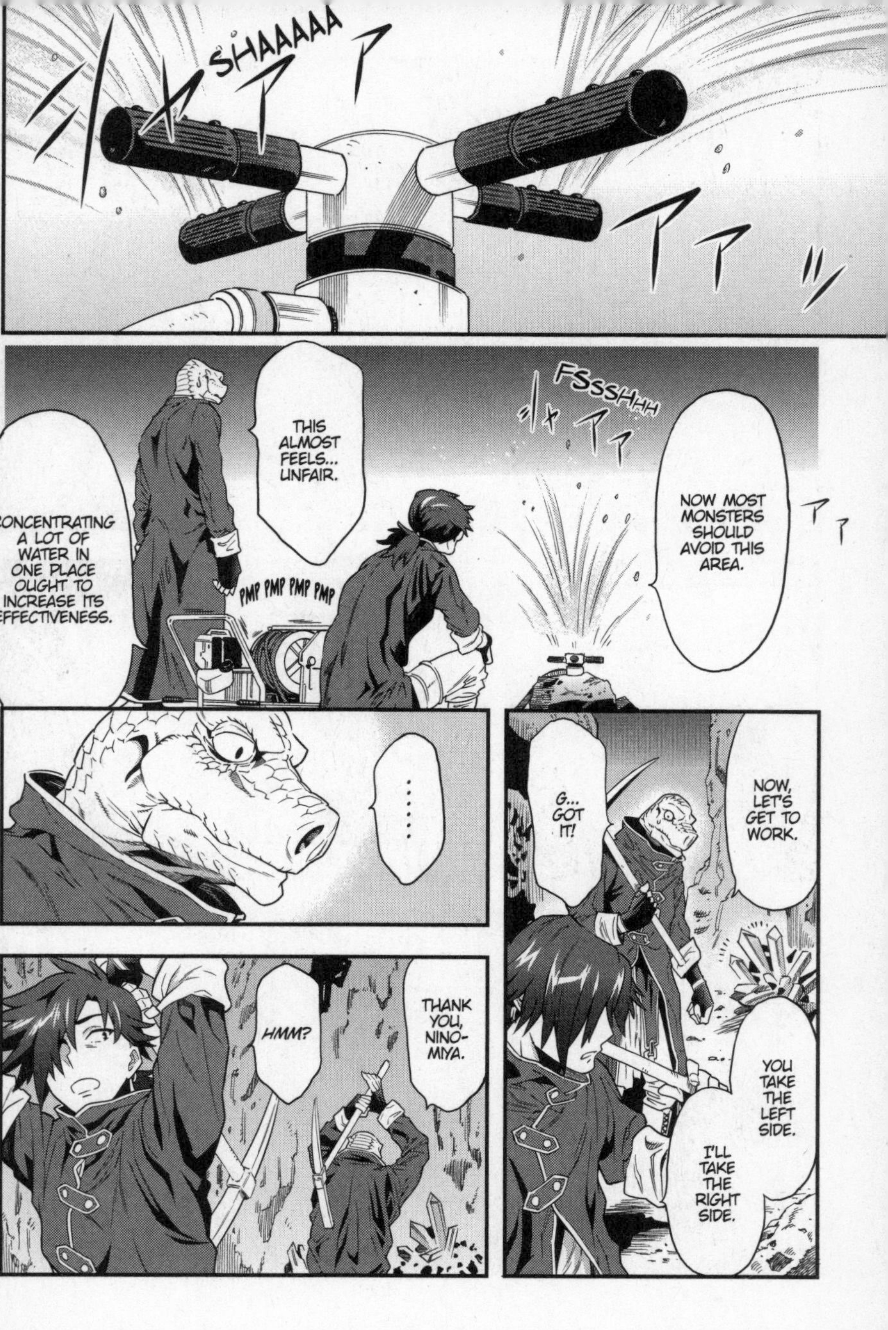
SHAAAAA
FSSSHHH
NOW MOST MONSTERS SHOULD AVOID THIS AREA.
THIS ALMOST FEELS... UNFAIR.
PMP PMP PMP PMP
CONCENTRATING A LOT OF WATER IN ONE PLACE OUGHT TO INCREASE ITS EFFECTIVENESS.
NOW, LET'S GET TO WORK.
G... GOT IT!
YOU TAKE THE LEFT SIDE.
I'LL TAKE THE RIGHT SIDE.
......
THANK YOU, NINO-MIYA.
HMM?

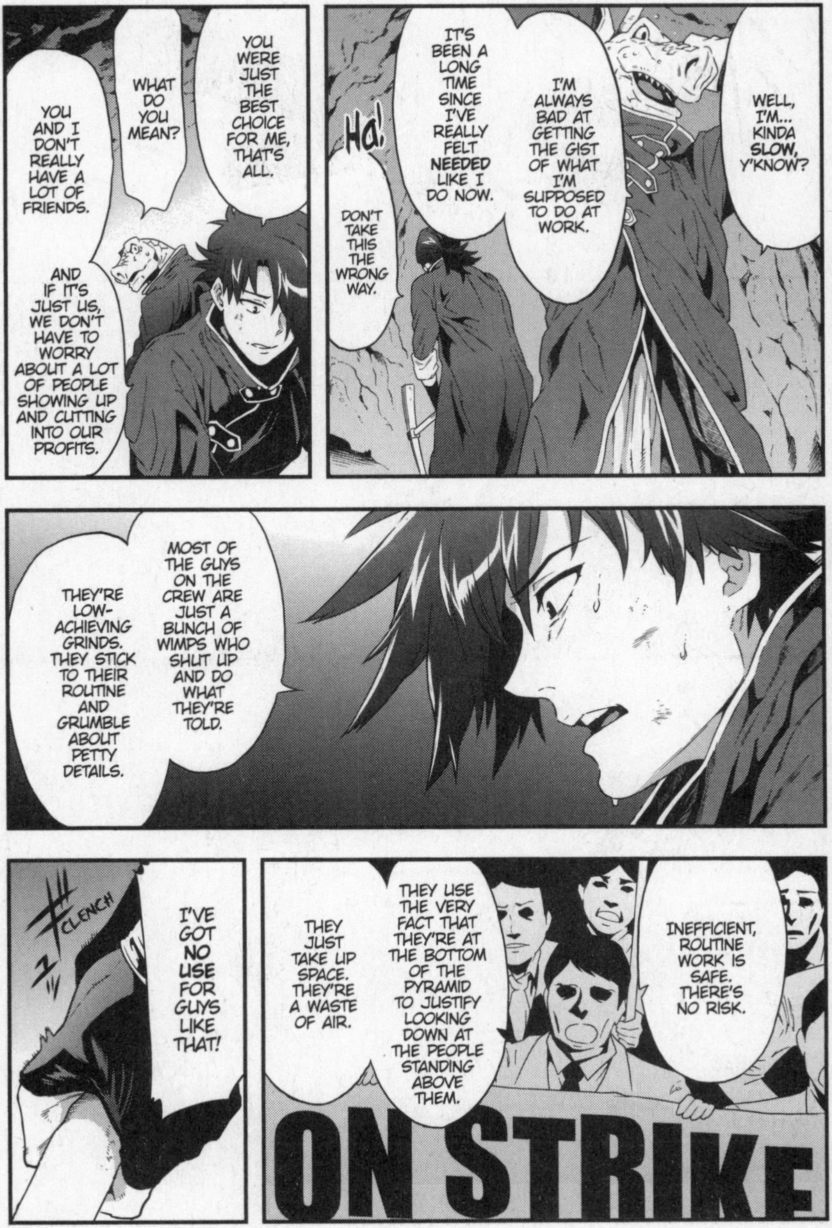
WELL, I'M... KINDA SLOW, Y'KNOW?
I'M ALWAYS BAD AT GETTING THE GIST OF WHAT I'M SUPPOSED TO DO AT WORK.
IT'S BEEN A LONG TIME SINCE I'VE REALLY FELT NEEDED LIKE I DO NOW.
Ha!
DON'T TAKE THIS THE WRONG WAY.
YOU WERE JUST THE BEST CHOICE FOR ME, THAT'S ALL.
WHAT DO YOU MEAN?
YOU AND I DON'T REALLY HAVE A LOT OF FRIENDS.
AND IF IT'S JUST US, WE DON'T HAVE TO WORRY ABOUT A LOT OF PEOPLE SHOWING UP AND CUTTING INTO OUR PROFITS.
MOST OF THE GUYS ON THE CREW ARE JUST A BUNCH OF WIMPS WHO SHUT UP AND DO WHAT THEY'RE TOLD.
THEY'RE LOW-ACHIEVING GRINDS. THEY STICK TO THEIR ROUTINE AND GRUMBLE ABOUT PETTY DETAILS.
INEFFICIENT, ROUTINE WORK IS SAFE. THERE'S NO RISK.
THEY USE THE VERY FACT THAT THEY'RE AT THE BOTTOM OF THE PYRAMID TO JUSTIFY LOOKING DOWN AT THE PEOPLE STANDING ABOVE THEM.
THEY JUST TAKE UP SPACE. THEY'RE A WASTE OF AIR.
ON STRIKE
I'VE GOT NO USE FOR GUYS LIKE THAT!
CLENCH

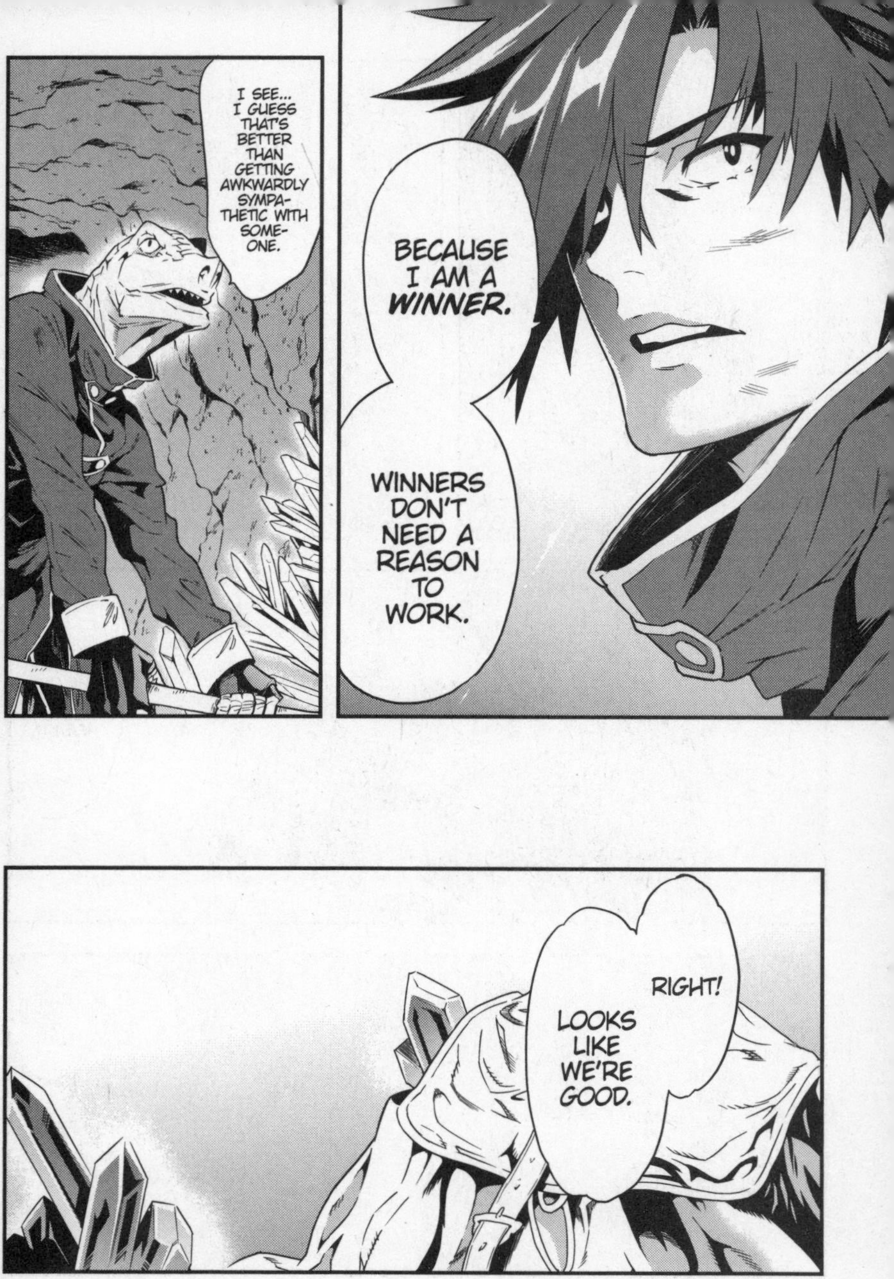
BECAUSE I AM A *WINNER.*
WINNERS DON'T NEED A REASON TO WORK.
I SEE... I GUESS THAT'S BETTER THAN GETTING AWKWARDLY SYMPATHETIC WITH SOMEONE.
RIGHT!
LOOKS LIKE WE'RE GOOD.

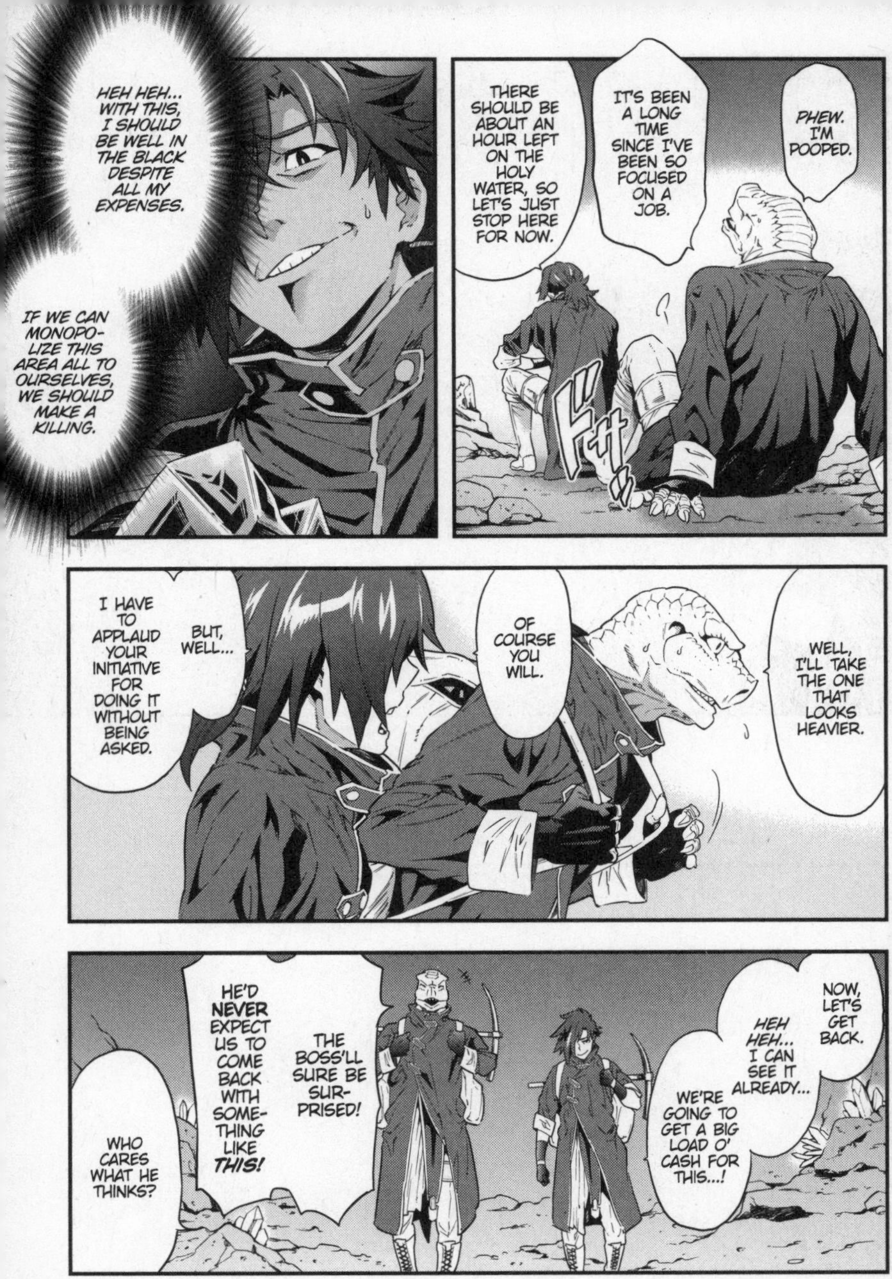
PHEW. I'M POOPED.
IT'S BEEN A LONG TIME SINCE I'VE BEEN SO FOCUSED ON A JOB.
THERE SHOULD BE ABOUT AN HOUR LEFT ON THE HOLY WATER, SO LET'S JUST STOP HERE FOR NOW.
ドサッ
HEH HEH... WITH THIS, I SHOULD BE WELL IN THE BLACK DESPITE ALL MY EXPENSES.
IF WE CAN MONOPOLIZE THIS AREA ALL TO OURSELVES, WE SHOULD MAKE A KILLING.
WELL, I'LL TAKE THE ONE THAT LOOKS HEAVIER.
OF COURSE YOU WILL.
BUT, WELL...
I HAVE TO APPLAUD YOUR INITIATIVE FOR DOING IT WITHOUT BEING ASKED.
NOW, LET'S GET BACK.
HEH HEH... I CAN SEE IT ALREADY...
WE'RE GOING TO GET A BIG LOAD O' CASH FOR THIS...!
THE BOSS'LL SURE BE SURPRISED!
HE'D **NEVER** EXPECT US TO COME BACK WITH SOMETHING LIKE ***THIS!***
WHO CARES WHAT HE THINKS?

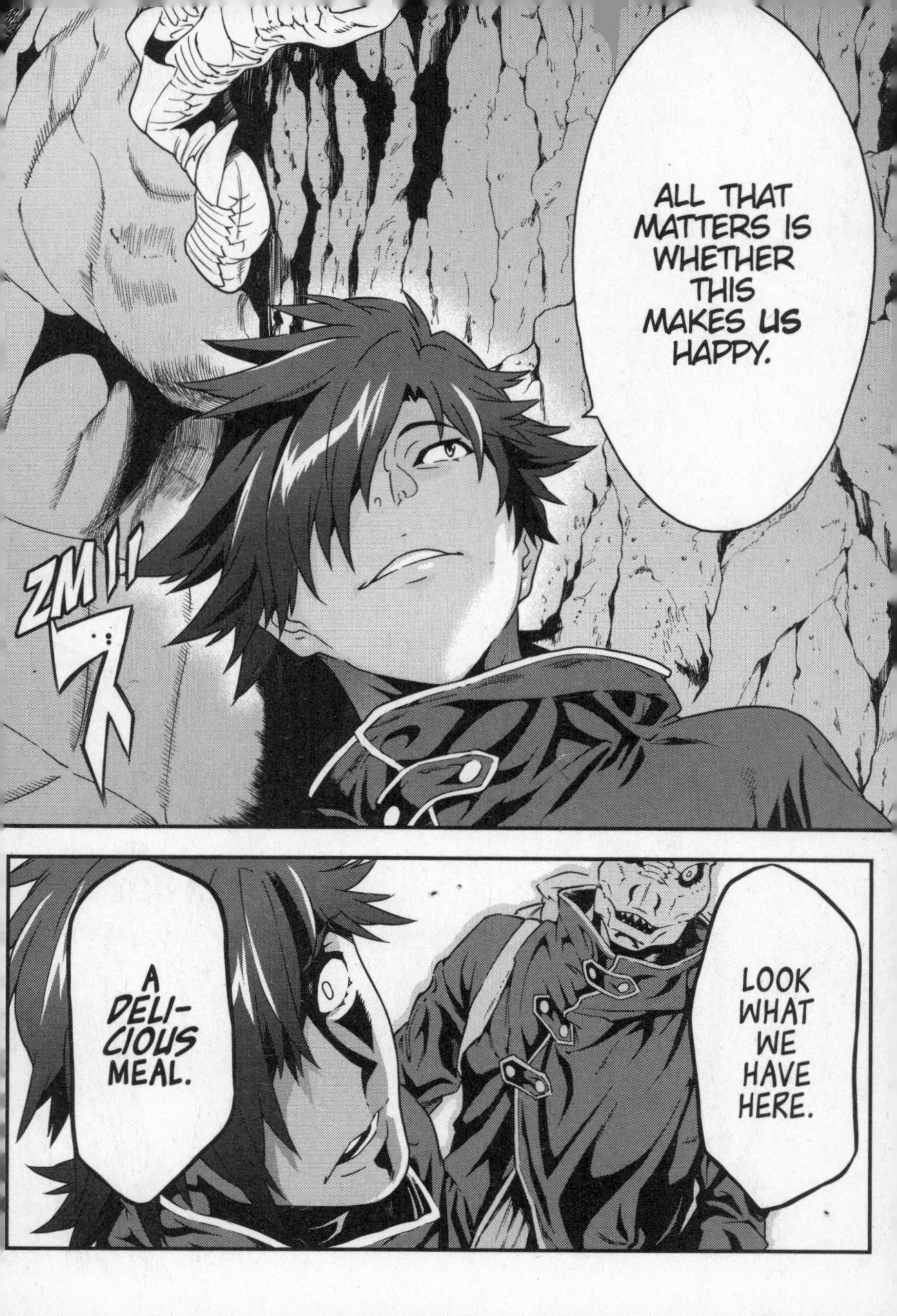
ALL THAT MATTERS IS WHETHER THIS MAKES US HAPPY.
ZMII
LOOK WHAT WE HAVE HERE.
A DELI-CIOUS MEAL.

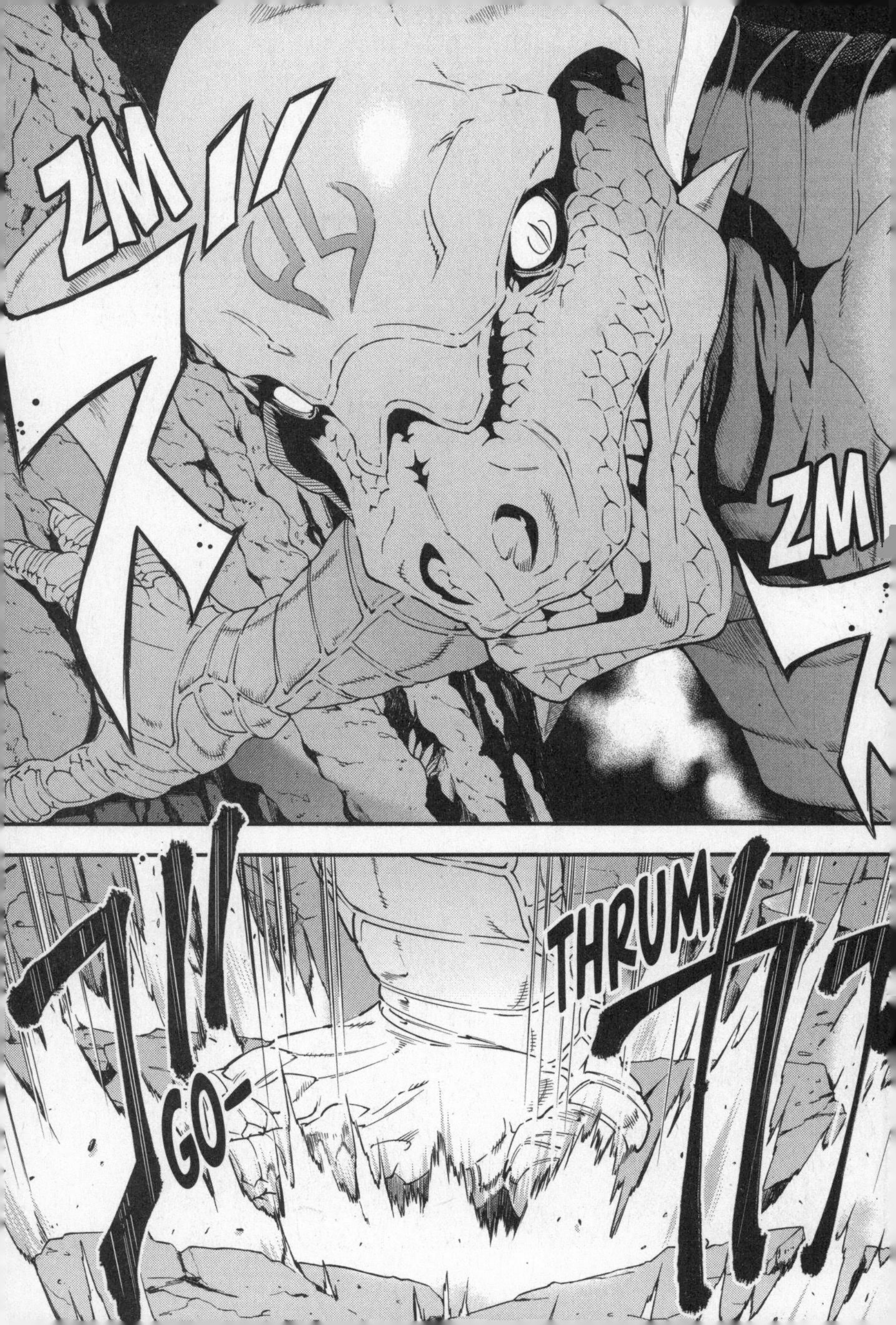
ZM
ZM
THRUM
GO-

HWOOOOO...

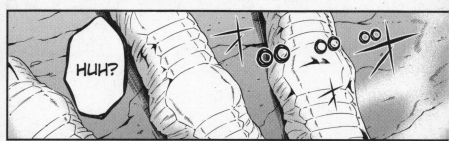

HUH?

THEY'RE GONE...?

WHERE DID THEY RUN OFF TO...?

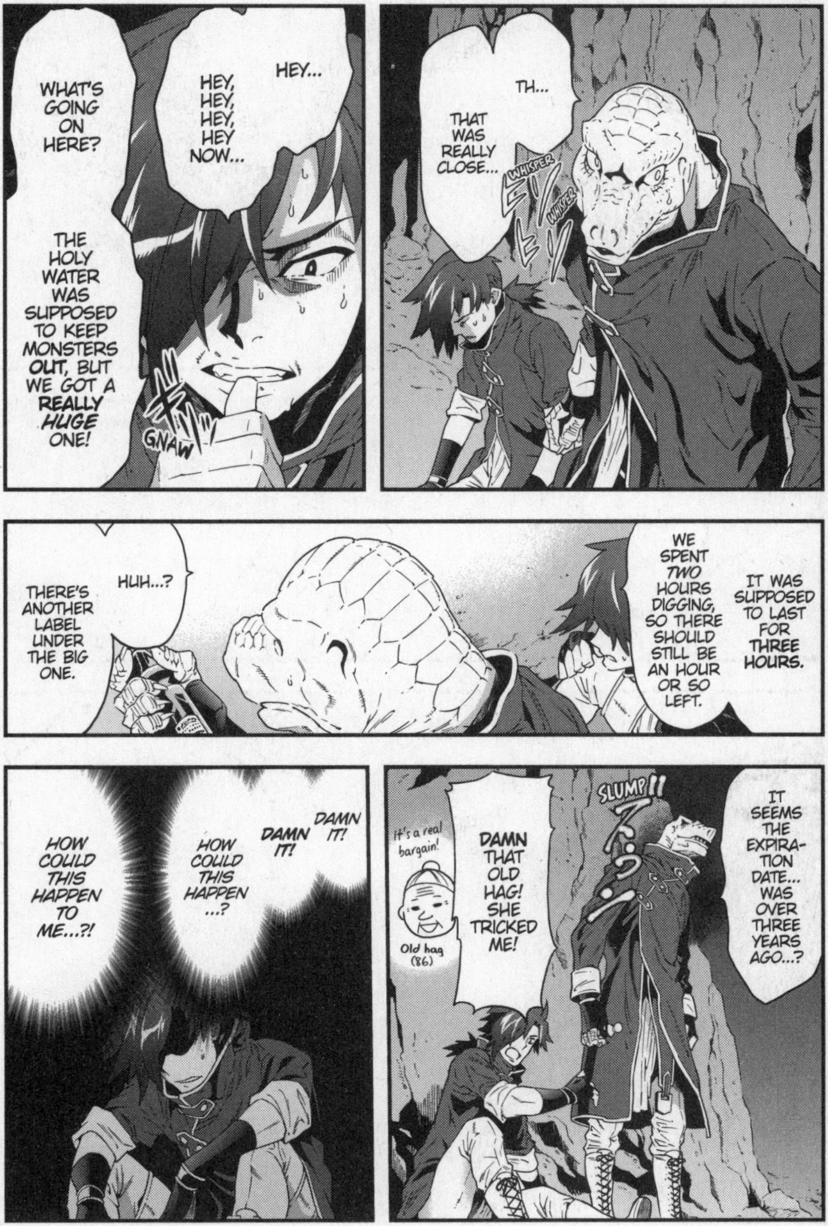
TH...
THAT WAS REALLY CLOSE...
WHISPER
WHISPER
HEY...
HEY, HEY, HEY, HEY NOW...
WHAT'S GOING ON HERE?
THE HOLY WATER WAS SUPPOSED TO KEEP MONSTERS OUT, BUT WE GOT A REALLY HUGE ONE!
GNAW
IT WAS SUPPOSED TO LAST FOR THREE HOURS.
WE SPENT TWO HOURS DIGGING, SO THERE SHOULD STILL BE AN HOUR OR SO LEFT.
HUH...?
THERE'S ANOTHER LABEL UNDER THE BIG ONE.
IT SEEMS THE EXPIRATION DATE... WAS OVER THREE YEARS AGO...?
SLUMP!!
DAMN THAT OLD HAG! SHE TRICKED ME!
It's a real bargain!
Old hag (86)
DAMN IT!
DAMN IT!
HOW COULD THIS HAPPEN...?
HOW COULD THIS HAPPEN TO ME...?!

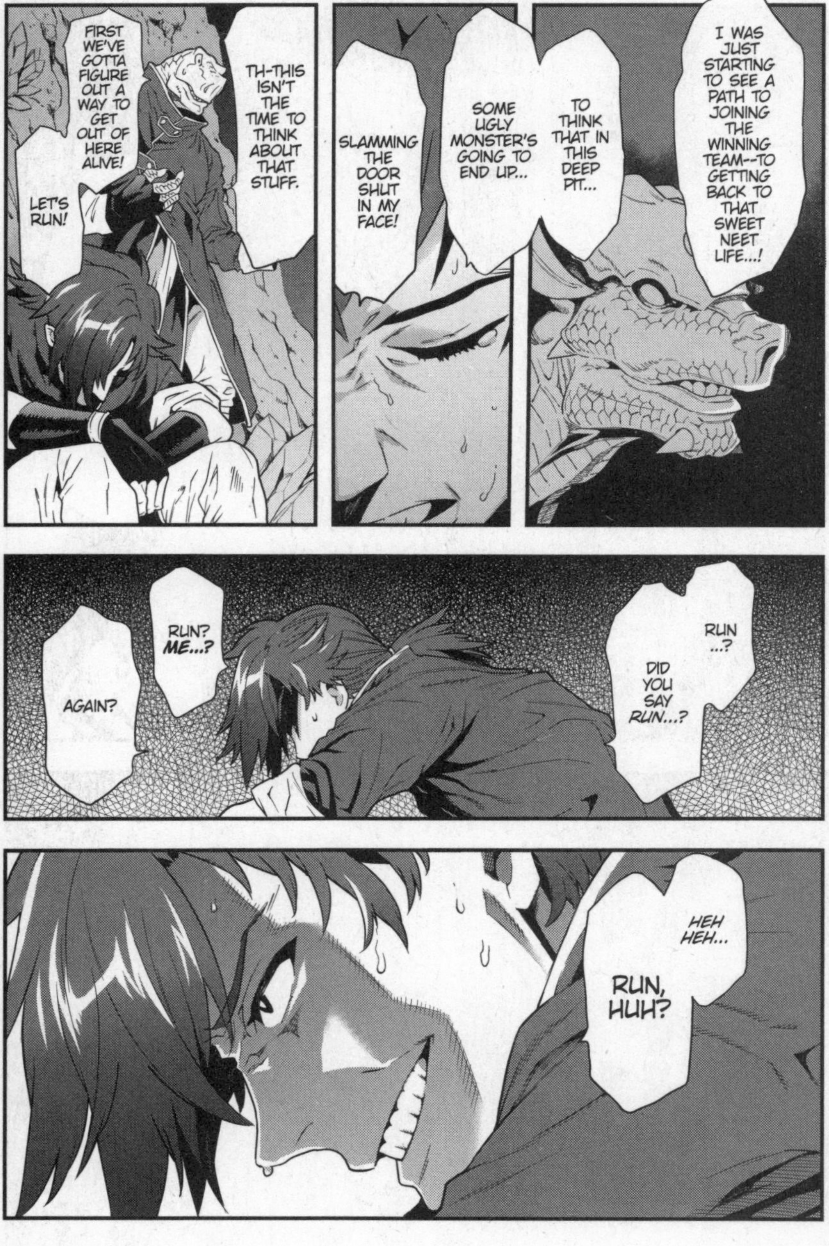
I WAS JUST STARTING TO SEE A PATH TO JOINING THE WINNING TEAM--TO GETTING BACK TO THAT SWEET NEET LIFE...!
TO THINK THAT IN THIS DEEP PIT...
SOME UGLY MONSTER'S GOING TO END UP...
SLAMMING THE DOOR SHUT IN MY FACE!
TH-THIS ISN'T THE TIME TO THINK ABOUT THAT STUFF.
FIRST WE'VE GOTTA FIGURE OUT A WAY TO GET OUT OF HERE ALIVE!
LET'S RUN!
RUN ...?
DID YOU SAY *RUN*...?
RUN? *ME*...?
AGAIN?
HEH HEH...
RUN, HUH?

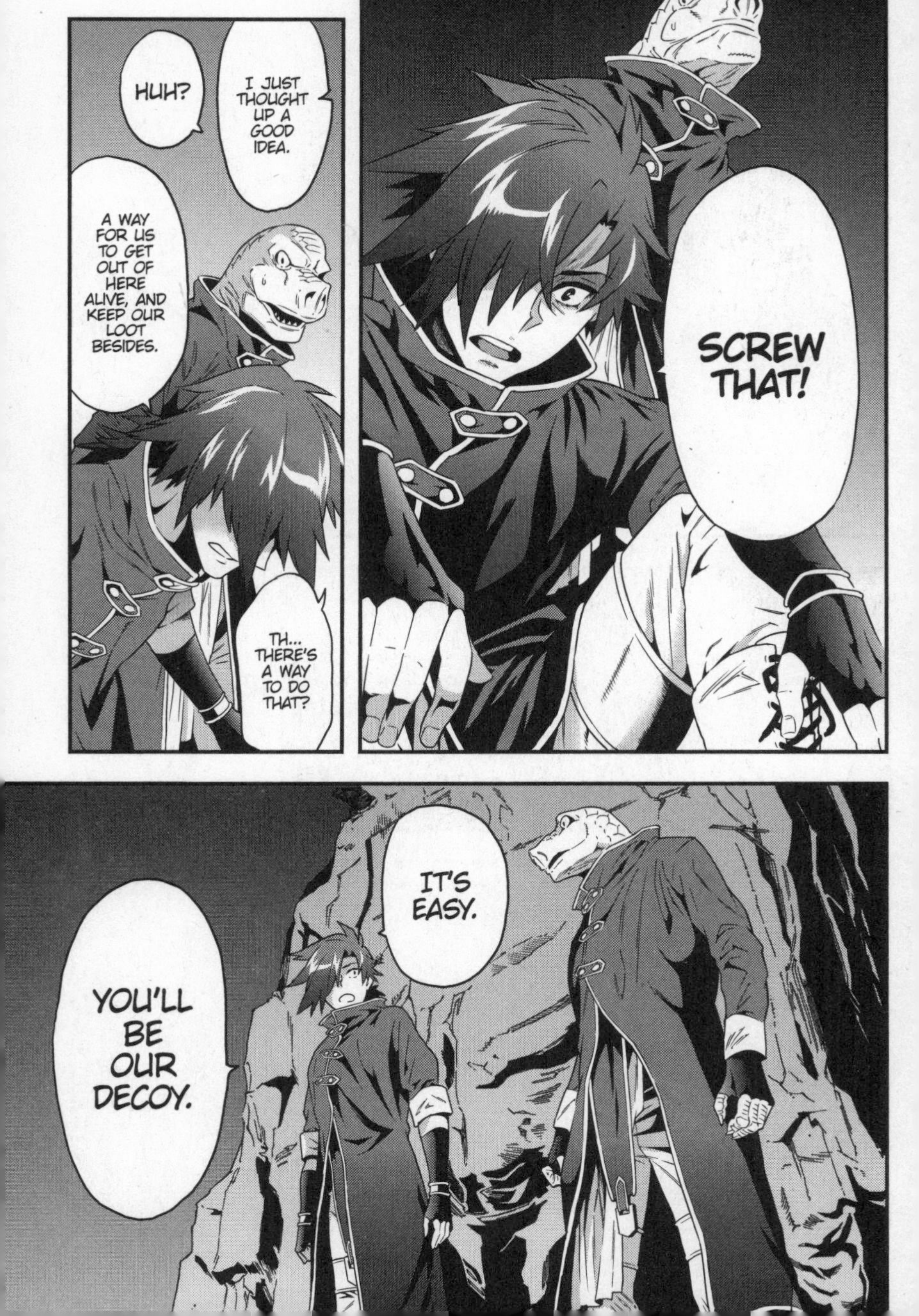
SCREW THAT!
I JUST THOUGHT UP A GOOD IDEA.
HUH?
A WAY FOR US TO GET OUT OF HERE ALIVE, AND KEEP OUR LOOT BESIDES.
TH... THERE'S A WAY TO DO THAT?
IT'S EASY.
YOU'LL BE OUR DECOY.

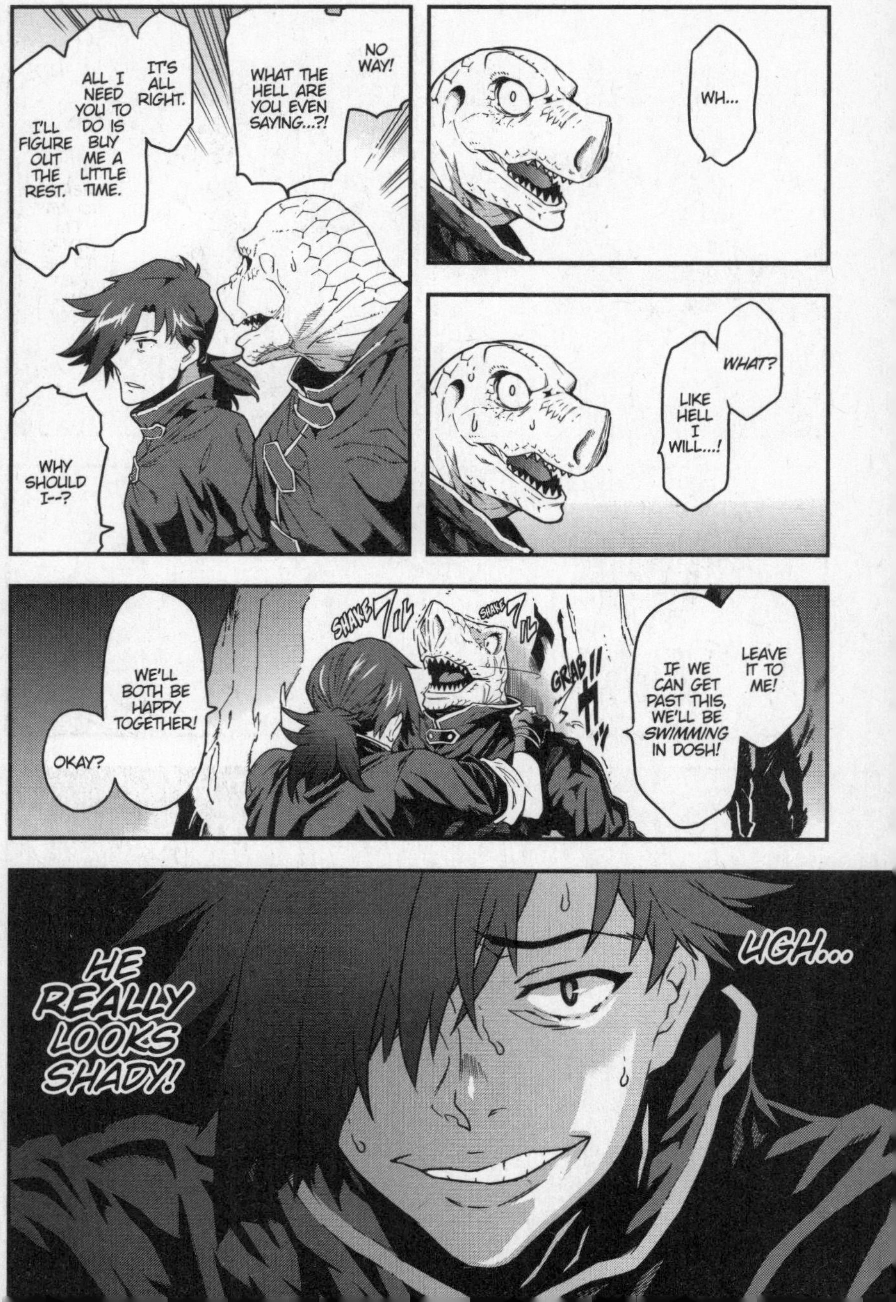
WH...
WHAT?
LIKE HELL I WILL...!
NO WAY!
WHAT THE HELL ARE YOU EVEN SAYING...?!
IT'S ALL RIGHT.
ALL I NEED YOU TO DO IS BUY ME A LITTLE TIME.
I'LL FIGURE OUT THE REST.
WHY SHOULD I--?
LEAVE IT TO ME!
IF WE CAN GET PAST THIS, WE'LL BE SWIMMING IN DOSH!
GRAB
SHAKE
SHAKE
WE'LL BOTH BE HAPPY TOGETHER!
OKAY?
UGH...
HE REALLY LOOKS SHADY!

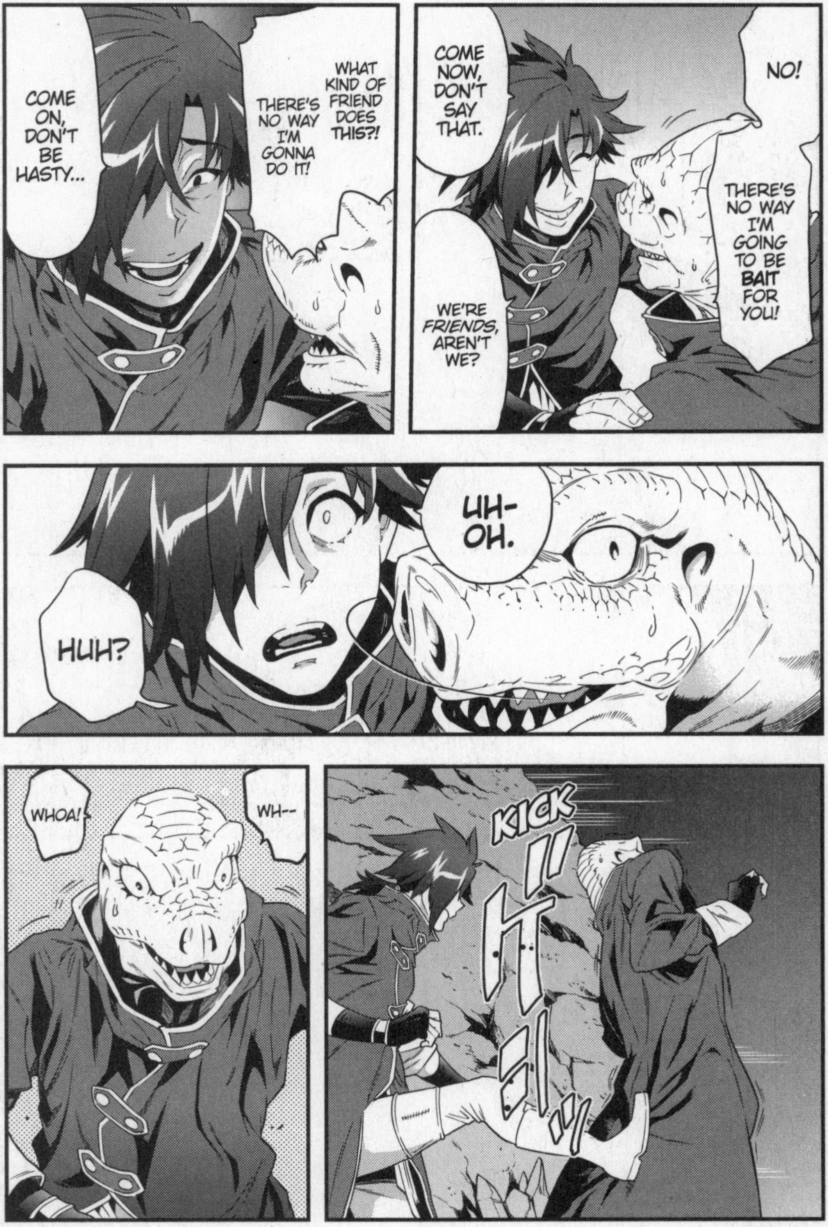
NO!
COME NOW, DON'T SAY THAT.
THERE'S NO WAY I'M GOING TO BE **BAIT** FOR YOU!
WE'RE *FRIENDS*, AREN'T WE?
WHAT KIND OF FRIEND DOES THIS?!
THERE'S NO WAY I'M GONNA DO IT!
COME ON, DON'T BE HASTY...
UH-OH.
HUH?
KICK
WH--
WHOA!

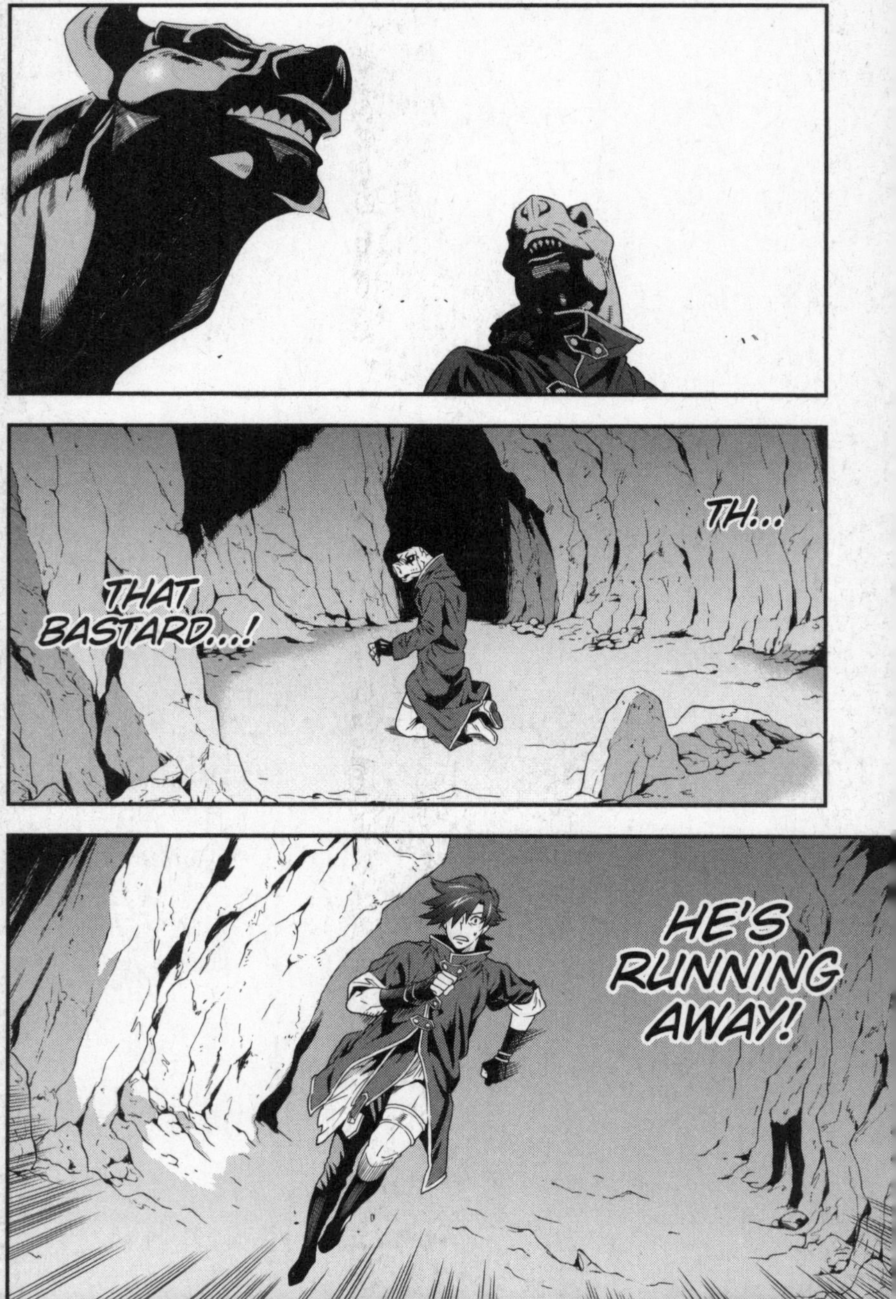
TH...
THAT BASTARD...!
HE'S RUNNING AWAY!

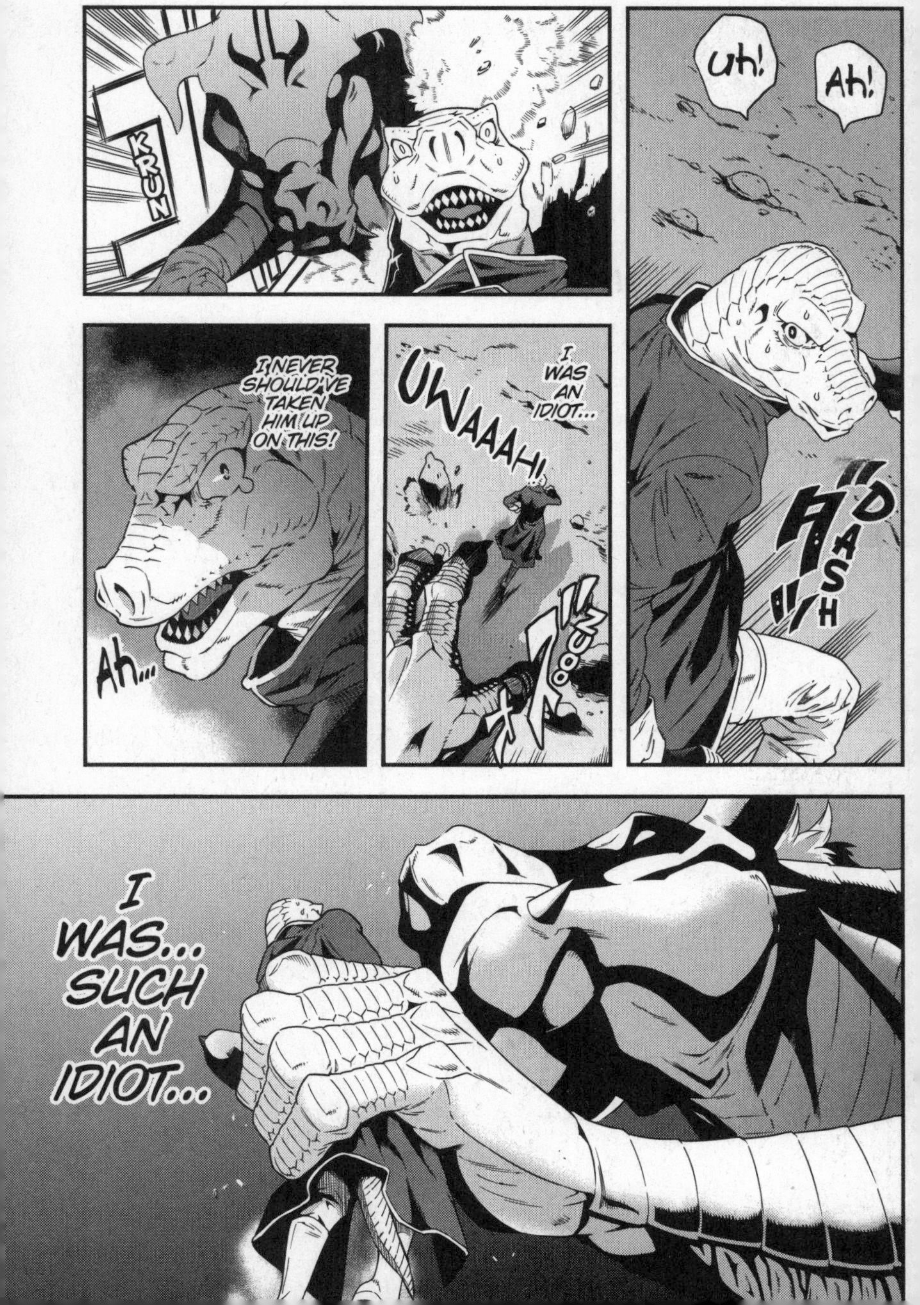

Uh!
Ah!
DASH
KRUN
I WAS AN IDIOT...
UWAAAAH!!
ZUOO...
I NEVER SHOULD'VE TAKEN HIM UP ON THIS!
Ah...
I WAS... SUCH AN IDIOT...

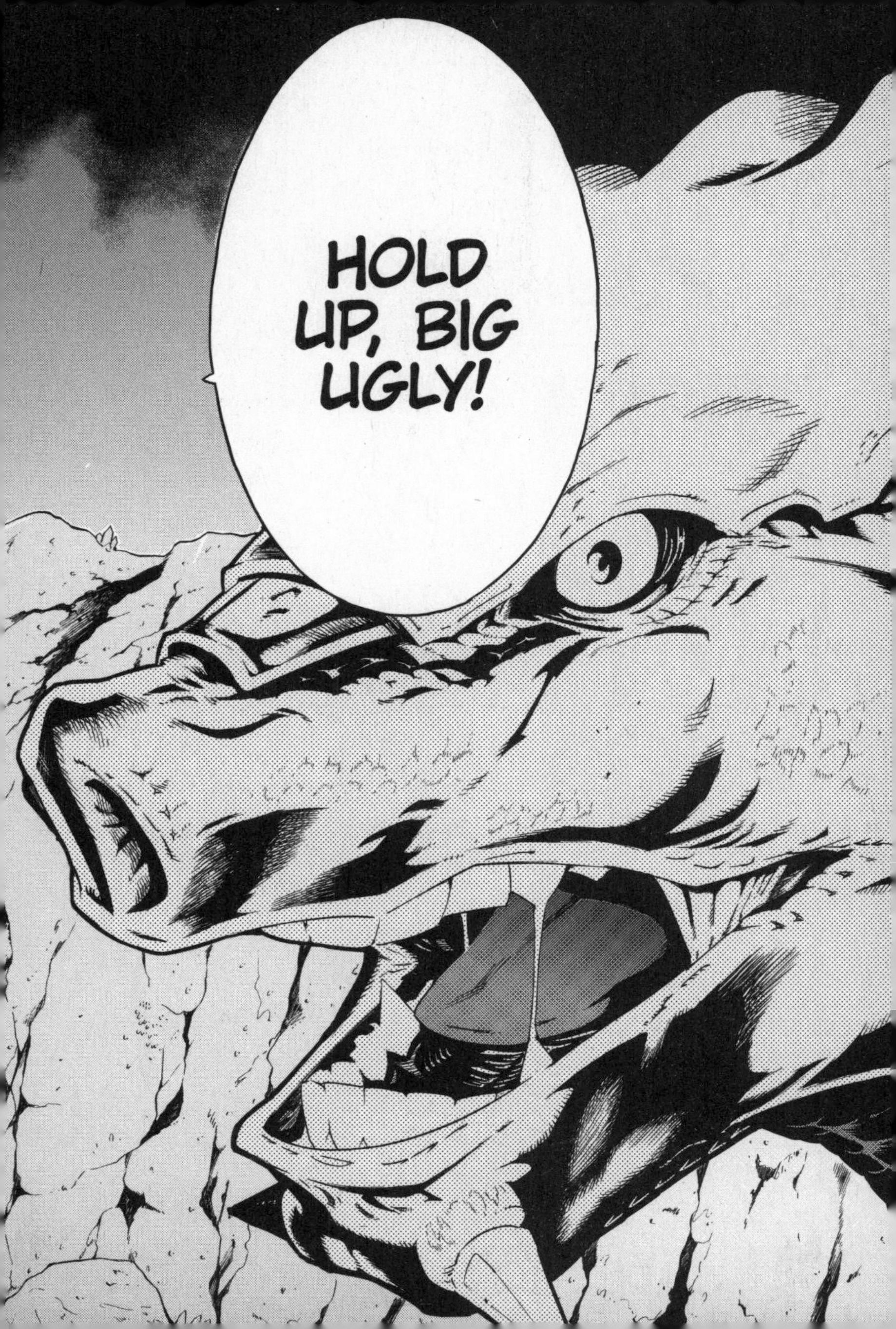
HOLD UP, BIG UGLY!

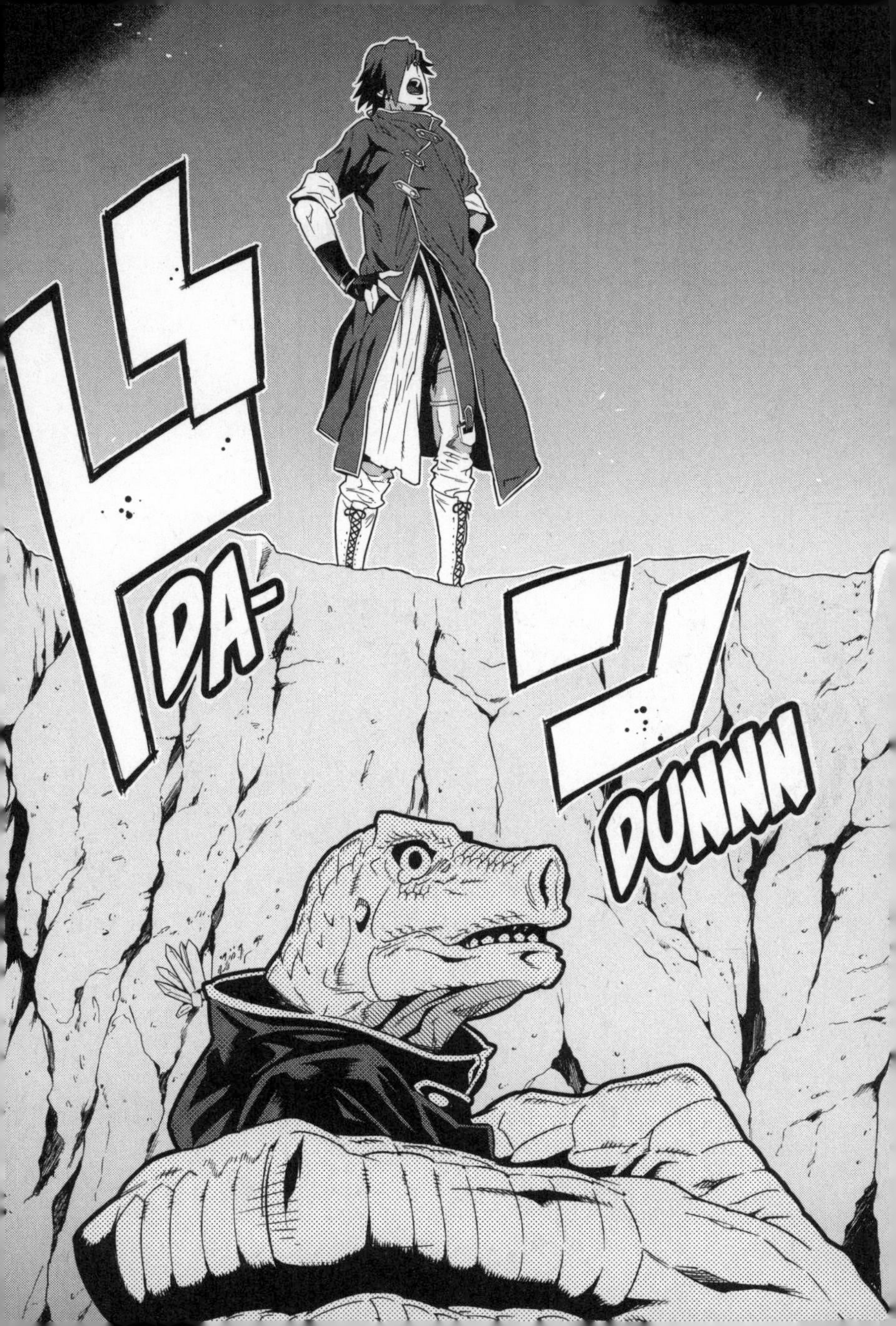

ドー
DA-
ン
DUNNN

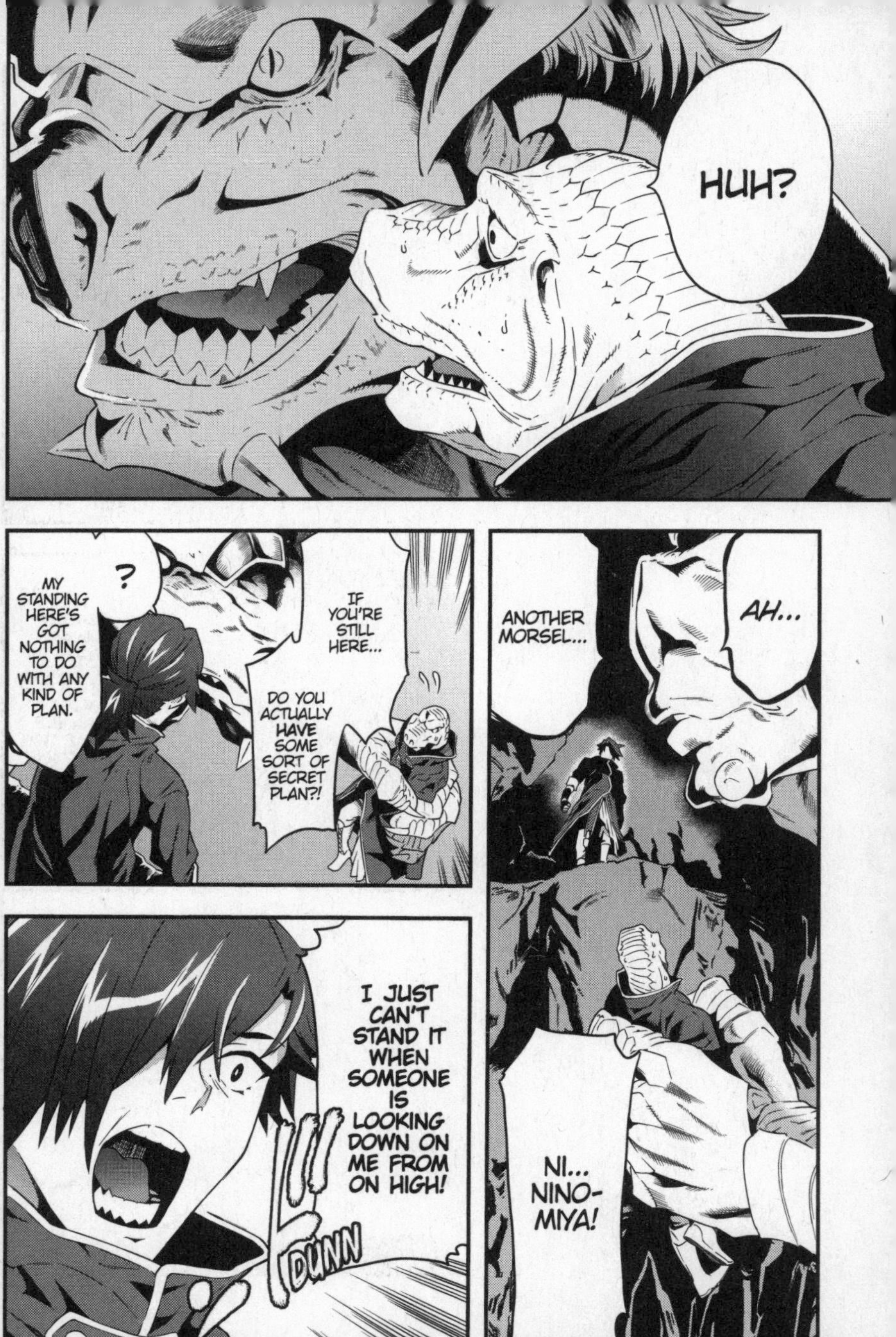
HUH?
AH...
ANOTHER MORSEL...
NI... NINO-MIYA!
IF YOU'RE STILL HERE...
DO YOU ACTUALLY HAVE SOME SORT OF SECRET PLAN?!
?
MY STANDING HERE'S GOT NOTHING TO DO WITH ANY KIND OF PLAN.
I JUST CAN'T STAND IT WHEN SOMEONE IS LOOKING DOWN ON ME FROM ON HIGH!
DUNN

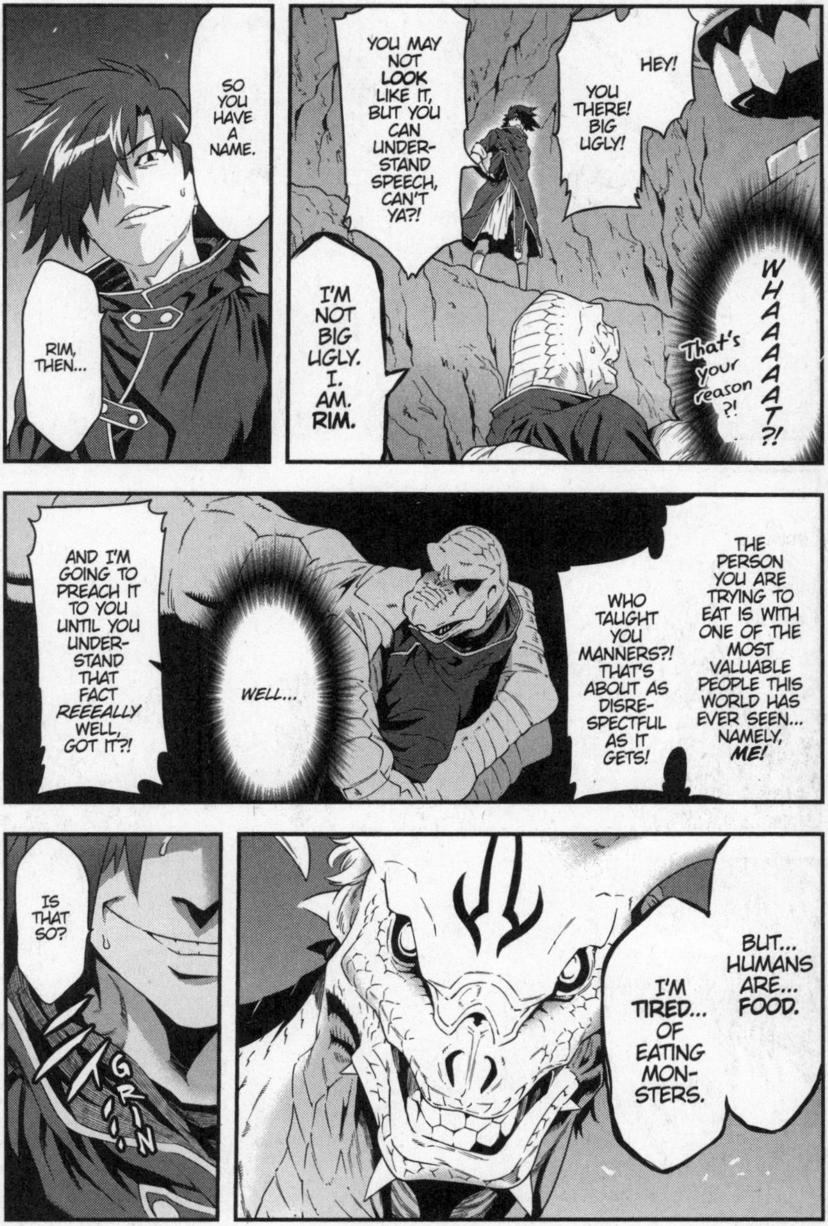
HEY!
YOU THERE! BIG UGLY!
YOU MAY NOT LOOK LIKE IT, BUT YOU CAN UNDERSTAND SPEECH, CAN'T YA?!
I'M NOT BIG UGLY. I. AM. RIM.
WHAAAAAAT?!
That's your reason?!
SO YOU HAVE A NAME.
RIM, THEN...
THE PERSON YOU ARE TRYING TO EAT IS WITH ONE OF THE MOST VALUABLE PEOPLE THIS WORLD HAS EVER SEEN... NAMELY, ME!
WHO TAUGHT YOU MANNERS?! THAT'S ABOUT AS DISRESPECTFUL AS IT GETS!
WELL...
AND I'M GOING TO PREACH IT TO YOU UNTIL YOU UNDERSTAND THAT FACT REEEALLY WELL, GOT IT?!
BUT... HUMANS ARE... FOOD.
I'M TIRED... OF EATING MONSTERS.
IS THAT SO?
GRIN

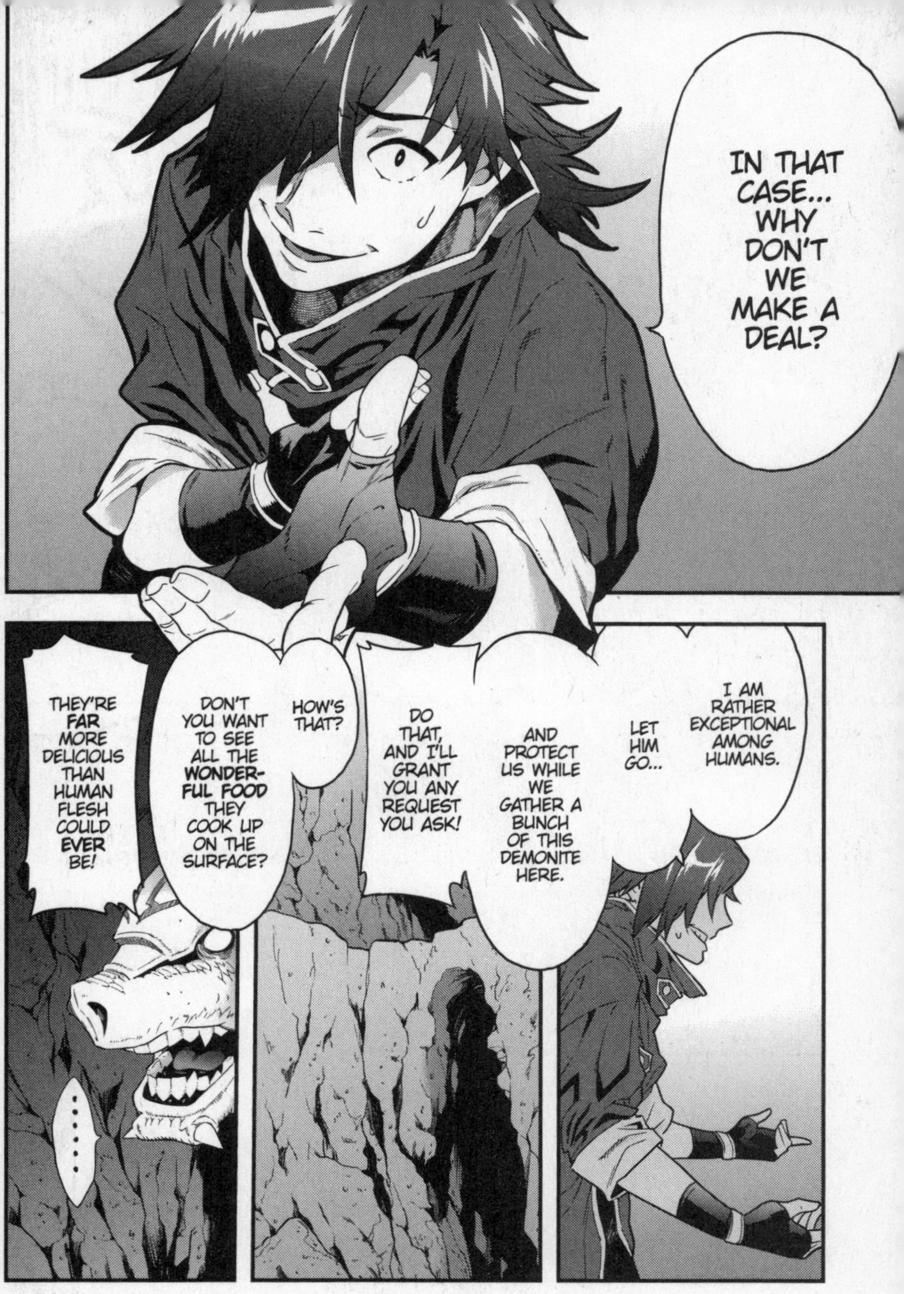
IN THAT CASE... WHY DON'T WE MAKE A DEAL?
I AM RATHER EXCEPTIONAL AMONG HUMANS.
LET HIM GO...
AND PROTECT US WHILE WE GATHER A BUNCH OF THIS DEMONITE HERE.
DO THAT, AND I'LL GRANT YOU ANY REQUEST YOU ASK!
HOW'S THAT?
DON'T YOU WANT TO SEE ALL THE WONDERFUL FOOD THEY COOK UP ON THE SURFACE?
THEY'RE FAR MORE DELICIOUS THAN HUMAN FLESH COULD EVER BE!
......

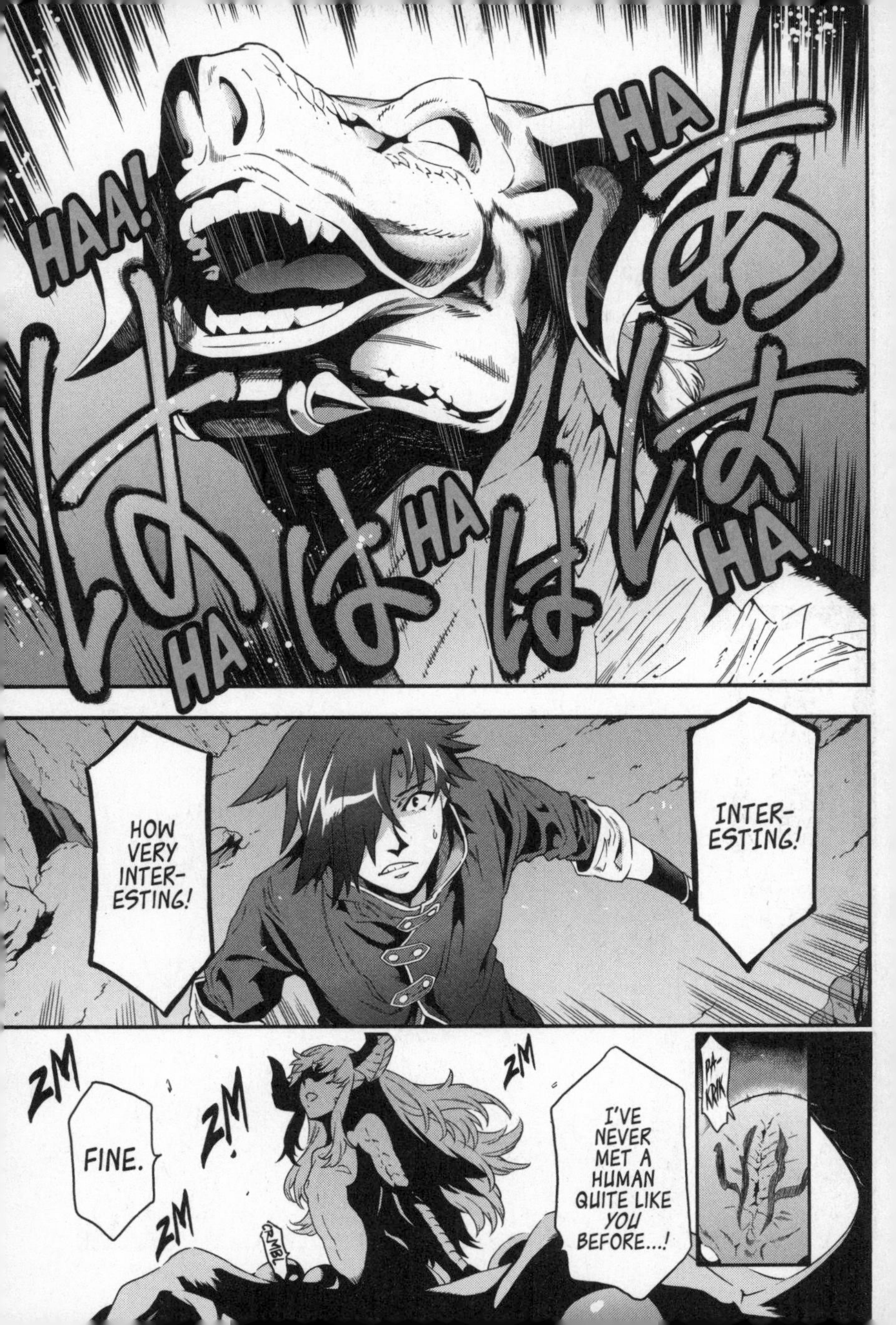
HA
HA
HA
HA
HA
HAA!
INTER-ESTING!
HOW VERY INTER-ESTING!
PA-KRIK
I'VE NEVER MET A HUMAN QUITE LIKE YOU BEFORE...!
ZM
ZM
FINE.
ZM
ZM
CRUMBL

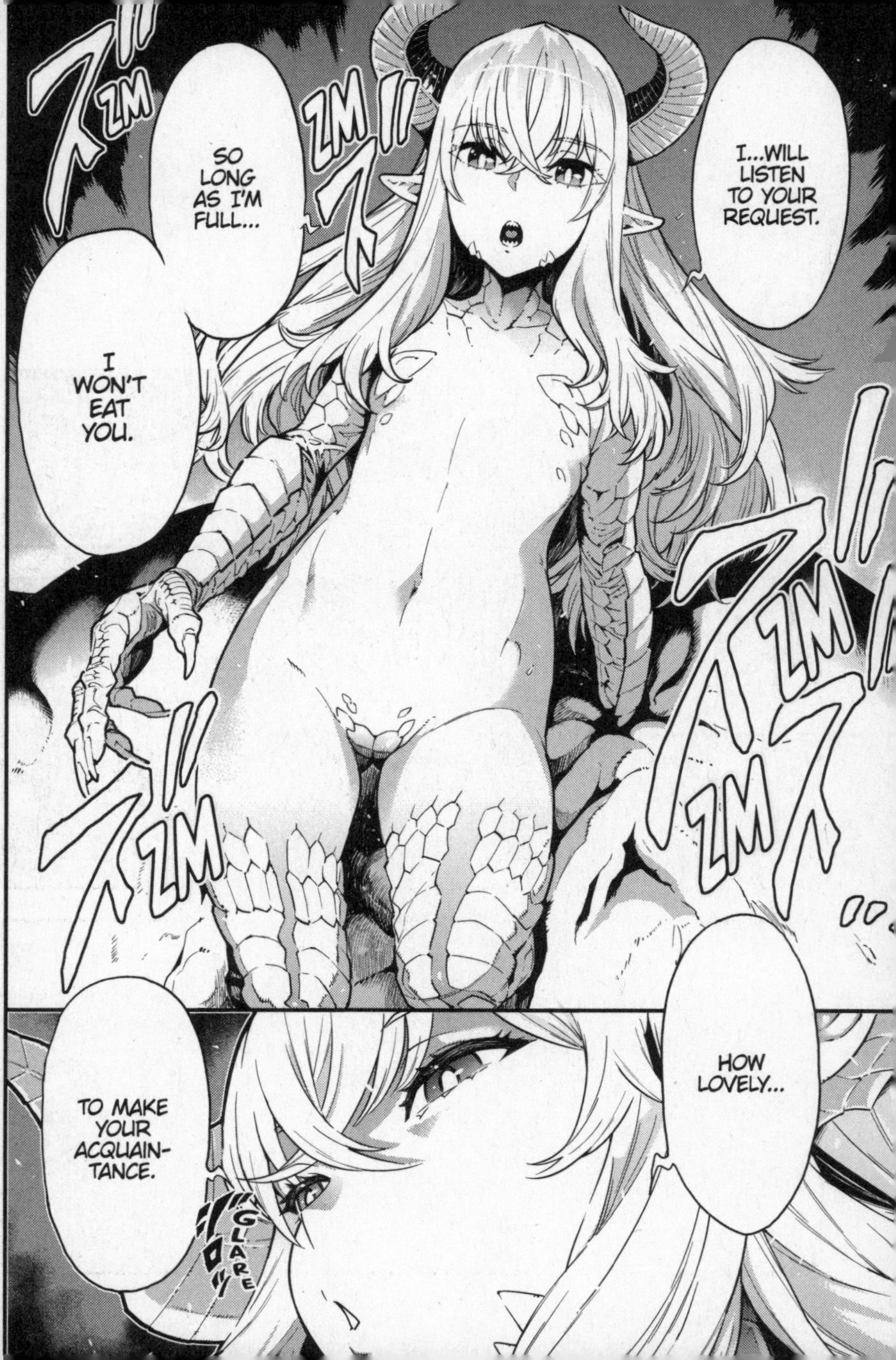
I...WILL LISTEN TO YOUR REQUEST.
ZM
ZM
SO LONG AS I'M FULL...
I WON'T EAT YOU.
ZM
ZM
ZM
HOW LOVELY...
TO MAKE YOUR ACQUAIN- TANCE.
GLARE

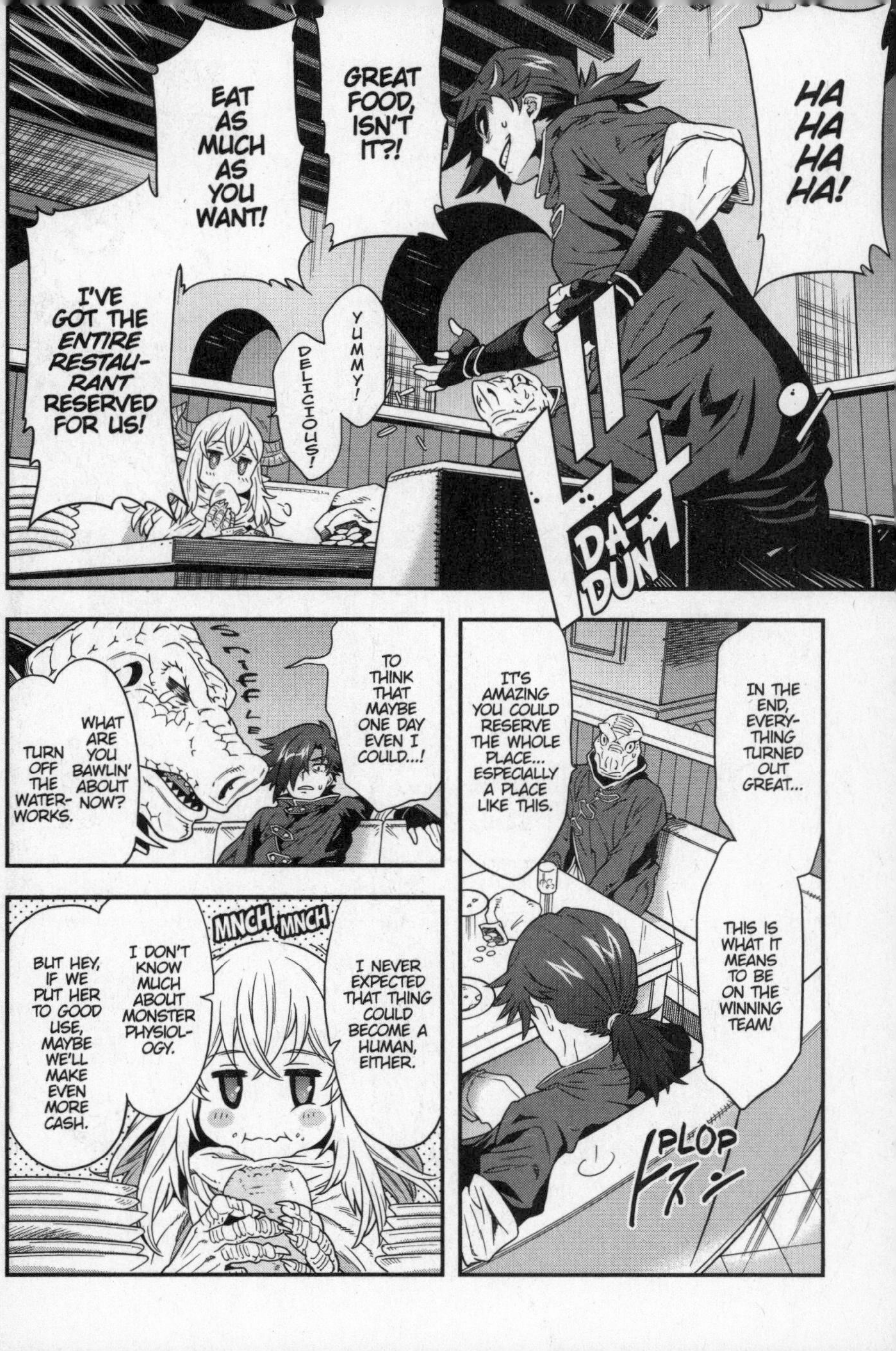
HA HA HA HA!
GREAT FOOD, ISN'T IT?!
EAT AS MUCH AS YOU WANT!
I'VE GOT THE *ENTIRE RESTAURANT* RESERVED FOR US!
YUMMY!
DELICIOUS!
DA-DUN
IN THE END, EVERYTHING TURNED OUT GREAT...
IT'S AMAZING YOU COULD RESERVE THE WHOLE PLACE... ESPECIALLY A PLACE LIKE THIS.
THIS IS WHAT IT MEANS TO BE ON THE WINNING TEAM!
PLOP
TO THINK THAT MAYBE ONE DAY EVEN I COULD...!
SNIFFLE
WHAT ARE YOU BAWLIN' ABOUT NOW?
TURN OFF THE WATERWORKS.
MNCH MNCH
I NEVER EXPECTED THAT THING COULD BECOME A HUMAN, EITHER.
I DON'T KNOW MUCH ABOUT MONSTER PHYSIOLOGY.
BUT HEY, IF WE PUT HER TO GOOD USE, MAYBE WE'LL MAKE EVEN MORE CASH.

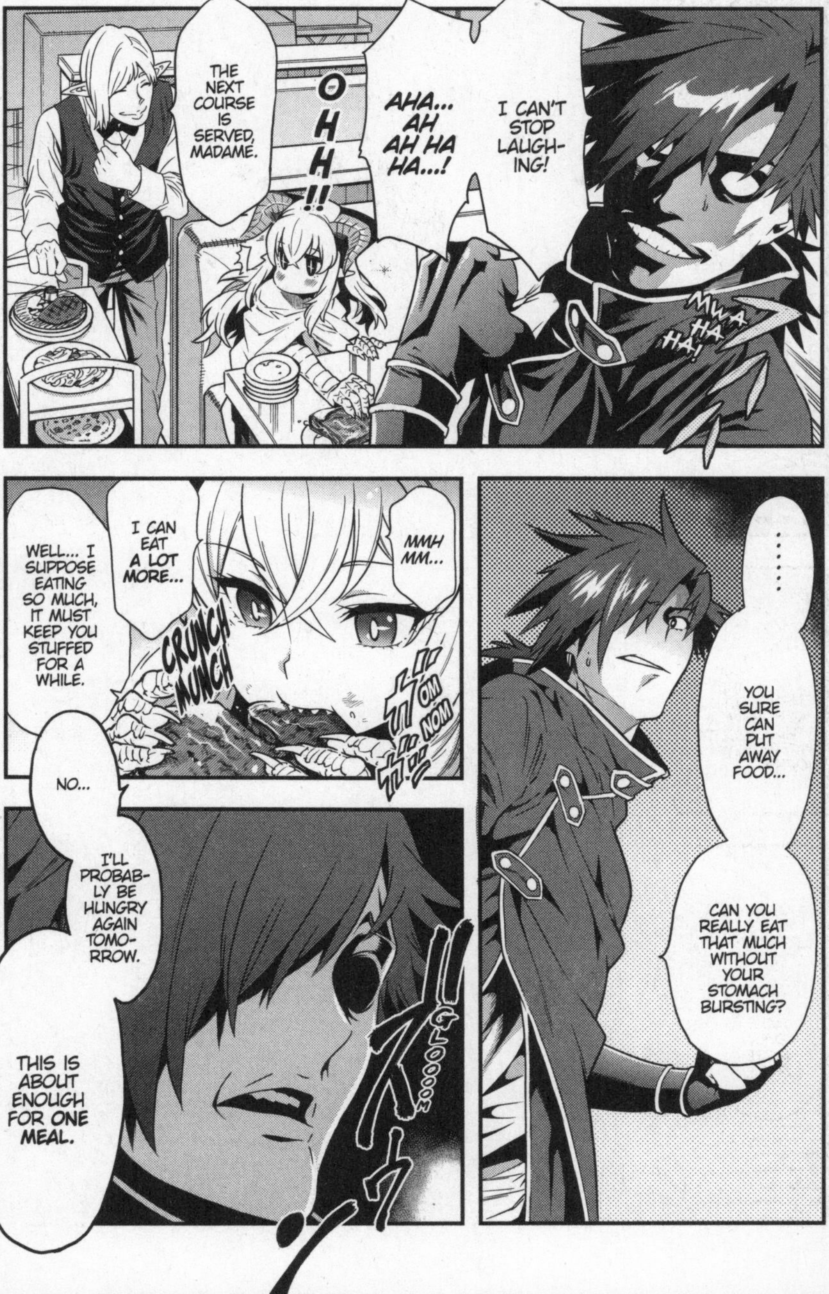
I CAN'T STOP LAUGHING!
AHA... AH AH HA HA...!
MWA HA HA!
OHH!!
THE NEXT COURSE IS SERVED, MADAME.
......
YOU SURE CAN PUT AWAY FOOD...
CAN YOU REALLY EAT THAT MUCH WITHOUT YOUR STOMACH BURSTING?
MMH MM...
I CAN EAT A LOT MORE...
WELL... I SUPPOSE EATING SO MUCH, IT MUST KEEP YOU STUFFED FOR A WHILE.
CRUNCH MUNCH
OM NOM
NO...
I'LL PROBABLY BE HUNGRY AGAIN TOMORROW.
THIS IS ABOUT ENOUGH FOR ONE MEAL.
GLOOOOOM

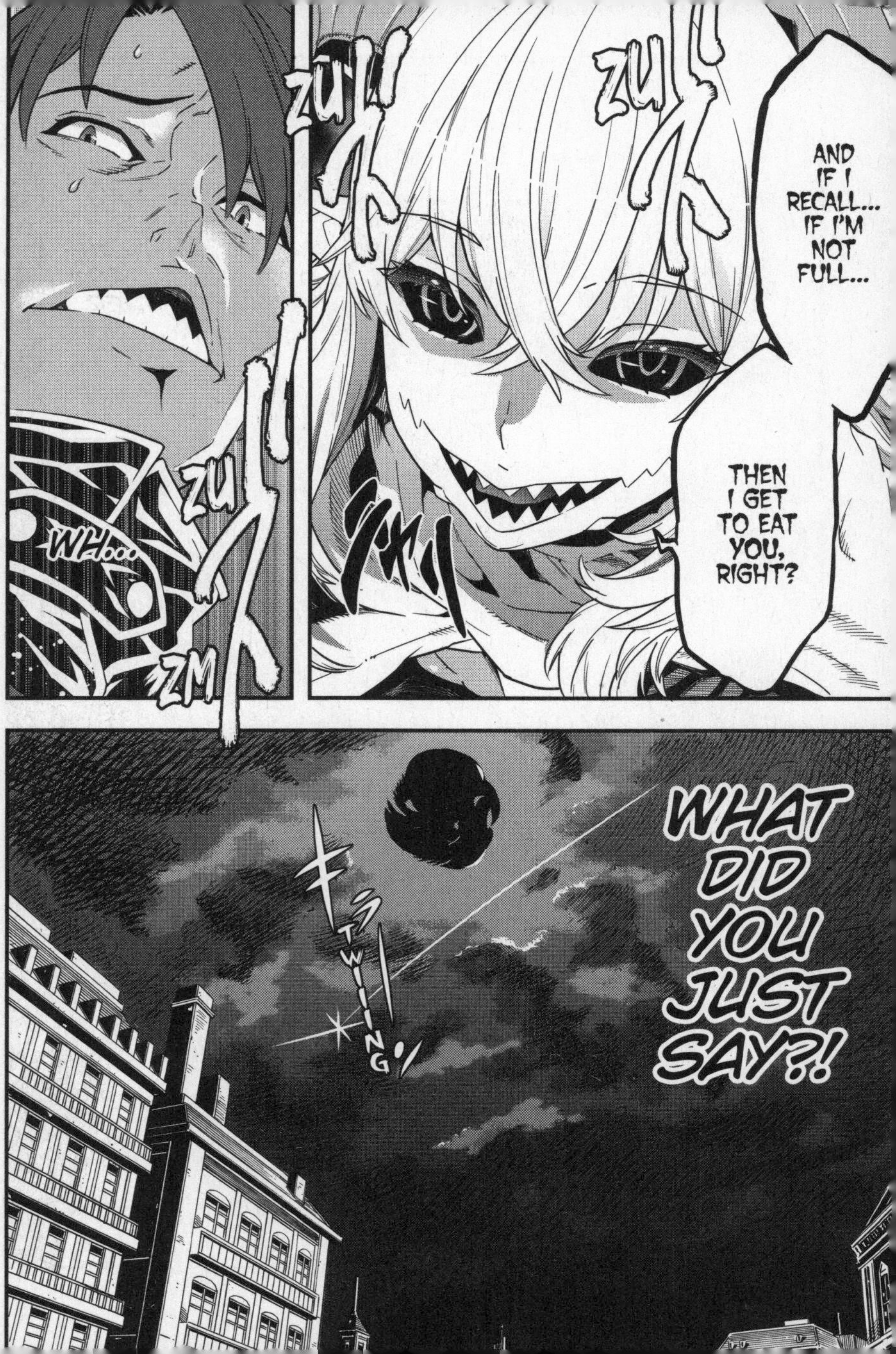
AND IF I RECALL... IF I'M NOT FULL...
THEN I GET TO EAT YOU, RIGHT?
ZU
WH-...
ZM
TWING
WHAT DID YOU JUST SAY?!

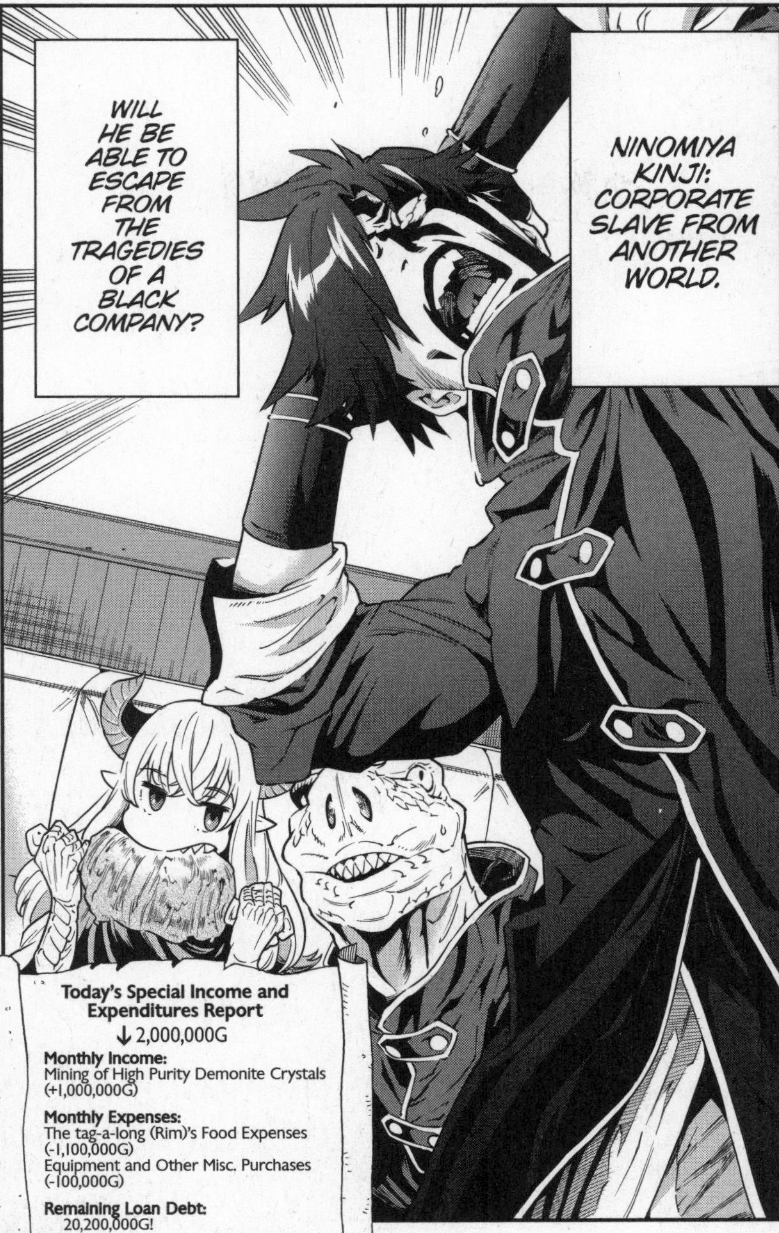
NINOMIYA KINJI: CORPORATE SLAVE FROM ANOTHER WORLD.
WILL HE BE ABLE TO ESCAPE FROM THE TRAGEDIES OF A BLACK COMPANY?
Today's Special Income and Expenditures Report
↓2,000,000G
Monthly Income:
Mining of High Purity Demonite Crystals (+1,000,000G)
Monthly Expenses:
The tag-a-long (Rim)'s Food Expenses (-1,100,000G)
Equipment and Other Misc. Purchases (-100,000G)
Remaining Loan Debt:
20,200,000G!

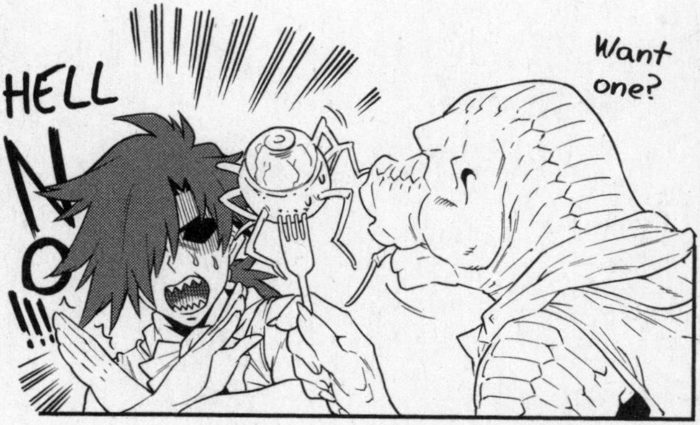
Want one?
HELL NO!!!!

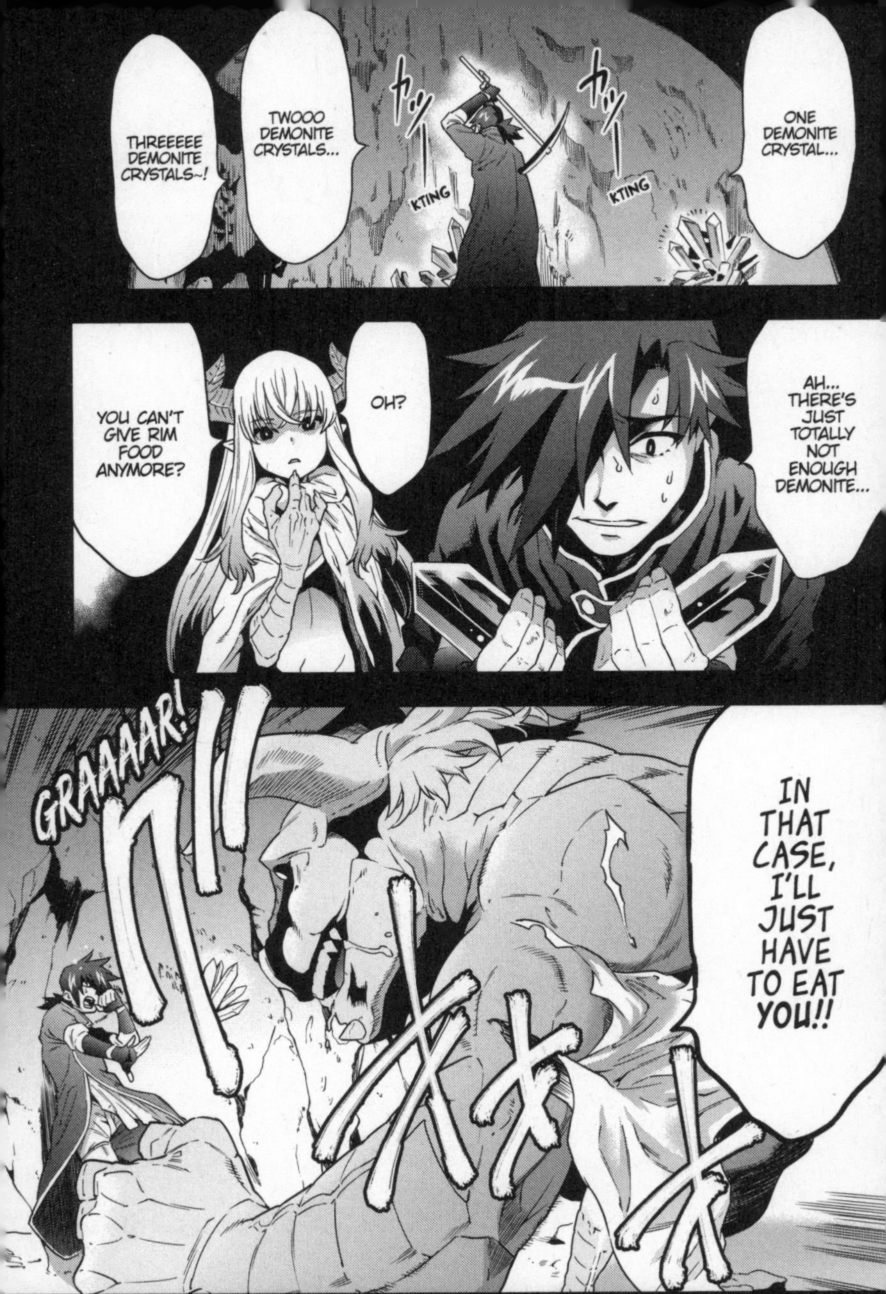
ONE DEMONITE CRYSTAL...
KTING
KTING
TWOOO DEMONITE CRYSTALS...
THREEEEE DEMONITE CRYSTALS~!
AH... THERE'S JUST TOTALLY NOT ENOUGH DEMONITE...
OH?
YOU CAN'T GIVE RIM FOOD ANYMORE?
IN THAT CASE, I'LL JUST HAVE TO EAT YOU!!
GRAAAAR!

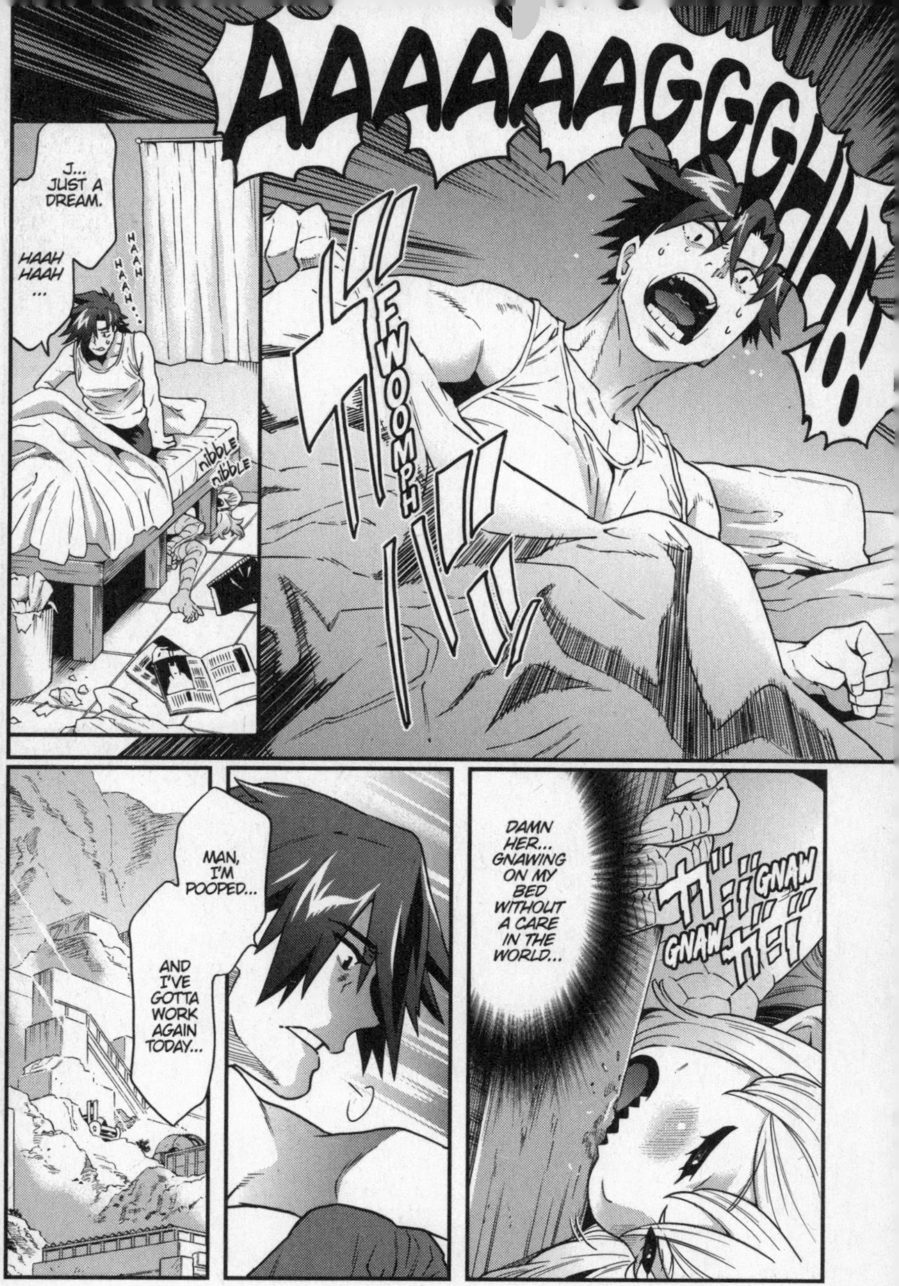
AAAAAAAGGGHHH!!
FWOOMPH
J... JUST A DREAM.
HAAH HAAH...
HAAH HAAH...
nibble nibble
DAMN HER... GNAWING ON MY BED WITHOUT A CARE IN THE WORLD...
GNAW GNAW
MAN, I'M POOPED...
AND I'VE GOTTA WORK AGAIN TODAY...

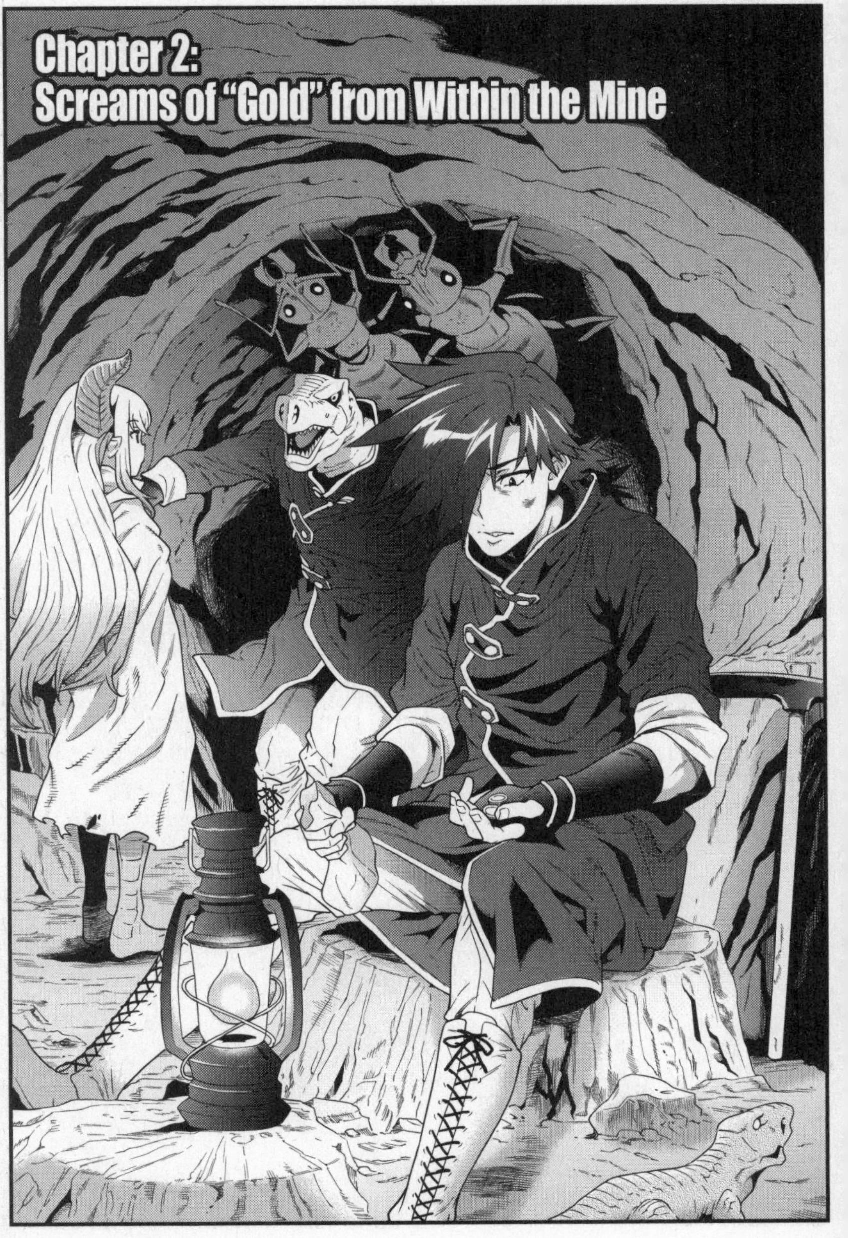
Chapter 2:
Screams of "Gold" from Within the Mine

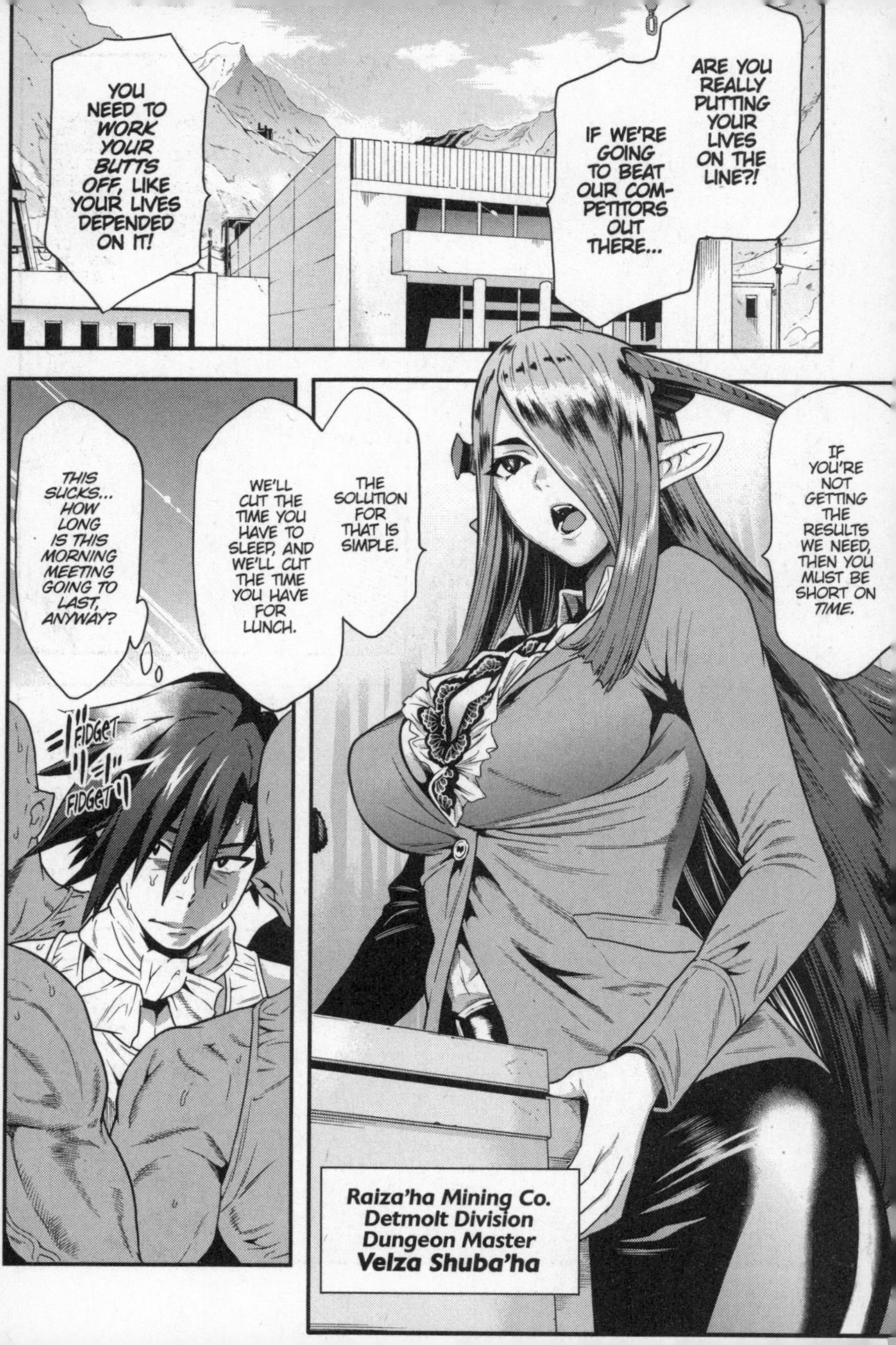
ARE YOU REALLY PUTTING YOUR LIVES ON THE LINE?!
IF WE'RE GOING TO BEAT OUR COMPETITORS OUT THERE...
YOU NEED TO WORK YOUR BUTTS OFF, LIKE YOUR LIVES DEPENDED ON IT!
IF YOU'RE NOT GETTING THE RESULTS WE NEED, THEN YOU MUST BE SHORT ON TIME.
THE SOLUTION FOR THAT IS SIMPLE.
WE'LL CUT THE TIME YOU HAVE TO SLEEP, AND WE'LL CUT THE TIME YOU HAVE FOR LUNCH.
Raiza'ha Mining Co.
Detmolt Division
Dungeon Master
Velza Shuba'ha
THIS SUCKS... HOW LONG IS THIS MORNING MEETING GOING TO LAST, ANYWAY?
FIDGET
FIDGET

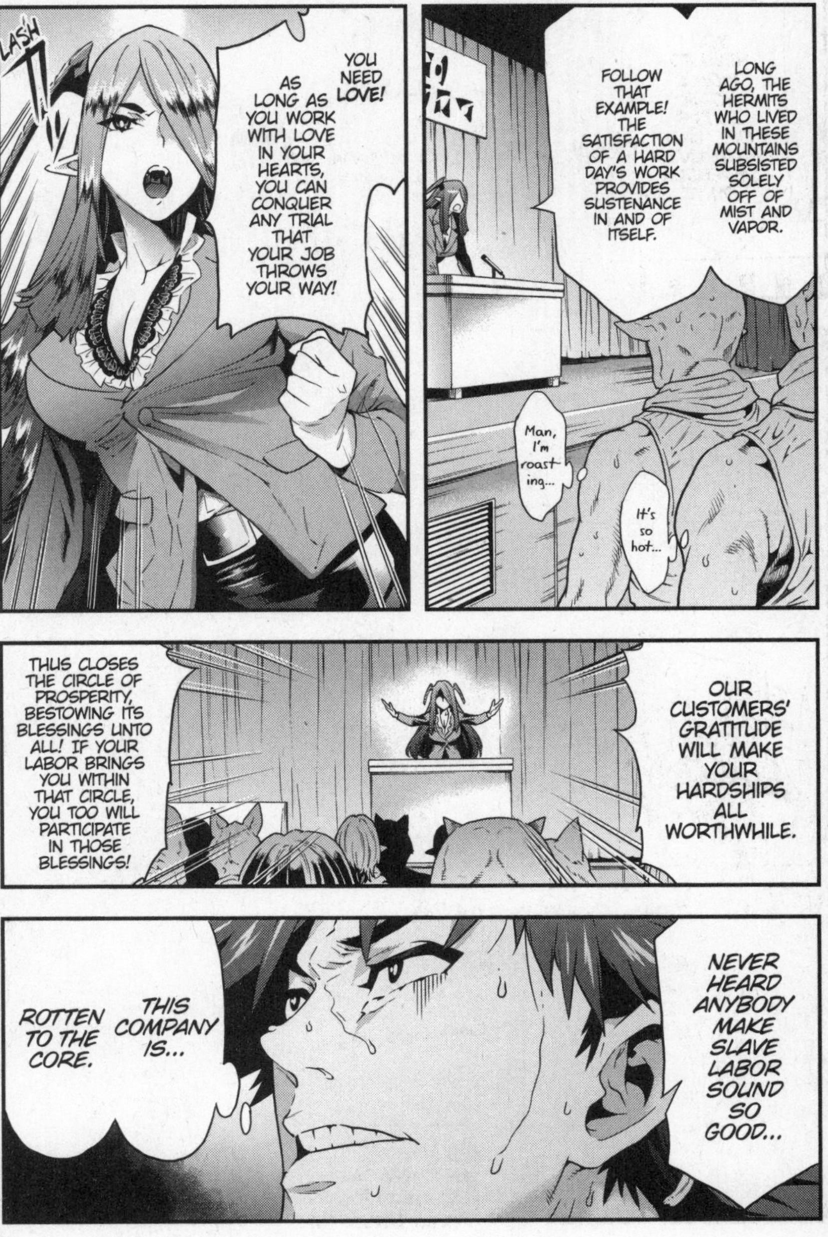
LONG AGO, THE HERMITS WHO LIVED IN THESE MOUNTAINS SUBSISTED SOLELY OFF OF MIST AND VAPOR.
FOLLOW THAT EXAMPLE! THE SATISFACTION OF A HARD DAY'S WORK PROVIDES SUSTENANCE IN AND OF ITSELF.
Man, I'm roasting...
It's so hot...
YOU NEED LOVE!
AS LONG AS YOU WORK WITH LOVE IN YOUR HEARTS, YOU CAN CONQUER ANY TRIAL THAT YOUR JOB THROWS YOUR WAY!
FLASH
OUR CUSTOMERS' GRATITUDE WILL MAKE YOUR HARDSHIPS ALL WORTHWHILE.
THUS CLOSES THE CIRCLE OF PROSPERITY, BESTOWING ITS BLESSINGS UNTO ALL! IF YOUR LABOR BRINGS YOU WITHIN THAT CIRCLE, YOU TOO WILL PARTICIPATE IN THOSE BLESSINGS!
NEVER HEARD ANYBODY MAKE SLAVE LABOR SOUND SO GOOD...
THIS COMPANY IS...
ROTTEN TO THE CORE.

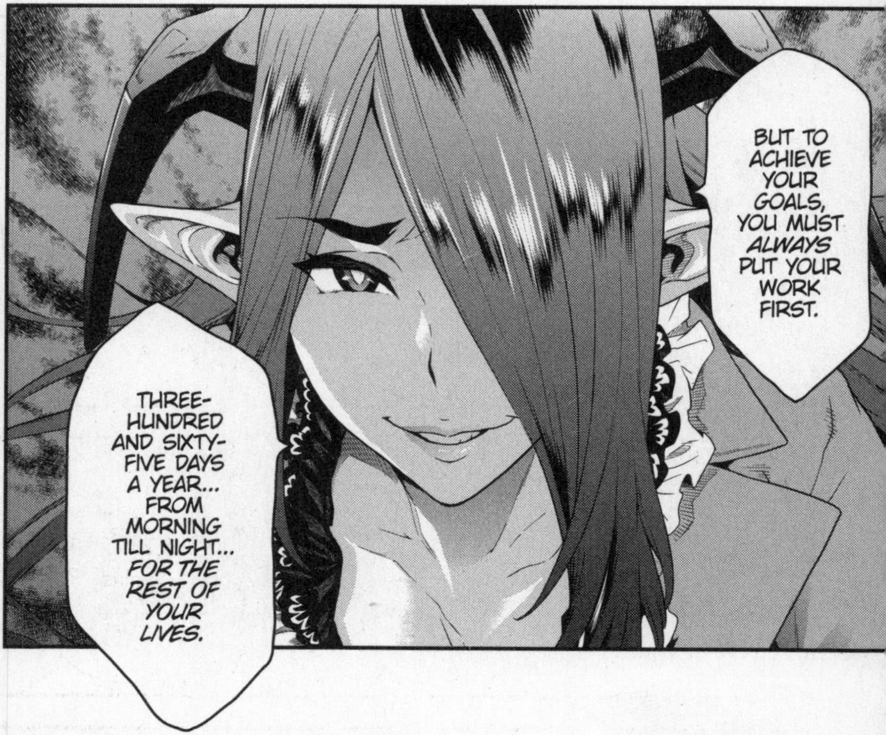
BUT TO ACHIEVE YOUR GOALS, YOU MUST *ALWAYS* PUT YOUR WORK FIRST.
THREE-HUNDRED AND SIXTY-FIVE DAYS A YEAR... FROM MORNING TILL NIGHT... *FOR THE REST OF YOUR LIVES.*

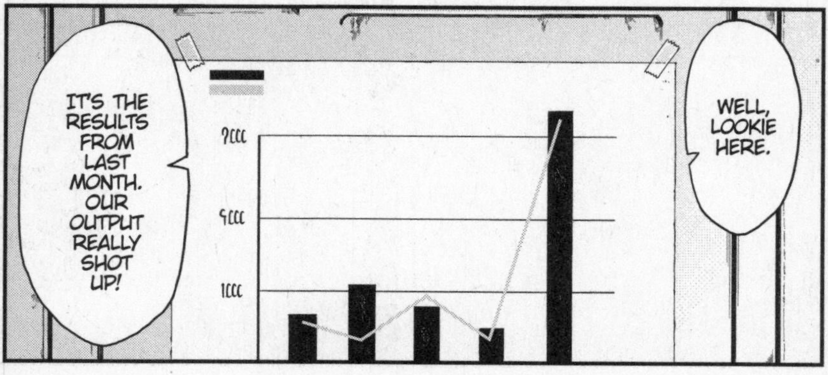
WELL, LOOKIE HERE.
IT'S THE RESULTS FROM LAST MONTH. OUR OUTPUT REALLY SHOT UP!

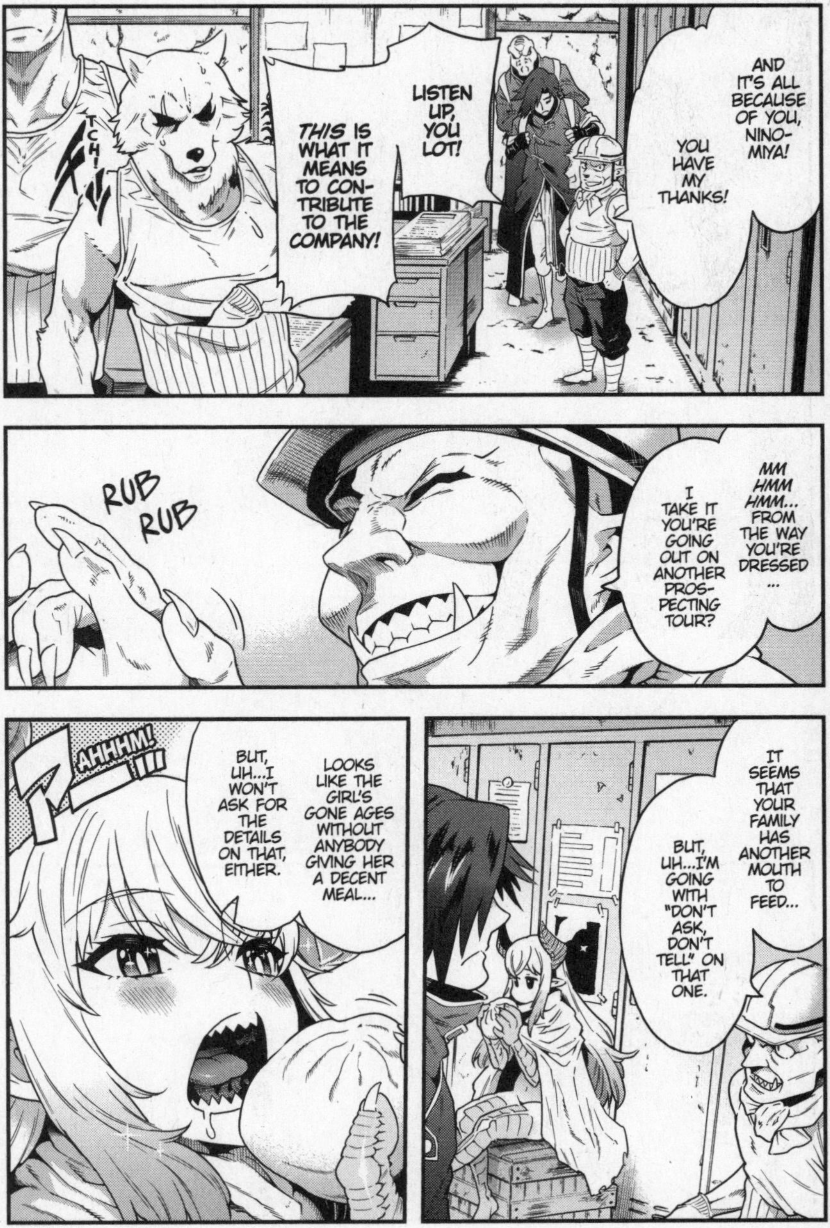
AND IT'S ALL BECAUSE OF YOU, NINOMIYA!
YOU HAVE MY THANKS!
LISTEN UP, YOU LOT!
THIS IS WHAT IT MEANS TO CONTRIBUTE TO THE COMPANY!
TCH!!
MM HMM HMM... FROM THE WAY YOU'RE DRESSED...
I TAKE IT YOU'RE GOING OUT ON ANOTHER PROSPECTING TOUR?
RUB RUB
IT SEEMS THAT YOUR FAMILY HAS ANOTHER MOUTH TO FEED...
BUT, UH...I'M GOING WITH "DON'T ASK, DON'T TELL" ON THAT ONE.
LOOKS LIKE THE GIRL'S GONE AGES WITHOUT ANYBODY GIVING HER A DECENT MEAL...
BUT, UH...I WON'T ASK FOR THE DETAILS ON THAT, EITHER.
AHHHM!!!

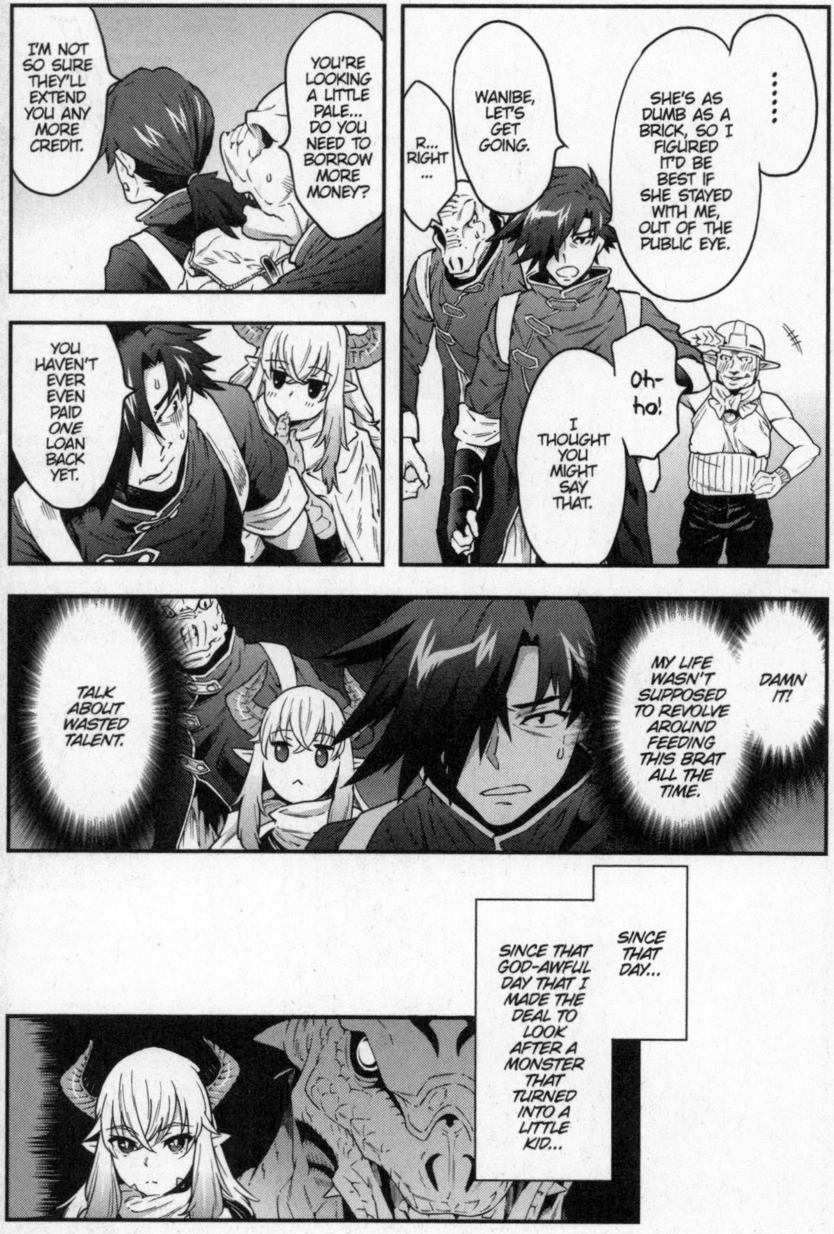
......
SHE'S AS DUMB AS A BRICK, SO I FIGURED IT'D BE BEST IF SHE STAYED WITH ME, OUT OF THE PUBLIC EYE.
WANIBE, LET'S GET GOING.
R... RIGHT ...
Oh-ho!
I THOUGHT YOU MIGHT SAY THAT.
YOU'RE LOOKING A LITTLE PALE... DO YOU NEED TO BORROW MORE MONEY?
I'M NOT SO SURE THEY'LL EXTEND YOU ANY MORE CREDIT.
YOU HAVEN'T EVER EVEN PAID ONE LOAN BACK YET.
DAMN IT!
MY LIFE WASN'T SUPPOSED TO REVOLVE AROUND FEEDING THIS BRAT ALL THE TIME.
TALK ABOUT WASTED TALENT.
SINCE THAT DAY...
SINCE THAT GOD-AWFUL DAY THAT I MADE THE DEAL TO LOOK AFTER A MONSTER THAT TURNED INTO A LITTLE KID...

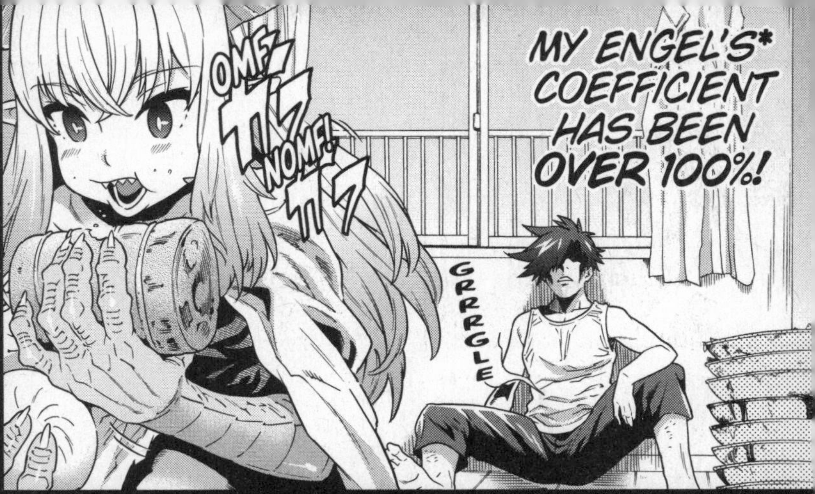
MY ENGEL'S* COEFFICIENT HAS BEEN OVER 100%!
GRRRGLE
OMF!
NOMF!

*Engel's law is sometimes used in economics to describe how much of their income people spend on food

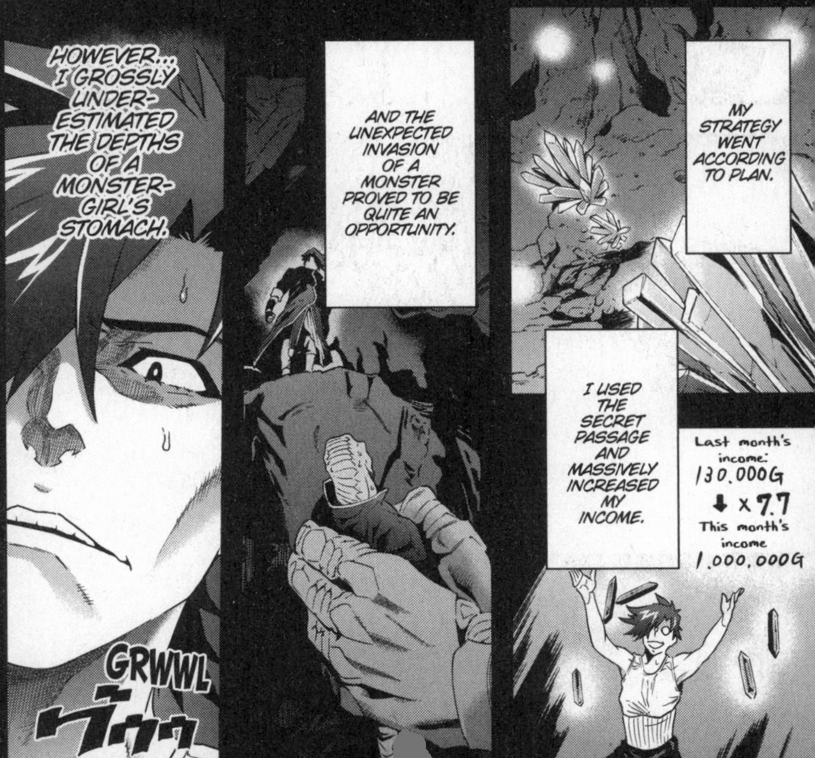
MY STRATEGY WENT ACCORDING TO PLAN.
I USED THE SECRET PASSAGE AND MASSIVELY INCREASED MY INCOME.
Last month's income: 130,000G
↓ x 7.7
This month's income 1,000,000G
AND THE UNEXPECTED INVASION OF A MONSTER PROVED TO BE QUITE AN OPPORTUNITY.
HOWEVER... I GROSSLY UNDER-ESTIMATED THE DEPTHS OF A MONSTER-GIRL'S STOMACH.
GRWWL

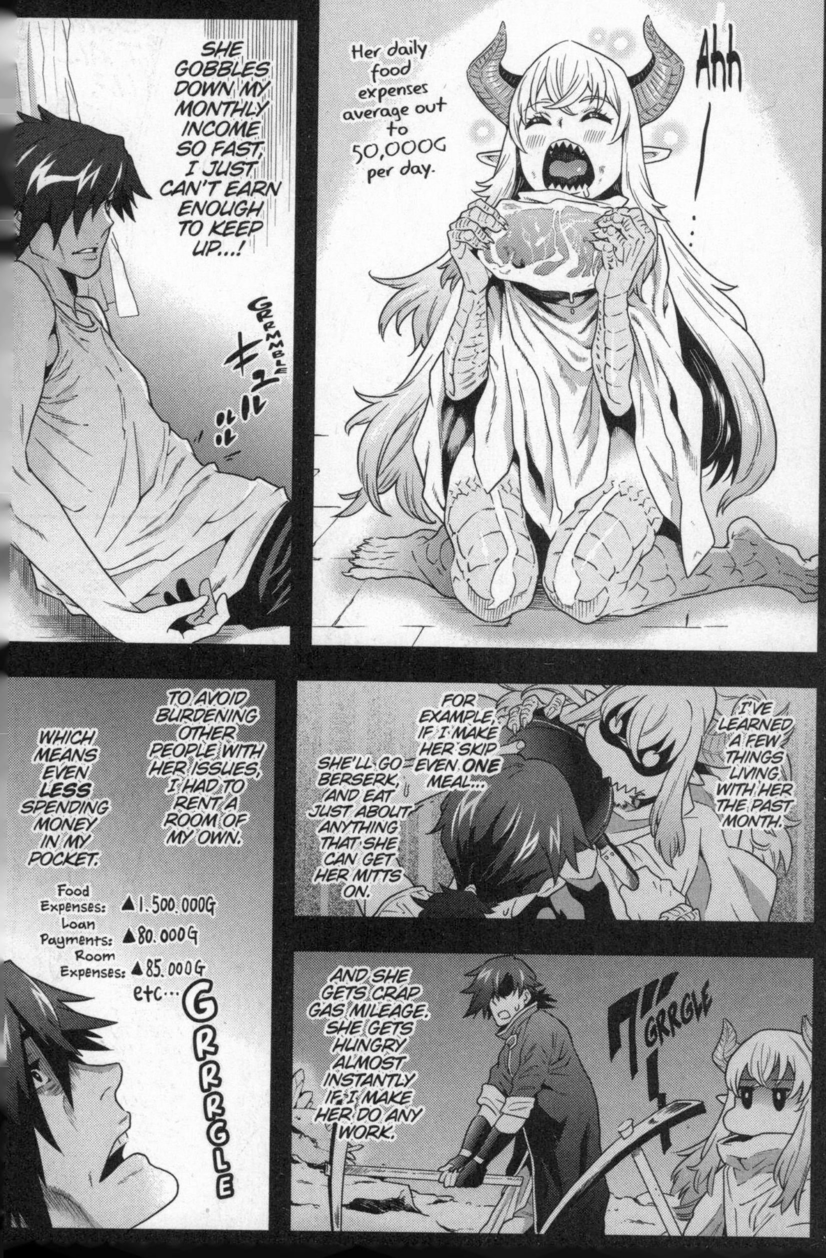
Her daily food expenses average out to 50,000G per day.
Ahh...!
SHE GOBBLES DOWN MY MONTHLY INCOME SO FAST, I JUST CAN'T EARN ENOUGH TO KEEP UP...!
GRRMMBLE
I'VE LEARNED A FEW THINGS LIVING WITH HER THE PAST MONTH.
FOR EXAMPLE, IF I MAKE HER SKIP EVEN ONE MEAL...
SHE'LL GO BERSERK, AND EAT JUST ABOUT ANYTHING THAT SHE CAN GET HER MITTS ON.
AND SHE GETS CRAP GAS MILEAGE. SHE GETS HUNGRY ALMOST INSTANTLY IF I MAKE HER DO ANY WORK.
GRRGLE
TO AVOID BURDENING OTHER PEOPLE WITH HER ISSUES, I HAD TO RENT A ROOM OF MY OWN.
WHICH MEANS EVEN LESS SPENDING MONEY IN MY POCKET.
Food Expenses: ▲1.500.000G
Loan Payments: ▲80.000G
Room Expenses: ▲85.000G
etc...
GRRRGLE

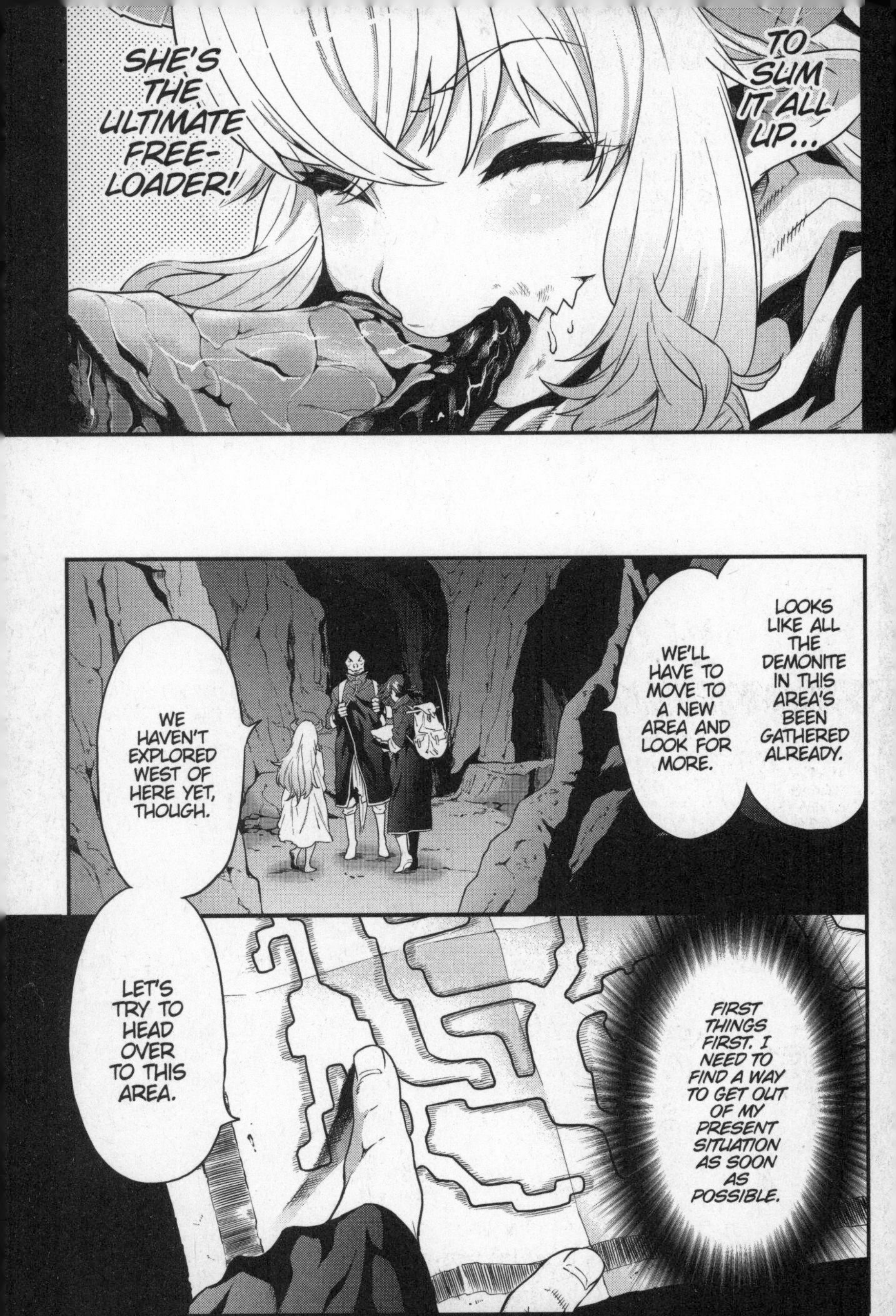
TO SUM IT ALL UP...
SHE'S THE ULTIMATE FREE-LOADER!
LOOKS LIKE ALL THE DEMONITE IN THIS AREA'S BEEN GATHERED ALREADY.
WE'LL HAVE TO MOVE TO A NEW AREA AND LOOK FOR MORE.
WE HAVEN'T EXPLORED WEST OF HERE YET, THOUGH.
LET'S TRY TO HEAD OVER TO THIS AREA.
FIRST THINGS FIRST. I NEED TO FIND A WAY TO GET OUT OF MY PRESENT SITUATION AS SOON AS POSSIBLE.

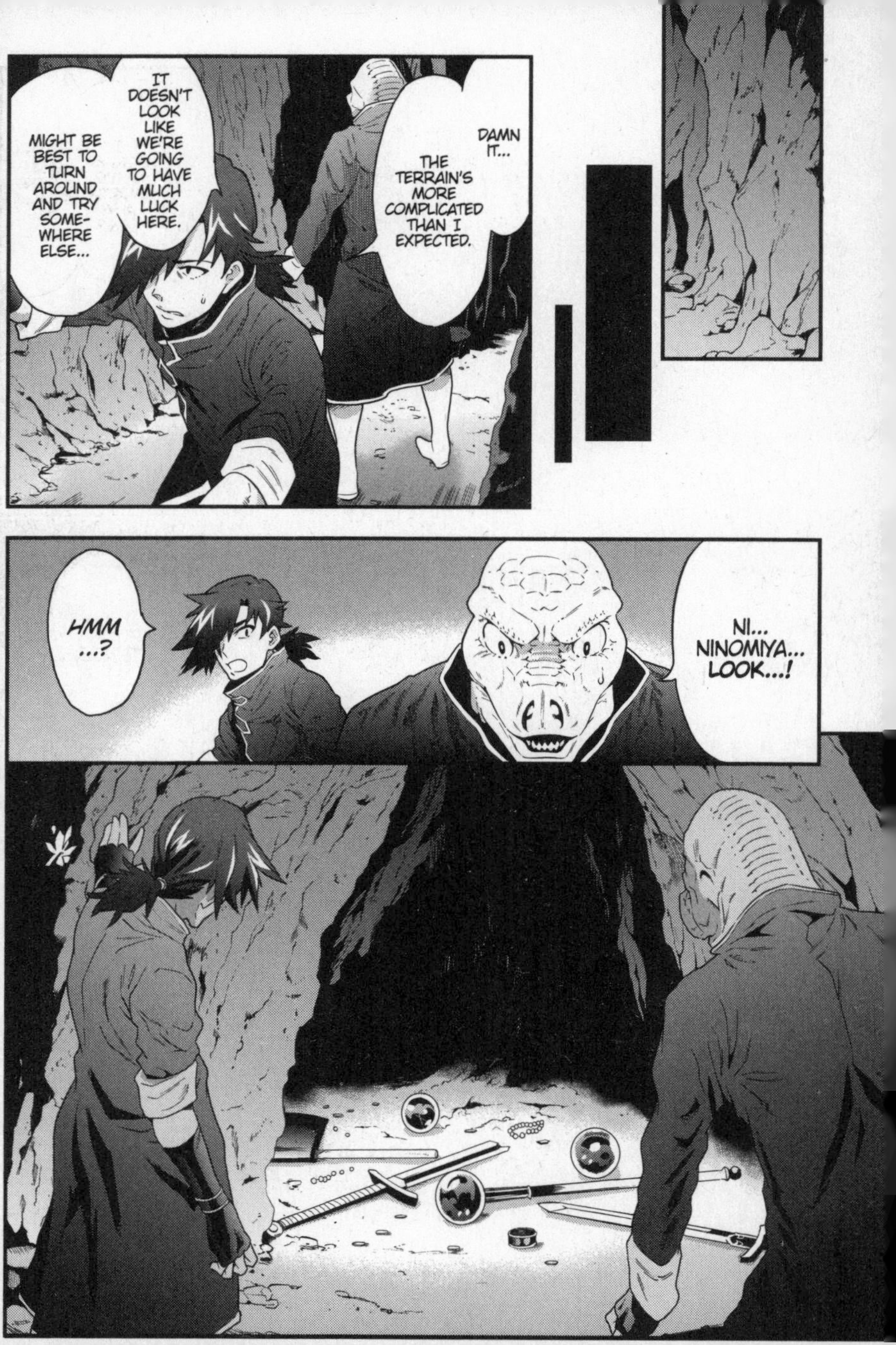
DAMN IT...
THE TERRAIN'S MORE COMPLICATED THAN I EXPECTED.
IT DOESN'T LOOK LIKE WE'RE GOING TO HAVE MUCH LUCK HERE.
MIGHT BE BEST TO TURN AROUND AND TRY SOME-WHERE ELSE...
NI... NINOMIYA... LOOK...!
HMM ...?

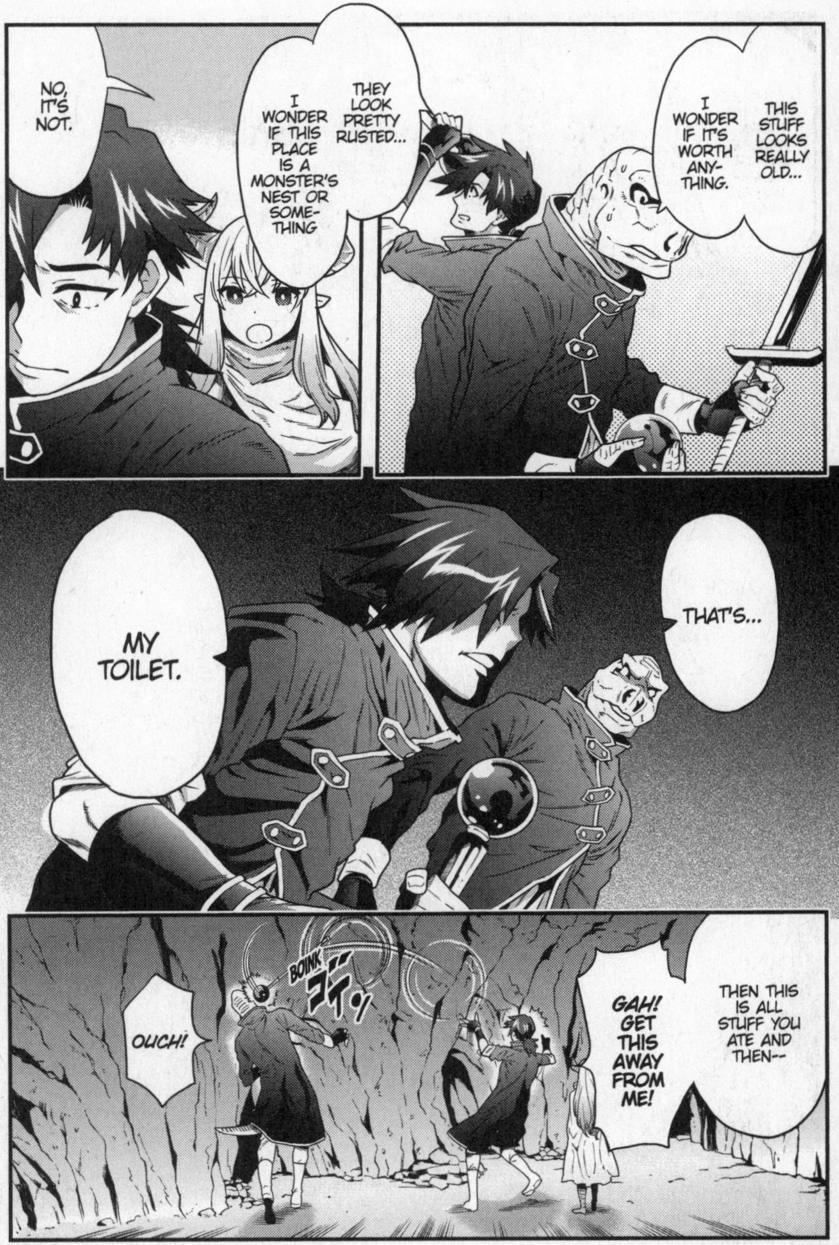
THIS STUFF LOOKS REALLY OLD...
I WONDER IF IT'S WORTH ANYTHING.
THEY LOOK PRETTY RUSTED...
I WONDER IF THIS PLACE IS A MONSTER'S NEST OR SOMETHING
NO, IT'S NOT.
THAT'S...
MY TOILET.
THEN THIS IS ALL STUFF YOU ATE AND THEN--
GAH! GET THIS AWAY FROM ME!
BOINK
OUCH!

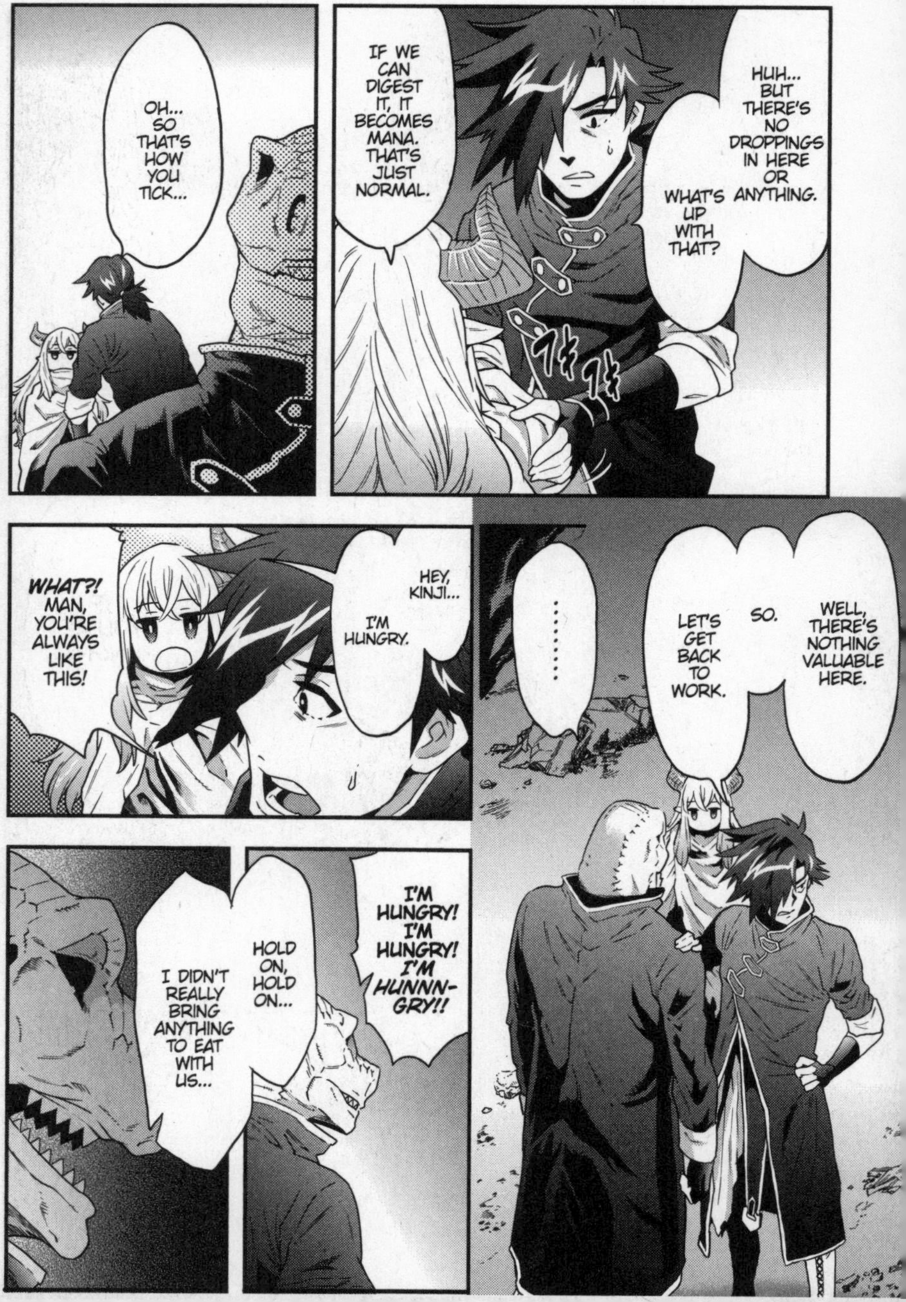
HUH... BUT THERE'S NO DROPPINGS IN HERE OR ANYTHING.
WHAT'S UP WITH THAT?
IF WE CAN DIGEST IT, IT BECOMES MANA. THAT'S JUST NORMAL.
OH... SO THAT'S HOW YOU TICK...
WELL, THERE'S NOTHING VALUABLE HERE.
SO.
LET'S GET BACK TO WORK.
......
HEY, KINJI...
I'M HUNGRY.
WHAT?! MAN, YOU'RE ALWAYS LIKE THIS!
I'M HUNGRY! I'M HUNGRY! I'M HUNNN-GRY!!
HOLD ON, HOLD ON...
I DIDN'T REALLY BRING ANYTHING TO EAT WITH US...

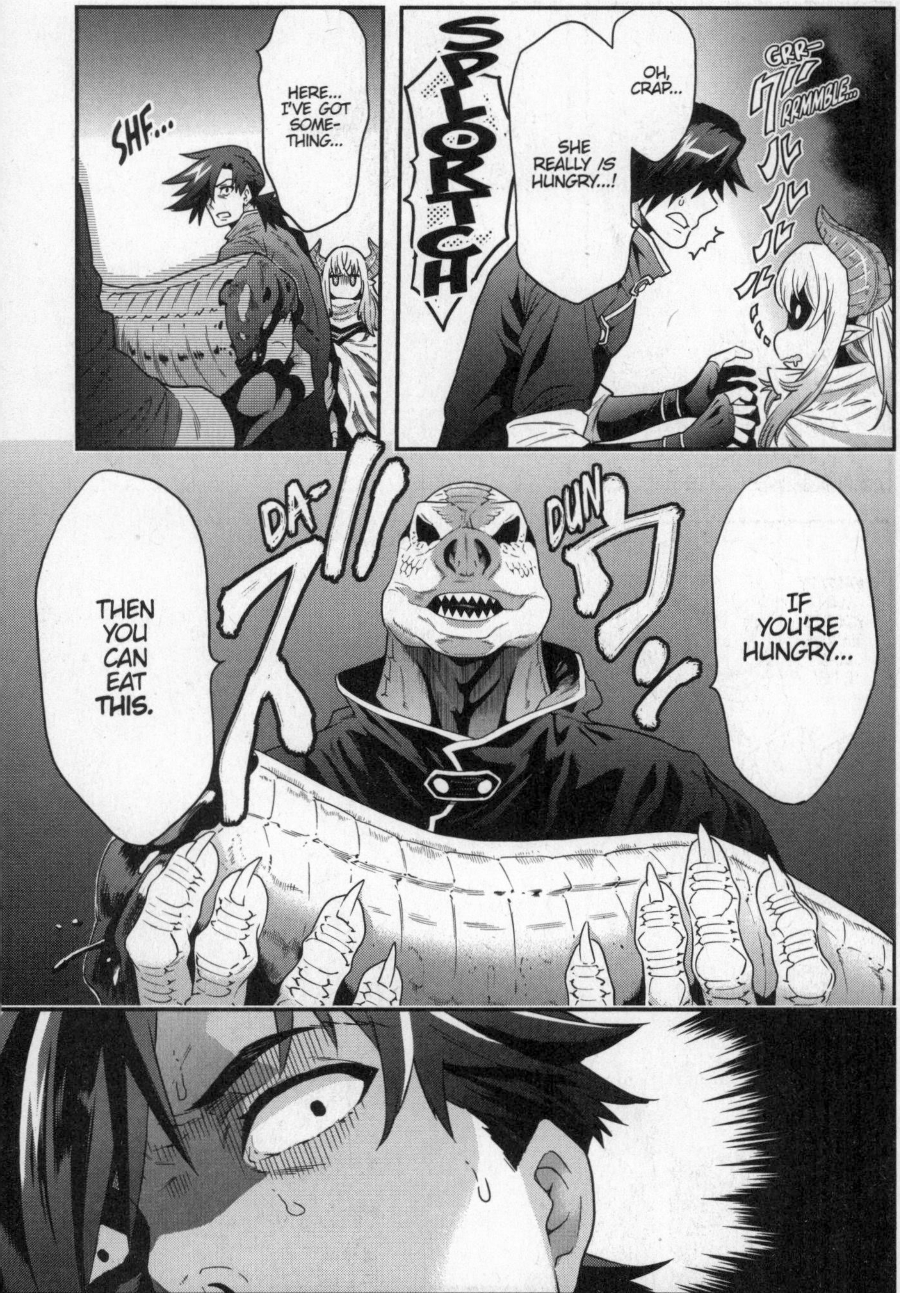
GRR-RRMMBLE...
OH, CRAP...
SHE REALLY IS HUNGRY...!
SPLORTCH
HERE... I'VE GOT SOME-THING...
SHF...
IF YOU'RE HUNGRY...
DA-DUN
THEN YOU CAN EAT THIS.

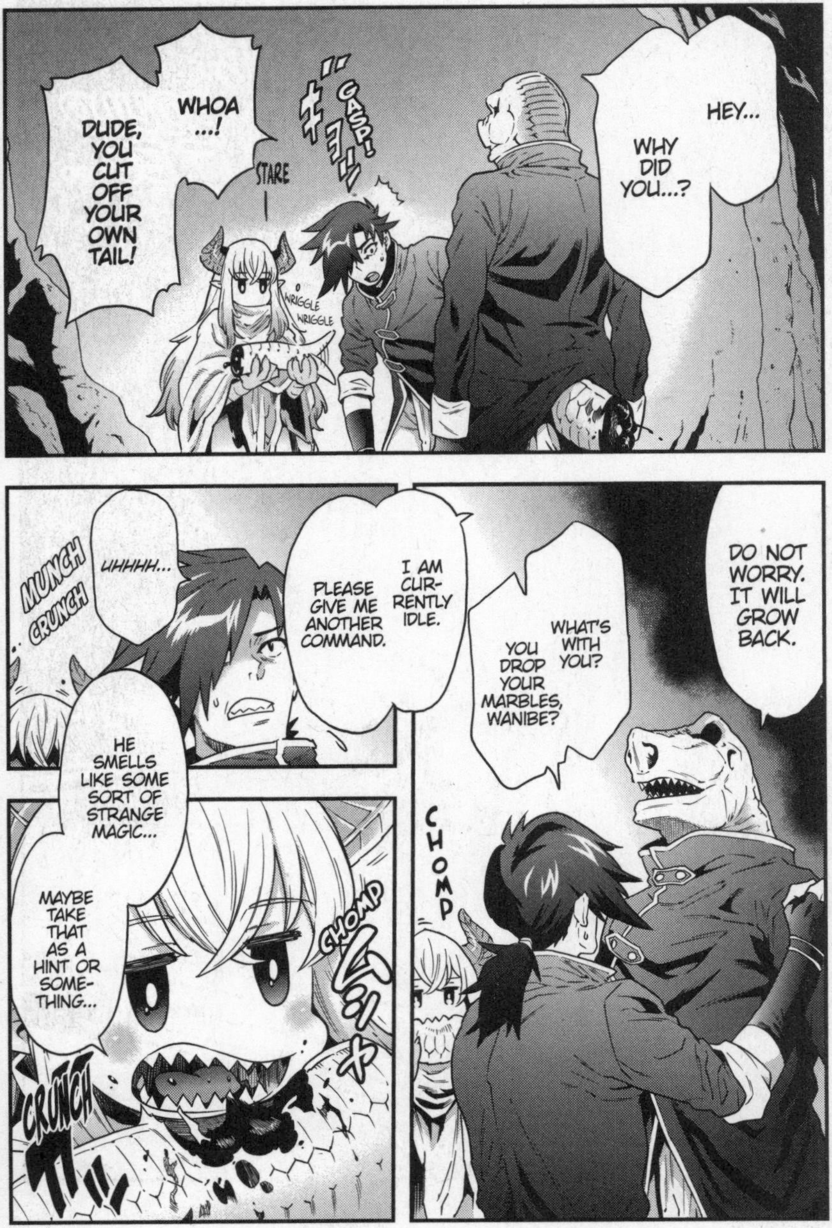
HEY...
WHY DID YOU...?
GASP!
STARE
WHOA ...!
DUDE, YOU CUT OFF YOUR OWN TAIL!
WRIGGLE WRIGGLE
DO NOT WORRY. IT WILL GROW BACK.
WHAT'S WITH YOU? YOU DROP YOUR MARBLES, WANIBE?
CHOMP
I AM CURRENTLY IDLE. PLEASE GIVE ME ANOTHER COMMAND.
UHHHH...
MUNCH
CRUNCH
HE SMELLS LIKE SOME SORT OF STRANGE MAGIC...
MAYBE TAKE THAT AS A HINT OR SOMETHING...
CHOMP
CRUNCH

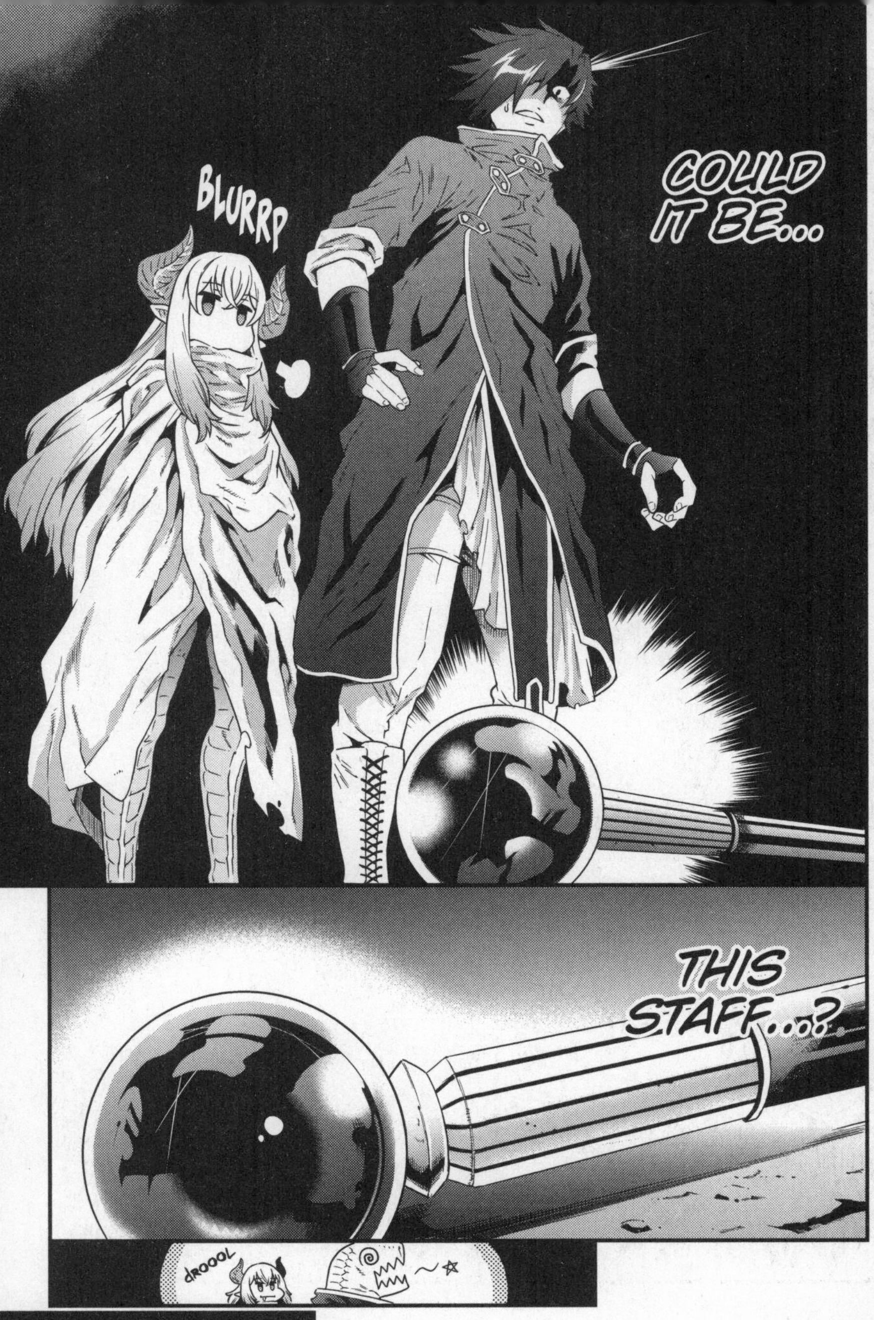
COULD IT BE...
BLURRP
THIS STAFF...?
DROOOL

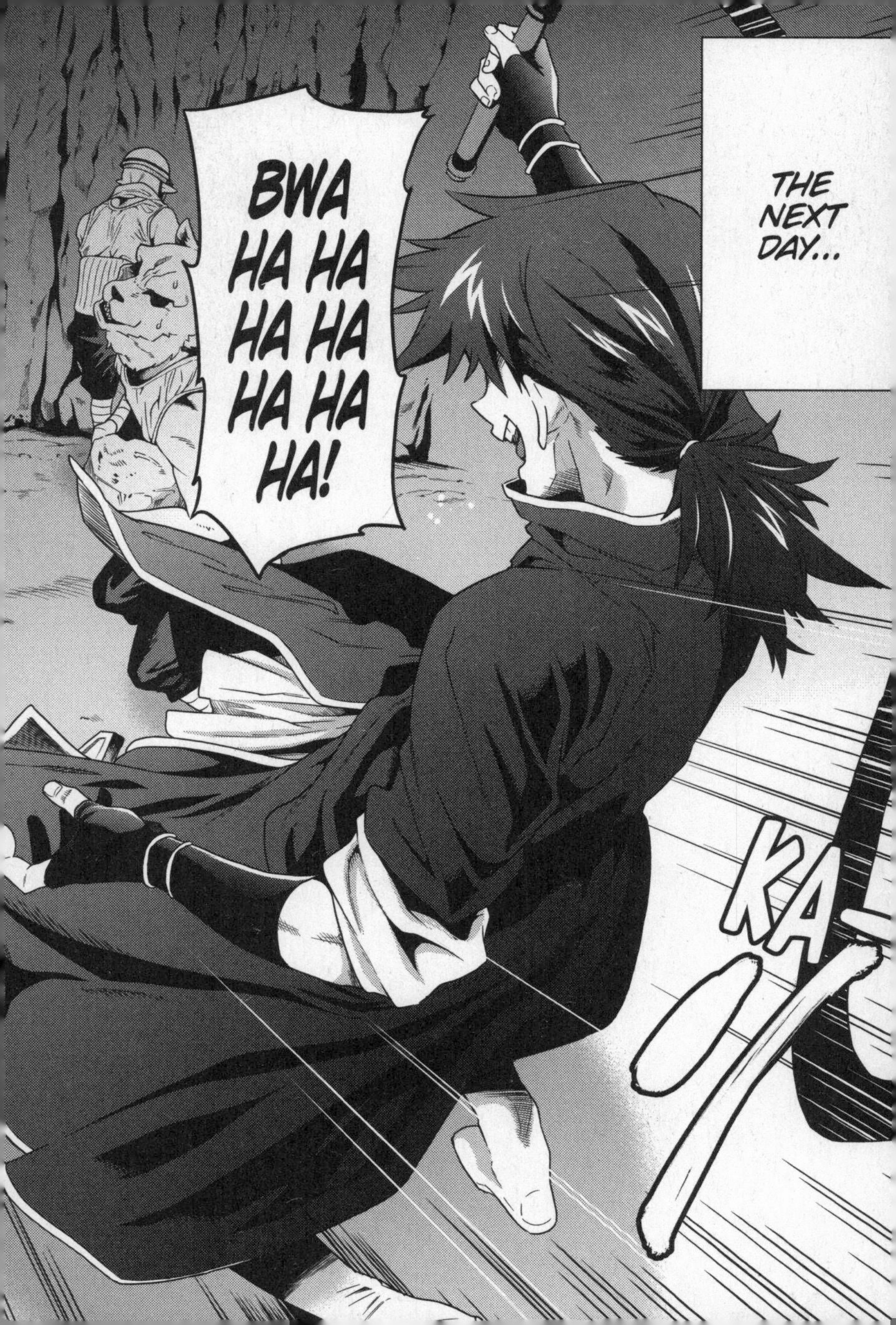
THE NEXT DAY...
BWA HA HA HA HA HA HA HA!
KA-

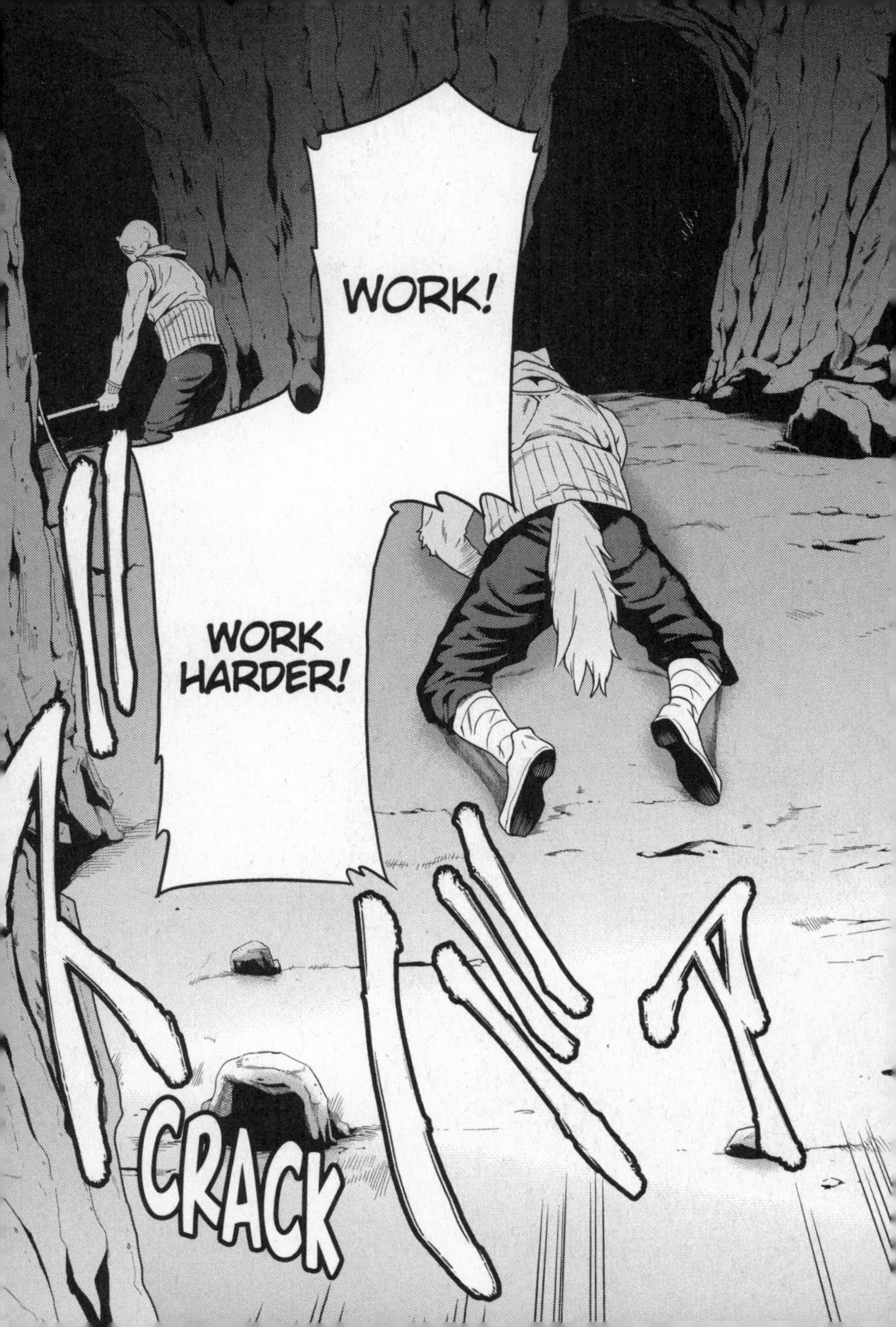
WORK!
WORK HARDER!
CRACK

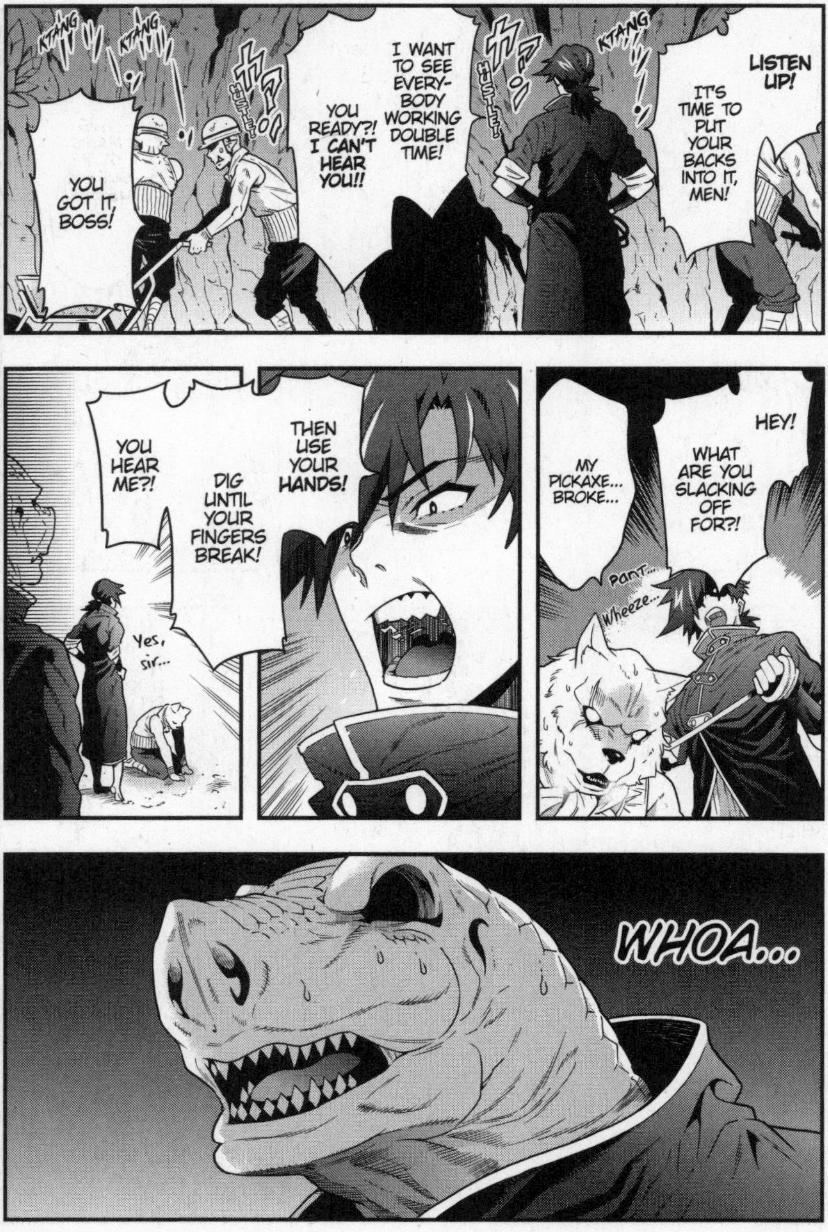
LISTEN UP!
IT'S TIME TO PUT YOUR BACKS INTO IT, MEN!
KTANG
HUSTLE!
I WANT TO SEE EVERYBODY WORKING DOUBLE TIME!
YOU READY?! I CAN'T HEAR YOU!!
HUSTLE!
YOU GOT IT, BOSS!
KTANG
KTANG
HEY!
WHAT ARE YOU SLACKING OFF FOR?!
MY PICKAXE... BROKE...
Pant...
Wheeze...
THEN USE YOUR HANDS!
DIG UNTIL YOUR FINGERS BREAK!
YOU HEAR ME?!
Yes, sir...
WHOA...

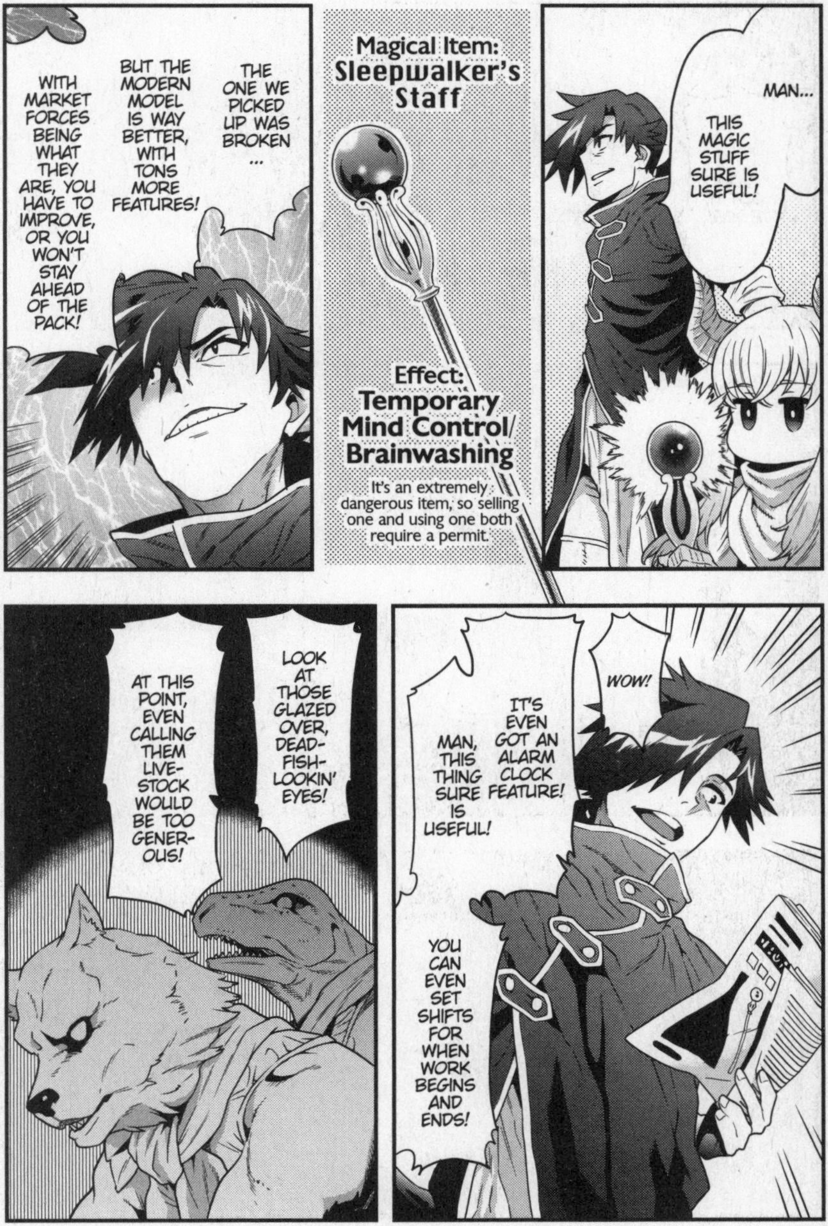
MAN...
THIS MAGIC STUFF SURE IS USEFUL!
Magical Item: Sleepwalker's Staff
Effect: Temporary Mind Control/ Brainwashing
It's an extremely dangerous item, so selling one and using one both require a permit.
THE ONE WE PICKED UP WAS BROKEN...
BUT THE MODERN MODEL IS WAY BETTER, WITH TONS MORE FEATURES!
WITH MARKET FORCES BEING WHAT THEY ARE, YOU HAVE TO IMPROVE, OR YOU WON'T STAY AHEAD OF THE PACK!
WOW!
IT'S EVEN GOT AN ALARM CLOCK FEATURE!
MAN, THIS THING SURE IS USEFUL!
YOU CAN EVEN SET SHIFTS FOR WHEN WORK BEGINS AND ENDS!
LOOK AT THOSE GLAZED OVER, DEAD-FISH-LOOKIN' EYES!
AT THIS POINT, EVEN CALLING THEM LIVE-STOCK WOULD BE TOO GENER-OUS!

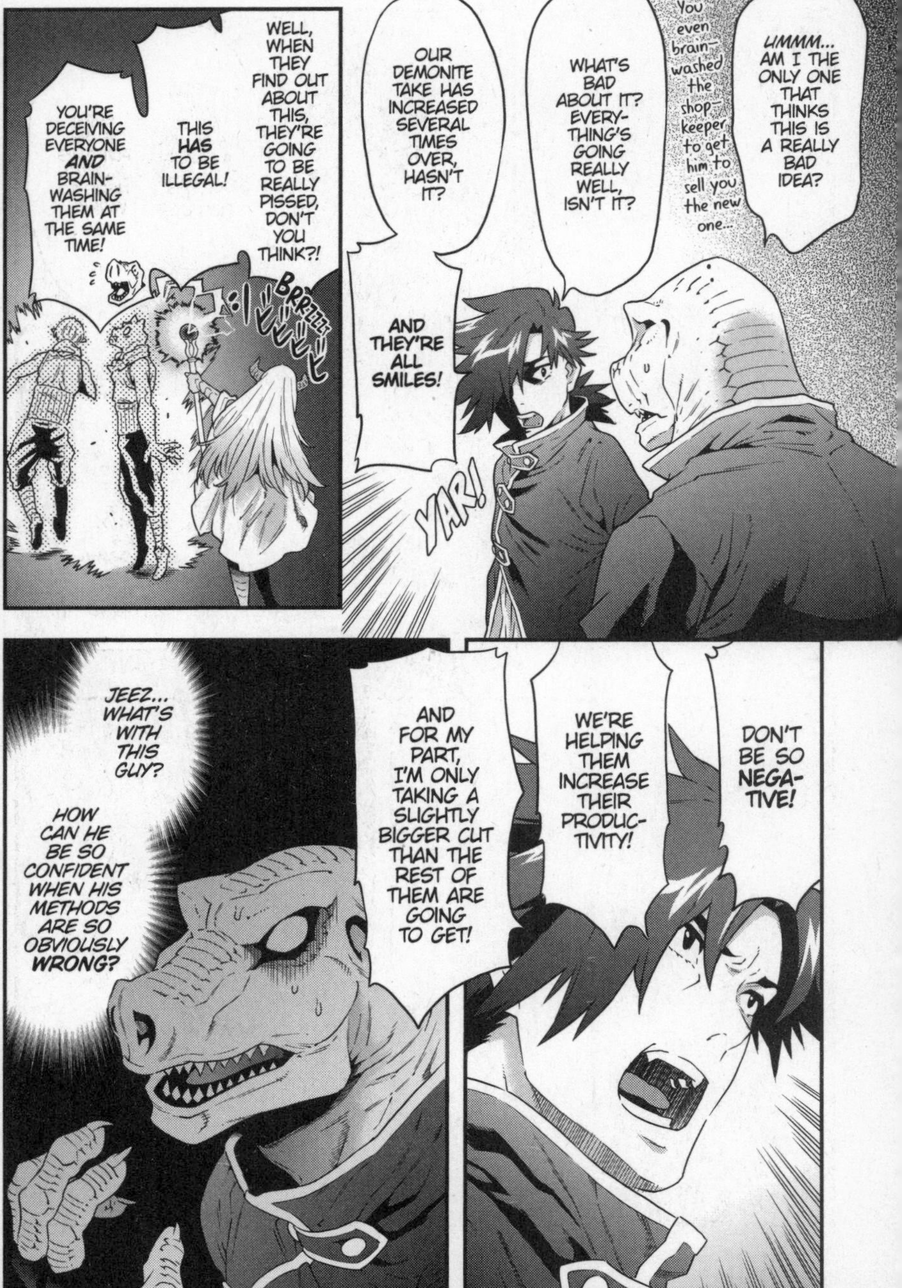
UMMM... AM I THE ONLY ONE THAT THINKS THIS IS A REALLY BAD IDEA?
You even brain-washed the shop-keeper to get him to sell you the new one...
WHAT'S BAD ABOUT IT? EVERYTHING'S GOING REALLY WELL, ISN'T IT?
OUR DEMONITE TAKE HAS INCREASED SEVERAL TIMES OVER, HASN'T IT?
AND THEY'RE ALL SMILES!
YAR!
WELL, WHEN THEY FIND OUT ABOUT THIS, THEY'RE GOING TO BE REALLY PISSED, DON'T YOU THINK?!
THIS HAS TO BE ILLEGAL!
YOU'RE DECEIVING EVERYONE AND BRAIN-WASHING THEM AT THE SAME TIME!
BRRZZZZ
DON'T BE SO NEGA-TIVE!
WE'RE HELPING THEM INCREASE THEIR PRODUC-TIVITY!
AND FOR MY PART, I'M ONLY TAKING A SLIGHTLY BIGGER CUT THAN THE REST OF THEM ARE GOING TO GET!
JEEZ... WHAT'S WITH THIS GUY?
HOW CAN HE BE SO CONFIDENT WHEN HIS METHODS ARE SO OBVIOUSLY WRONG?

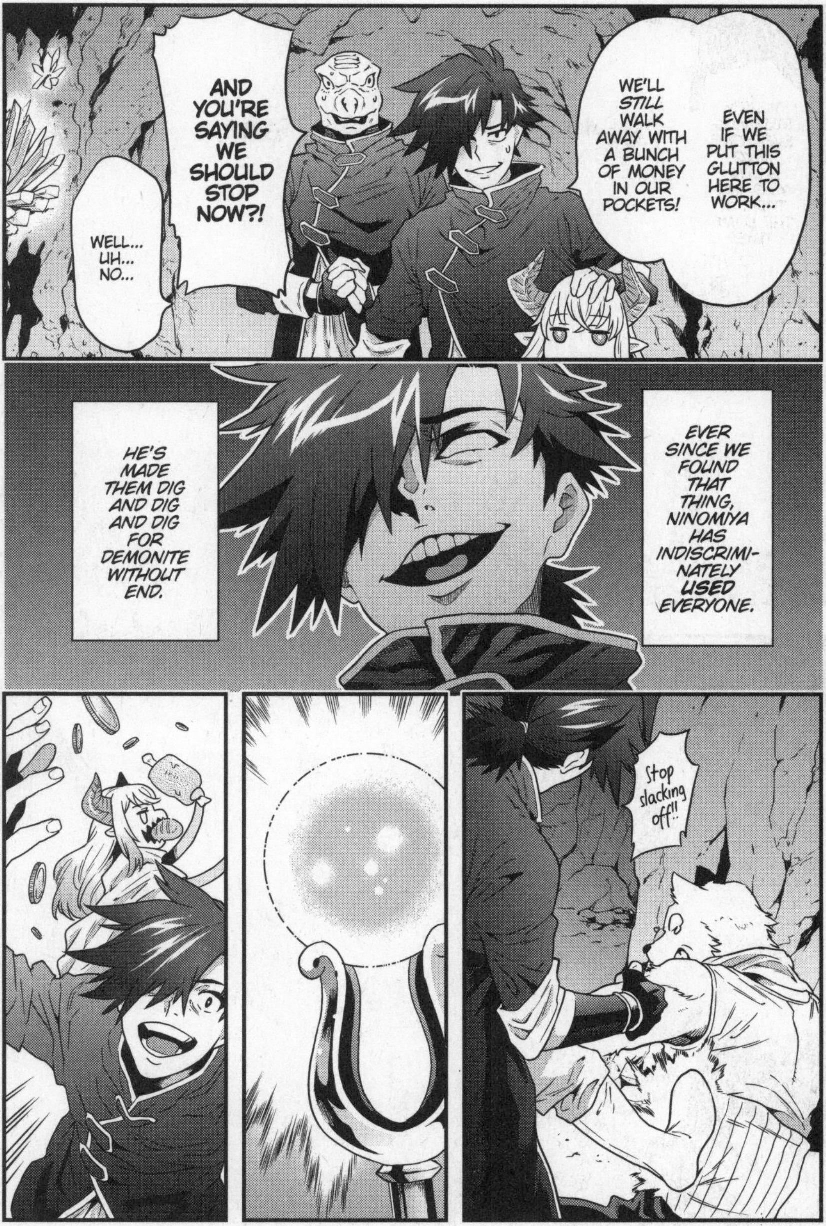
EVEN IF WE PUT THIS GLUTTON HERE TO WORK...
WE'LL STILL WALK AWAY WITH A BUNCH OF MONEY IN OUR POCKETS!
AND YOU'RE SAYING WE SHOULD STOP NOW?!
WELL... UH... NO...
EVER SINCE WE FOUND THAT THING, NINOMIYA HAS INDISCRIMINATELY USED EVERYONE.
HE'S MADE THEM DIG AND DIG AND DIG FOR DEMONITE WITHOUT END.
Stop slacking off!!

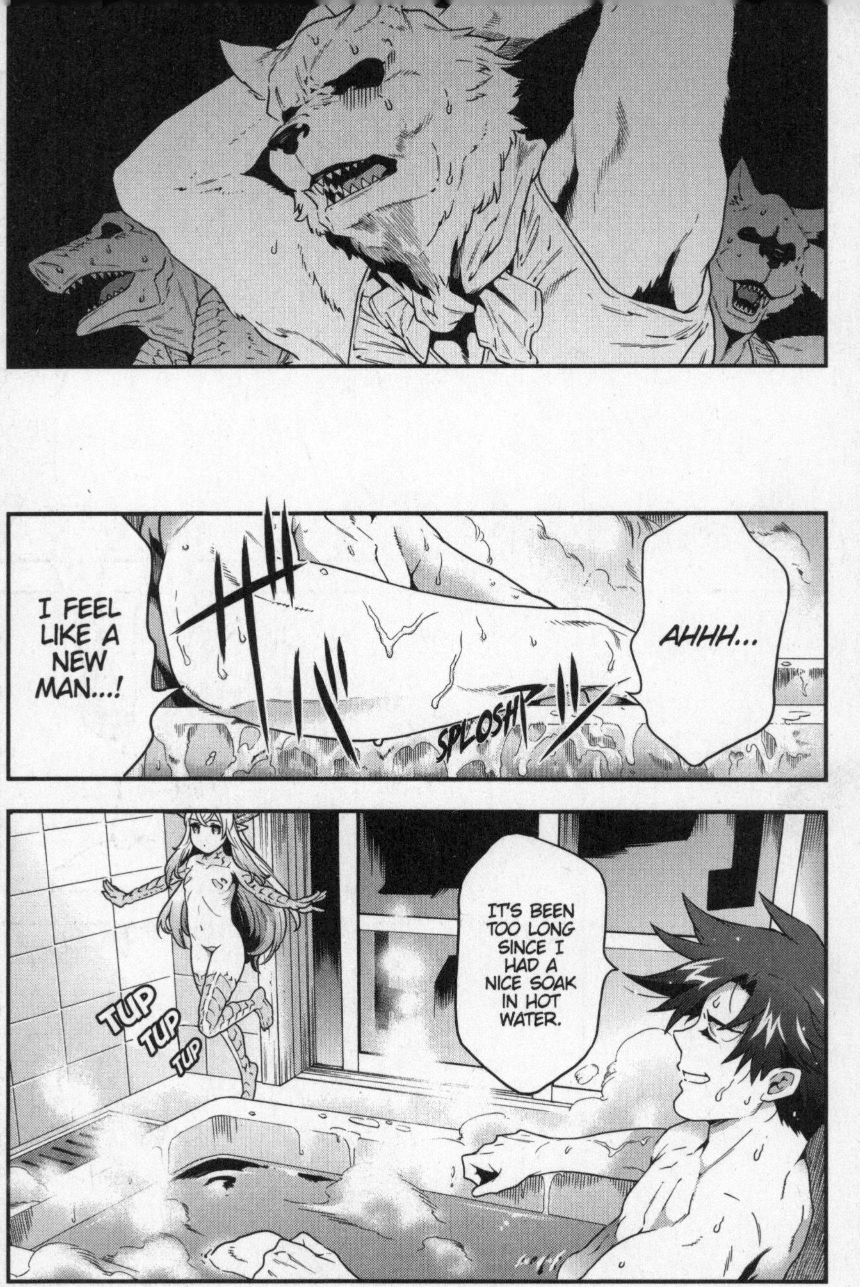
AHHH...
SPLOSH
I FEEL LIKE A NEW MAN...!
IT'S BEEN TOO LONG SINCE I HAD A NICE SOAK IN HOT WATER.
TUP TUP TUP

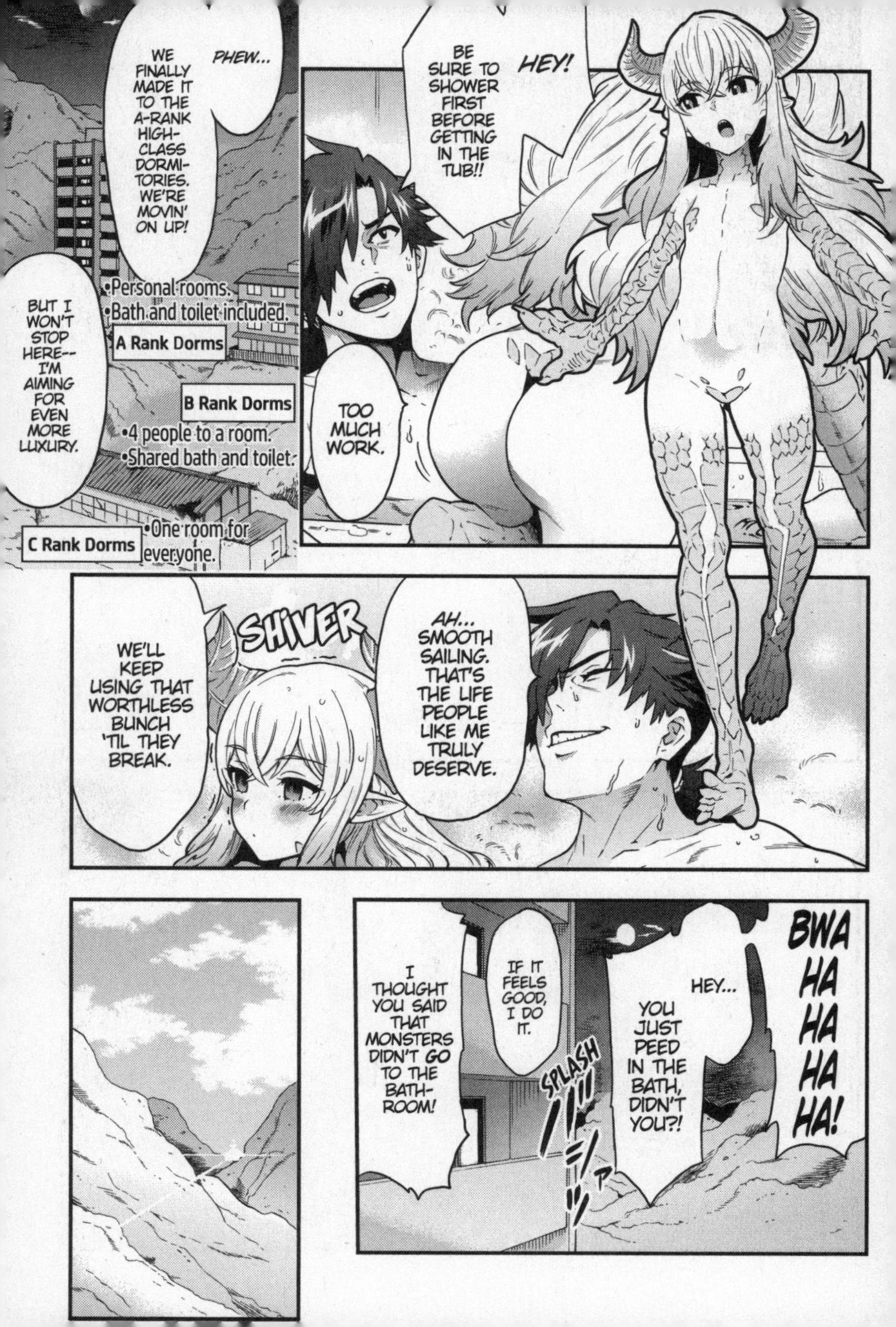
HEY!
BE SURE TO SHOWER FIRST BEFORE GETTING IN THE TUB!!
TOO MUCH WORK.
PHEW...
WE FINALLY MADE IT TO THE A-RANK HIGH-CLASS DORMITORIES. WE'RE MOVIN' ON UP!
BUT I WON'T STOP HERE-- I'M AIMING FOR EVEN MORE LUXURY.
•Personal rooms.
•Bath and toilet included.
A Rank Dorms
B Rank Dorms
•4 people to a room.
•Shared bath and toilet.
•One room for everyone.
C Rank Dorms
AH... SMOOTH SAILING. THAT'S THE LIFE PEOPLE LIKE ME TRULY DESERVE.
SHIVER
WE'LL KEEP USING THAT WORTHLESS BUNCH 'TIL THEY BREAK.
BWA HA HA HA HA HA!
HEY...
YOU JUST PEED IN THE BATH, DIDN'T YOU?!
IF IT FEELS GOOD, I DO IT.
I THOUGHT YOU SAID THAT MONSTERS DIDN'T GO TO THE BATH-ROOM!
SPLASH

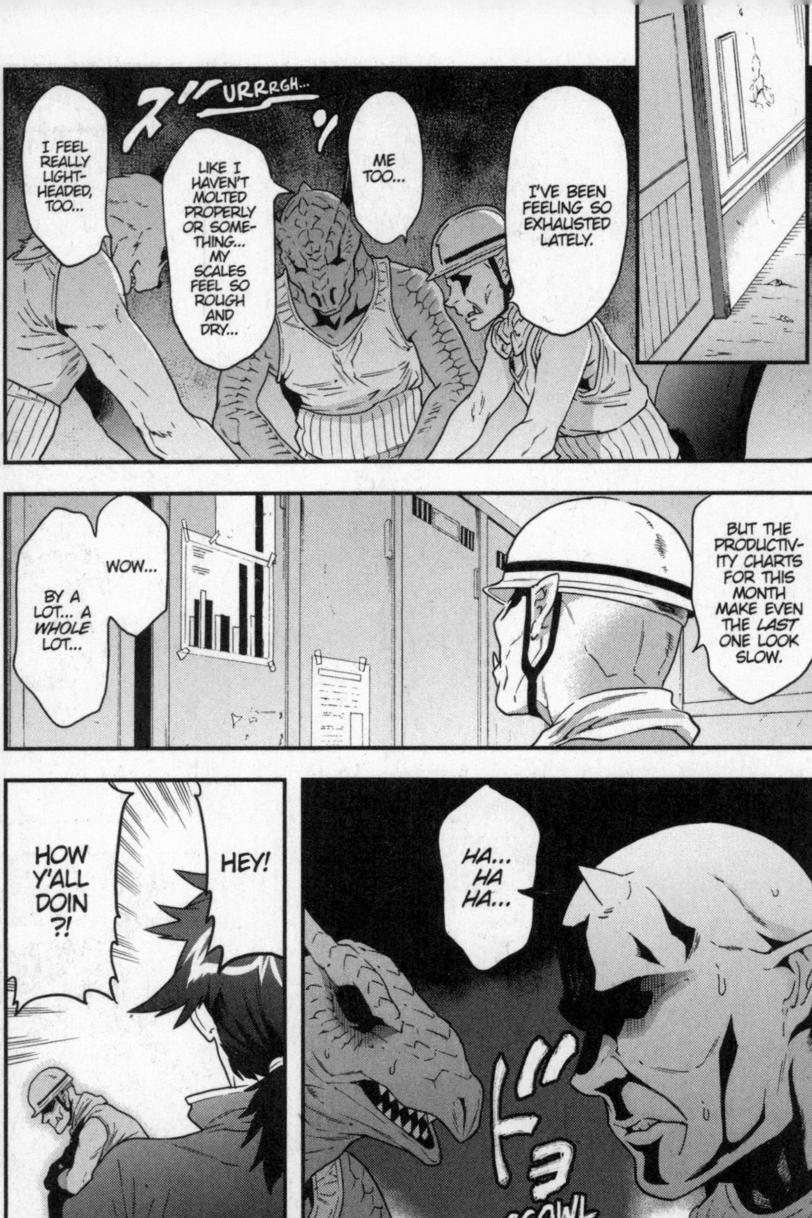
I'VE BEEN FEELING SO EXHAUSTED LATELY.
ME TOO...
LIKE I HAVEN'T MOLTED PROPERLY OR SOMETHING... MY SCALES FEEL SO ROUGH AND DRY...
URRRGH...
I FEEL REALLY LIGHT-HEADED, TOO...
BUT THE PRODUCTIVITY CHARTS FOR THIS MONTH MAKE EVEN THE *LAST* ONE LOOK SLOW.
WOW...
BY A LOT... A *WHOLE* LOT...
HA... HA HA...
SCOWL
HEY!
HOW Y'ALL DOIN?!

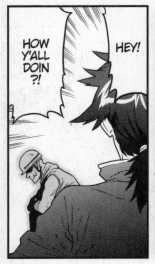

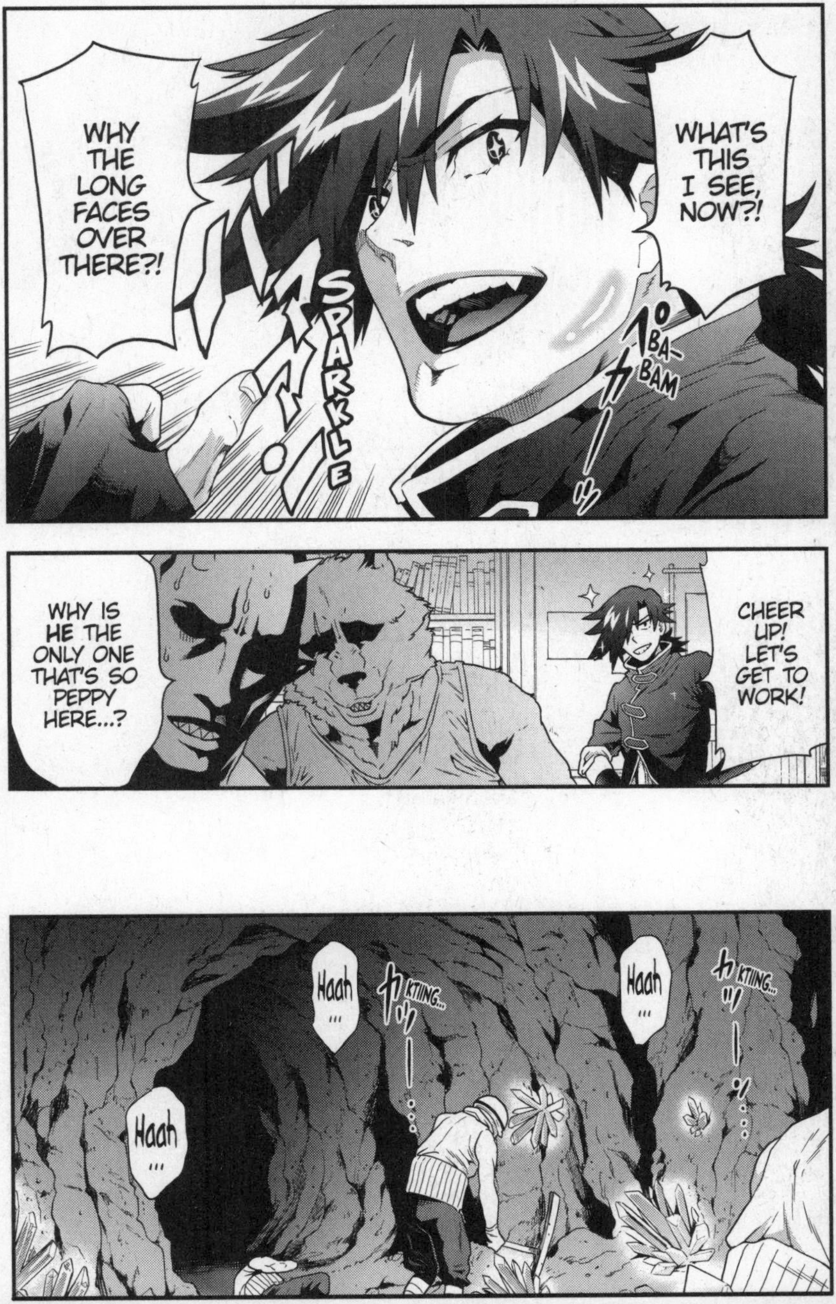
WHAT'S THIS I SEE, NOW?!
BA-BAM
SPARKLE
WHY THE LONG FACES OVER THERE?!
CHEER UP! LET'S GET TO WORK!
WHY IS HE THE ONLY ONE THAT'S SO PEPPY HERE...?
KTIING...
Haah ...
KTIING...
Haah ...
Haah ...

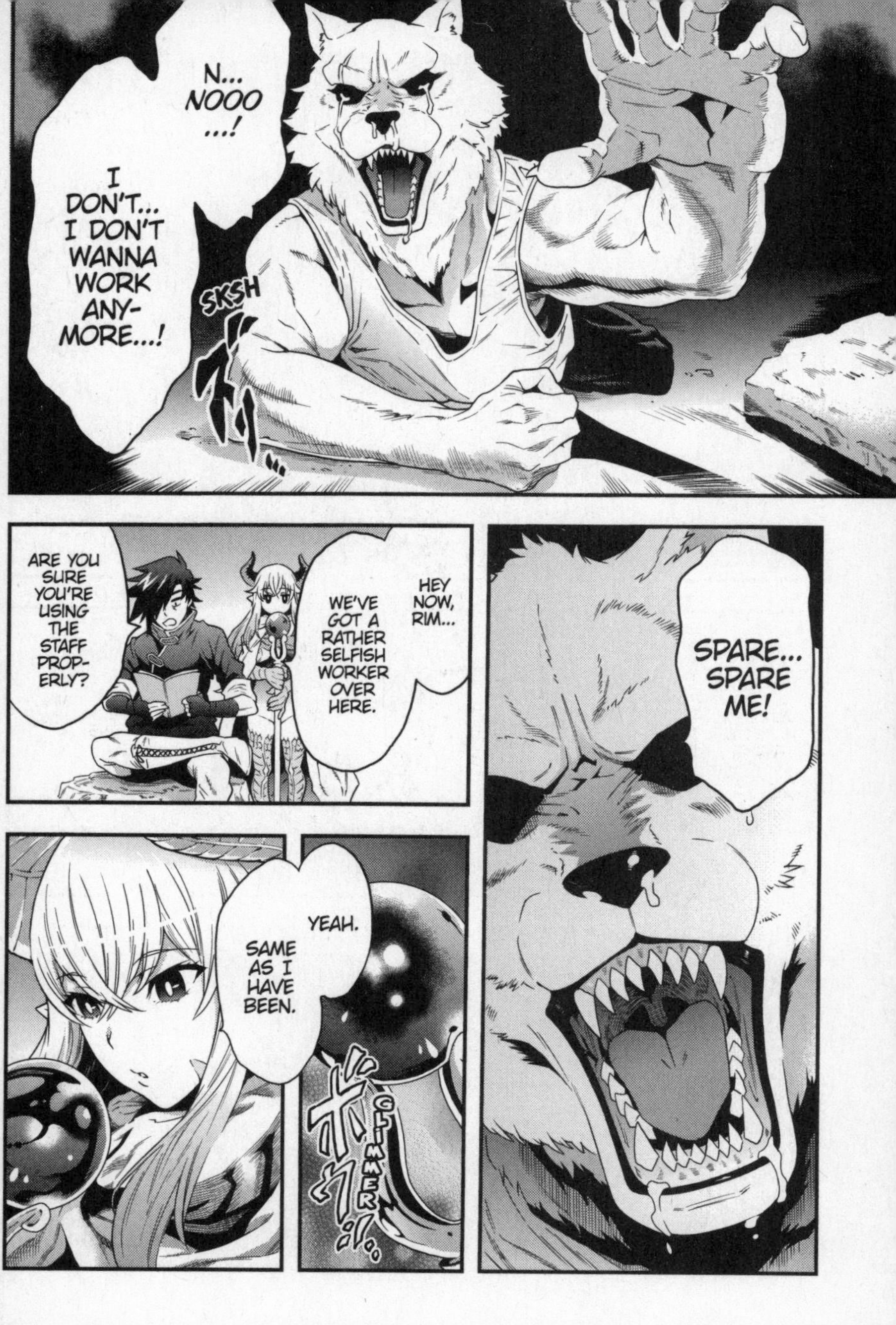
N... NOOO ...!
I DON'T... I DON'T WANNA WORK ANY-MORE...!
SKSH
SPARE... SPARE ME!
HEY NOW, RIM...
WE'VE GOT A RATHER SELFISH WORKER OVER HERE.
ARE YOU SURE YOU'RE USING THE STAFF PROP-ERLY?
YEAH.
SAME AS I HAVE BEEN.
GLIMMER

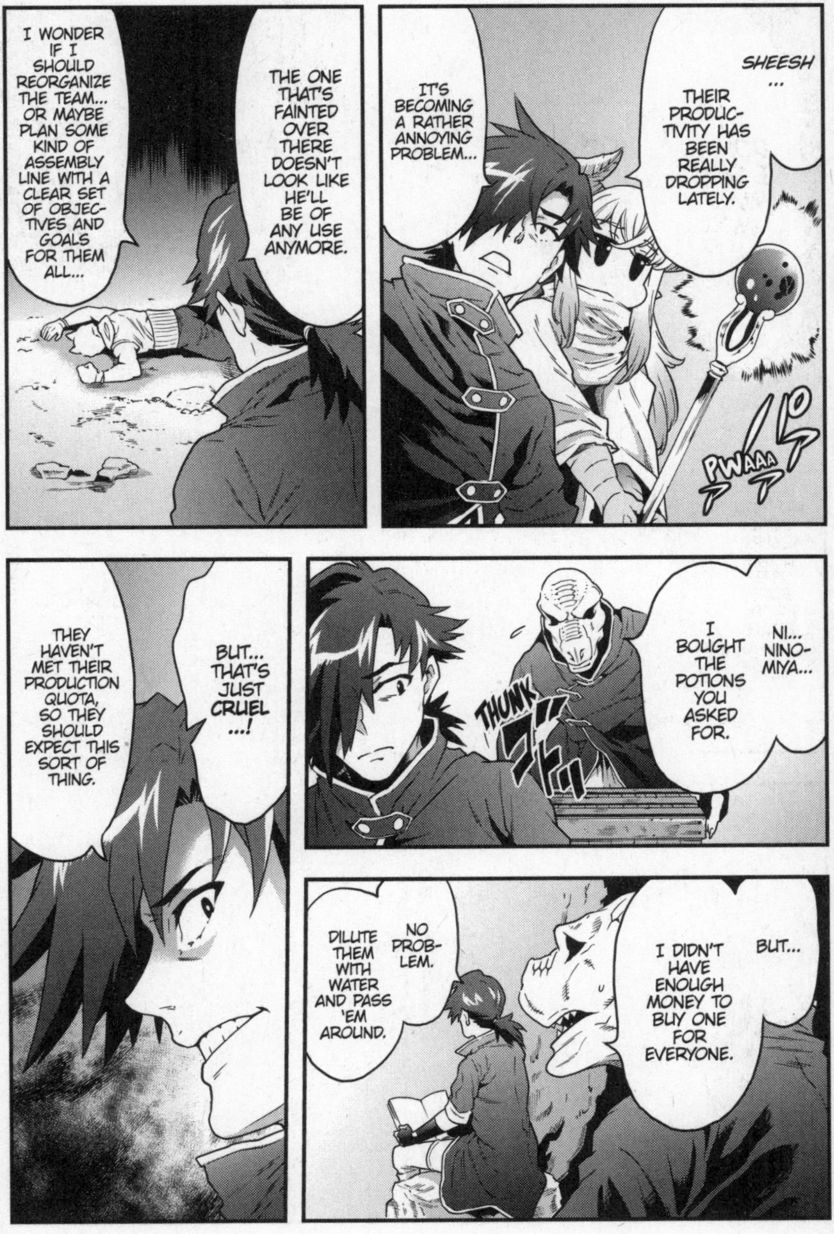
SHEESH ...
THEIR PRODUCTIVITY HAS BEEN REALLY DROPPING LATELY.
IT'S BECOMING A RATHER ANNOYING PROBLEM...
PWAAA
THE ONE THAT'S FAINTED OVER THERE DOESN'T LOOK LIKE HE'LL BE OF ANY USE ANYMORE.
I WONDER IF I SHOULD REORGANIZE THE TEAM... OR MAYBE PLAN SOME KIND OF ASSEMBLY LINE WITH A CLEAR SET OF OBJECTIVES AND GOALS FOR THEM ALL...
NI... NINOMIYA...
I BOUGHT THE POTIONS YOU ASKED FOR.
THUNK
BUT...
I DIDN'T HAVE ENOUGH MONEY TO BUY ONE FOR EVERYONE.
NO PROBLEM.
DILUTE THEM WITH WATER AND PASS 'EM AROUND.
BUT... THAT'S JUST CRUEL ...!
THEY HAVEN'T MET THEIR PRODUCTION QUOTA, SO THEY SHOULD EXPECT THIS SORT OF THING.

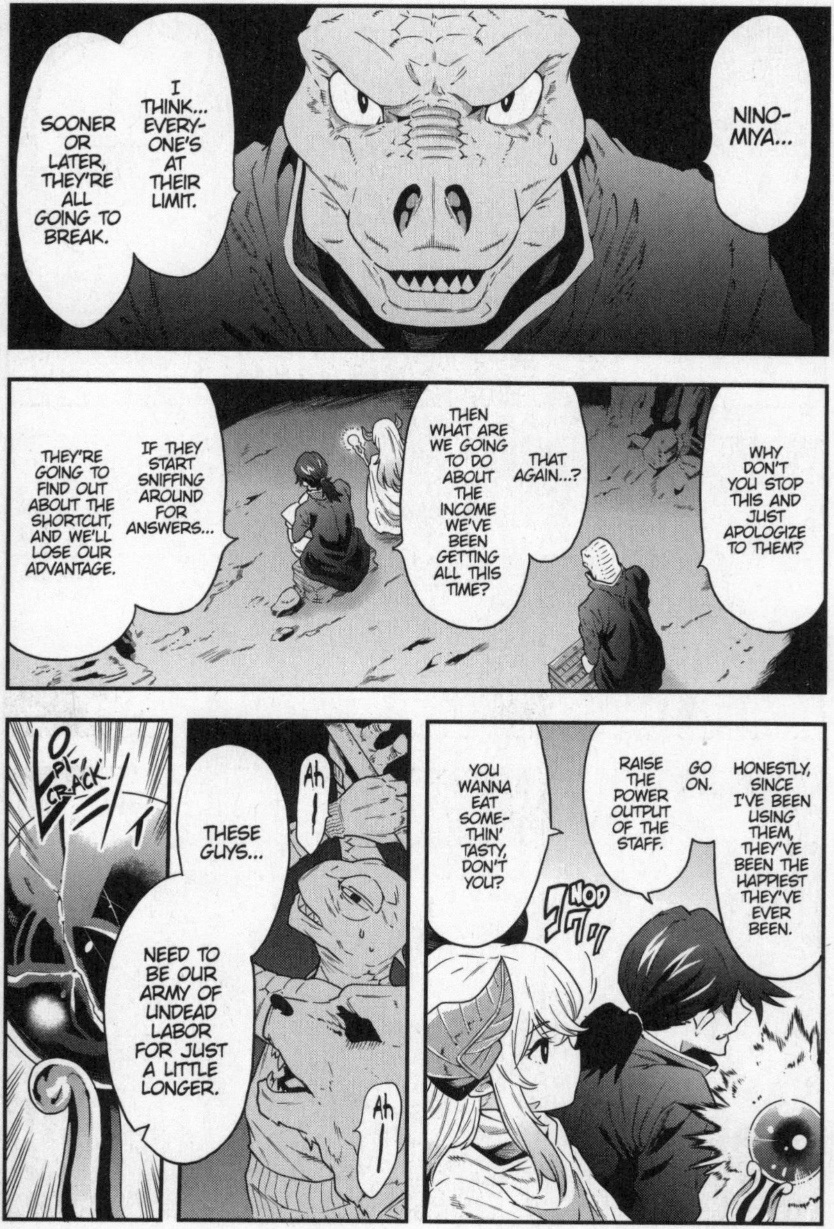
NINO-MIYA...
I THINK... EVERY-ONE'S AT THEIR LIMIT.
SOONER OR LATER, THEY'RE ALL GOING TO BREAK.
WHY DON'T YOU STOP THIS AND JUST APOLOGIZE TO THEM?
THAT AGAIN...?
THEN WHAT ARE WE GOING TO DO ABOUT THE INCOME WE'VE BEEN GETTING ALL THIS TIME?
IF THEY START SNIFFING AROUND FOR ANSWERS...
THEY'RE GOING TO FIND OUT ABOUT THE SHORTCUT, AND WE'LL LOSE OUR ADVANTAGE.
HONESTLY, SINCE I'VE BEEN USING THEM, THEY'VE BEEN THE HAPPIEST THEY'VE EVER BEEN.
GO ON.
RAISE THE POWER OUTPUT OF THE STAFF.
YOU WANNA EAT SOME-THIN' TASTY, DON'T YOU?
NOD
Ah
THESE GUYS...
NEED TO BE OUR ARMY OF UNDEAD LABOR FOR JUST A LITTLE LONGER.
Ah
PI-CRACK

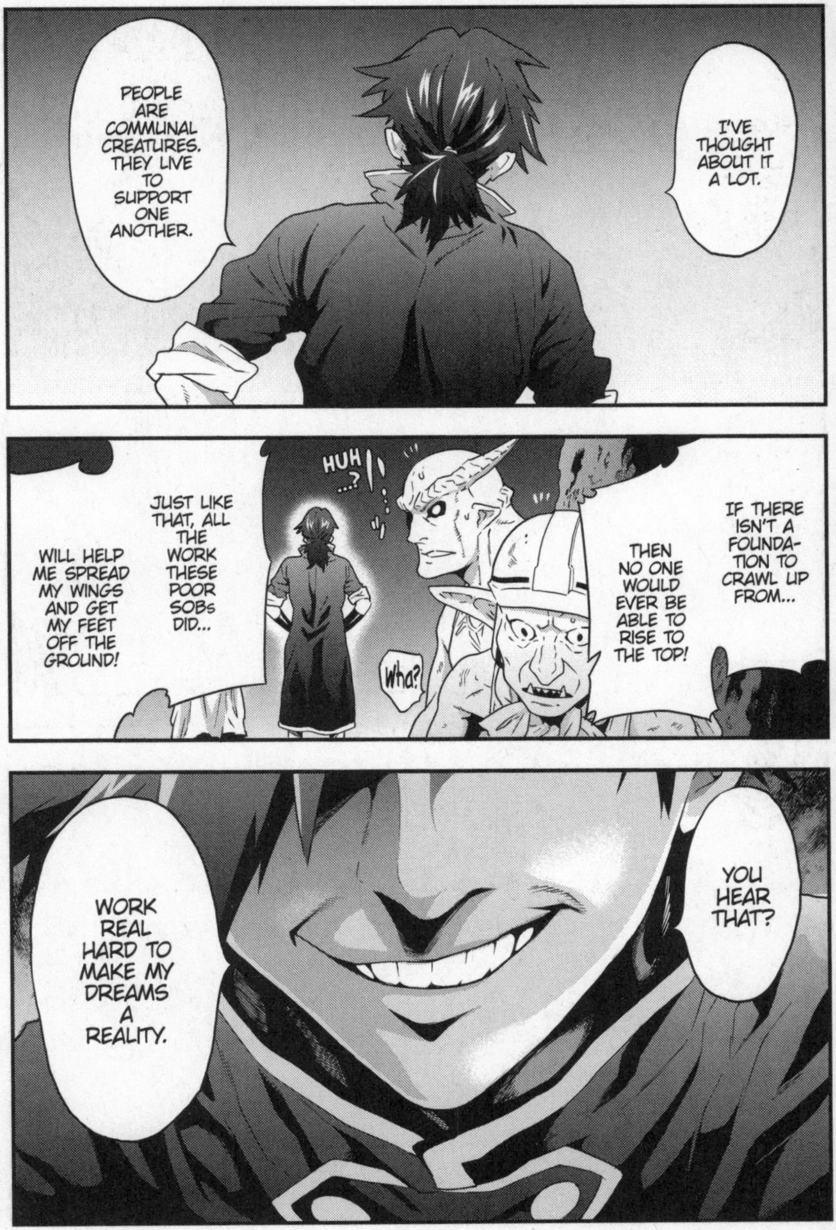
I'VE THOUGHT ABOUT IT A LOT.
PEOPLE ARE COMMUNAL CREATURES. THEY LIVE TO SUPPORT ONE ANOTHER.
IF THERE ISN'T A FOUNDATION TO CRAWL UP FROM...
THEN NO ONE WOULD EVER BE ABLE TO RISE TO THE TOP!
Wha?
HUH ...?
JUST LIKE THAT, ALL THE WORK THESE POOR SOBs DID...
WILL HELP ME SPREAD MY WINGS AND GET MY FEET OFF THE GROUND!
YOU HEAR THAT?
WORK REAL HARD TO MAKE MY DREAMS A REALITY.

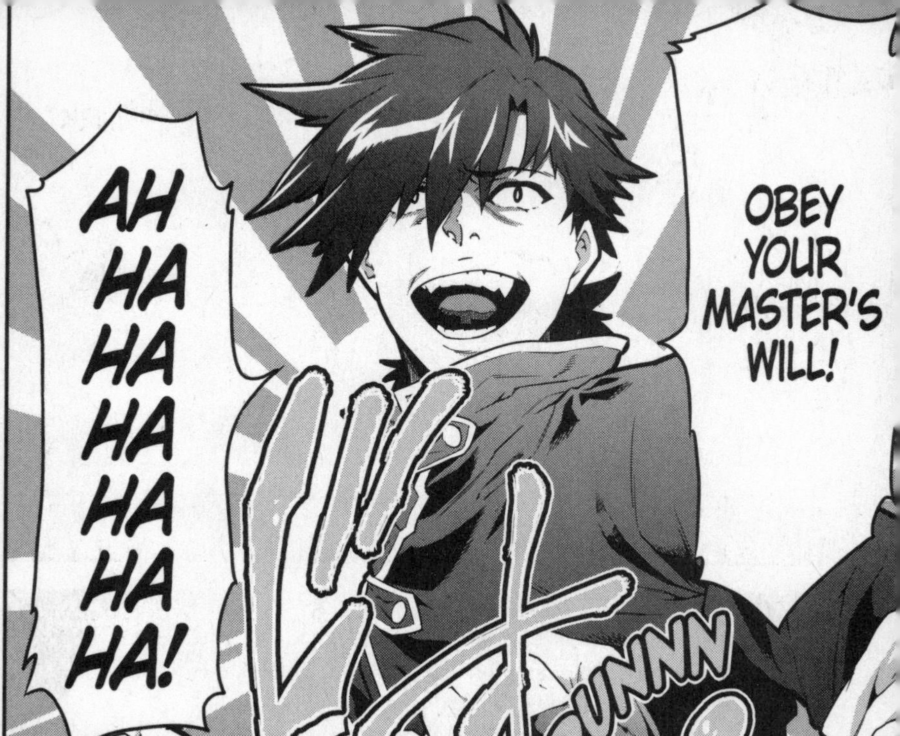
OBEY YOUR MASTER'S WILL!
AH HA HA HA HA HA HA HA HA!
DU-DUNNN
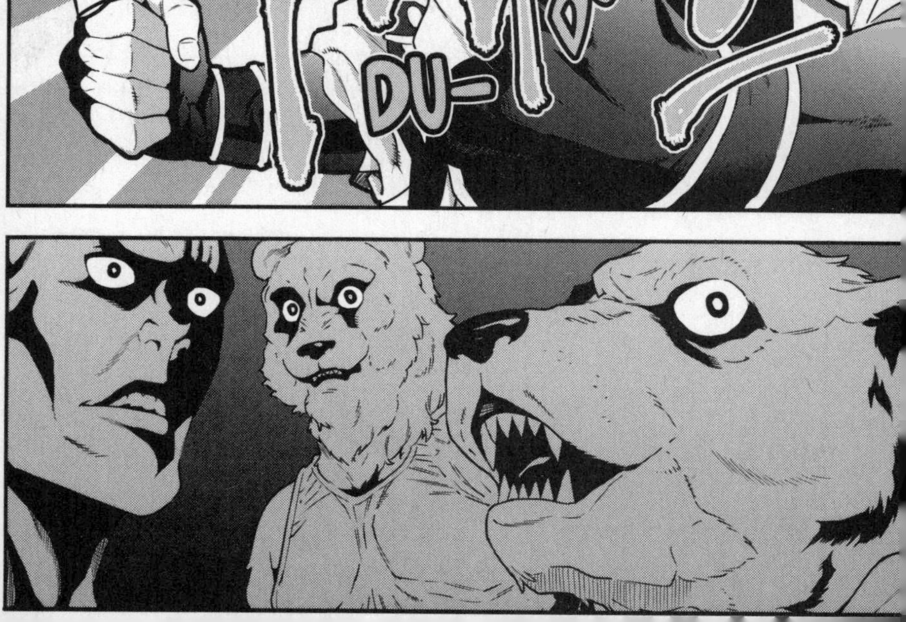

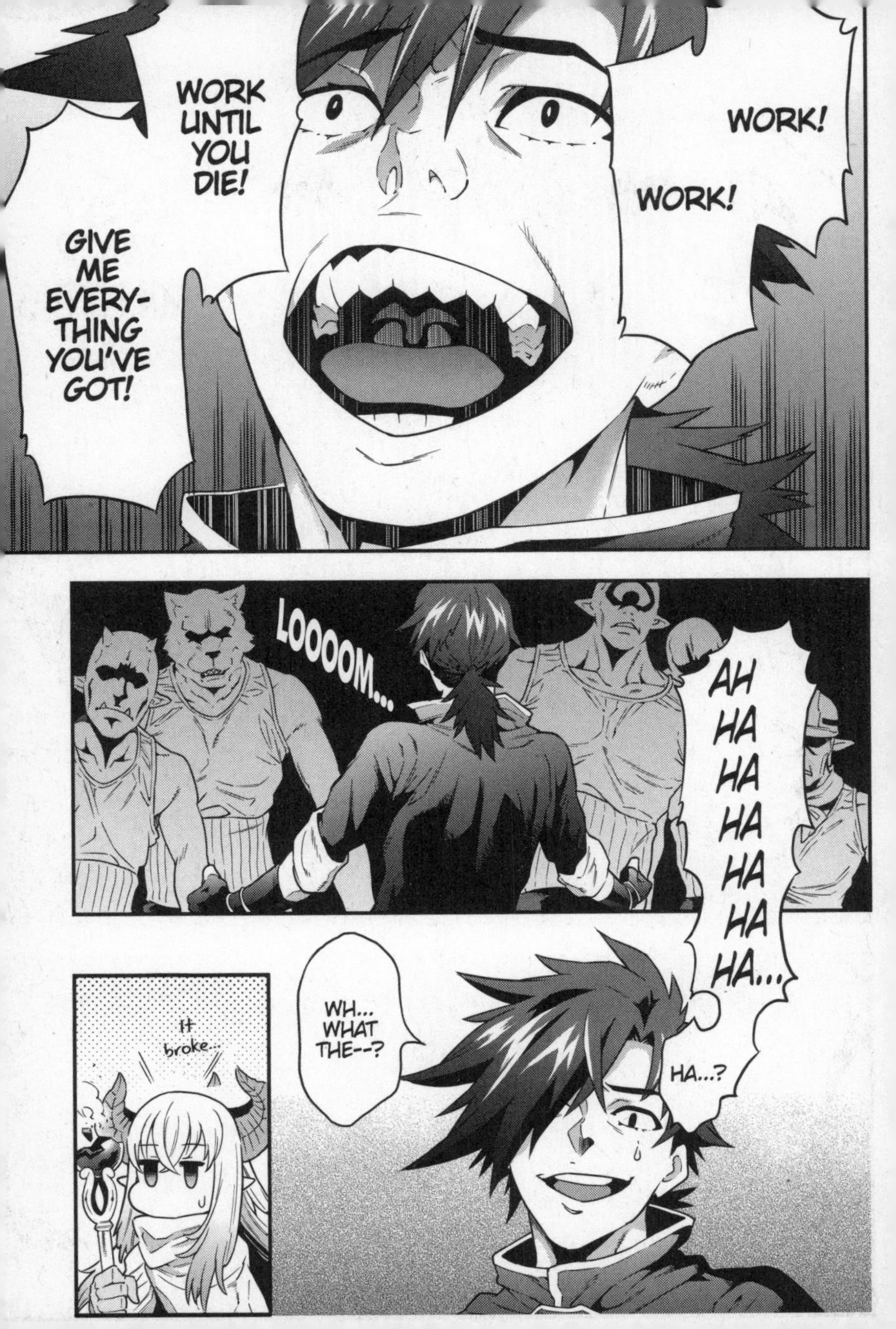
WORK!
WORK!
WORK UNTIL YOU DIE!
GIVE ME EVERY-THING YOU'VE GOT!
AH HA HA HA HA HA HA HA...
LOOOOM...
HA...?
WH... WHAT THE--?
It broke...

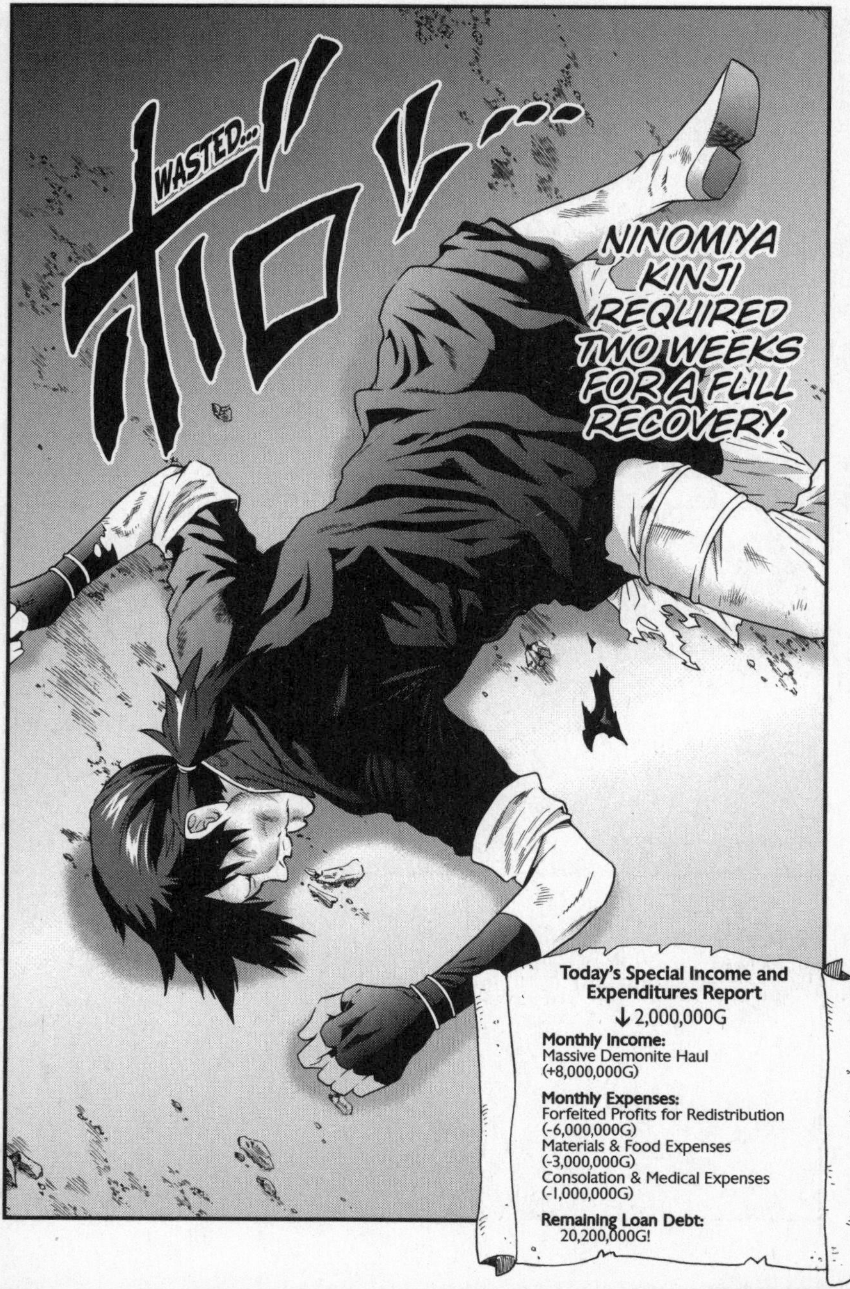
オロ〜…
WASTED…
NINOMIYA KINJI REQUIRED TWO WEEKS FOR A FULL RECOVERY.
Today's Special Income and Expenditures Report
↓2,000,000G
Monthly Income:
Massive Demonite Haul
(+8,000,000G)
Monthly Expenses:
Forfeited Profits for Redistribution
(-6,000,000G)
Materials & Food Expenses
(-3,000,000G)
Consolation & Medical Expenses
(-1,000,000G)
Remaining Loan Debt:
20,200,000G!

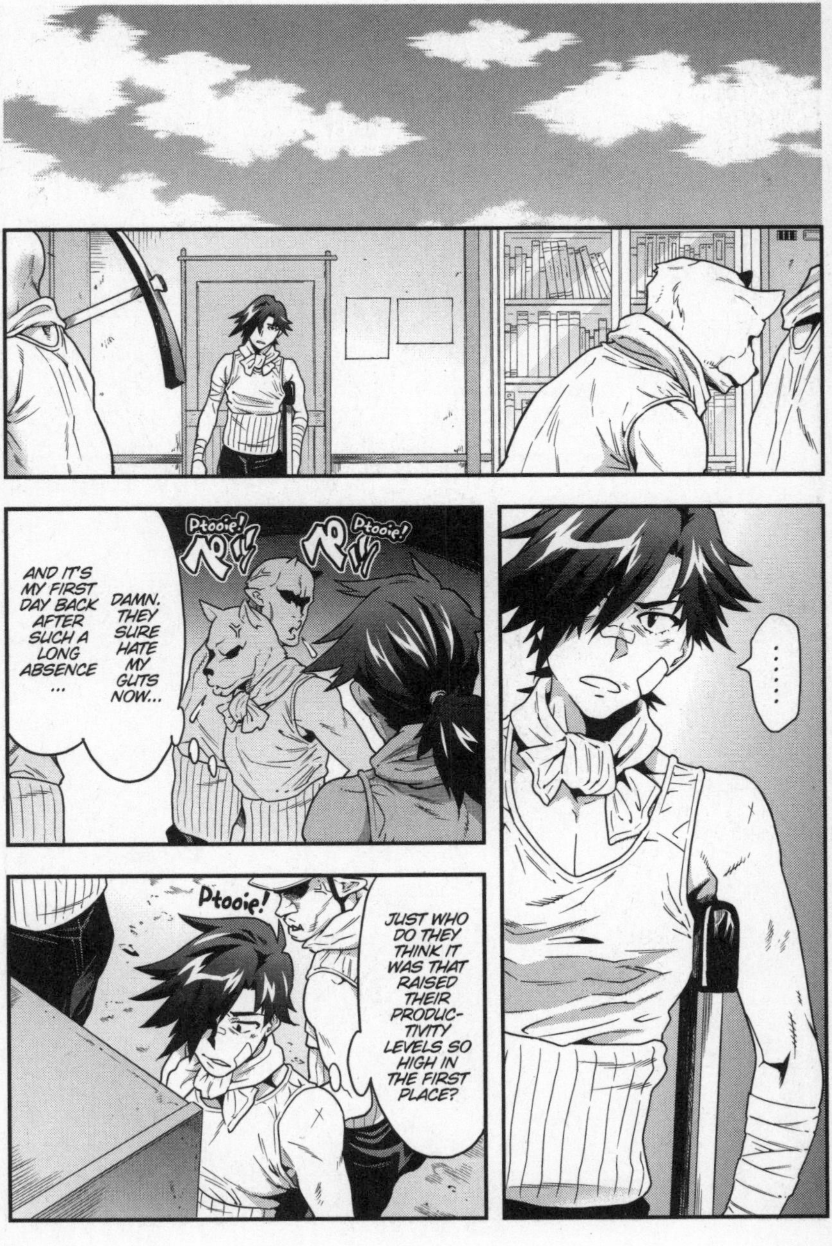

......
Ptooie! ペッ
Ptooie! ペッ
DAMN. THEY SURE HATE MY GUTS NOW...
AND IT'S MY FIRST DAY BACK AFTER SUCH A LONG ABSENCE ...
Ptooie!
JUST WHO DO THEY THINK IT WAS THAT RAISED THEIR PRODUC-TIVITY LEVELS SO HIGH IN THE FIRST PLACE?

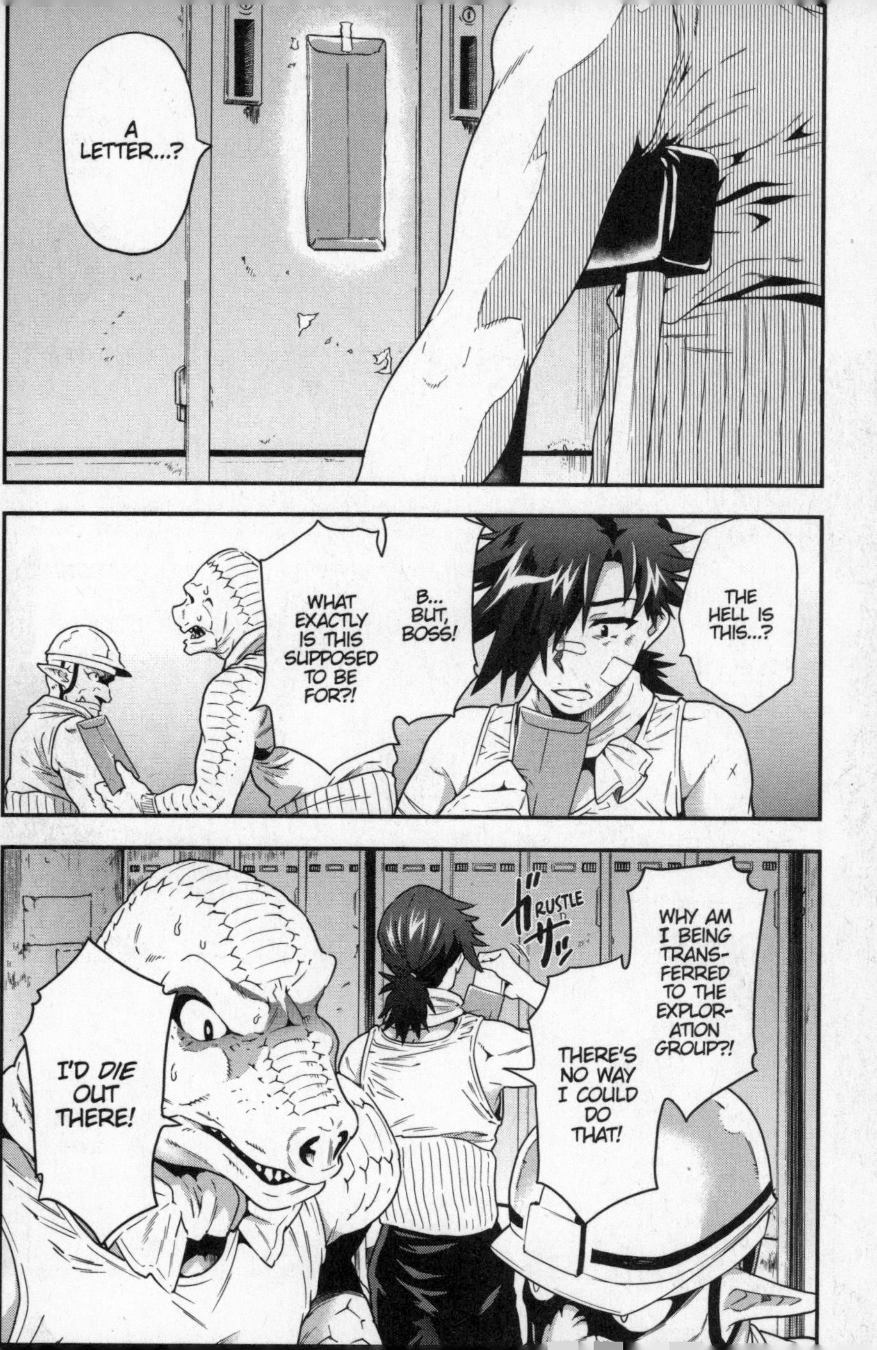
A LETTER...?
THE HELL IS THIS...?
B... BUT, BOSS!
WHAT EXACTLY IS THIS SUPPOSED TO BE FOR?!
RUSTLE
WHY AM I BEING TRANS-FERRED TO THE EXPLOR-ATION GROUP?!
THERE'S NO WAY I COULD DO THAT!
I'D DIE OUT THERE!

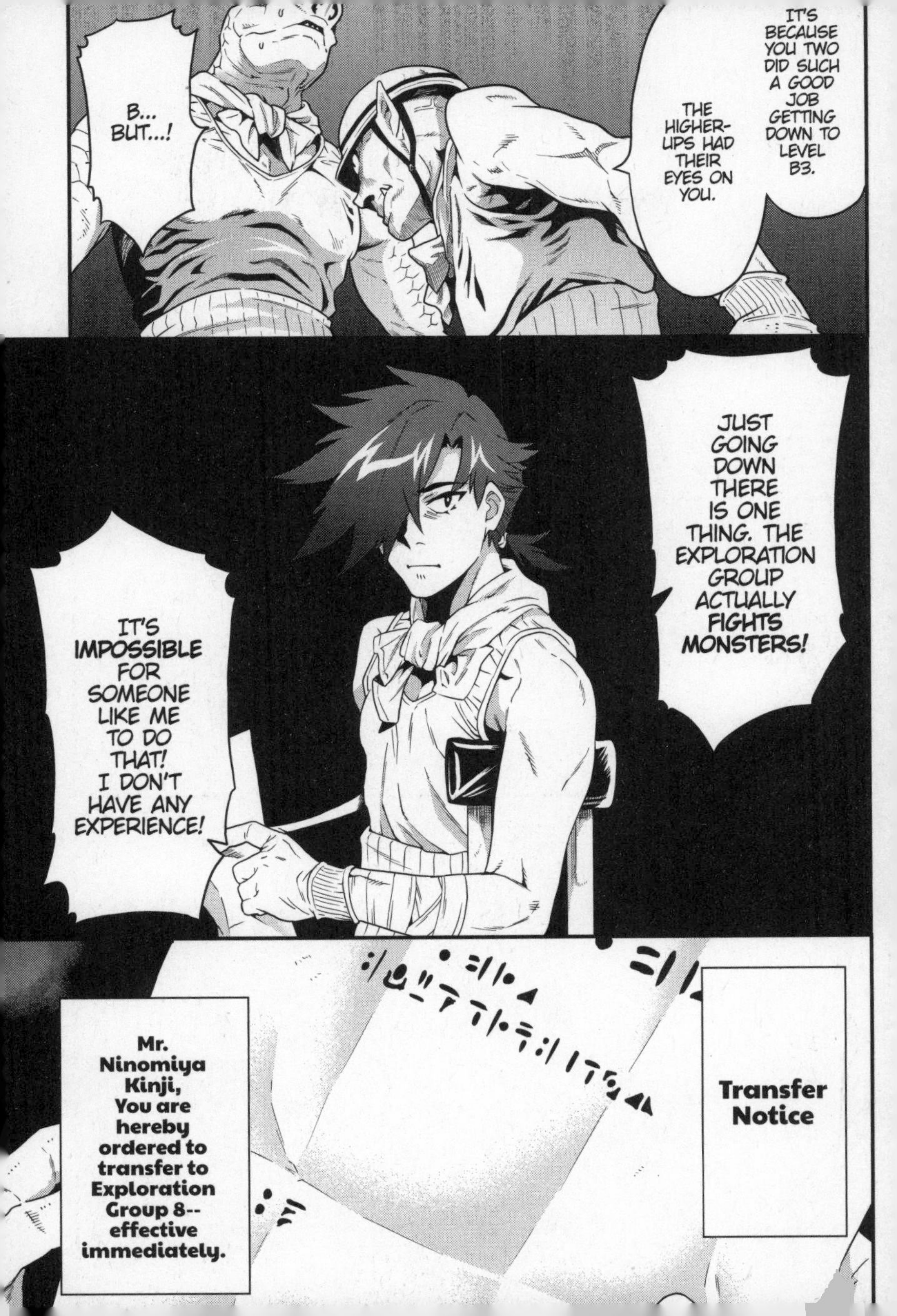
IT'S BECAUSE YOU TWO DID SUCH A GOOD JOB GETTING DOWN TO LEVEL B3.
THE HIGHER-UPS HAD THEIR EYES ON YOU.
B... BUT...!
JUST GOING DOWN THERE IS ONE THING. THE EXPLORATION GROUP ACTUALLY FIGHTS MONSTERS!
IT'S IMPOSSIBLE FOR SOMEONE LIKE ME TO DO THAT! I DON'T HAVE ANY EXPERIENCE!
Transfer Notice
Mr. Ninomiya Kinji, You are hereby ordered to transfer to Exploration Group 8-- effective immediately.

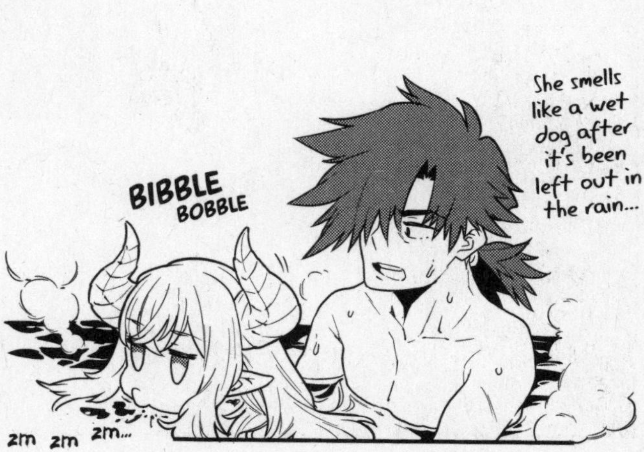
She smells like a wet dog after it's been left out in the rain...
BIBBLE BOBBLE
zm zm zm...

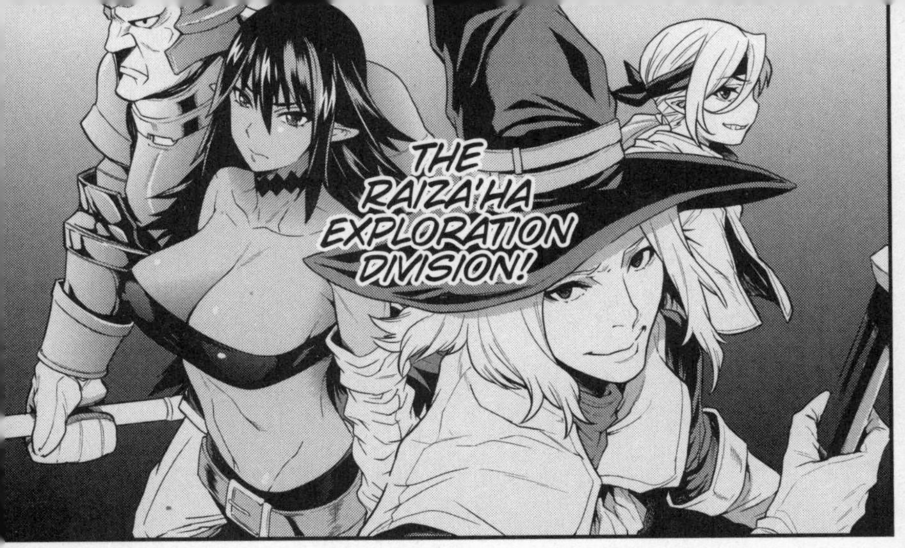
THE RAIZA'HA EXPLORATION DIVISION!

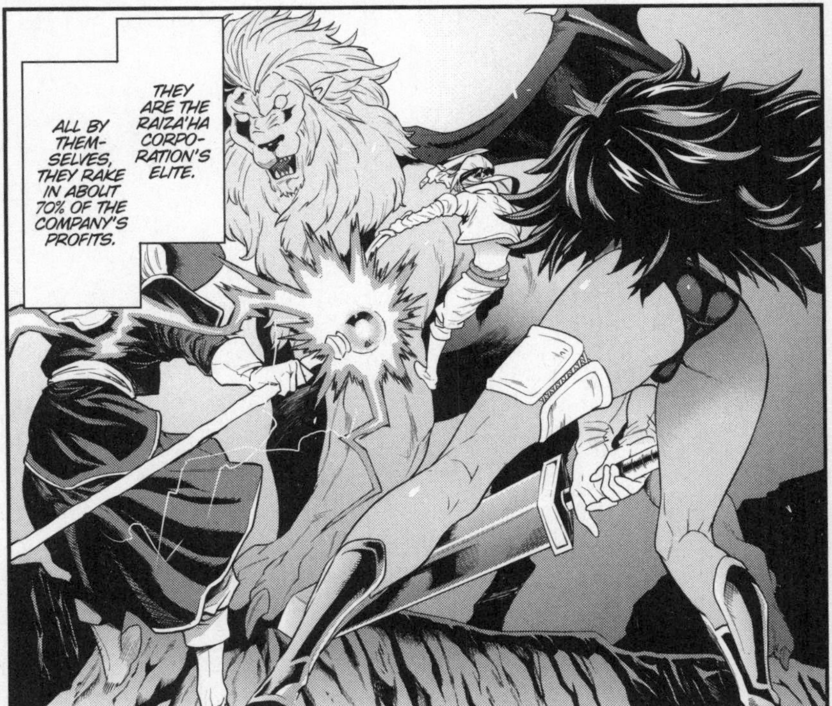
THEY ARE THE RAIZA'HA CORPO-RATION'S ELITE.
ALL BY THEM-SELVES, THEY RAKE IN ABOUT 70% OF THE COMPANY'S PROFITS.

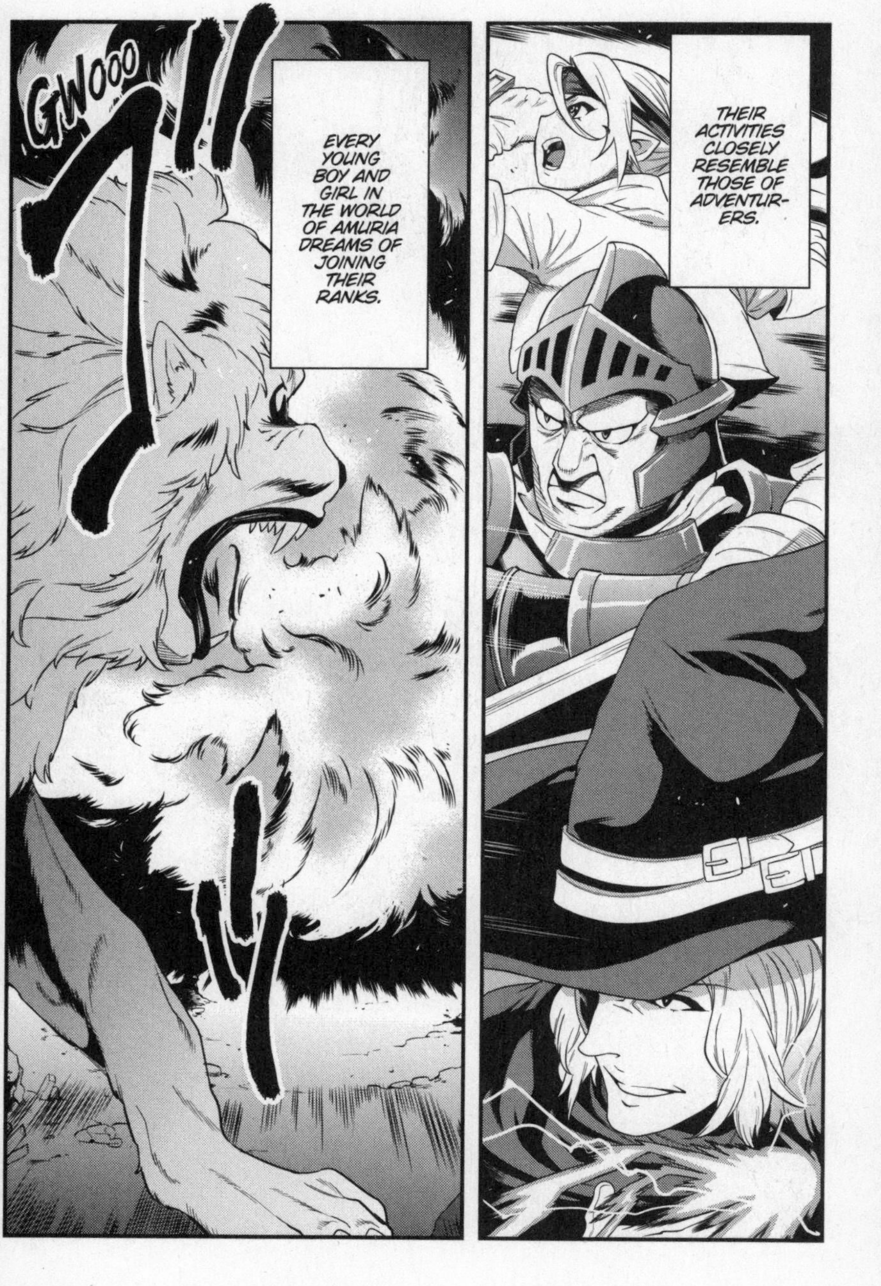
THEIR ACTIVITIES CLOSELY RESEMBLE THOSE OF ADVENTURERS.
GWOOO
EVERY YOUNG BOY AND GIRL IN THE WORLD OF AMURIA DREAMS OF JOINING THEIR RANKS.

FOR NINOMIYA KINJI, BURDENED BY A TRULY STUPENDOUS DEBT...

THIS STAGE OF FIERCE AND GLORIOUS BATTLES IS AN OPPORTUNITY.

NOW...

Hey, one went that way.

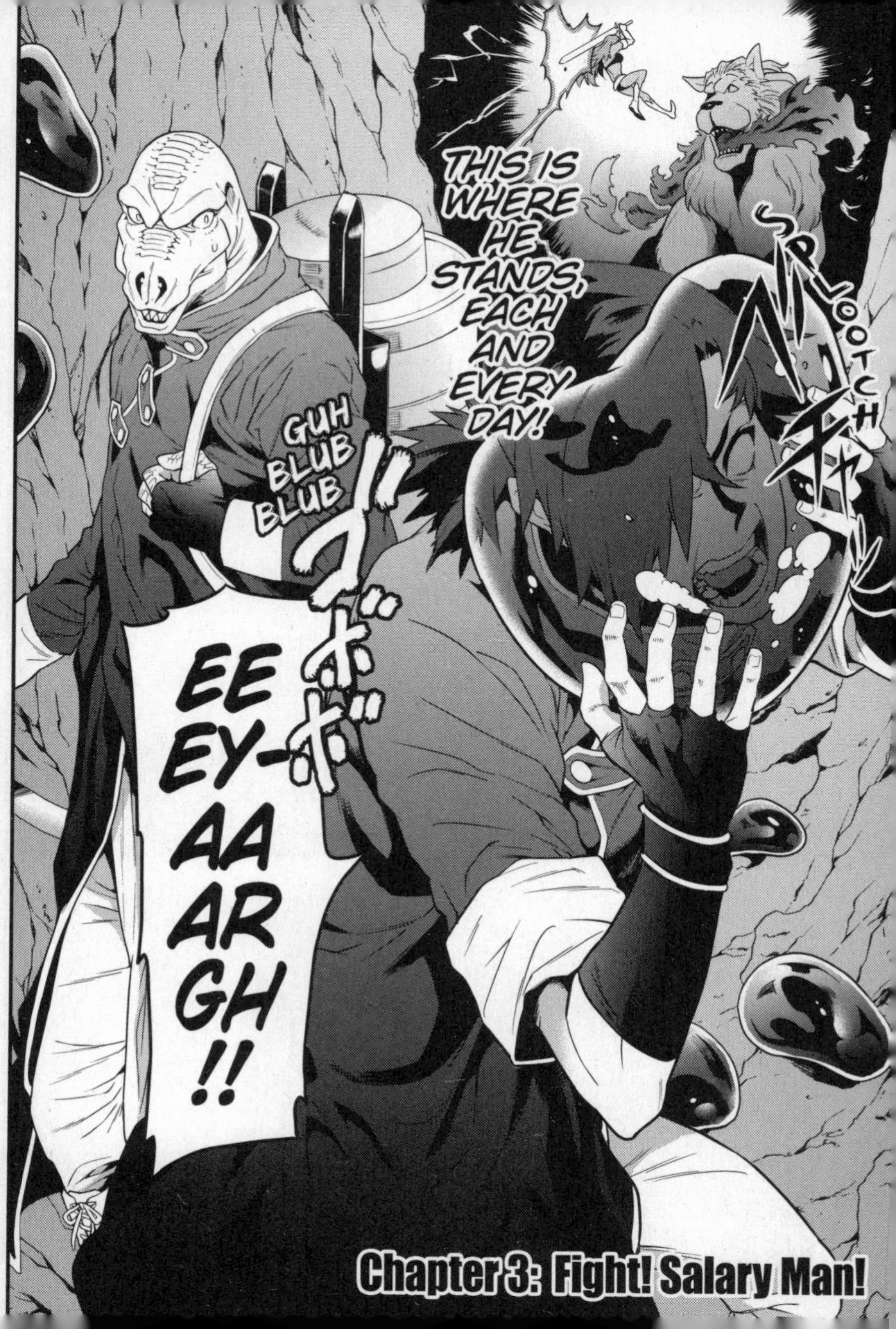
SPLOOTCH
THIS IS WHERE HE STANDS, EACH AND EVERY DAY!
GUH BLUB BLUB
EEEY-AAAARGH!!
Chapter 3: Fight! Salary Man!

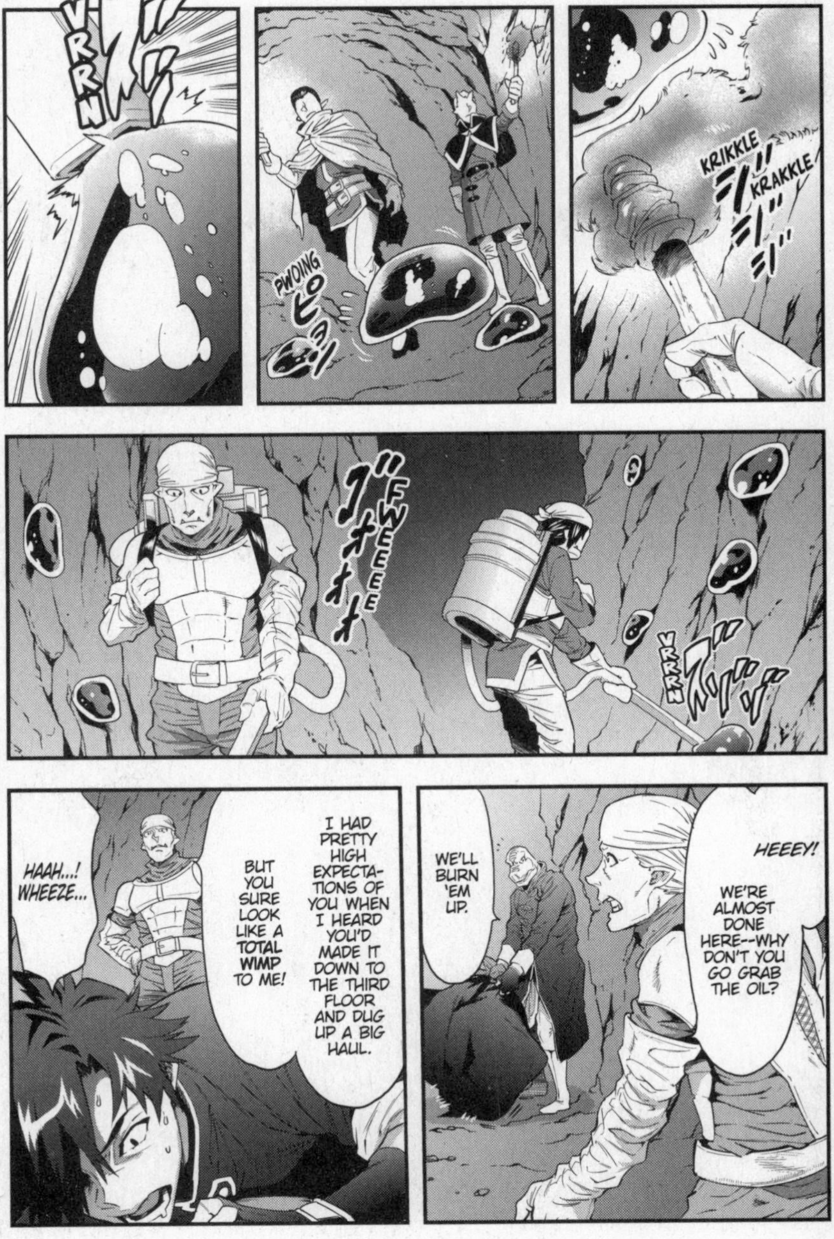
KRIKKLE
KRAKKLE
PWOING
VRRN
FWEEEE
VRRRN
HEEEY!
WE'RE ALMOST DONE HERE--WHY DON'T YOU GO GRAB THE OIL?
WE'LL BURN 'EM UP.
I HAD PRETTY HIGH EXPECTATIONS OF YOU WHEN I HEARD YOU'D MADE IT DOWN TO THE THIRD FLOOR AND DUG UP A BIG HAUL.
BUT YOU SURE LOOK LIKE A TOTAL WIMP TO ME!
HAAH...! WHEEZE...

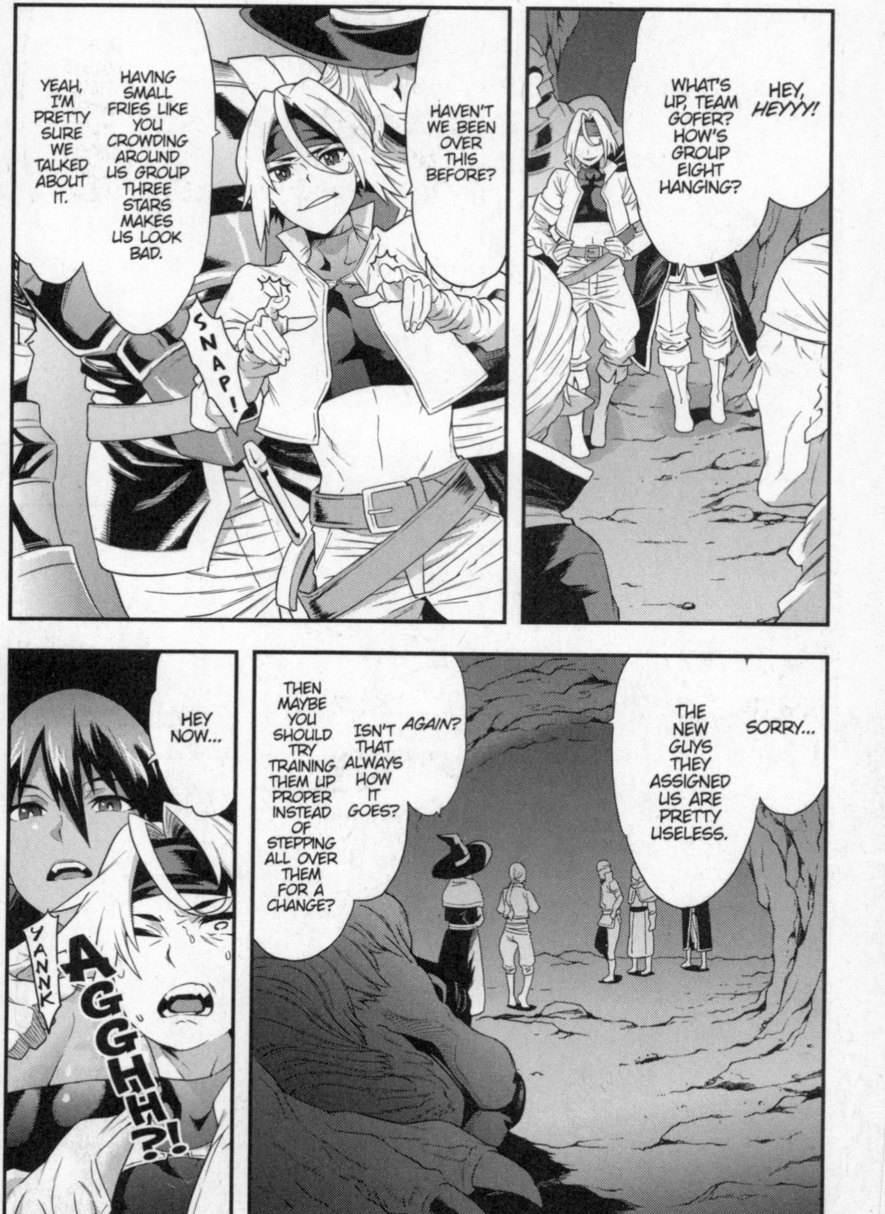
HEY, HEYYY!
WHAT'S UP, TEAM GOFER? HOW'S GROUP EIGHT HANGING?
HAVEN'T WE BEEN OVER THIS BEFORE?
HAVING SMALL FRIES LIKE YOU CROWDING AROUND US GROUP THREE STARS MAKES US LOOK BAD.
YEAH, I'M PRETTY SURE WE TALKED ABOUT IT.
SNAP!
SORRY...
THE NEW GUYS THEY ASSIGNED US ARE PRETTY USELESS.
AGAIN?
ISN'T THAT ALWAYS HOW IT GOES?
THEN MAYBE YOU SHOULD TRY TRAINING THEM UP PROPER INSTEAD OF STEPPING ALL OVER THEM FOR A CHANGE?
HEY NOW...
YANNK
AGGHH?!

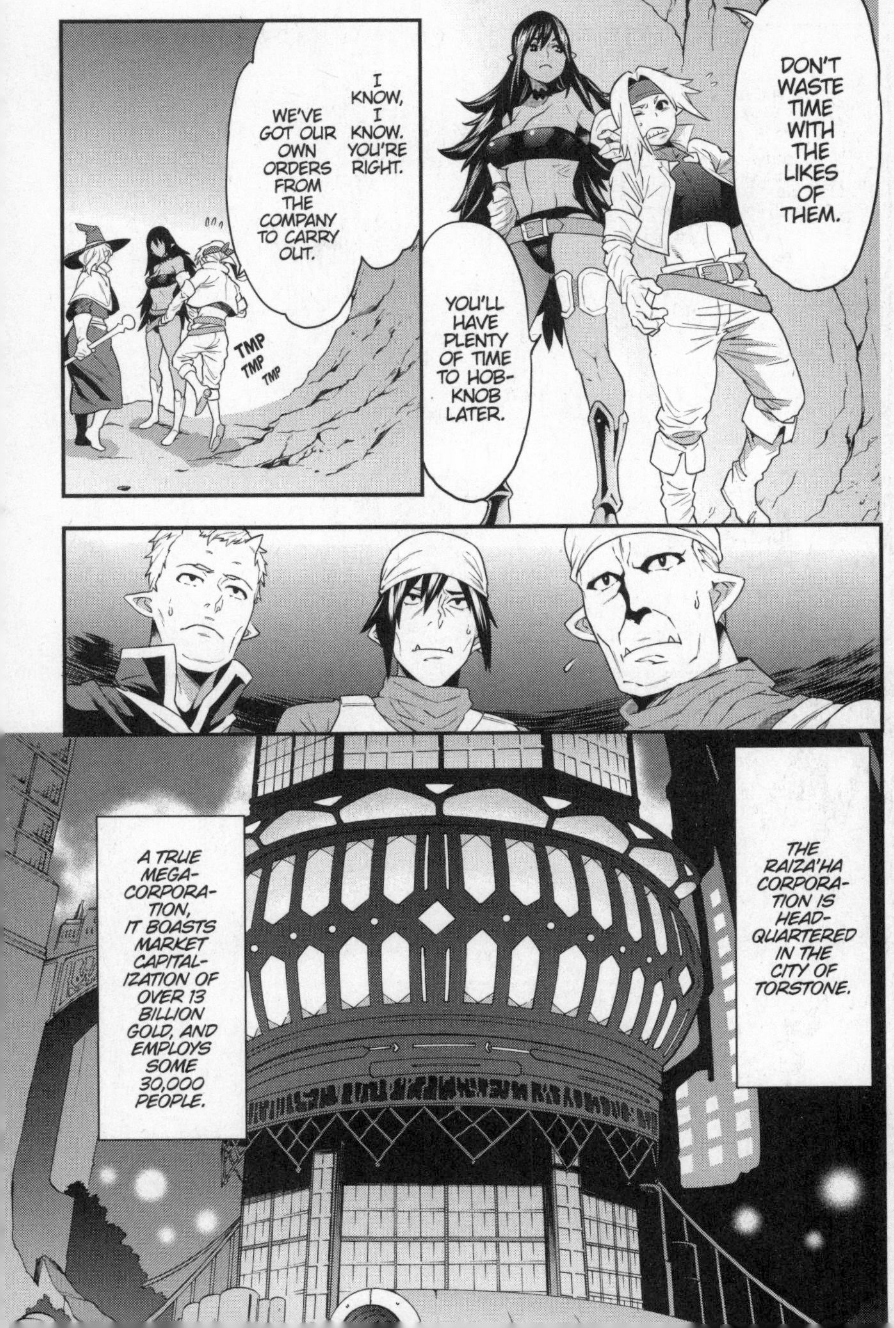
DON'T WASTE TIME WITH THE LIKES OF THEM.
YOU'LL HAVE PLENTY OF TIME TO HOB-KNOB LATER.
I KNOW, I KNOW. YOU'RE RIGHT.
WE'VE GOT OUR OWN ORDERS FROM THE COMPANY TO CARRY OUT.
TMP TMP TMP
THE RAIZA'HA CORPORATION IS HEADQUARTERED IN THE CITY OF TORSTONE.
A TRUE MEGA-CORPORATION, IT BOASTS MARKET CAPITALIZATION OF OVER 13 BILLION GOLD, AND EMPLOYS SOME 30,000 PEOPLE.

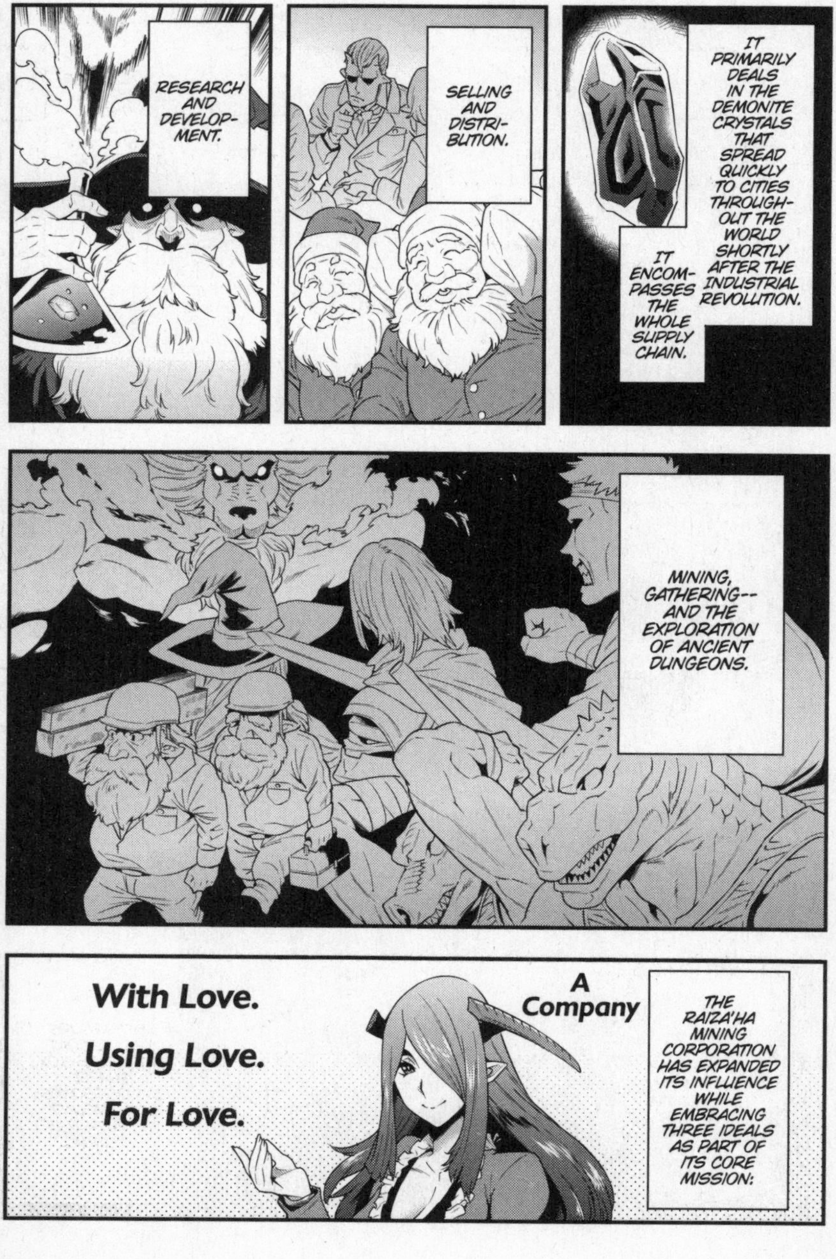
IT PRIMARILY DEALS IN THE DEMONITE CRYSTALS THAT SPREAD QUICKLY TO CITIES THROUGHOUT THE WORLD SHORTLY AFTER THE INDUSTRIAL REVOLUTION.
IT ENCOMPASSES THE WHOLE SUPPLY CHAIN.
SELLING AND DISTRIBUTION.
RESEARCH AND DEVELOPMENT.
MINING, GATHERING-- AND THE EXPLORATION OF ANCIENT DUNGEONS.
THE RAIZA'HA MINING CORPORATION HAS EXPANDED ITS INFLUENCE WHILE EMBRACING THREE IDEALS AS PART OF ITS CORE MISSION:
A Company
With Love.
Using Love.
For Love.

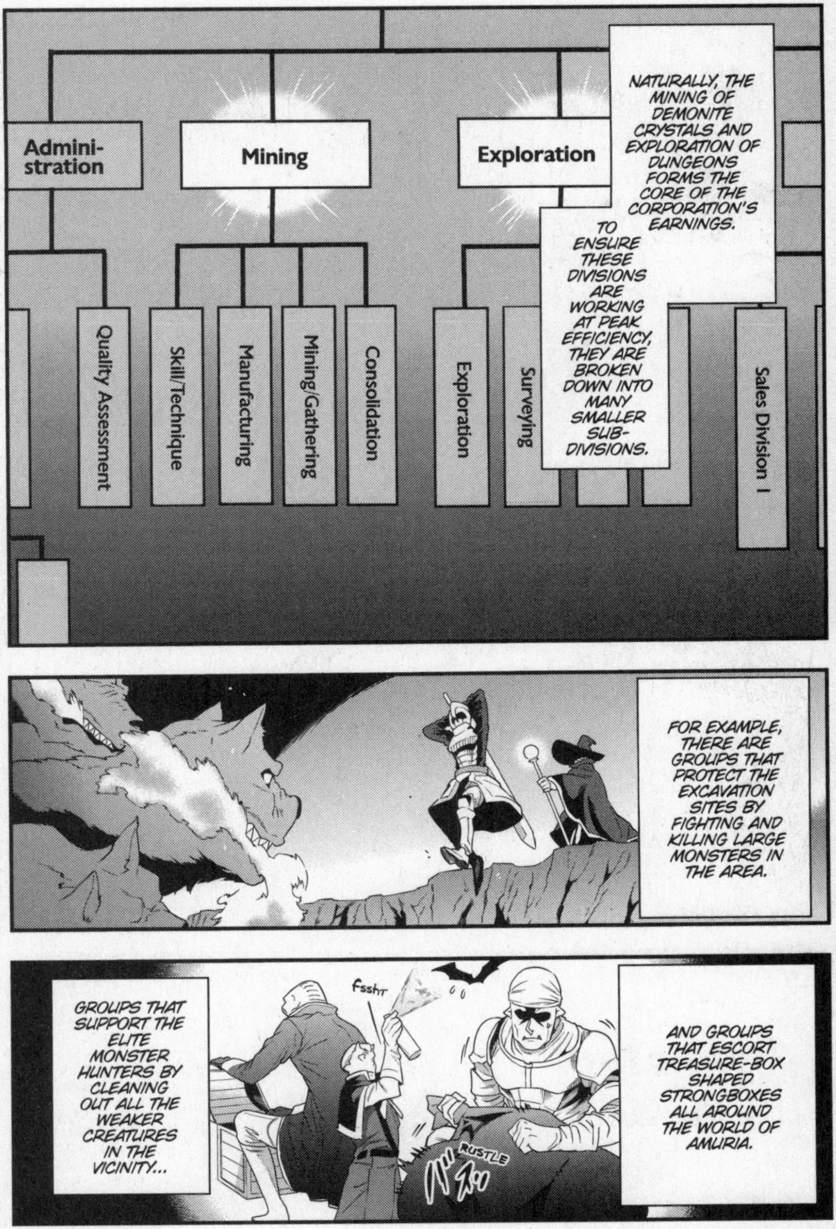
NATURALLY, THE MINING OF DEMONITE CRYSTALS AND EXPLORATION OF DUNGEONS FORMS THE CORE OF THE CORPORATION'S EARNINGS.
TO ENSURE THESE DIVISIONS ARE WORKING AT PEAK EFFICIENCY, THEY ARE BROKEN DOWN INTO MANY SMALLER SUB-DIVISIONS.
Exploration
Mining
Administration
Sales Division 1
Surveying
Exploration
Consolidation
Mining/Gathering
Manufacturing
Skill/Technique
Quality Assessment
FOR EXAMPLE, THERE ARE GROUPS THAT PROTECT THE EXCAVATION SITES BY FIGHTING AND KILLING LARGE MONSTERS IN THE AREA.
GROUPS THAT SUPPORT THE ELITE MONSTER HUNTERS BY CLEANING OUT ALL THE WEAKER CREATURES IN THE VICINITY...
fsshT
RUSTLE
AND GROUPS THAT ESCORT TREASURE-BOX SHAPED STRONGBOXES ALL AROUND THE WORLD OF AMURIA.

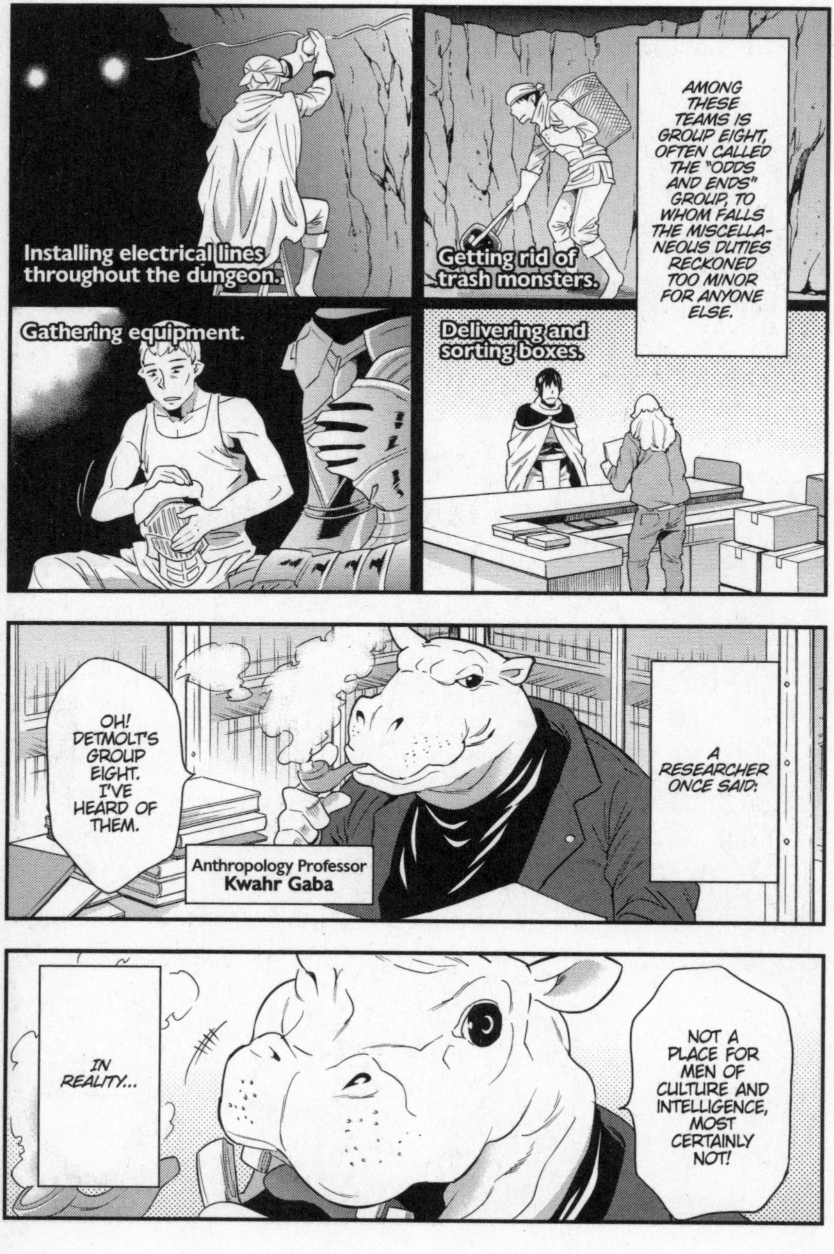

AMONG THESE TEAMS IS GROUP EIGHT, OFTEN CALLED THE "ODDS AND ENDS" GROUP, TO WHOM FALLS THE MISCELLANEOUS DUTIES RECKONED TOO MINOR FOR ANYONE ELSE.
Getting rid of trash monsters.
Installing electrical lines throughout the dungeon.
Delivering and sorting boxes.
Gathering equipment.
A RESEARCHER ONCE SAID:
OH! DETMOLT'S GROUP EIGHT. I'VE HEARD OF THEM.
Anthropology Professor Kwahr Gaba
NOT A PLACE FOR MEN OF CULTURE AND INTELLIGENCE, MOST CERTAINLY NOT!
IN REALITY...

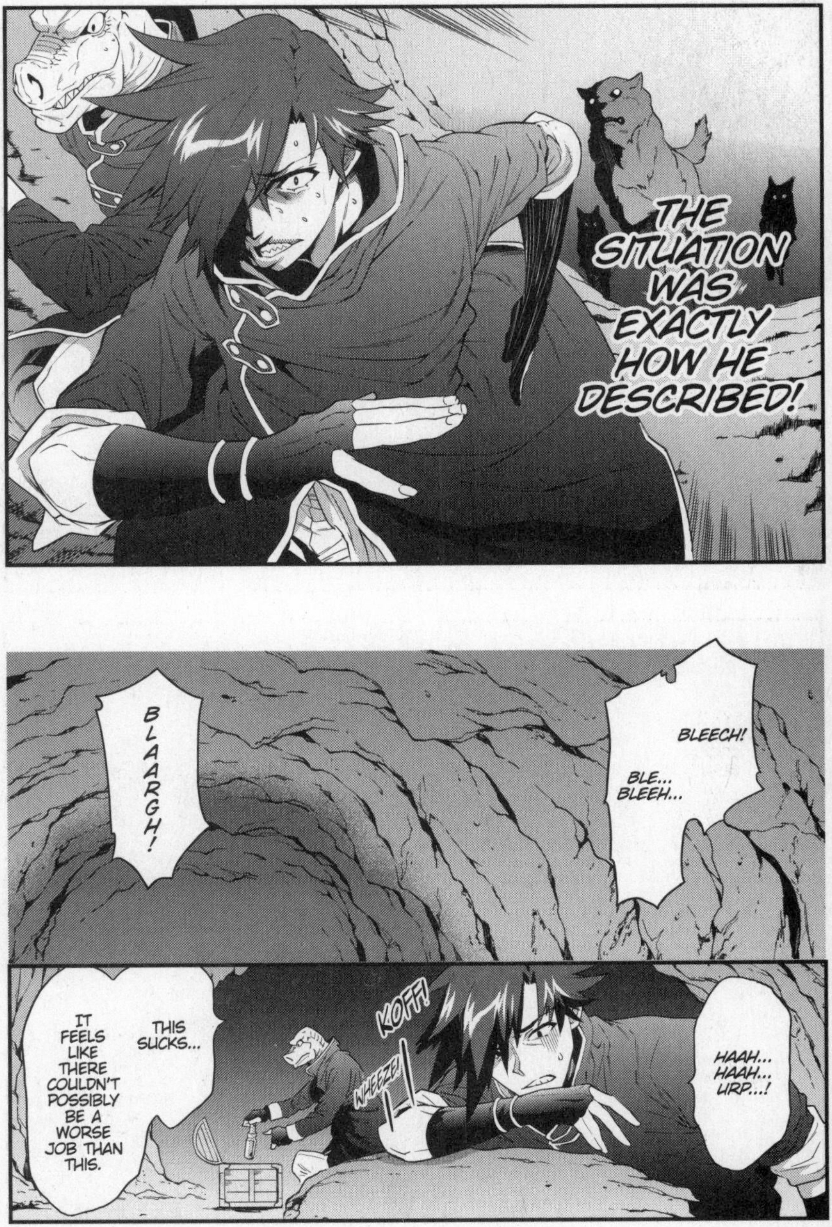
THE SITUATION WAS EXACTLY HOW HE DESCRIBED!
BLEECH!
BLE... BLEEH...
BLAARGH!
HAAH... HAAH... URP...!
KOFF!
WHEEZE!
THIS SUCKS...
IT FEELS LIKE THERE COULDN'T POSSIBLY BE A WORSE JOB THAN THIS.

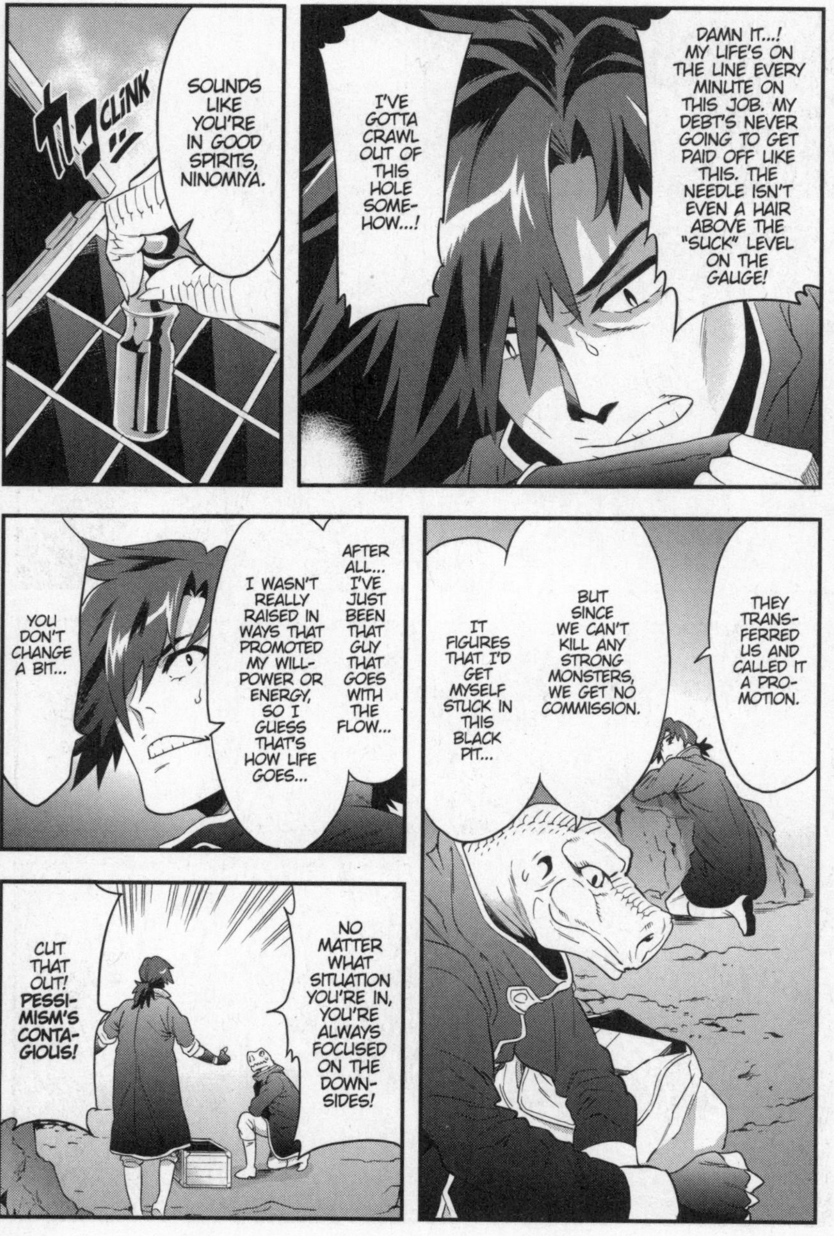
DAMN IT...! MY LIFE'S ON THE LINE EVERY MINUTE ON THIS JOB. MY DEBT'S NEVER GOING TO GET PAID OFF LIKE THIS. THE NEEDLE ISN'T EVEN A HAIR ABOVE THE "SUCK" LEVEL ON THE GAUGE!
I'VE GOTTA CRAWL OUT OF THIS HOLE SOMEHOW...!
CLINK
SOUNDS LIKE YOU'RE IN GOOD SPIRITS, NINOMIYA.
THEY TRANSFERRED US AND CALLED IT A PROMOTION.
BUT SINCE WE CAN'T KILL ANY STRONG MONSTERS, WE GET NO COMMISSION.
IT FIGURES THAT I'D GET MYSELF STUCK IN THIS BLACK PIT...
AFTER ALL... I'VE JUST BEEN THAT GUY THAT GOES WITH THE FLOW...
I WASN'T REALLY RAISED IN WAYS THAT PROMOTED MY WILLPOWER OR ENERGY, SO I GUESS THAT'S HOW LIFE GOES...
YOU DON'T CHANGE A BIT...
NO MATTER WHAT SITUATION YOU'RE IN, YOU'RE ALWAYS FOCUSED ON THE DOWNSIDES!
CUT THAT OUT! PESSIMISM'S CONTAGIOUS!

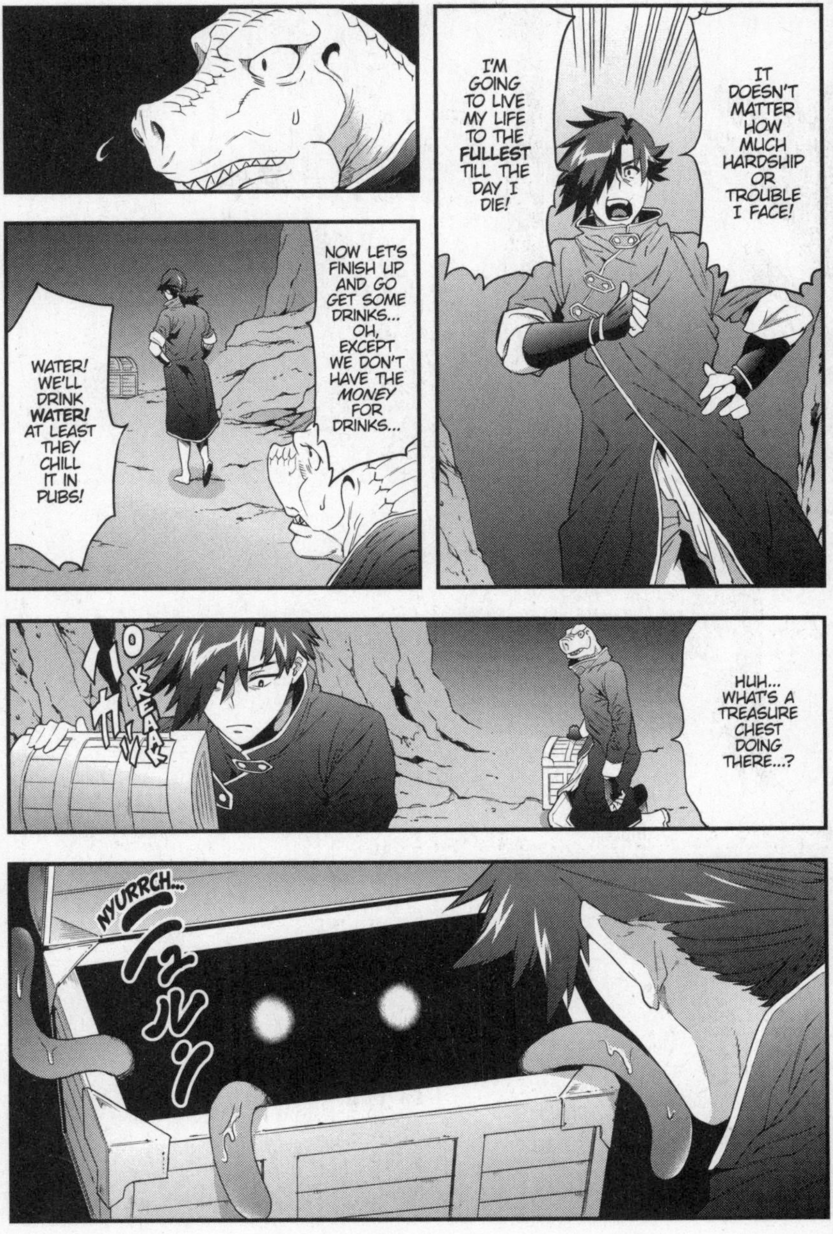
IT DOESN'T MATTER HOW MUCH HARDSHIP OR TROUBLE I FACE!
I'M GOING TO LIVE MY LIFE TO THE **FULLEST** TILL THE DAY I DIE!
NOW LET'S FINISH UP AND GO GET SOME DRINKS... OH, EXCEPT WE DON'T HAVE THE *MONEY* FOR DRINKS...
WATER! WE'LL DRINK **WATER!** AT LEAST THEY CHILL IT IN PUBS!
HUH... WHAT'S A TREASURE CHEST DOING THERE...?
KREAAK
NYURRCH...

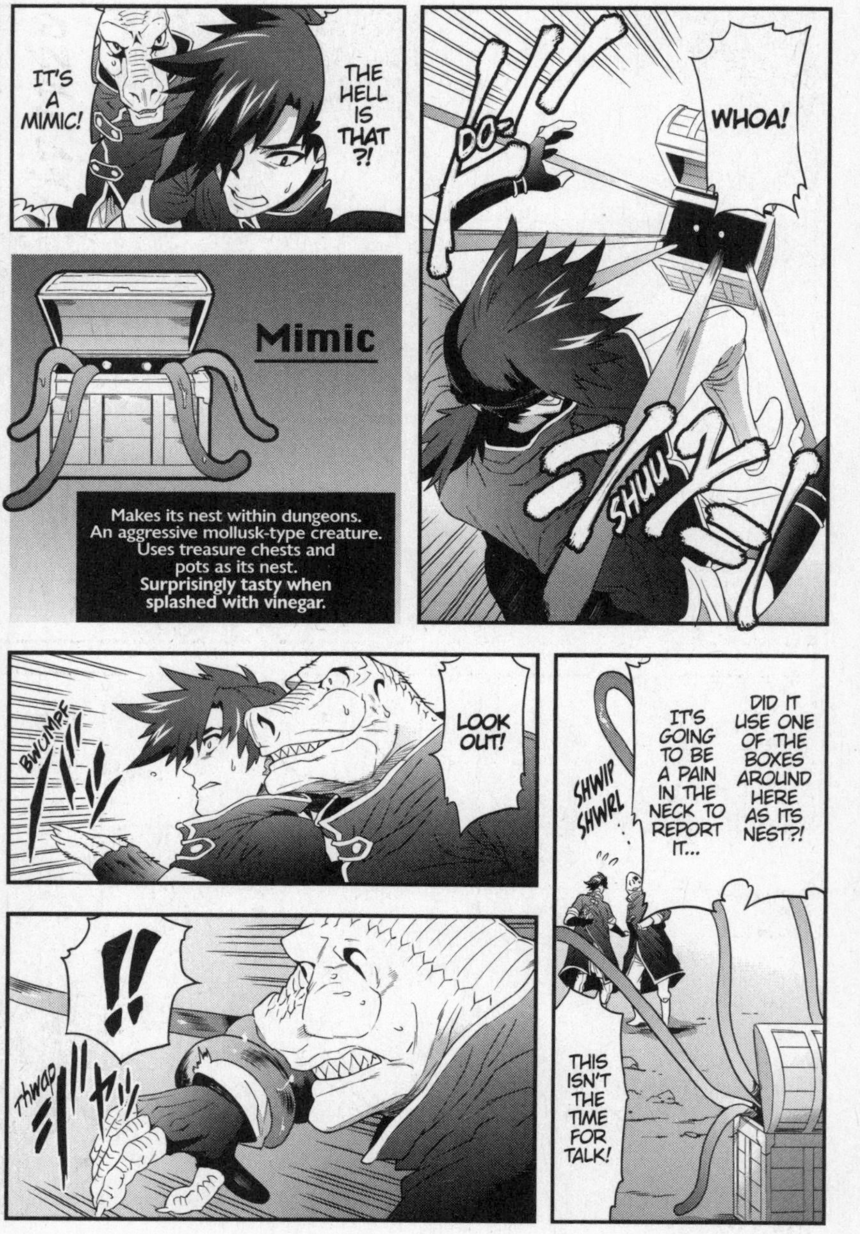
WHOA!
DO-
SHUU
THE HELL IS THAT?!
IT'S A MIMIC!
Mimic
Makes its nest within dungeons.
An aggressive mollusk-type creature.
Uses treasure chests and pots as its nest.
Surprisingly tasty when splashed with vinegar.
DID IT USE ONE OF THE BOXES AROUND HERE AS ITS NEST?!
IT'S GOING TO BE A PAIN IN THE NECK TO REPORT IT...
SHWIP SHWRL
THIS ISN'T THE TIME FOR TALK!
LOOK OUT!
BWUMPF
!!
thwap

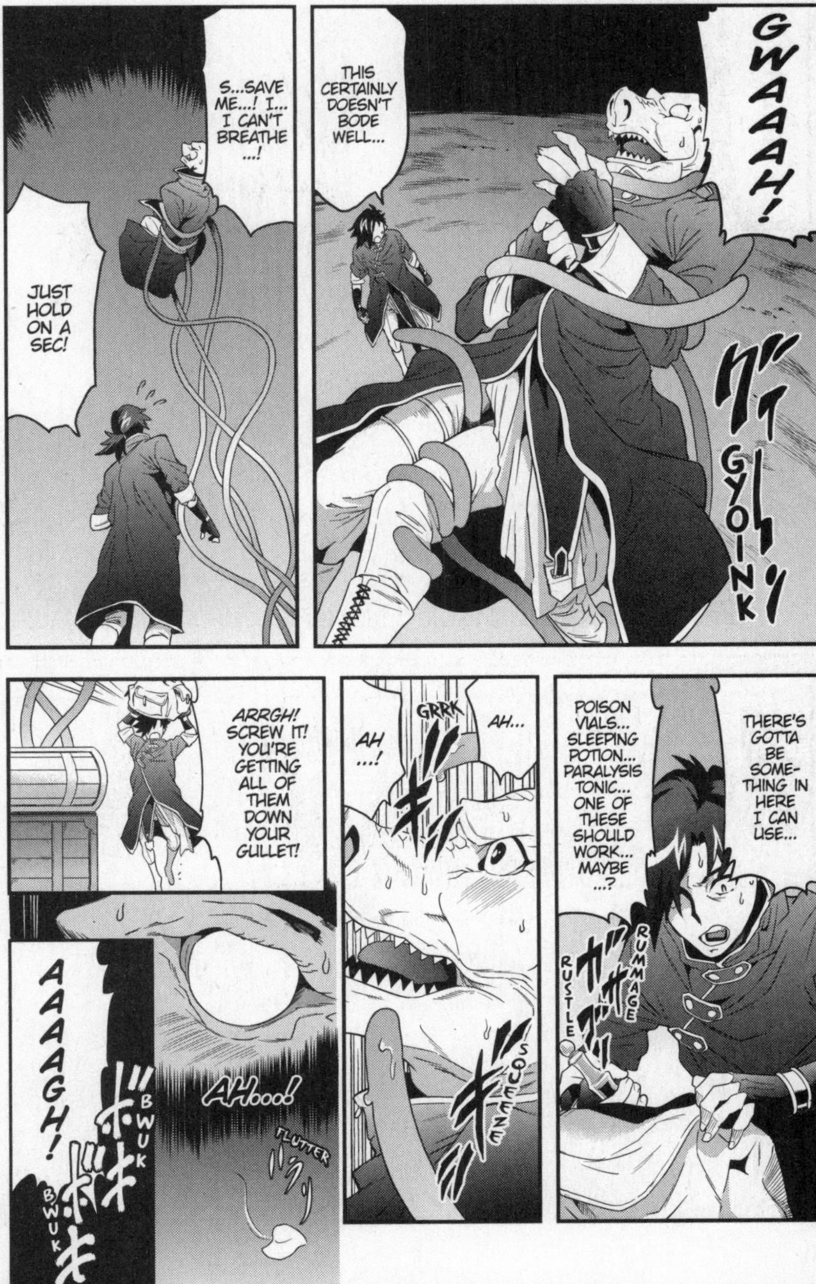
GWAAAH!
THIS CERTAINLY DOESN'T BODE WELL...
GYOINK
S...SAVE ME...! I... I CAN'T BREATHE ...!
JUST HOLD ON A SEC!
THERE'S GOTTA BE SOME-THING IN HERE I CAN USE...
POISON VIALS... SLEEPING POTION... PARALYSIS TONIC... ONE OF THESE SHOULD WORK... MAYBE ...?
RUMMAGE
RUSTLE
AH...
AH ...!
GRRK
SQUEEZE
ARRGH! SCREW IT! YOU'RE GETTING ALL OF THEM DOWN YOUR GULLET!
AAAAAGH!
AH...!
BWUK
BWUK
FLUTTER

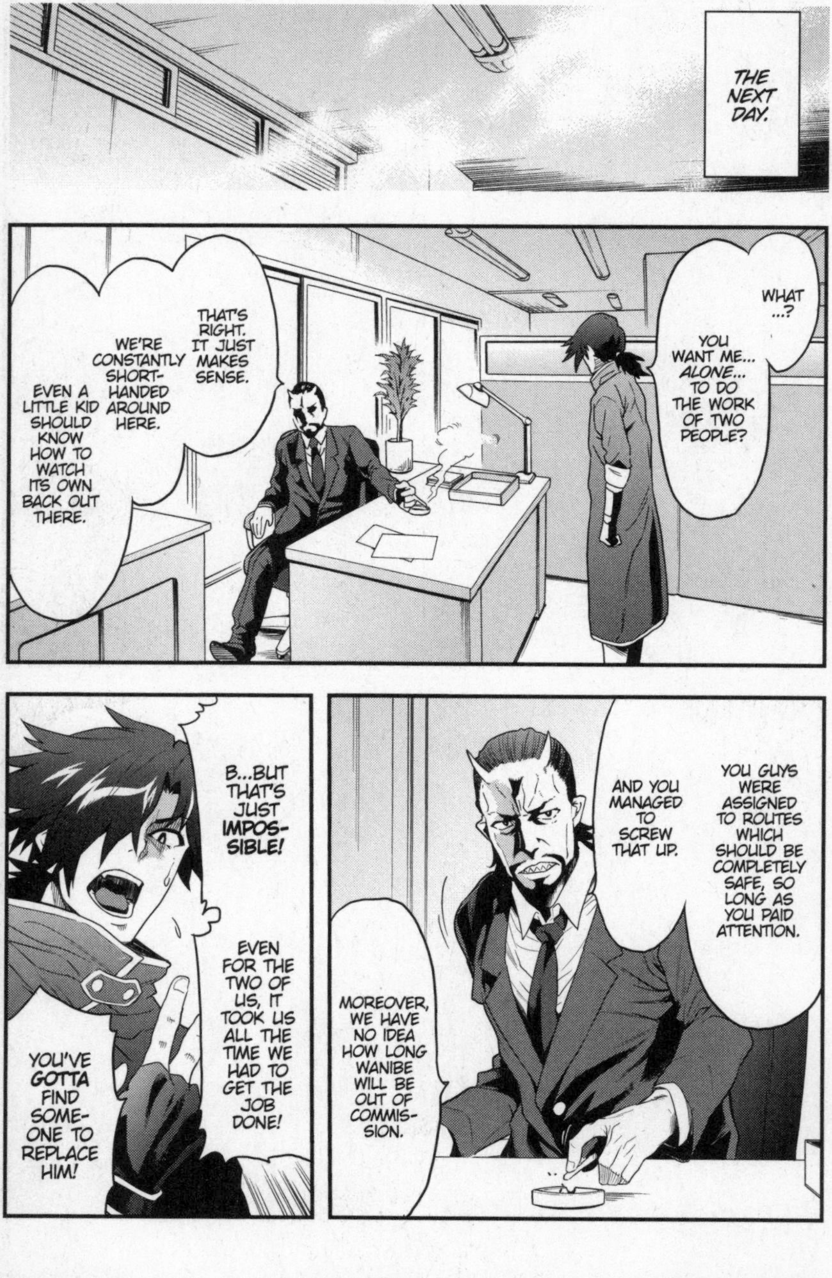
THE NEXT DAY.
WHAT ...?
YOU WANT ME... ALONE... TO DO THE WORK OF TWO PEOPLE?
THAT'S RIGHT. IT JUST MAKES SENSE.
WE'RE CONSTANTLY SHORT-HANDED AROUND HERE.
EVEN A LITTLE KID SHOULD KNOW HOW TO WATCH ITS OWN BACK OUT THERE.
YOU GUYS WERE ASSIGNED TO ROUTES WHICH SHOULD BE COMPLETELY SAFE, SO LONG AS YOU PAID ATTENTION.
AND YOU MANAGED TO SCREW THAT UP.
MOREOVER, WE HAVE NO IDEA HOW LONG WANIBE WILL BE OUT OF COMMISSION.
B...BUT THAT'S JUST IMPOSSIBLE!
EVEN FOR THE TWO OF US, IT TOOK US ALL THE TIME WE HAD TO GET THE JOB DONE!
YOU'VE GOTTA FIND SOMEONE TO REPLACE HIM!

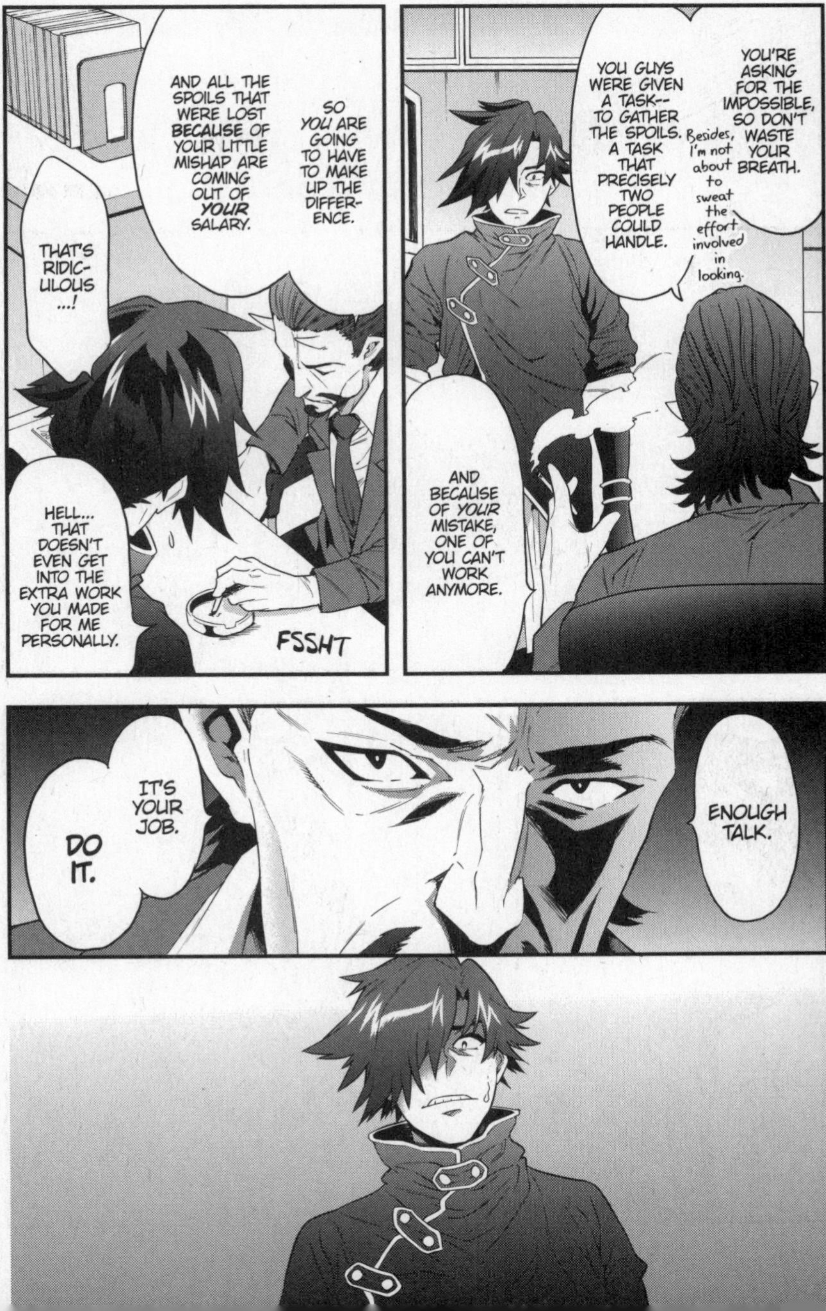
YOU'RE ASKING FOR THE IMPOSSIBLE, SO DON'T WASTE YOUR BREATH.
Besides, I'm not about to sweat the effort involved in looking.
YOU GUYS WERE GIVEN A TASK-- TO GATHER THE SPOILS. A TASK THAT PRECISELY TWO PEOPLE COULD HANDLE.
AND BECAUSE OF YOUR MISTAKE, ONE OF YOU CAN'T WORK ANYMORE.
SO YOU ARE GOING TO HAVE TO MAKE UP THE DIFFER-ENCE.
AND ALL THE SPOILS THAT WERE LOST BECAUSE OF YOUR LITTLE MISHAP ARE COMING OUT OF YOUR SALARY.
THAT'S RIDIC-ULOUS ...!
HELL... THAT DOESN'T EVEN GET INTO THE EXTRA WORK YOU MADE FOR ME PERSONALLY.
FSSHT
ENOUGH TALK.
IT'S YOUR JOB.
DO IT.

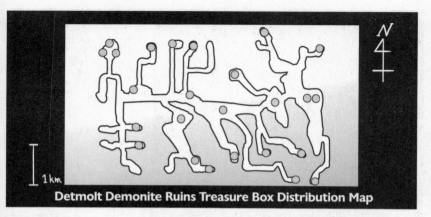

4

Detmolt Demonite Ruins Treasure Box Distribution Map

1 km

Sector B-1:
Treasure Box 1.

Sector B-1:
Treasure Box 3.

Sector D-4:
Treasure Box 2.

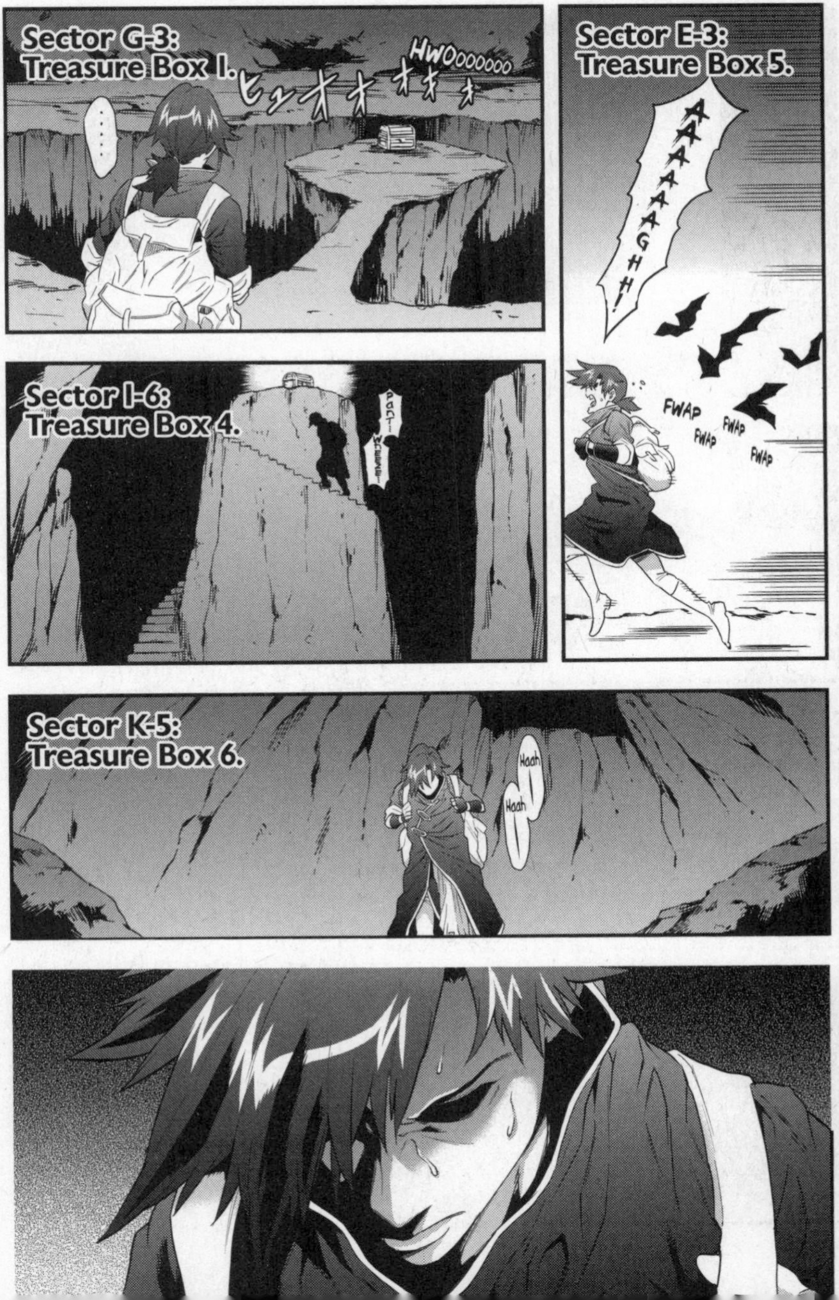
Sector E-3: Treasure Box 5.
AAAAAAGHH!
FWAP
FWAP
FWAP
FWAP
Sector G-3: Treasure Box 1.
HWOOOOOOO
ヒュオオオオォォ
. . . . . .
Sector I-6: Treasure Box 4.
Pant...
Wheeze...
Sector K-5: Treasure Box 6.
Haah
Haah

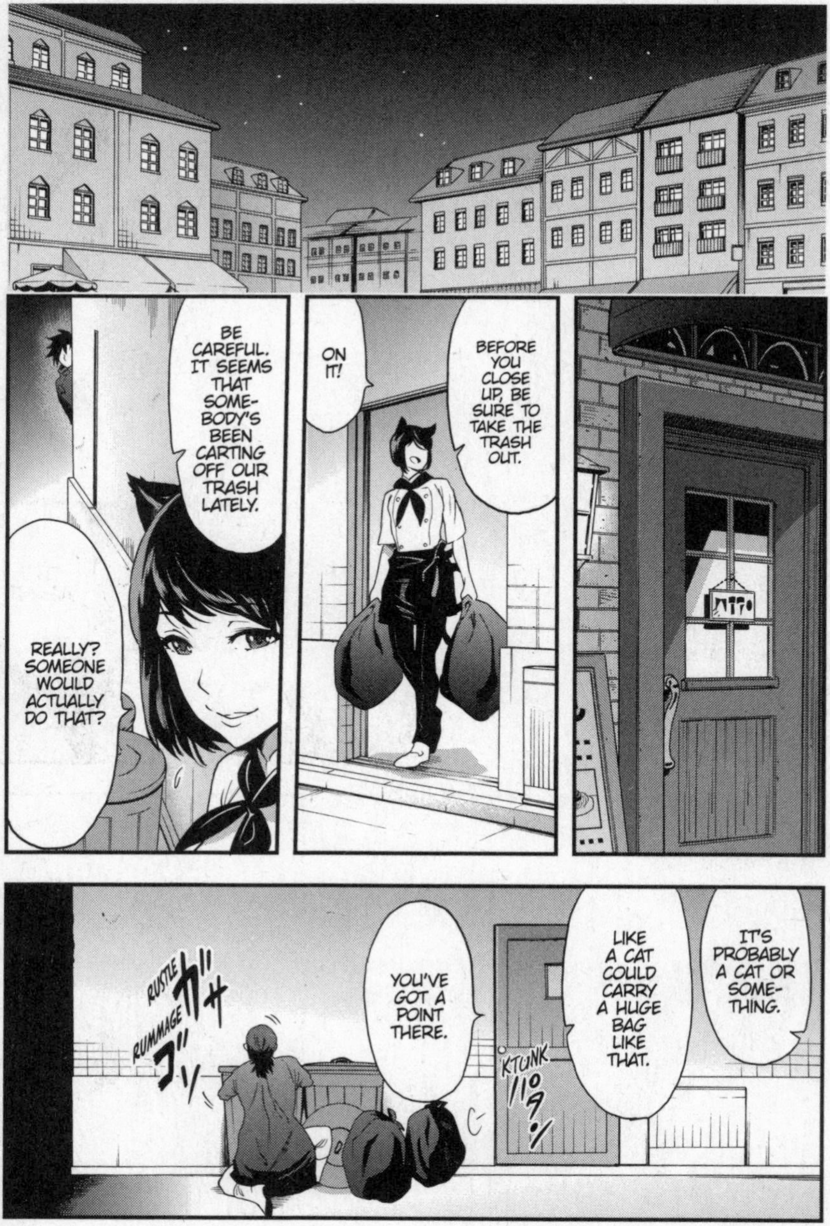
BEFORE YOU CLOSE UP, BE SURE TO TAKE THE TRASH OUT.
ON IT!
BE CAREFUL. IT SEEMS THAT SOME-BODY'S BEEN CARTING OFF OUR TRASH LATELY.
REALLY? SOMEONE WOULD ACTUALLY DO THAT?
IT'S PROBABLY A CAT OR SOME-THING.
LIKE A CAT COULD CARRY A HUGE BAG LIKE THAT.
KTUNK
バタン
YOU'VE GOT A POINT THERE.
RUSTLE
ガサ
RUMMAGE
ゴソ

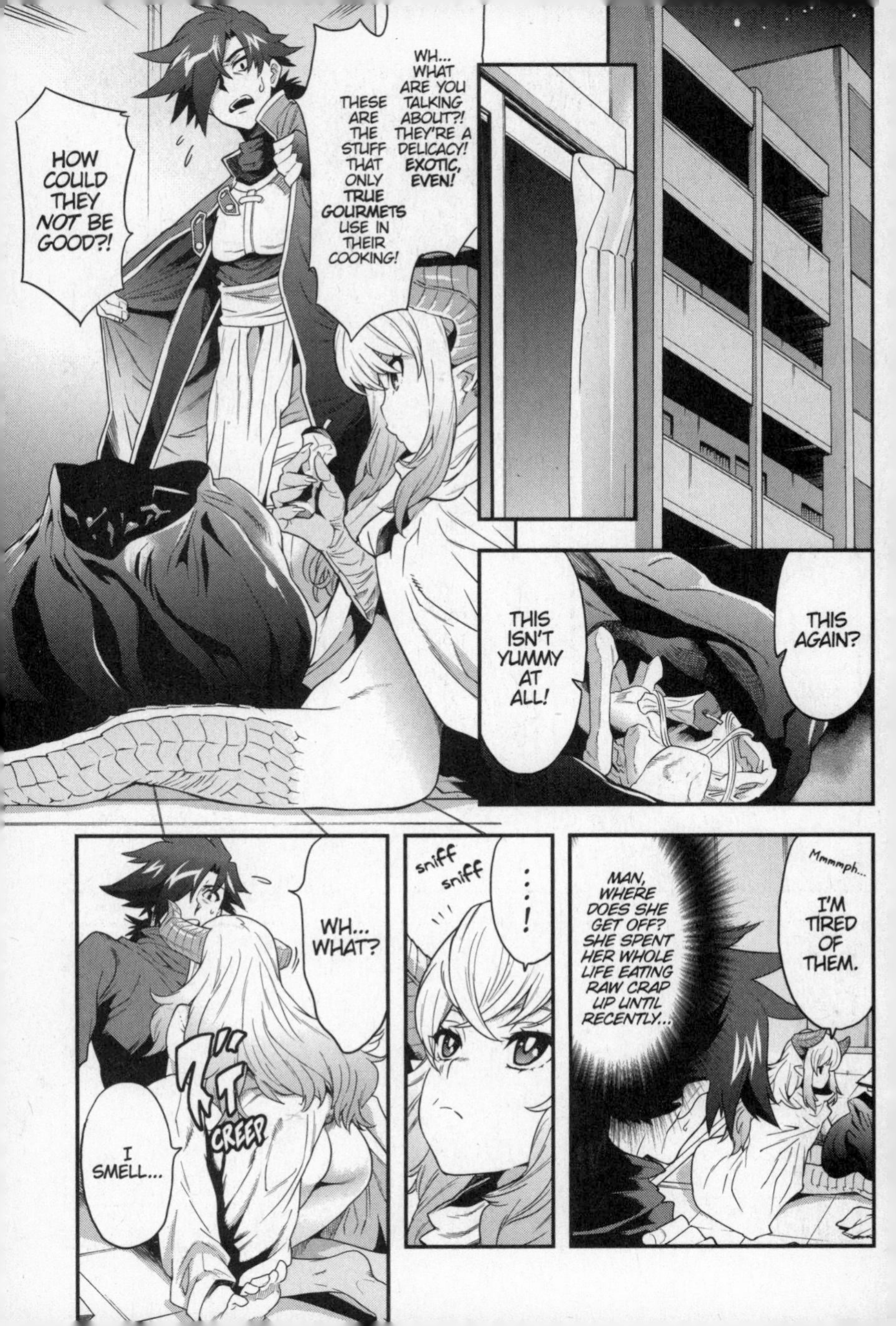
THIS AGAIN?
THIS ISN'T YUMMY AT ALL!
WH... WHAT ARE YOU TALKING ABOUT?! THEY'RE A DELICACY! EXOTIC, EVEN!
THESE ARE THE STUFF THAT ONLY TRUE GOURMETS USE IN THEIR COOKING!
HOW COULD THEY NOT BE GOOD?!
Mmmmph...
I'M TIRED OF THEM.
MAN, WHERE DOES SHE GET OFF? SHE SPENT HER WHOLE LIFE EATING RAW CRAP UP UNTIL RECENTLY...
sniff sniff
...!
WH... WHAT?
CREEP
I SMELL...

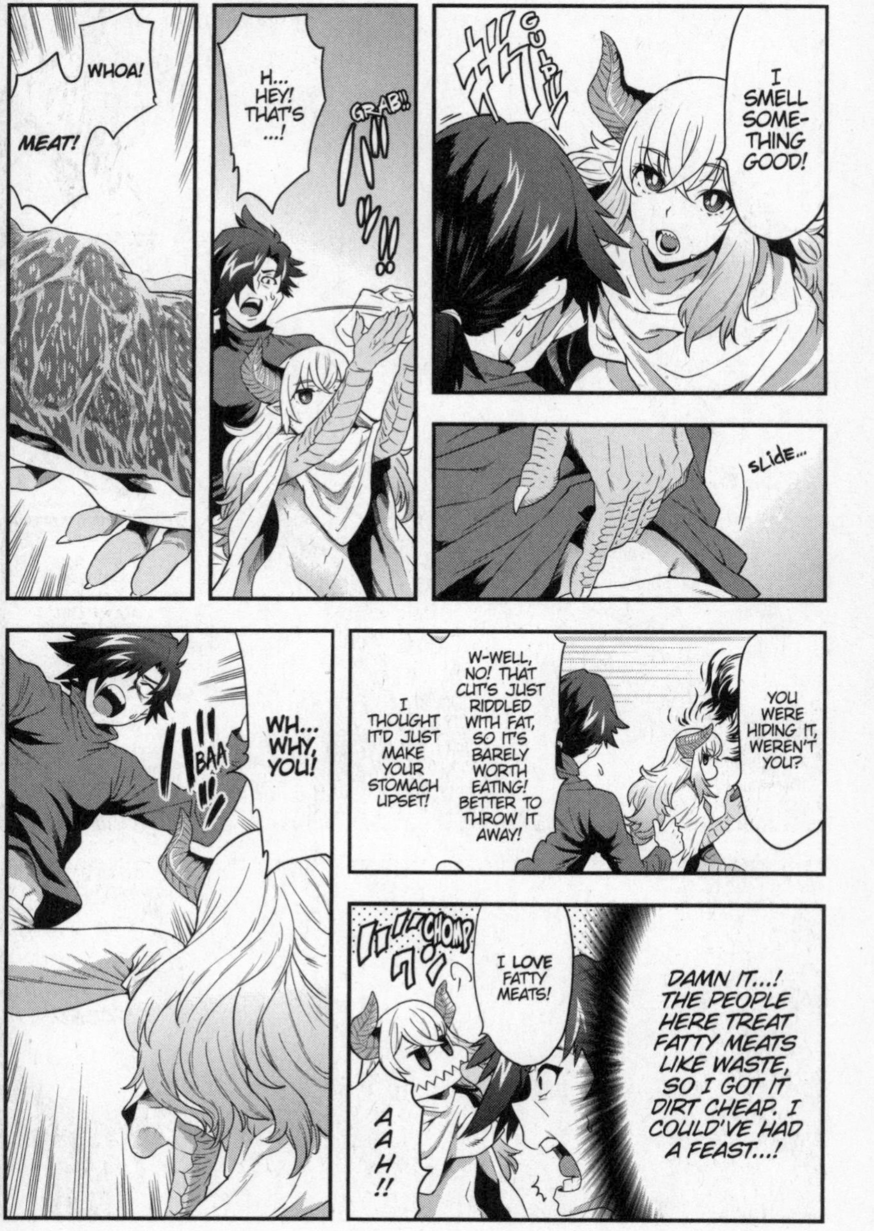
GULP!!
I SMELL SOME-THING GOOD!
SLIDE...
H... HEY! THAT'S ...!
GRAB!!
WHOA!
MEAT!
YOU WERE HIDING IT, WEREN'T YOU?
W-WELL, NO! THAT CUT'S JUST RIDDLED WITH FAT, SO IT'S BARELY WORTH EATING! BETTER TO THROW IT AWAY!
I THOUGHT IT'D JUST MAKE YOUR STOMACH UPSET!
CHOMP
I LOVE FATTY MEATS!
DAMN IT...! THE PEOPLE HERE TREAT FATTY MEATS LIKE WASTE, SO I GOT IT DIRT CHEAP. I COULD'VE HAD A FEAST...!
AAH!!
WH... WHY, YOU!
BAA

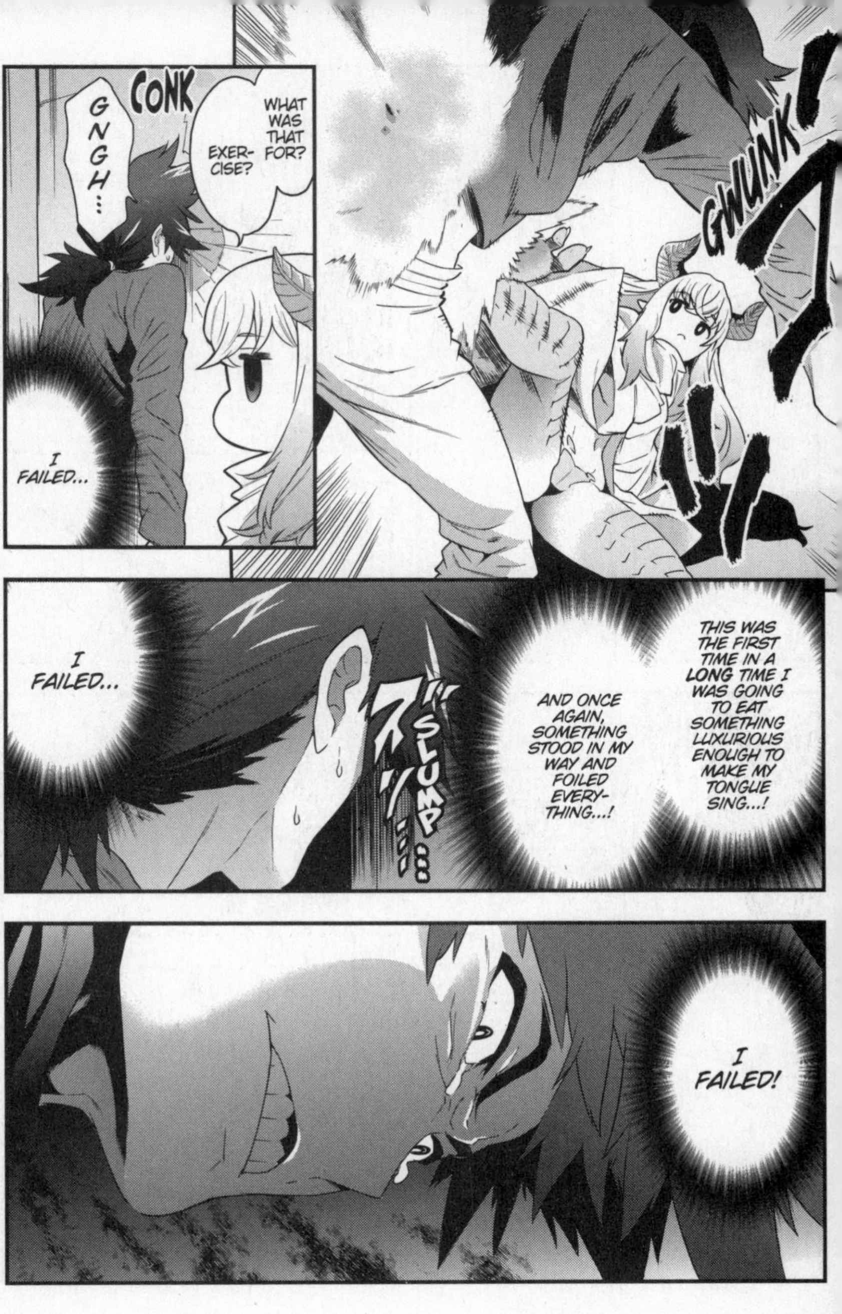
GWUNK!
CONK
WHAT WAS THAT FOR? EXERCISE?
GNGH...
I FAILED...
THIS WAS THE FIRST TIME IN A LONG TIME I WAS GOING TO EAT SOMETHING LUXURIOUS ENOUGH TO MAKE MY TONGUE SING...!
AND ONCE AGAIN, SOMETHING STOOD IN MY WAY AND FOILED EVERYTHING...!
SLUMP...
I FAILED...
I FAILED!

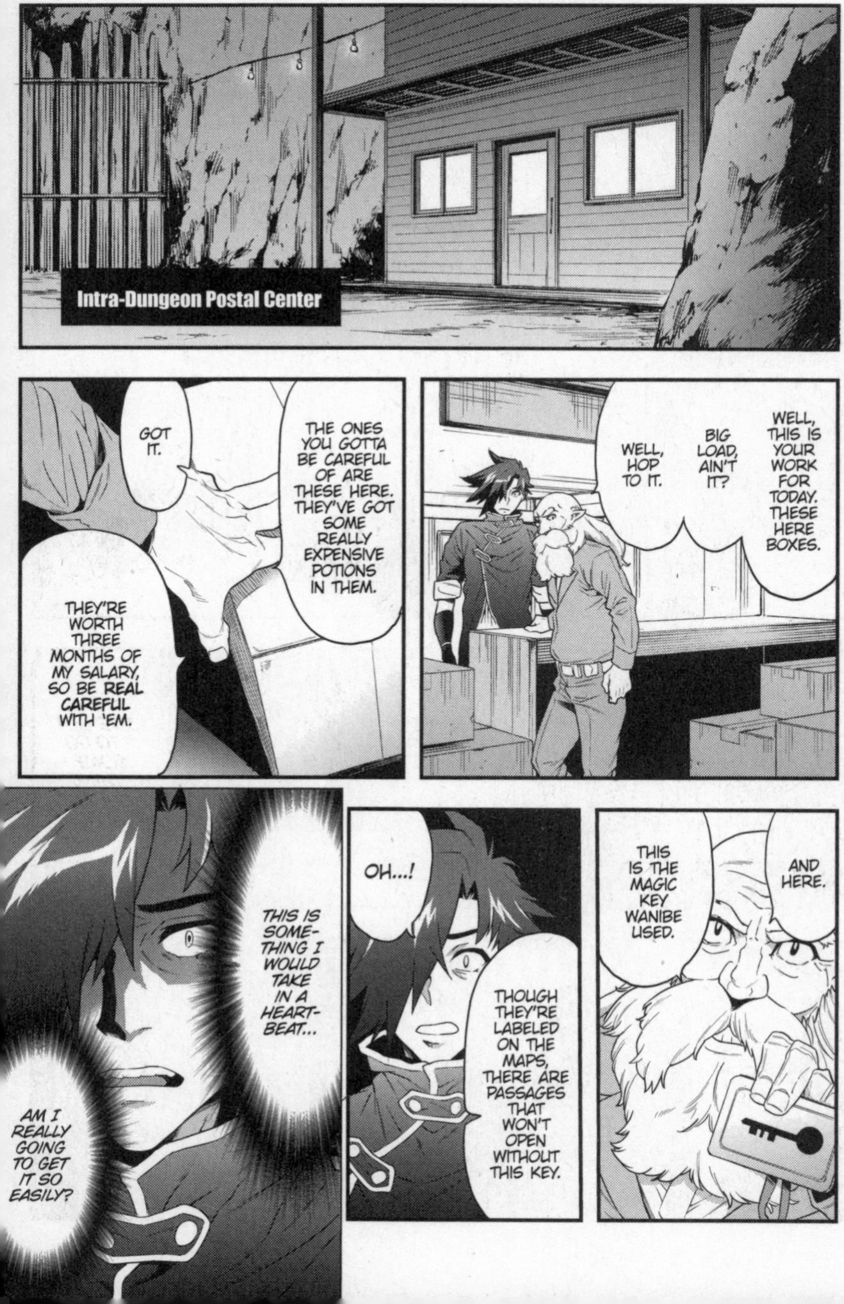
Intra-Dungeon Postal Center
WELL, THIS IS YOUR WORK FOR TODAY. THESE HERE BOXES.
BIG LOAD, AIN'T IT?
WELL, HOP TO IT.
THE ONES YOU GOTTA BE CAREFUL OF ARE THESE HERE. THEY'VE GOT SOME REALLY EXPENSIVE POTIONS IN THEM.
GOT IT.
THEY'RE WORTH THREE MONTHS OF MY SALARY, SO BE REAL CAREFUL WITH 'EM.
AND HERE.
THIS IS THE MAGIC KEY WANIBE USED.
THOUGH THEY'RE LABELED ON THE MAPS, THERE ARE PASSAGES THAT WON'T OPEN WITHOUT THIS KEY.
OH...!
THIS IS SOME-THING I WOULD TAKE IN A HEART-BEAT...
AM I REALLY GOING TO GET IT SO EASILY?

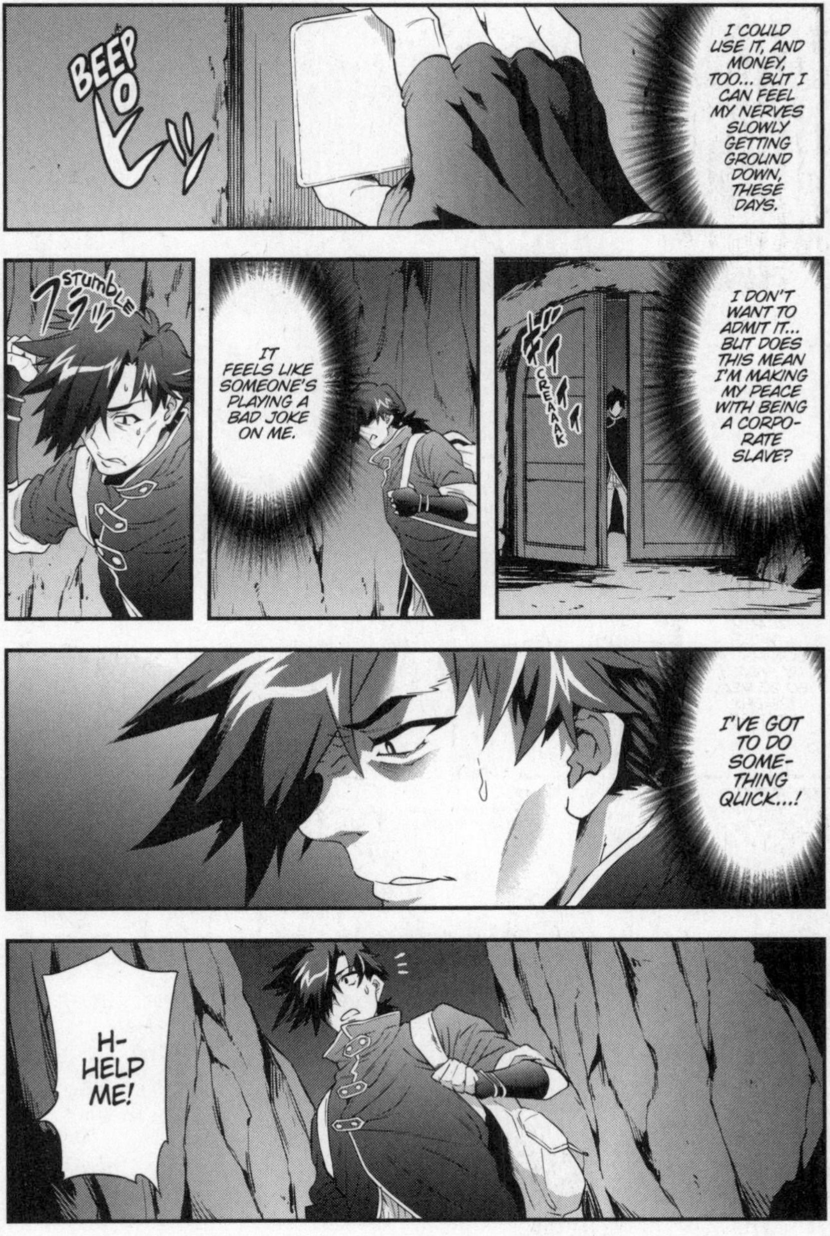
I COULD USE IT, AND MONEY, TOO... BUT I CAN FEEL MY NERVES SLOWLY GETTING GROUND DOWN, THESE DAYS.
BEEP
I DON'T WANT TO ADMIT IT... BUT DOES THIS MEAN I'M MAKING MY PEACE WITH BEING A CORPO-RATE SLAVE?
CREAAAK
IT FEELS LIKE SOMEONE'S PLAYING A BAD JOKE ON ME.
stumble
I'VE GOT TO DO SOME-THING QUICK...!
H-HELP ME!

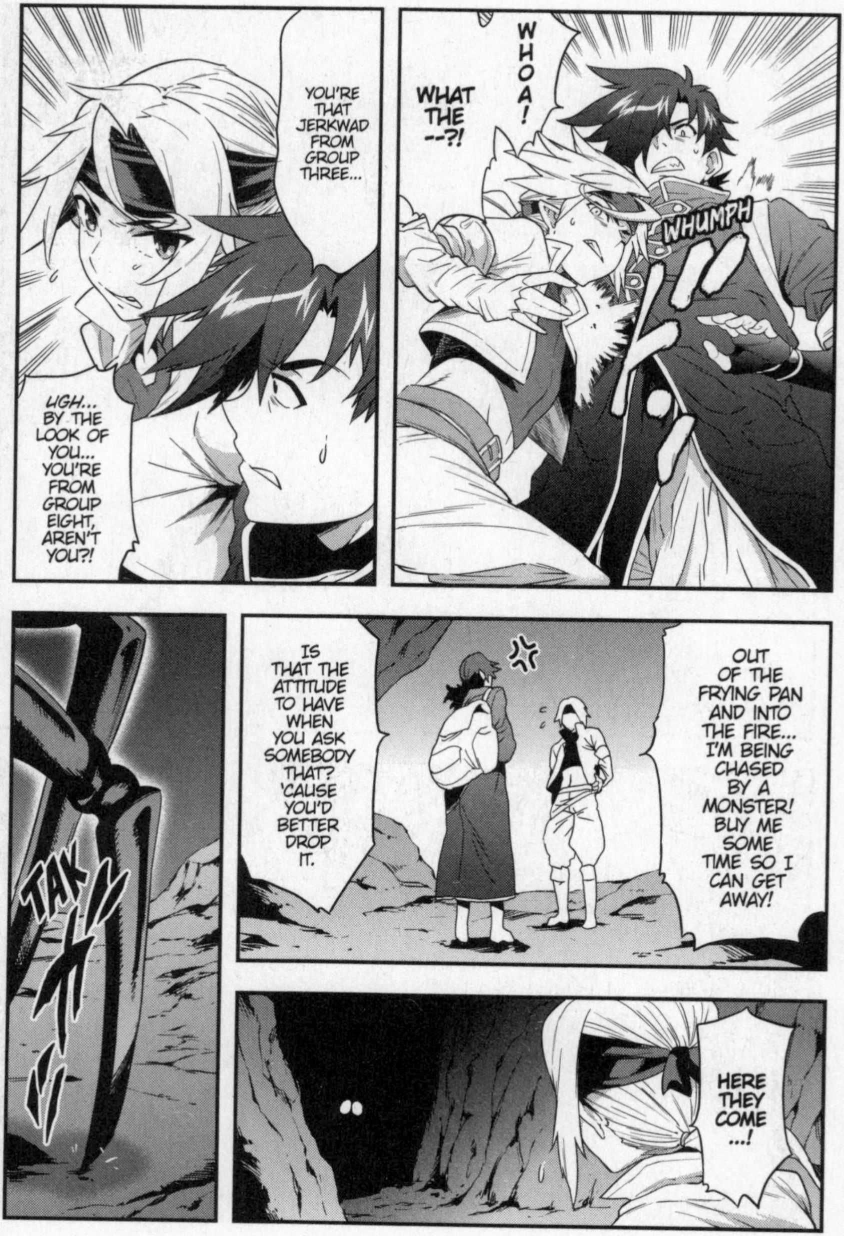
WHOA!
WHAT THE --?!
WHUMPH
YOU'RE THAT JERKWAD FROM GROUP THREE...
UGH... BY THE LOOK OF YOU... YOU'RE FROM GROUP EIGHT, AREN'T YOU?!
OUT OF THE FRYING PAN AND INTO THE FIRE... I'M BEING CHASED BY A MONSTER! BUY ME SOME TIME SO I CAN GET AWAY!
IS THAT THE ATTITUDE TO HAVE WHEN YOU ASK SOMEBODY THAT? 'CAUSE YOU'D BETTER DROP IT.
HERE THEY COME ...!
TAK

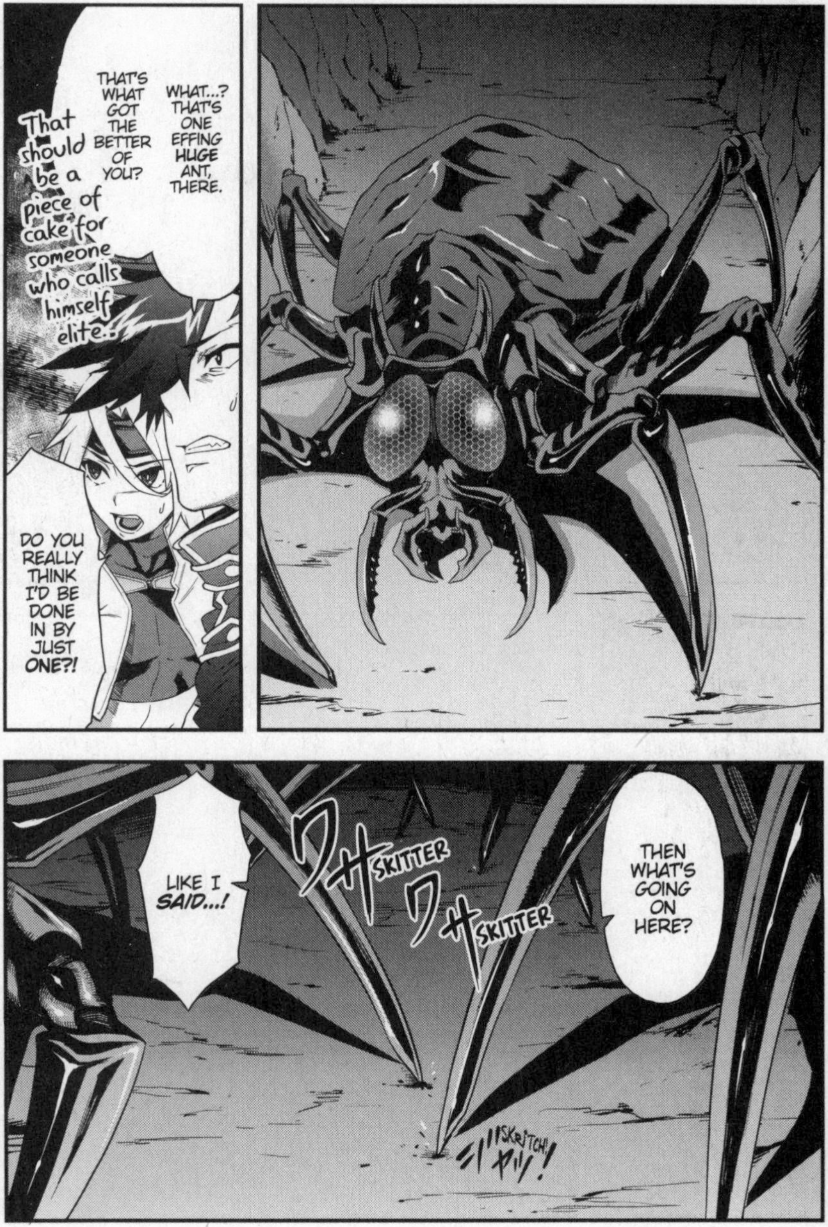
WHAT...? THAT'S ONE EFFING HUGE ANT, THERE.
THAT'S WHAT GOT THE BETTER OF YOU?
That should be a piece of cake for someone who calls himself elite...
DO YOU REALLY THINK I'D BE DONE IN BY JUST ONE?!
THEN WHAT'S GOING ON HERE?
SKITTER
SKITTER
LIKE I SAID...!
SKRITCH!

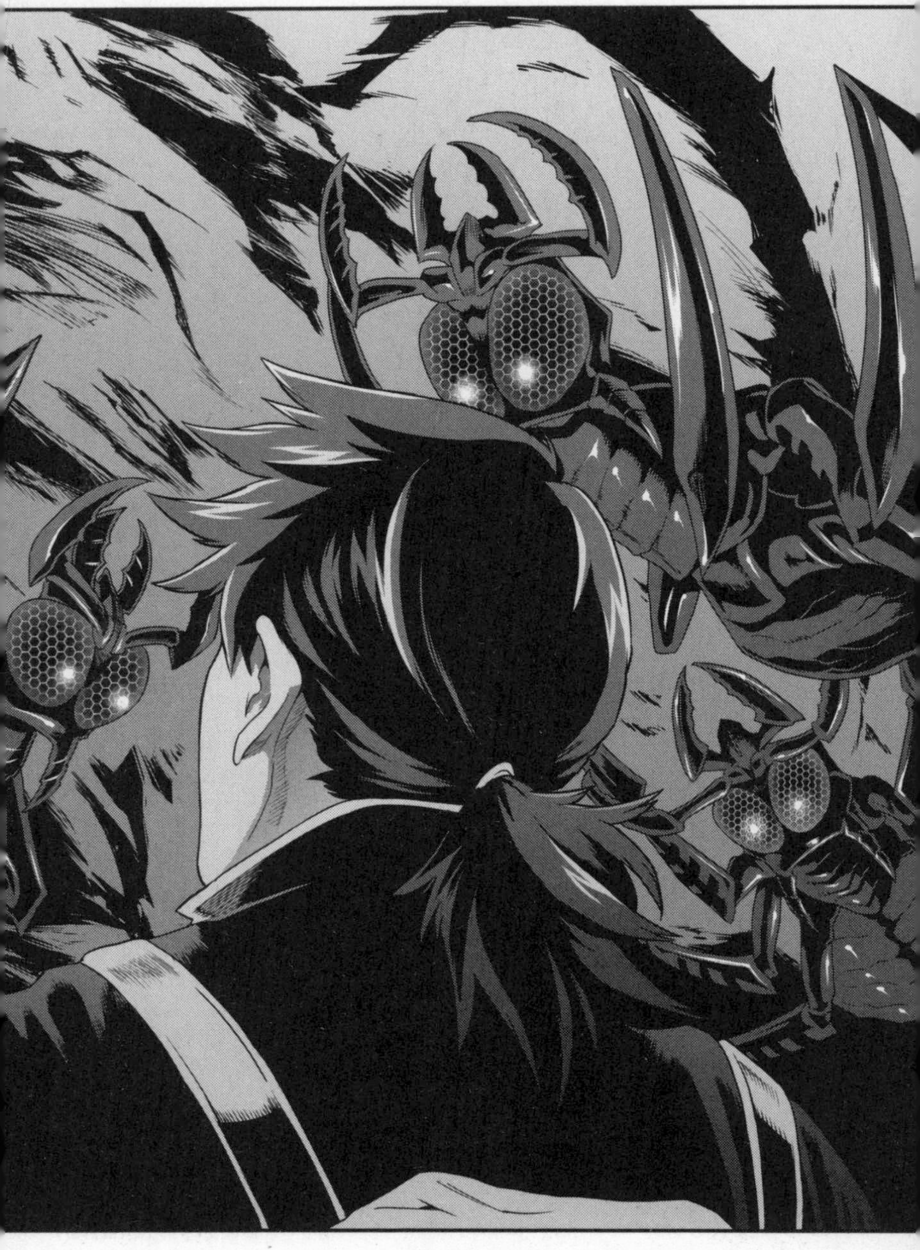

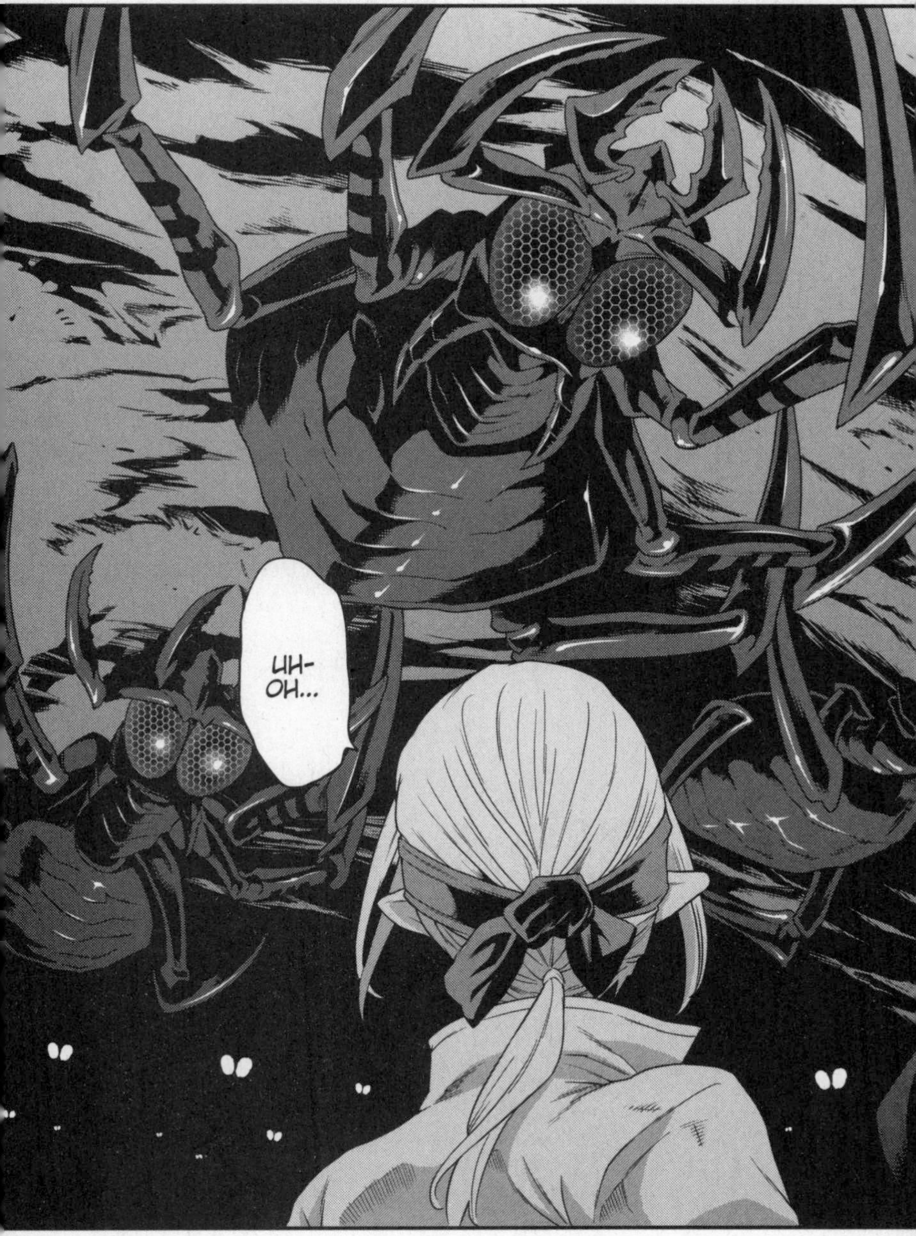
UH-OH...

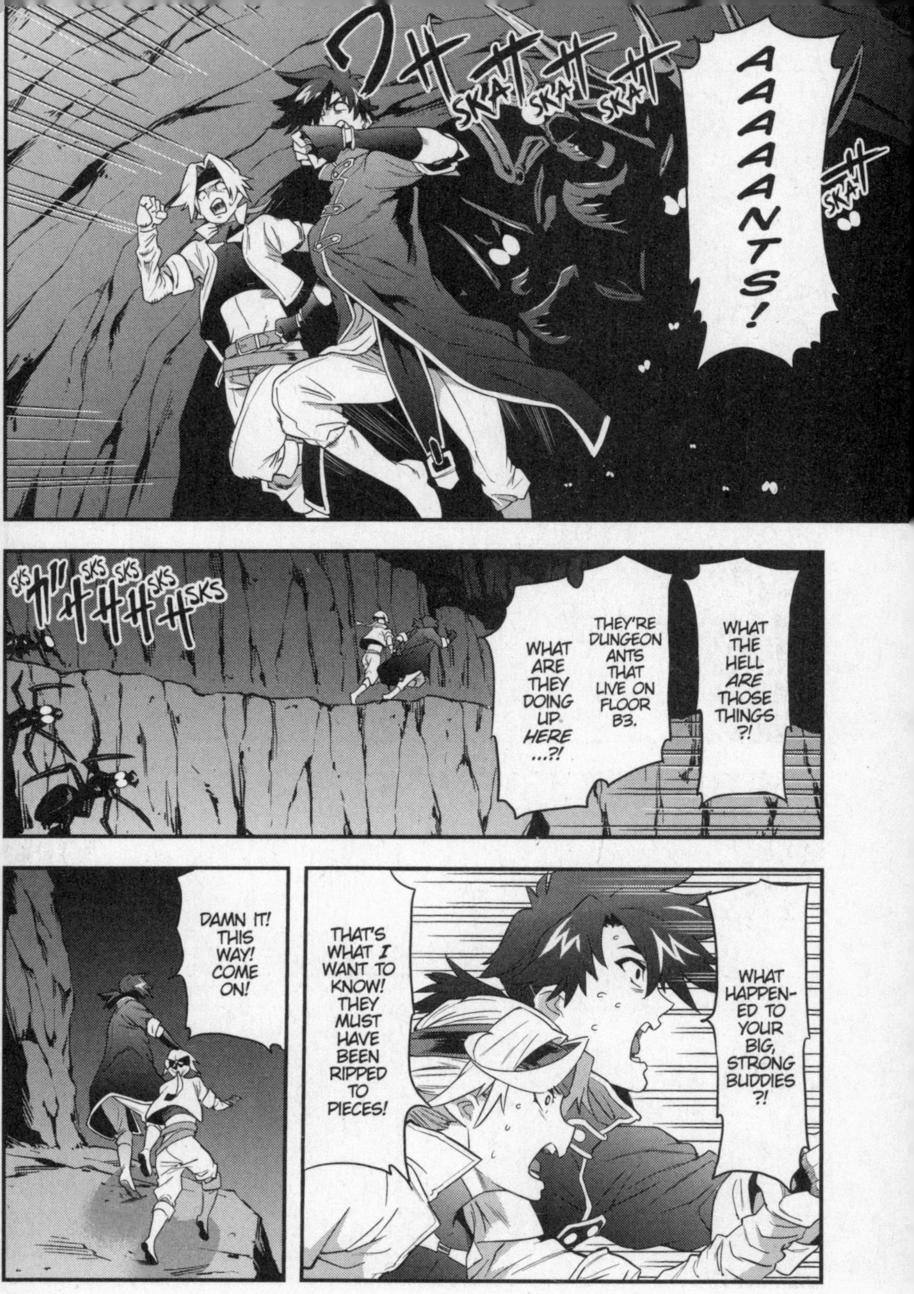

SKA SKA SKA
SKA
AAAAAANTS!
WHAT THE HELL *ARE* THOSE THINGS?!
THEY'RE DUNGEON ANTS THAT LIVE ON FLOOR B3.
WHAT ARE THEY DOING UP *HERE*...?!
SKS SKS SKS SKS SKS
WHAT HAPPENED TO YOUR BIG, STRONG BUDDIES?!
THAT'S WHAT *I* WANT TO KNOW! THEY MUST HAVE BEEN RIPPED TO PIECES!
DAMN IT! THIS WAY! COME ON!

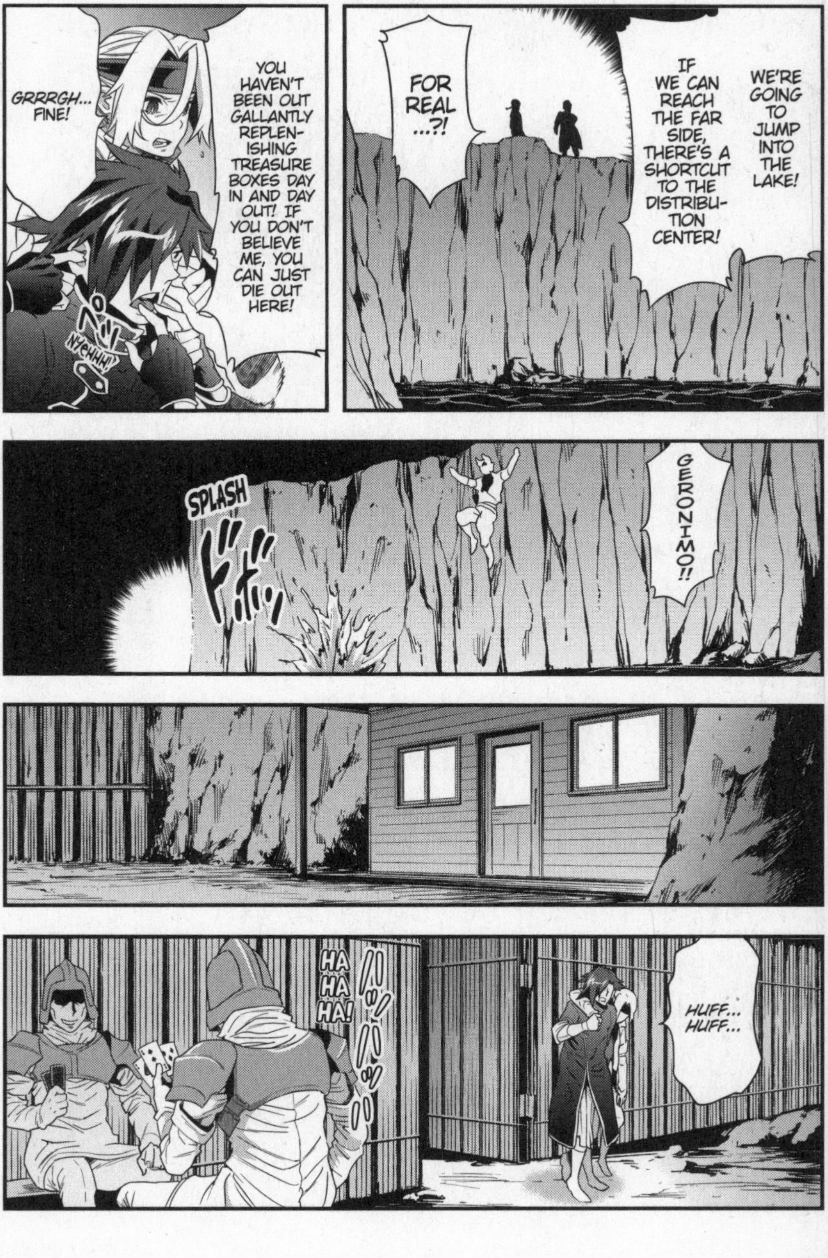
WE'RE GOING TO JUMP INTO THE LAKE!
IF WE CAN REACH THE FAR SIDE, THERE'S A SHORTCUT TO THE DISTRIBUTION CENTER!
FOR REAL...?!
YOU HAVEN'T BEEN OUT GALLANTLY REPLENISHING TREASURE BOXES DAY IN AND DAY OUT! IF YOU DON'T BELIEVE ME, YOU CAN JUST DIE OUT HERE!
GRRRGH... FINE!
NYEHHH!
GERONIMO!!
SPLASH
HUFF... HUFF...
HA HA HA!

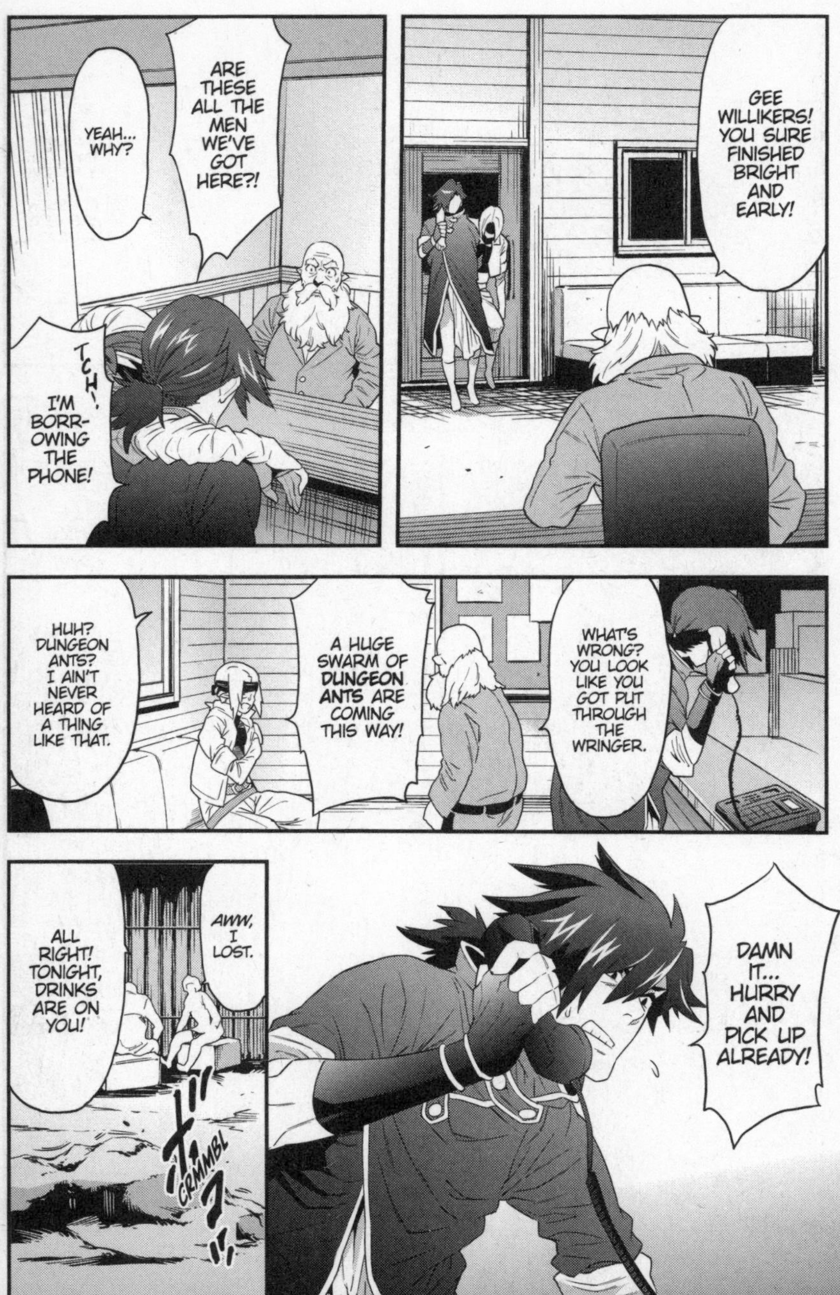
GEE WILLIKERS! YOU SURE FINISHED BRIGHT AND EARLY!
ARE THESE ALL THE MEN WE'VE GOT HERE?!
YEAH... WHY?
TCH!
I'M BORROWING THE PHONE!
WHAT'S WRONG? YOU LOOK LIKE YOU GOT PUT THROUGH THE WRINGER.
A HUGE SWARM OF DUNGEON ANTS ARE COMING THIS WAY!
HUH? DUNGEON ANTS? I AIN'T NEVER HEARD OF A THING LIKE THAT.
DAMN IT... HURRY AND PICK UP ALREADY!
AWW, I LOST.
ALL RIGHT! TONIGHT, DRINKS ARE ON YOU!
CRMMBL

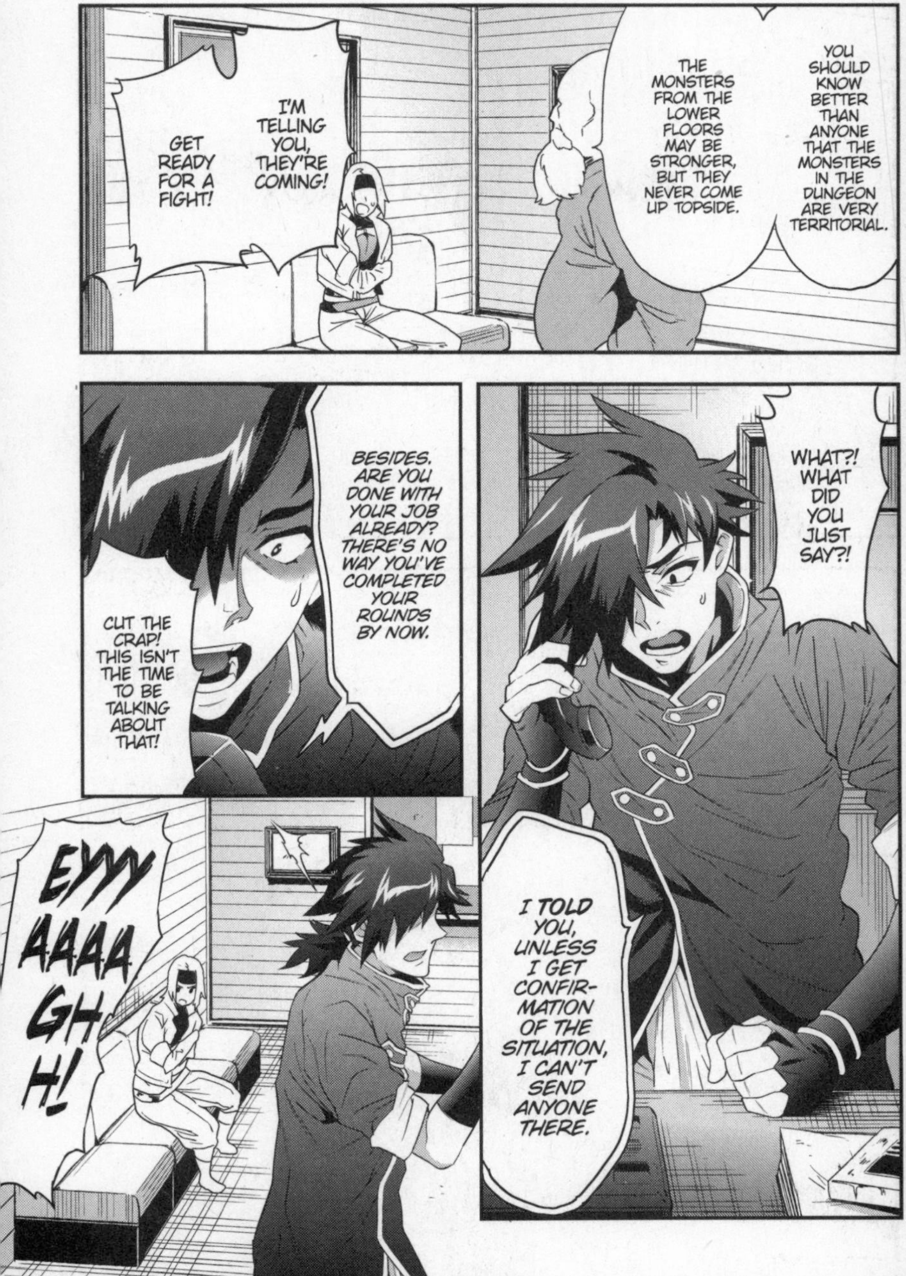
YOU SHOULD KNOW BETTER THAN ANYONE THAT THE MONSTERS IN THE DUNGEON ARE VERY TERRITORIAL.
THE MONSTERS FROM THE LOWER FLOORS MAY BE STRONGER, BUT THEY NEVER COME UP TOPSIDE.
I'M TELLING YOU, THEY'RE COMING!
GET READY FOR A FIGHT!
WHAT?! WHAT DID YOU JUST SAY?!
I TOLD YOU, UNLESS I GET CONFIRMATION OF THE SITUATION, I CAN'T SEND ANYONE THERE.
BESIDES. ARE YOU DONE WITH YOUR JOB ALREADY? THERE'S NO WAY YOU'VE COMPLETED YOUR ROUNDS BY NOW.
CUT THE CRAP! THIS ISN'T THE TIME TO BE TALKING ABOUT THAT!
EYYY AAAAGHH!

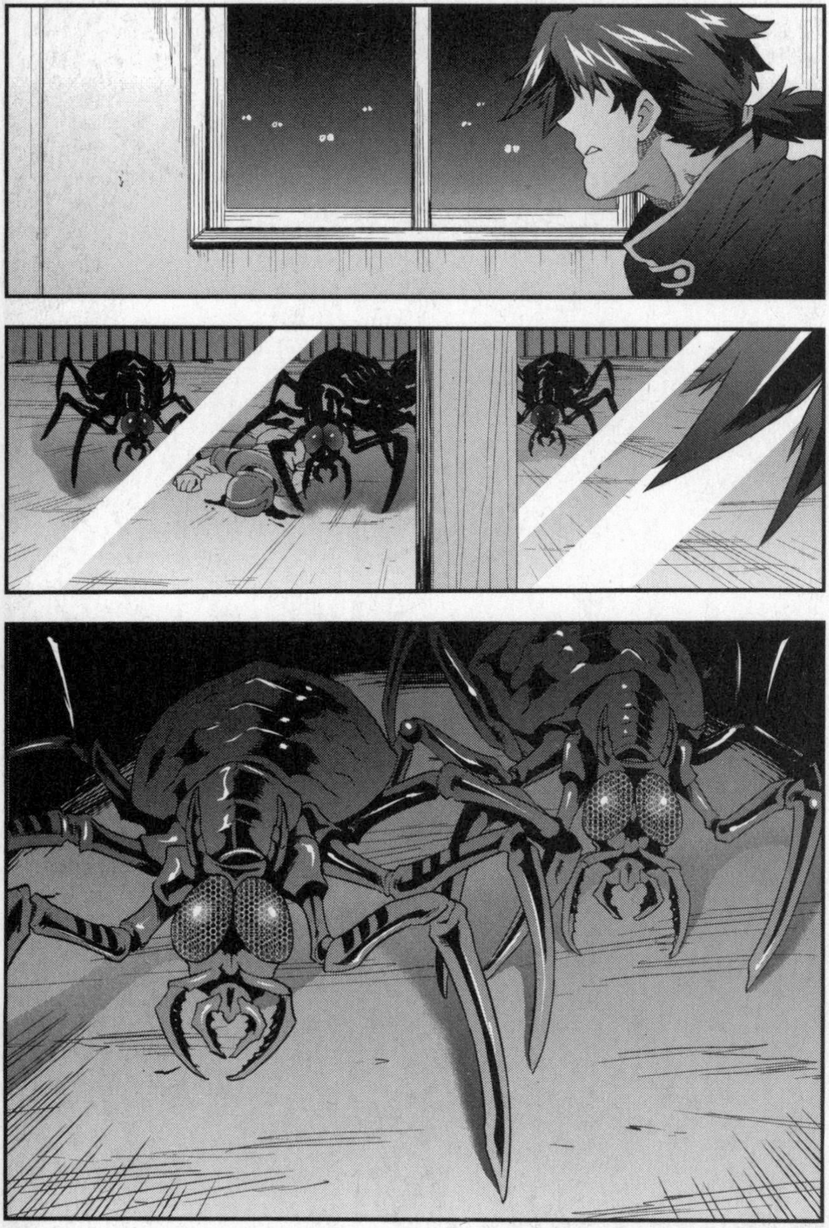

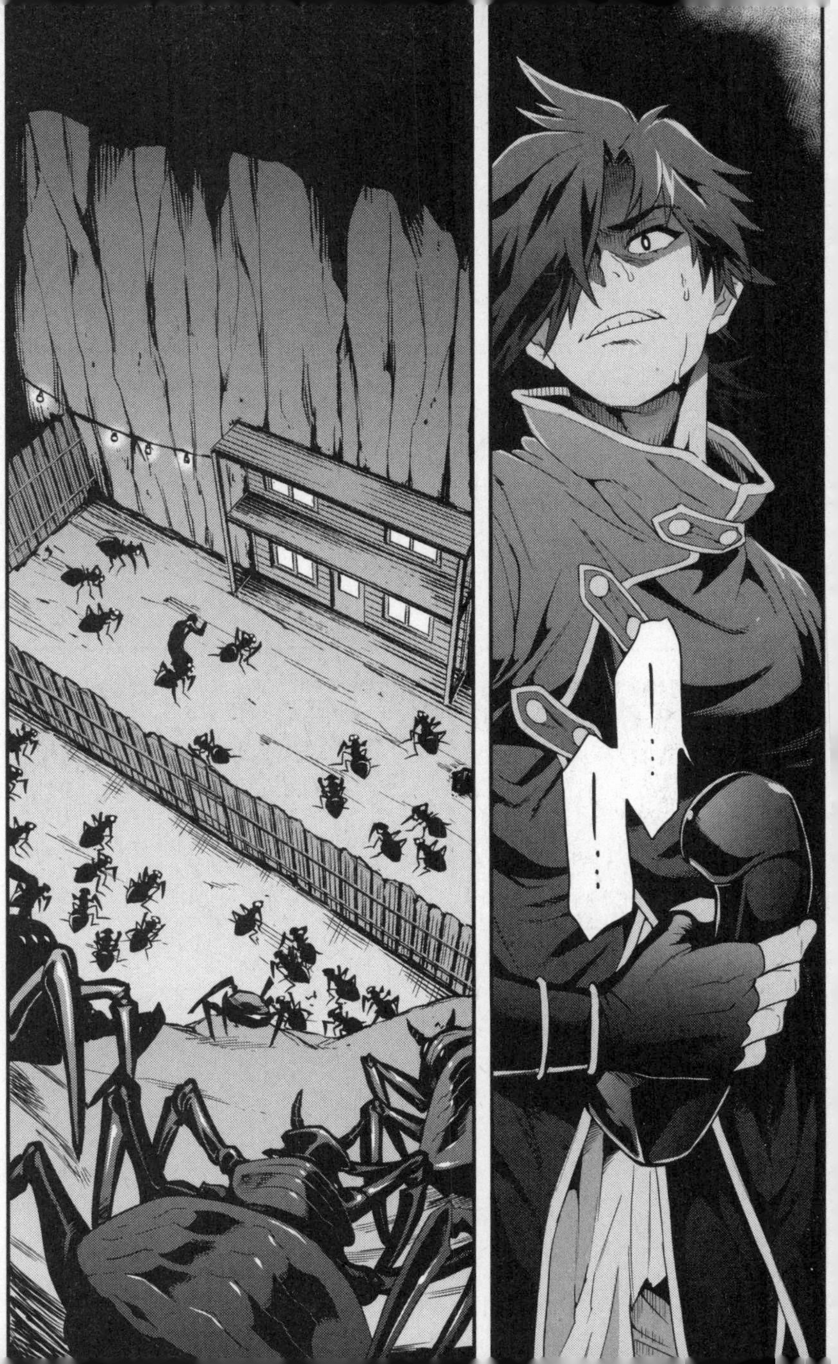
—...
—...

We didn't have anything to treat your injuries.

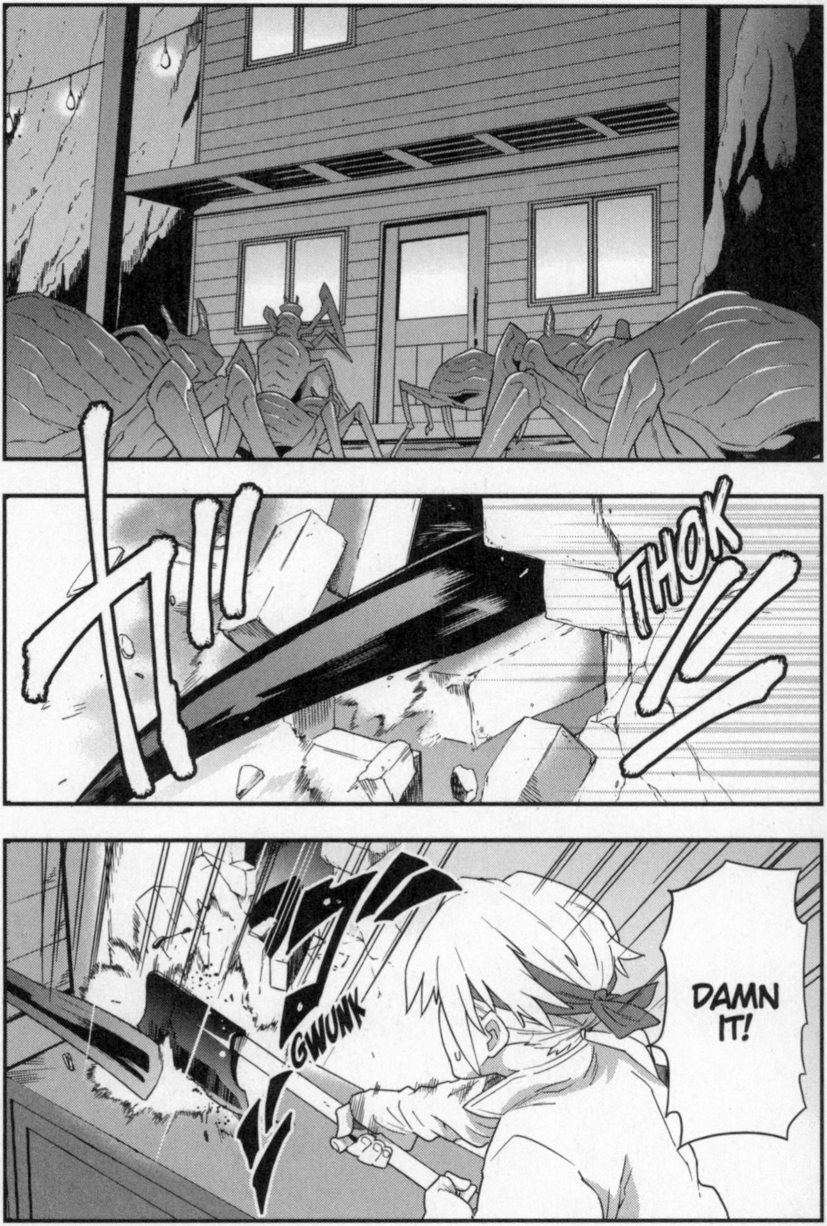
THOK
DAMN IT!
GWUNK

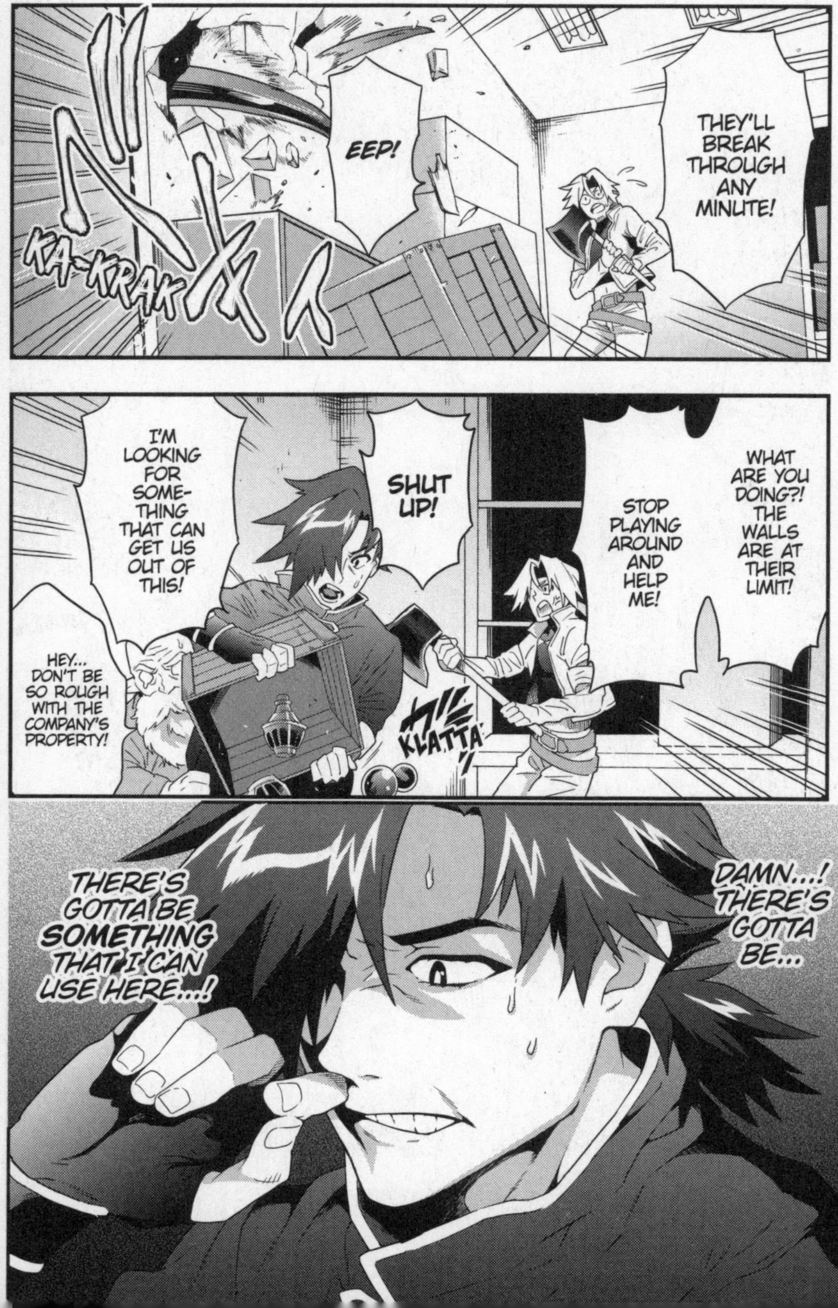
THEY'LL BREAK THROUGH ANY MINUTE!
EEP!
KA-KRAK
WHAT ARE YOU DOING?! THE WALLS ARE AT THEIR LIMIT!
STOP PLAYING AROUND AND HELP ME!
SHUT UP!
I'M LOOKING FOR SOME-THING THAT CAN GET US OUT OF THIS!
KLATTA
HEY... DON'T BE SO ROUGH WITH THE COMPANY'S PROPERTY!
DAMN...! THERE'S GOTTA BE...
THERE'S GOTTA BE SOMETHING THAT I CAN USE HERE...!

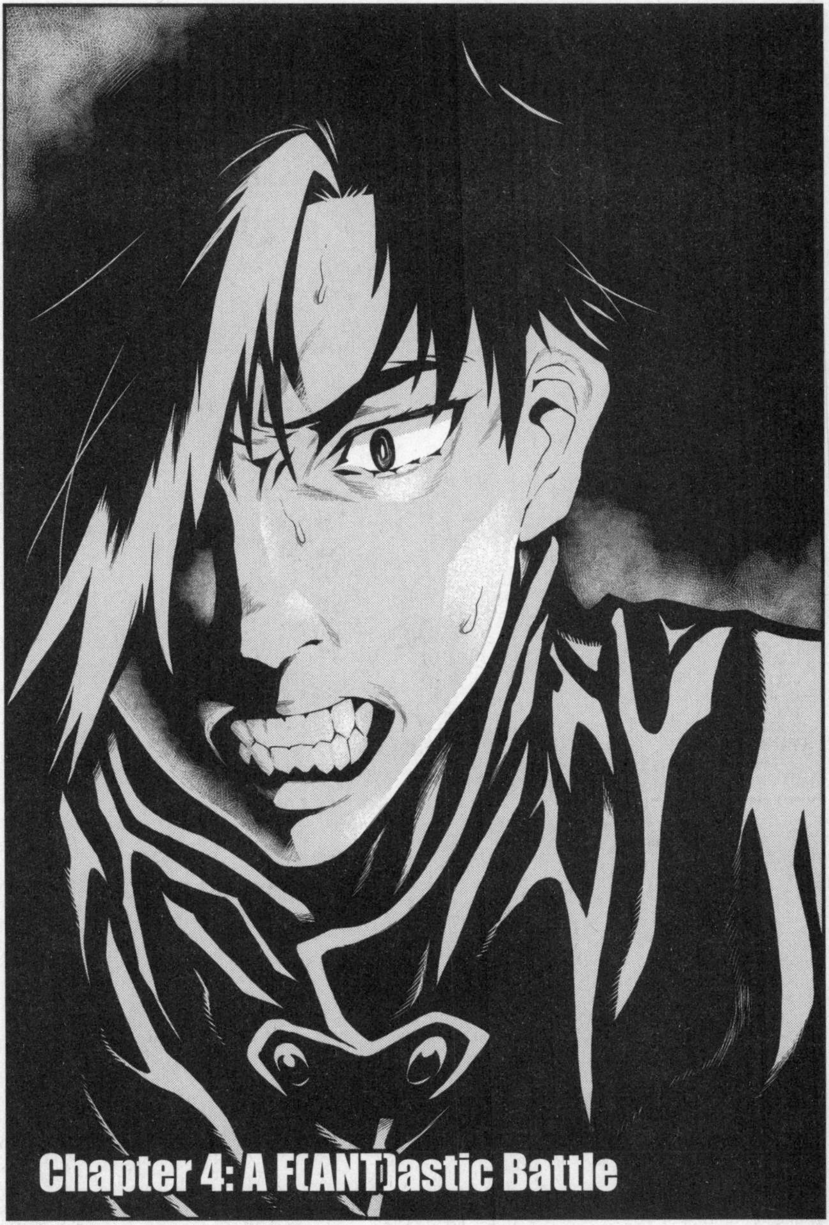
Chapter 4: A F(ANT)astic Battle

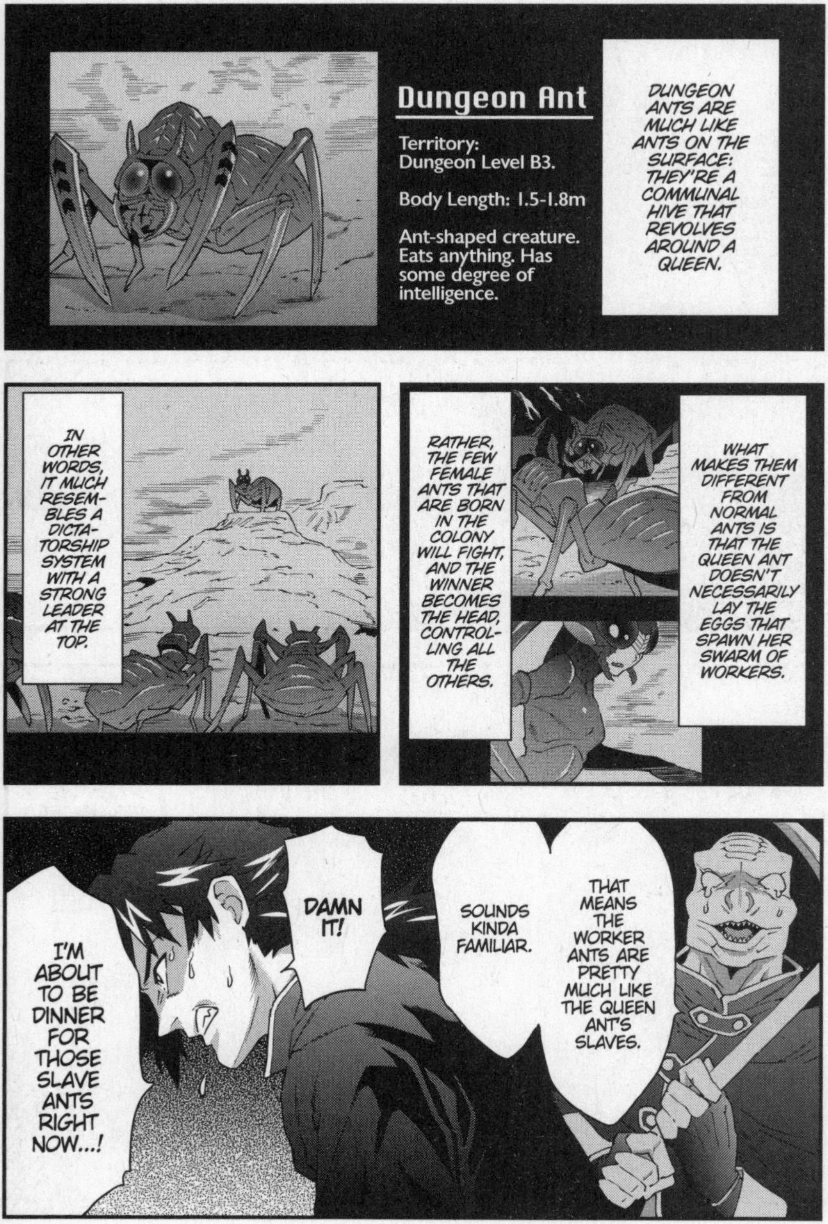
DUNGEON ANTS ARE MUCH LIKE ANTS ON THE SURFACE: THEY'RE A COMMUNAL HIVE THAT REVOLVES AROUND A QUEEN.
Dungeon Ant
Territory: Dungeon Level B3.
Body Length: 1.5-1.8m
Ant-shaped creature. Eats anything. Has some degree of intelligence.
WHAT MAKES THEM DIFFERENT FROM NORMAL ANTS IS THAT THE QUEEN ANT DOESN'T NECESSARILY LAY THE EGGS THAT SPAWN HER SWARM OF WORKERS.
RATHER, THE FEW FEMALE ANTS THAT ARE BORN IN THE COLONY WILL FIGHT, AND THE WINNER BECOMES THE HEAD, CONTROLLING ALL THE OTHERS.
IN OTHER WORDS, IT MUCH RESEMBLES A DICTATORSHIP SYSTEM WITH A STRONG LEADER AT THE TOP.
THAT MEANS THE WORKER ANTS ARE PRETTY MUCH LIKE THE QUEEN ANT'S SLAVES.
SOUNDS KINDA FAMILIAR.
DAMN IT!
I'M ABOUT TO BE DINNER FOR THOSE SLAVE ANTS RIGHT NOW...!

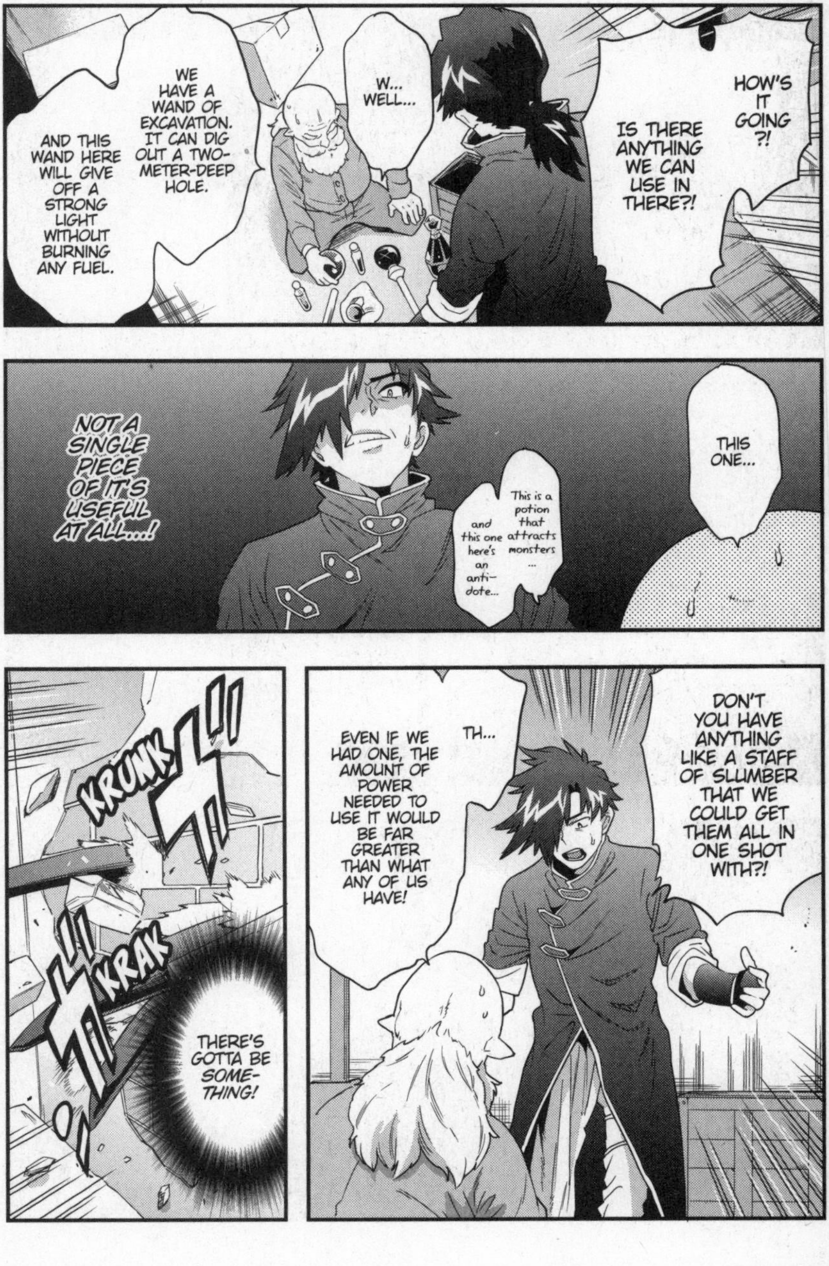
HOW'S IT GOING?!
IS THERE ANYTHING WE CAN USE IN THERE?!
W... WELL...
WE HAVE A WAND OF EXCAVATION. IT CAN DIG OUT A TWO-METER-DEEP HOLE.
AND THIS WAND HERE WILL GIVE OFF A STRONG LIGHT WITHOUT BURNING ANY FUEL.
THIS ONE...
This is a potion that attracts monsters...
and this one here's an anti-dote...
NOT A SINGLE PIECE OF IT'S USEFUL AT ALL...!
DON'T YOU HAVE ANYTHING LIKE A STAFF OF SLUMBER THAT WE COULD GET THEM ALL IN ONE SHOT WITH?!
TH...
EVEN IF WE HAD ONE, THE AMOUNT OF POWER NEEDED TO USE IT WOULD BE FAR GREATER THAN WHAT ANY OF US HAVE!
KRUNK
KRAK
THERE'S GOTTA BE SOME-THING!

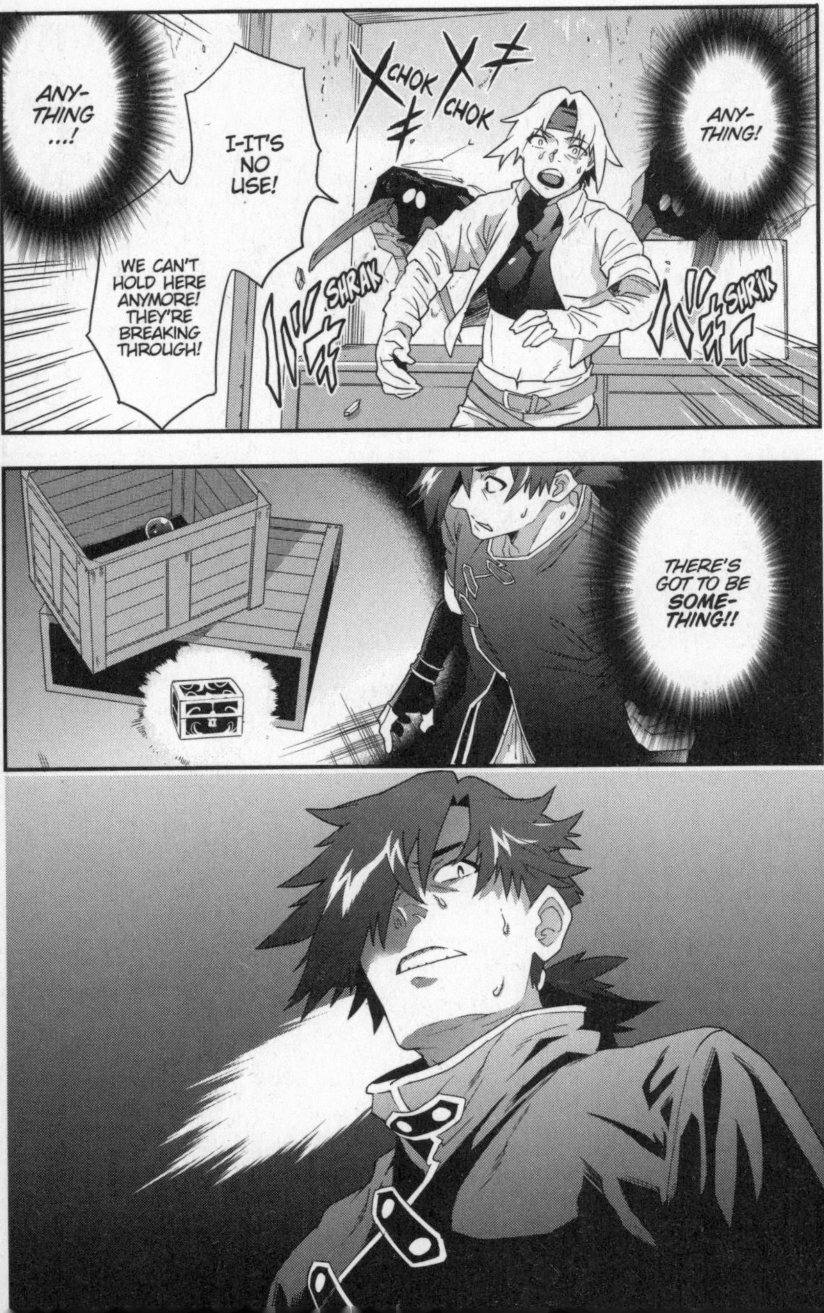
ANY-THING!
CHOK CHOK
I-IT'S NO USE!
ANY-THING...!
SHRIK
SHRAK
WE CAN'T HOLD HERE ANYMORE! THEY'RE BREAKING THROUGH!
THERE'S GOT TO BE SOME-THING!!

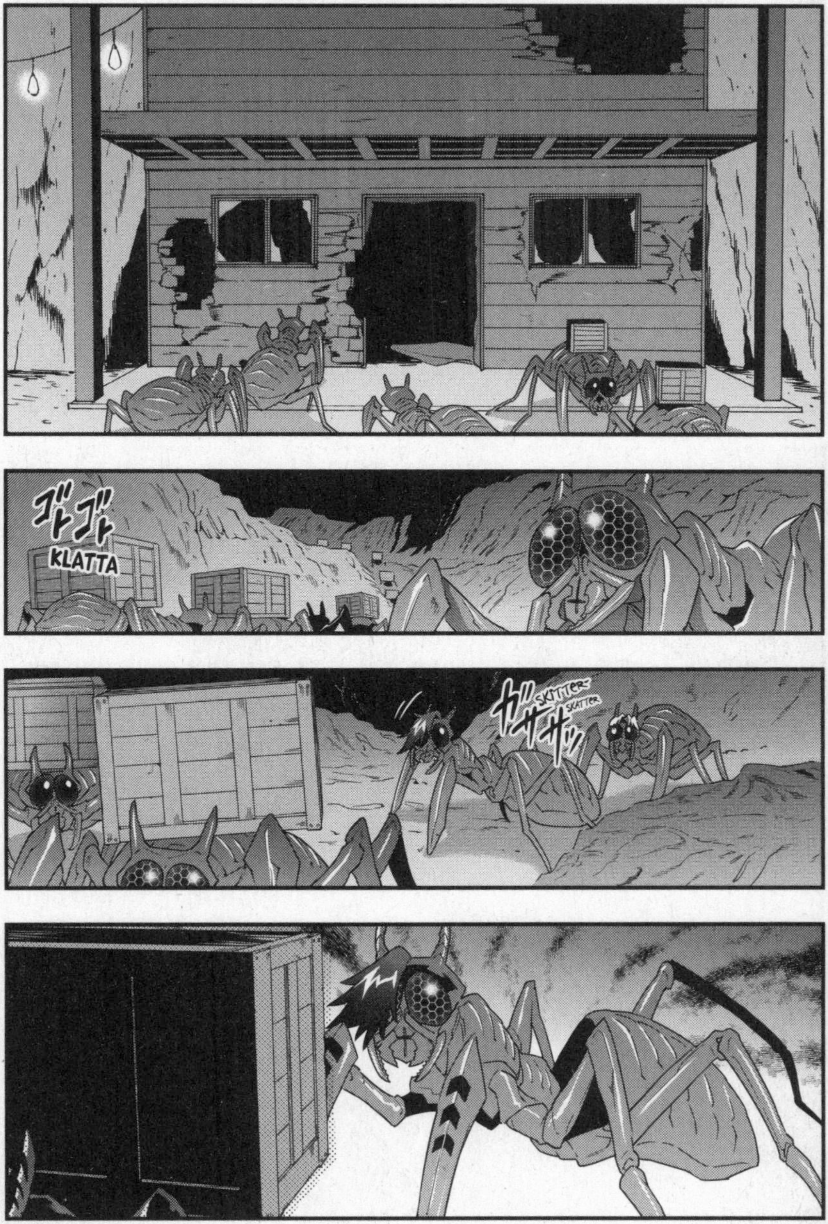
ゴトゴト
KLATTA
ガサササッ
SKITTER
SKATTER

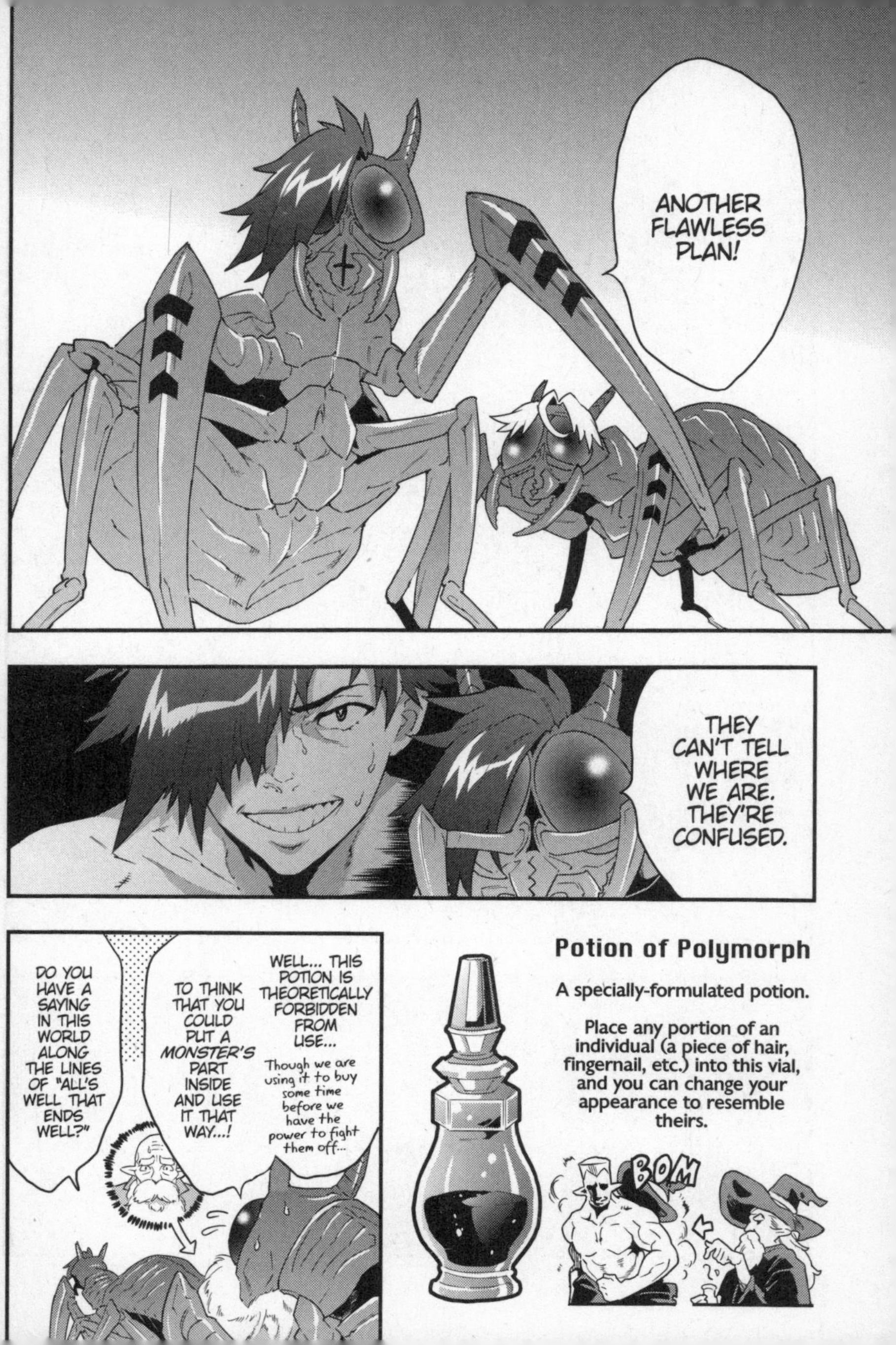
ANOTHER FLAWLESS PLAN!
THEY CAN'T TELL WHERE WE ARE. THEY'RE CONFUSED.
Potion of Polymorph
A specially-formulated potion.
Place any portion of an individual (a piece of hair, fingernail, etc.) into this vial, and you can change your appearance to resemble theirs.
BOM
WELL... THIS POTION IS THEORETICALLY FORBIDDEN FROM USE...
Though we are using it to buy some time before we have the power to fight them off...
TO THINK THAT YOU COULD PUT A *MONSTER'S* PART INSIDE AND USE IT THAT WAY...!
DO YOU HAVE A SAYING IN THIS WORLD ALONG THE LINES OF "ALL'S WELL THAT ENDS WELL?"

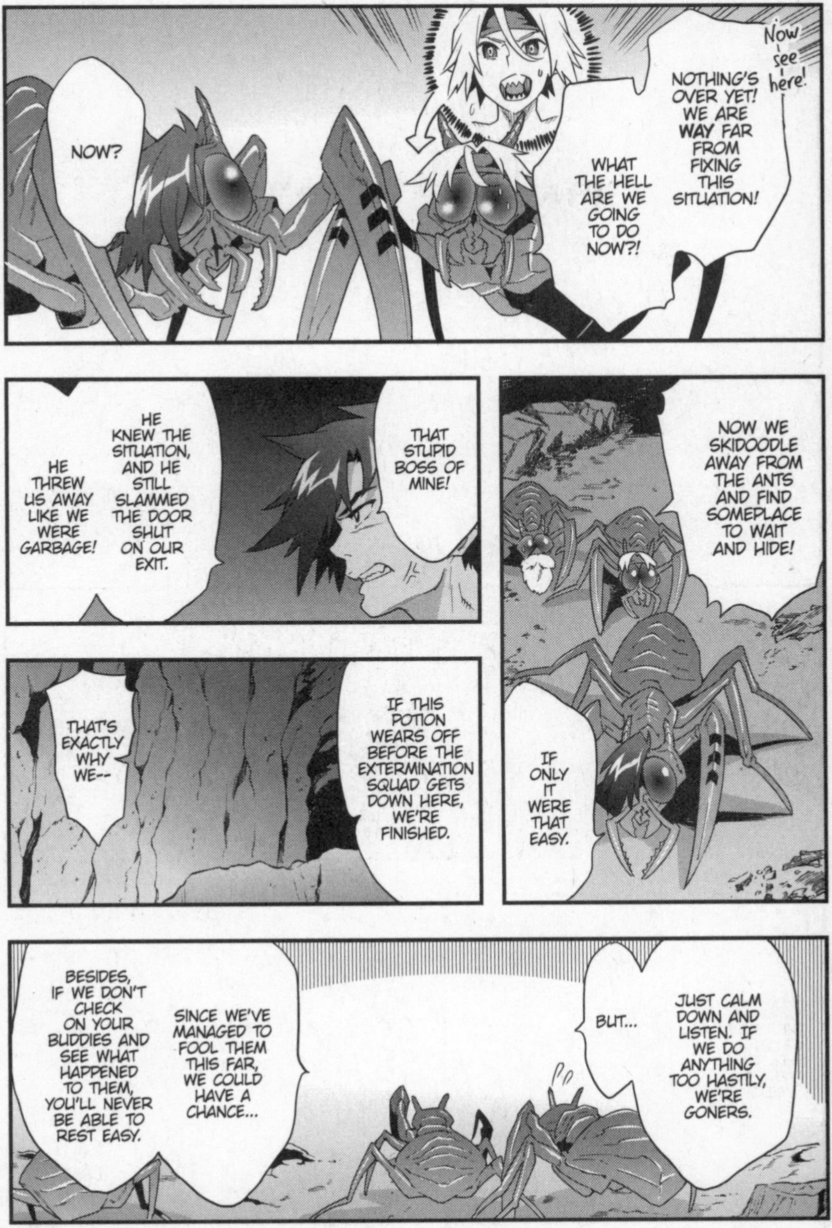
Now see here!
NOTHING'S OVER YET! WE ARE WAY FAR FROM FIXING THIS SITUATION!
WHAT THE HELL ARE WE GOING TO DO NOW?!
NOW?
NOW WE SKIDOODLE AWAY FROM THE ANTS AND FIND SOMEPLACE TO WAIT AND HIDE!
IF ONLY IT WERE THAT EASY.
THAT STUPID BOSS OF MINE!
HE KNEW THE SITUATION, AND HE STILL SLAMMED THE DOOR SHUT ON OUR EXIT.
HE THREW US AWAY LIKE WE WERE GARBAGE!
IF THIS POTION WEARS OFF BEFORE THE EXTERMINATION SQUAD GETS DOWN HERE, WE'RE FINISHED.
THAT'S EXACTLY WHY WE--
JUST CALM DOWN AND LISTEN. IF WE DO ANYTHING TOO HASTILY, WE'RE GONERS.
BUT...
SINCE WE'VE MANAGED TO FOOL THEM THIS FAR, WE COULD HAVE A CHANCE...
BESIDES, IF WE DON'T CHECK ON YOUR BUDDIES AND SEE WHAT HAPPENED TO THEM, YOU'LL NEVER BE ABLE TO REST EASY.

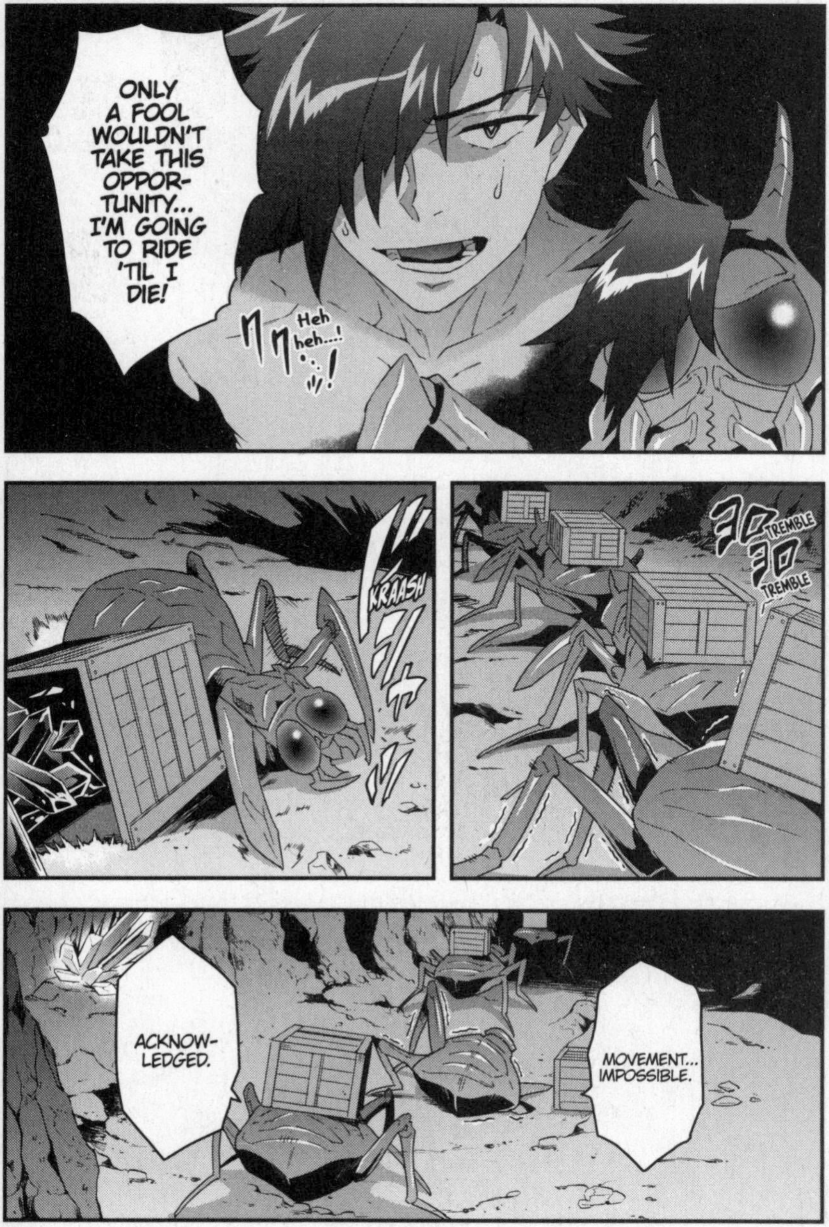
ONLY A FOOL WOULDN'T TAKE THIS OPPOR-TUNITY... I'M GOING TO RIDE 'TIL I DIE!
Heh heh...!
TREMBLE
TREMBLE
KRAASH
MOVEMENT... IMPOSSIBLE.
ACKNOW-LEDGED.

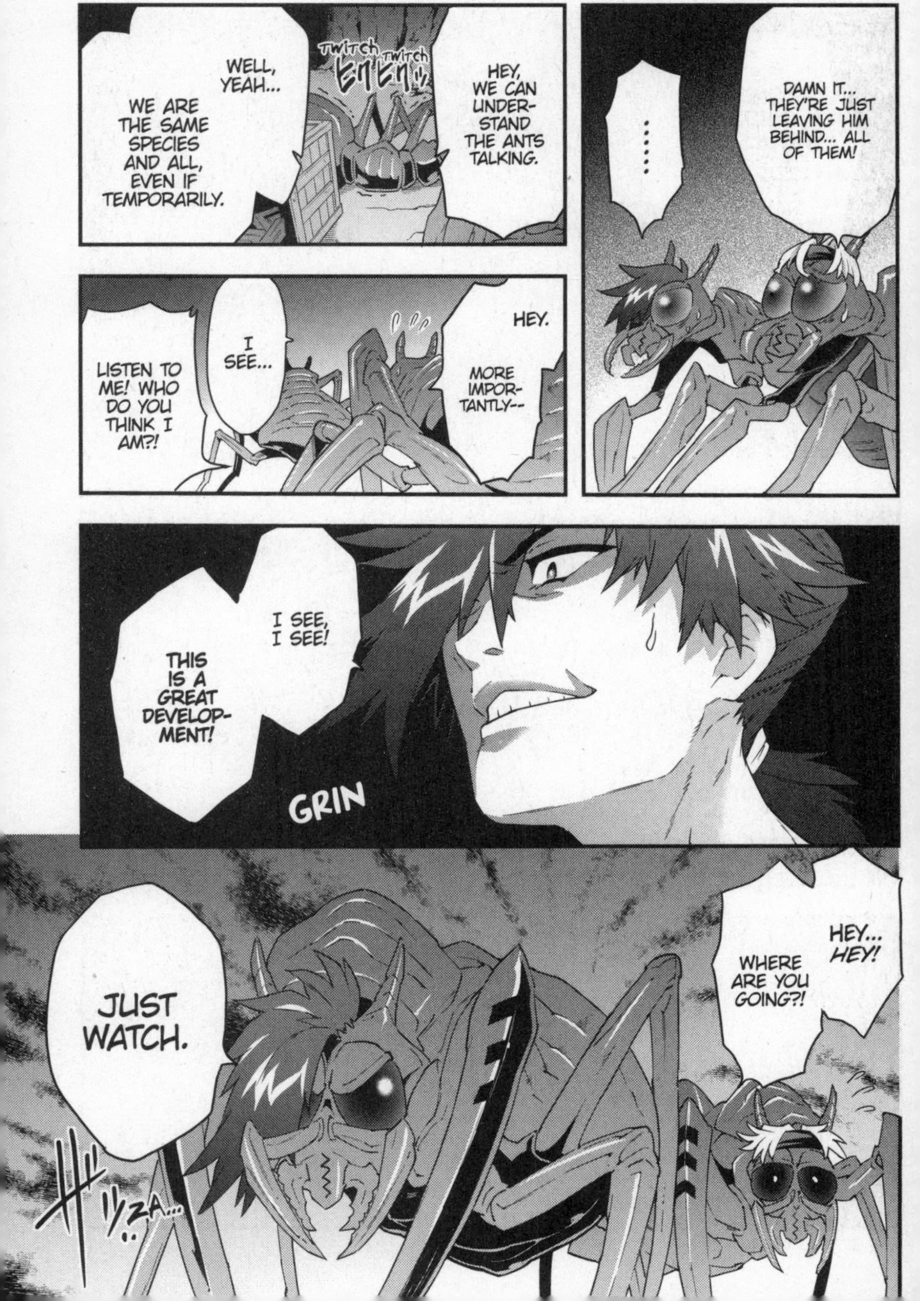
DAMN IT... THEY'RE JUST LEAVING HIM BEHIND... ALL OF THEM!
......
HEY, WE CAN UNDERSTAND THE ANTS TALKING.
TWITCH TWITCH
ピクピクッ
WELL, YEAH...
WE ARE THE SAME SPECIES AND ALL, EVEN IF TEMPORARILY.
HEY.
MORE IMPORTANTLY--
I SEE...
LISTEN TO ME! WHO DO YOU THINK I AM?!
I SEE, I SEE!
THIS IS A GREAT DEVELOPMENT!
GRIN
HEY... HEY!
WHERE ARE YOU GOING?!
JUST WATCH.
ZA...

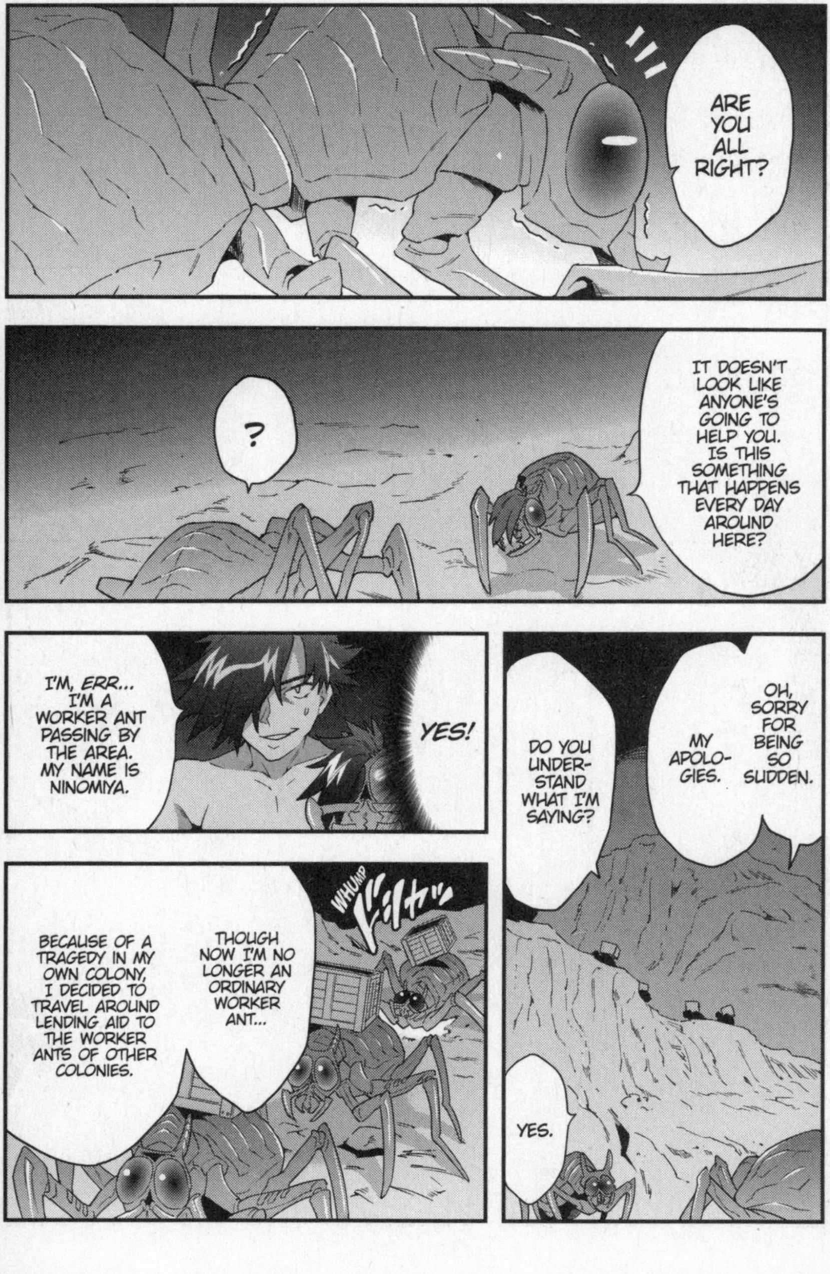
ARE YOU ALL RIGHT?
IT DOESN'T LOOK LIKE ANYONE'S GOING TO HELP YOU. IS THIS SOMETHING THAT HAPPENS EVERY DAY AROUND HERE?
?
OH, SORRY FOR BEING SO SUDDEN.
MY APOLO-GIES.
DO YOU UNDER-STAND WHAT I'M SAYING?
YES.
YES!
I'M, ERR... I'M A WORKER ANT PASSING BY THE AREA. MY NAME IS NINOMIYA.
WHUMP
THOUGH NOW I'M NO LONGER AN ORDINARY WORKER ANT...
BECAUSE OF A TRAGEDY IN MY OWN COLONY, I DECIDED TO TRAVEL AROUND LENDING AID TO THE WORKER ANTS OF OTHER COLONIES.

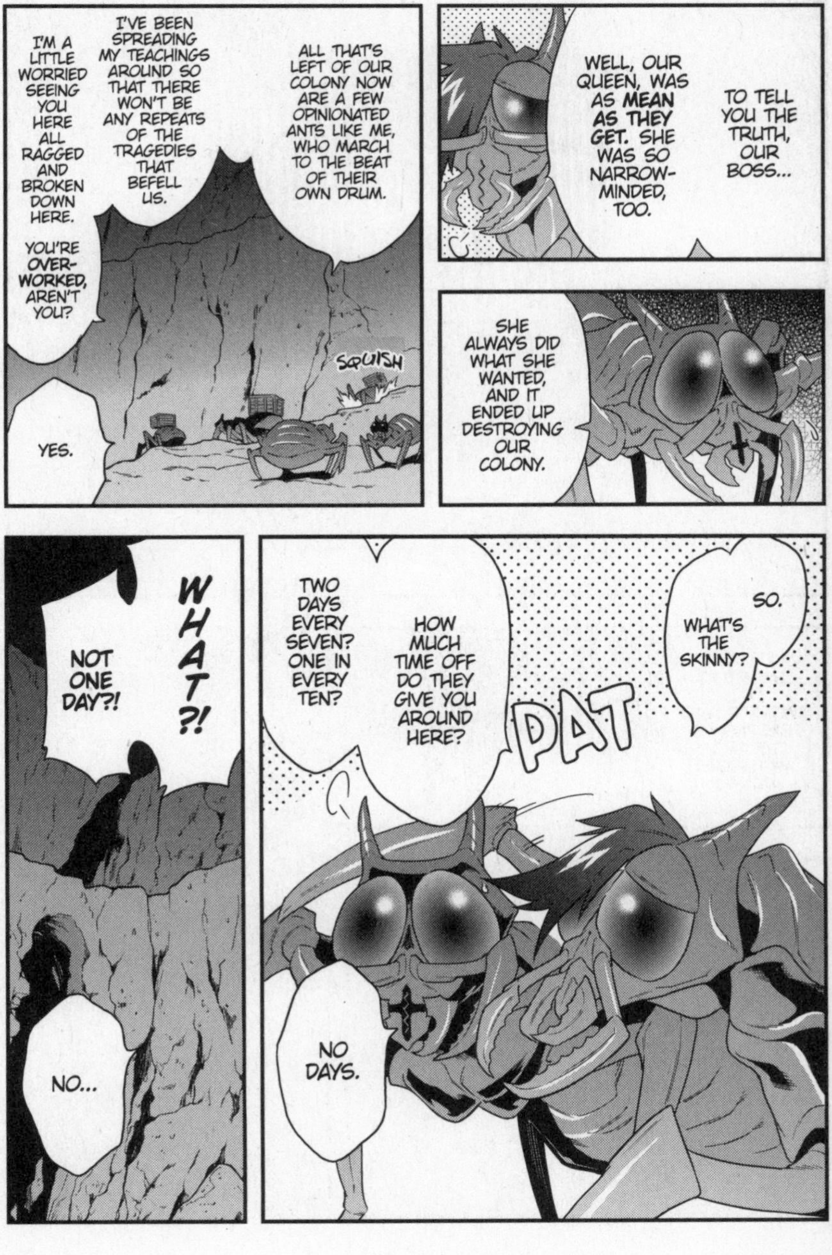
TO TELL YOU THE TRUTH, OUR BOSS...
WELL, OUR QUEEN, WAS AS **MEAN AS THEY GET**. SHE WAS SO NARROW-MINDED, TOO.
SHE ALWAYS DID WHAT SHE WANTED, AND IT ENDED UP DESTROYING OUR COLONY.
ALL THAT'S LEFT OF OUR COLONY NOW ARE A FEW OPINIONATED ANTS LIKE ME, WHO MARCH TO THE BEAT OF THEIR OWN DRUM.
I'VE BEEN SPREADING MY TEACHINGS AROUND SO THAT THERE WON'T BE ANY REPEATS OF THE TRAGEDIES THAT BEFELL US.
I'M A LITTLE WORRIED SEEING YOU HERE ALL RAGGED AND BROKEN DOWN HERE.
YOU'RE OVER-WORKED, AREN'T YOU?
SQUISH
YES.
SO.
WHAT'S THE SKINNY?
PAT
HOW MUCH TIME OFF DO THEY GIVE YOU AROUND HERE?
TWO DAYS EVERY SEVEN? ONE IN EVERY TEN?
NO DAYS.
WHAT?!
NOT ONE DAY?!
NO...

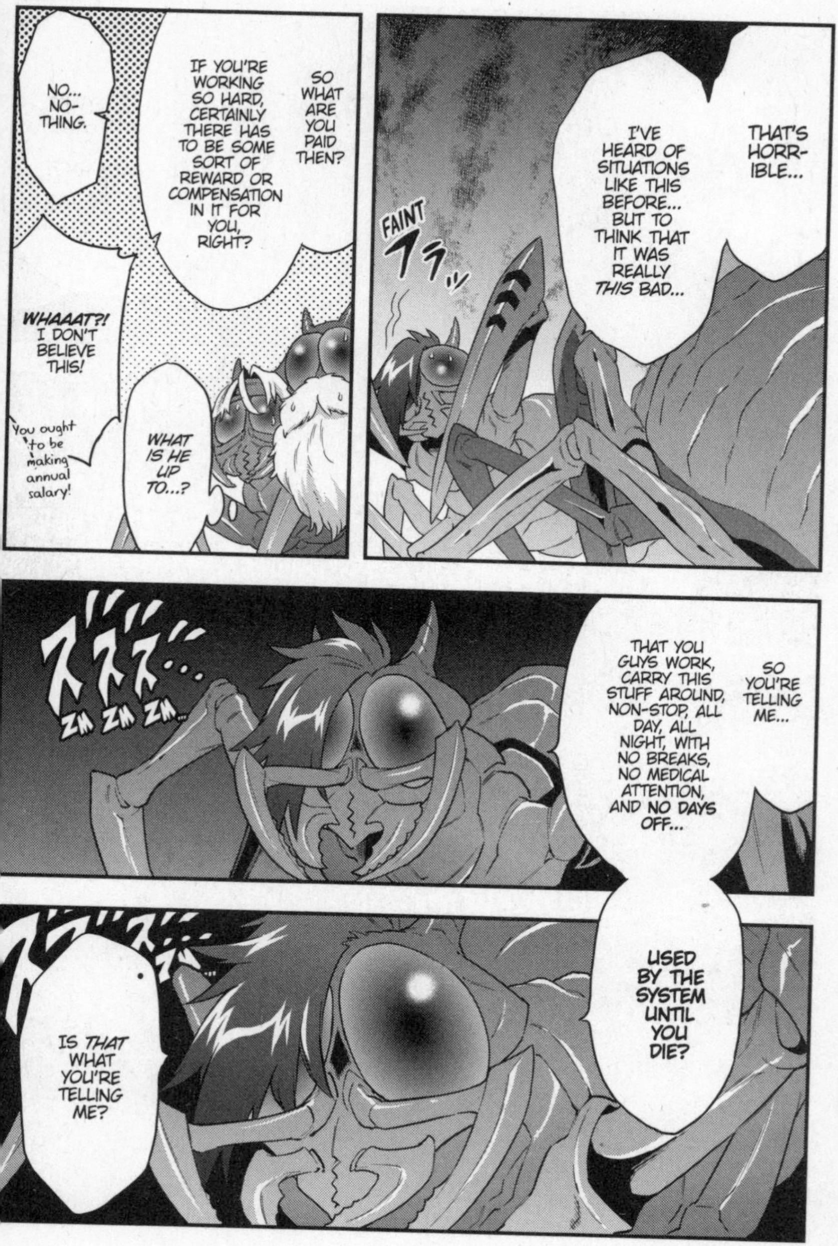
THAT'S HORRIBLE...
I'VE HEARD OF SITUATIONS LIKE THIS BEFORE... BUT TO THINK THAT IT WAS REALLY *THIS* BAD...
FAINT
SO WHAT ARE YOU PAID THEN?
IF YOU'RE WORKING SO HARD, CERTAINLY THERE HAS TO BE SOME SORT OF REWARD OR COMPENSATION IN IT FOR YOU, RIGHT?
NO... NO-THING.
WHAAAT?! I DON'T BELIEVE THIS!
You ought to be making annual salary!
WHAT IS HE UP TO...?
SO YOU'RE TELLING ME...
THAT YOU GUYS WORK, CARRY THIS STUFF AROUND, NON-STOP, ALL DAY, ALL NIGHT, WITH NO BREAKS, NO MEDICAL ATTENTION, AND **NO DAYS** OFF...
ZM ZM ZM...
USED BY THE SYSTEM UNTIL YOU DIE?
IS *THAT* WHAT YOU'RE TELLING ME?

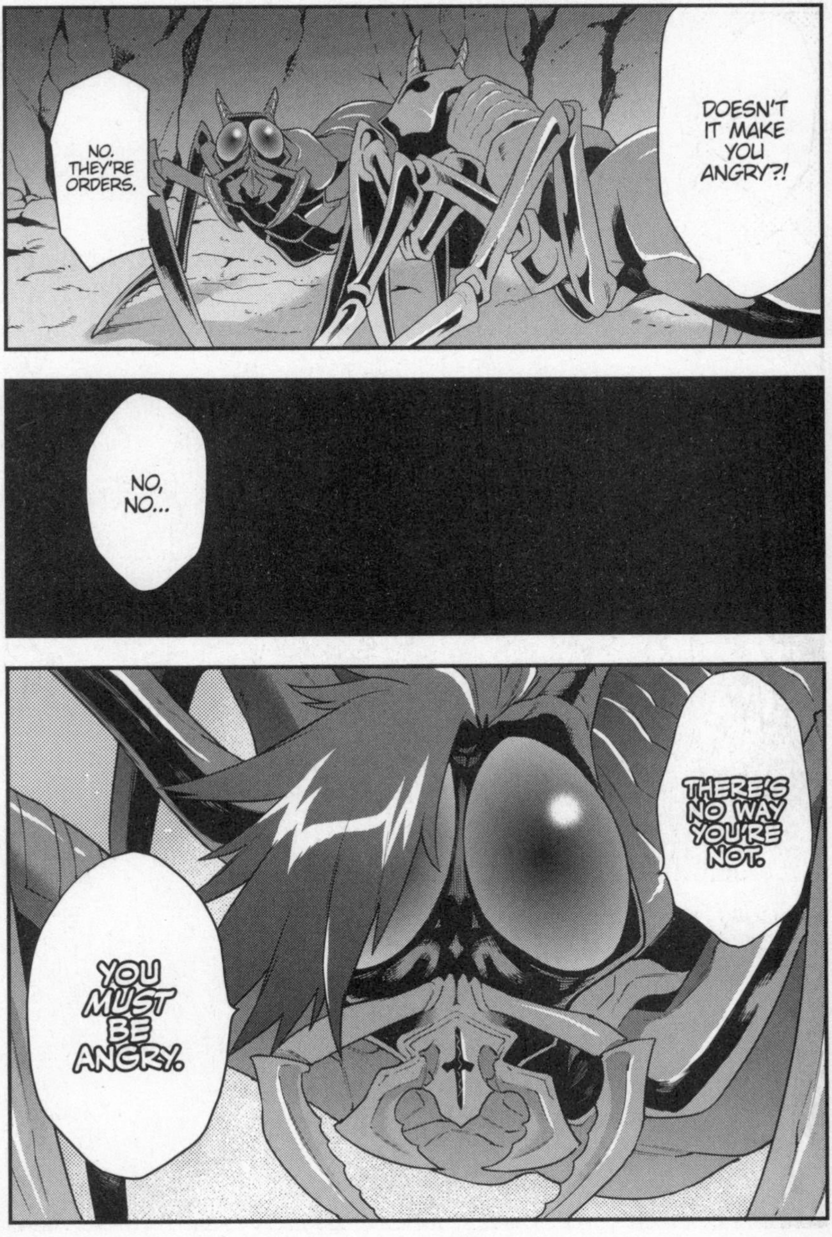
DOESN'T IT MAKE YOU ANGRY?!
NO. THEY'RE ORDERS.
NO, NO...
THERE'S NO WAY YOU'RE NOT.
YOU MUST BE ANGRY.

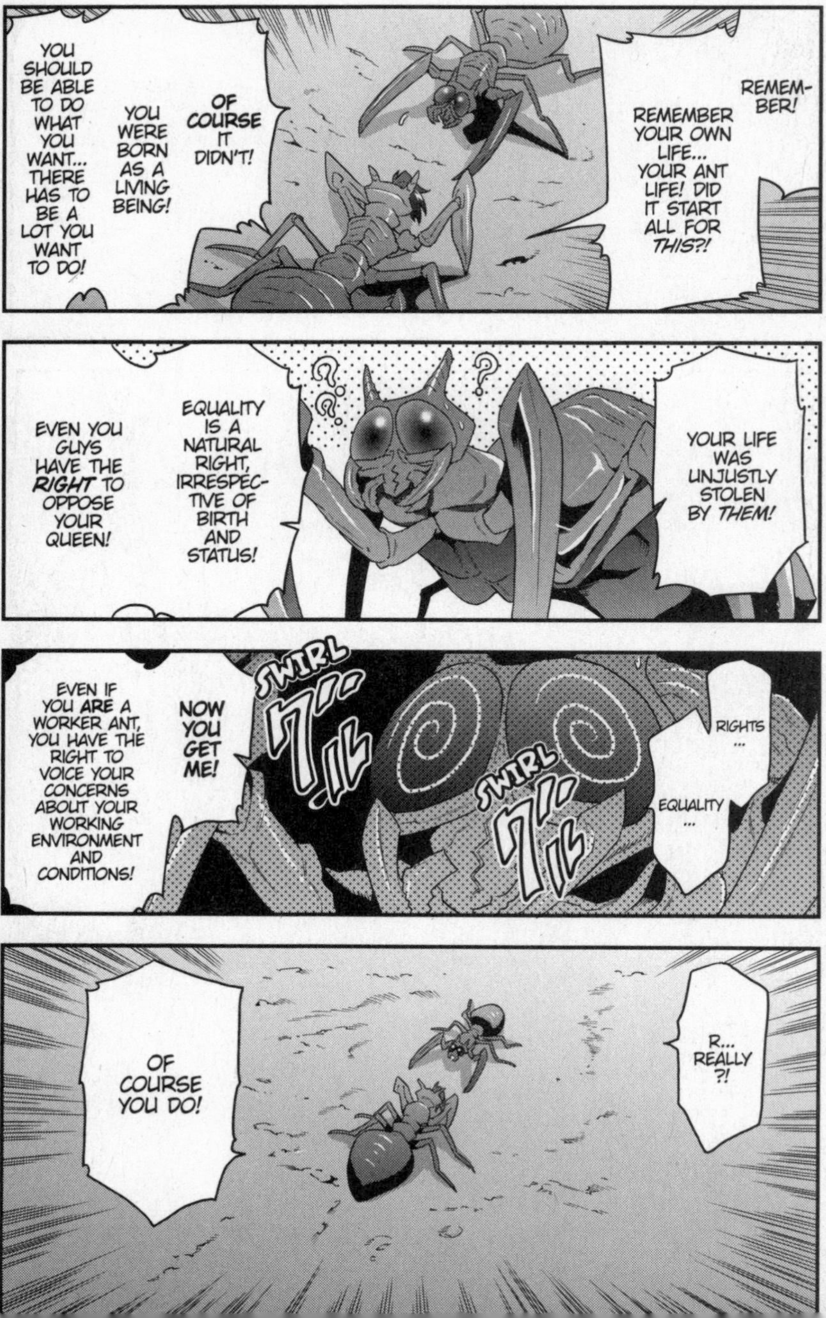
REMEMBER!
REMEMBER YOUR OWN LIFE... YOUR ANT LIFE! DID IT START ALL FOR *THIS?!*
OF **COURSE** IT DIDN'T!
YOU WERE BORN AS A LIVING BEING!
YOU SHOULD BE ABLE TO DO WHAT YOU WANT... THERE HAS TO BE A LOT YOU WANT TO DO!
YOUR LIFE WAS UNJUSTLY STOLEN BY *THEM!*
EQUALITY IS A NATURAL RIGHT, IRRESPECTIVE OF BIRTH AND STATUS!
EVEN YOU GUYS HAVE THE ***RIGHT*** TO OPPOSE YOUR QUEEN!
SWIRL
RIGHTS...
SWIRL
EQUALITY...
NOW YOU GET ME!
EVEN IF YOU **ARE** A WORKER ANT, YOU HAVE THE RIGHT TO VOICE YOUR CONCERNS ABOUT YOUR WORKING ENVIRONMENT AND CONDITIONS!
R... REALLY ?!
OF COURSE YOU DO!

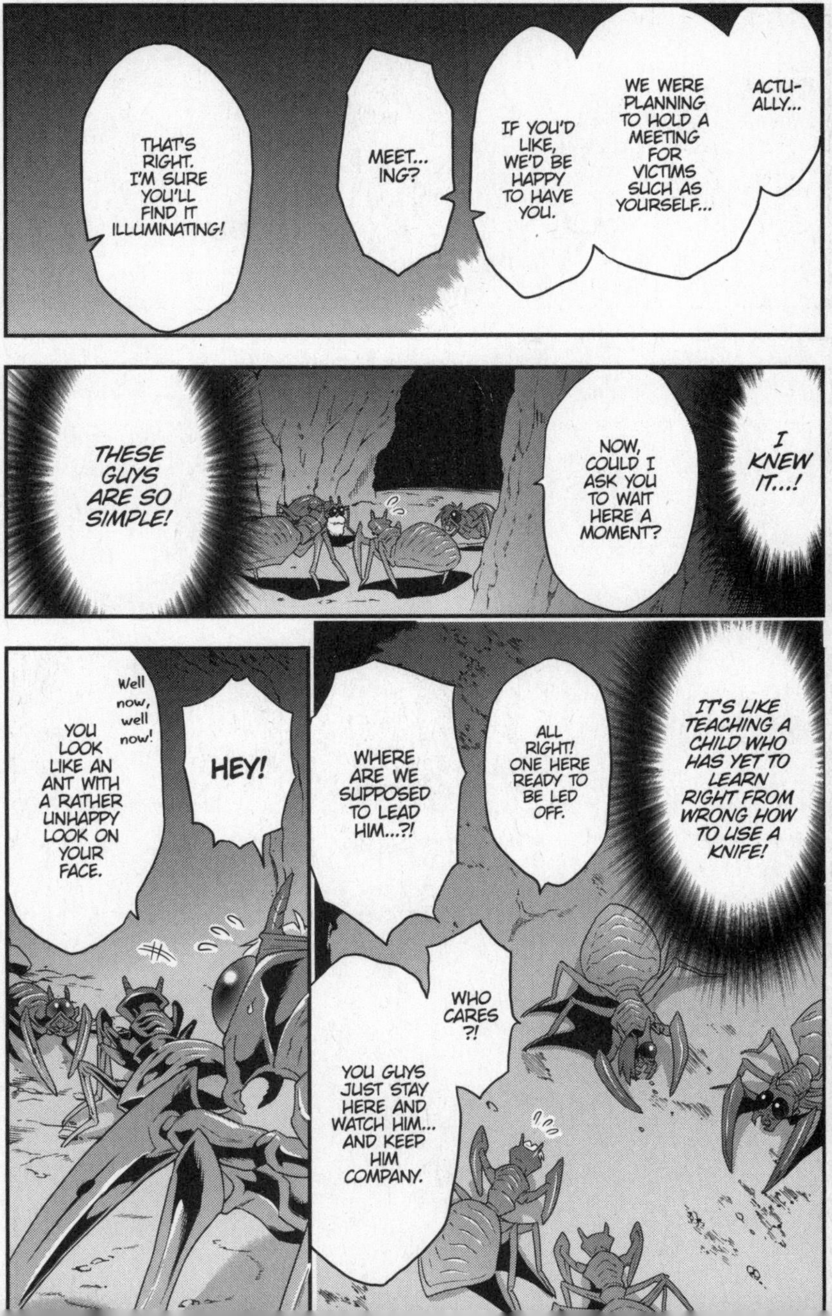
ACTU-ALLY...
WE WERE PLANNING TO HOLD A MEETING FOR VICTIMS SUCH AS YOURSELF...
IF YOU'D LIKE, WE'D BE HAPPY TO HAVE YOU.
MEET... ING?
THAT'S RIGHT. I'M SURE YOU'LL FIND IT ILLUMINATING!
I KNEW IT...!
NOW, COULD I ASK YOU TO WAIT HERE A MOMENT?
THESE GUYS ARE SO SIMPLE!
IT'S LIKE TEACHING A CHILD WHO HAS YET TO LEARN RIGHT FROM WRONG HOW TO USE A KNIFE!
ALL RIGHT! ONE HERE READY TO BE LED OFF.
WHERE ARE WE SUPPOSED TO LEAD HIM...?!
WHO CARES?!
YOU GUYS JUST STAY HERE AND WATCH HIM... AND KEEP HIM COMPANY.
HEY!
Well now, well now!
YOU LOOK LIKE AN ANT WITH A RATHER UNHAPPY LOOK ON YOUR FACE.

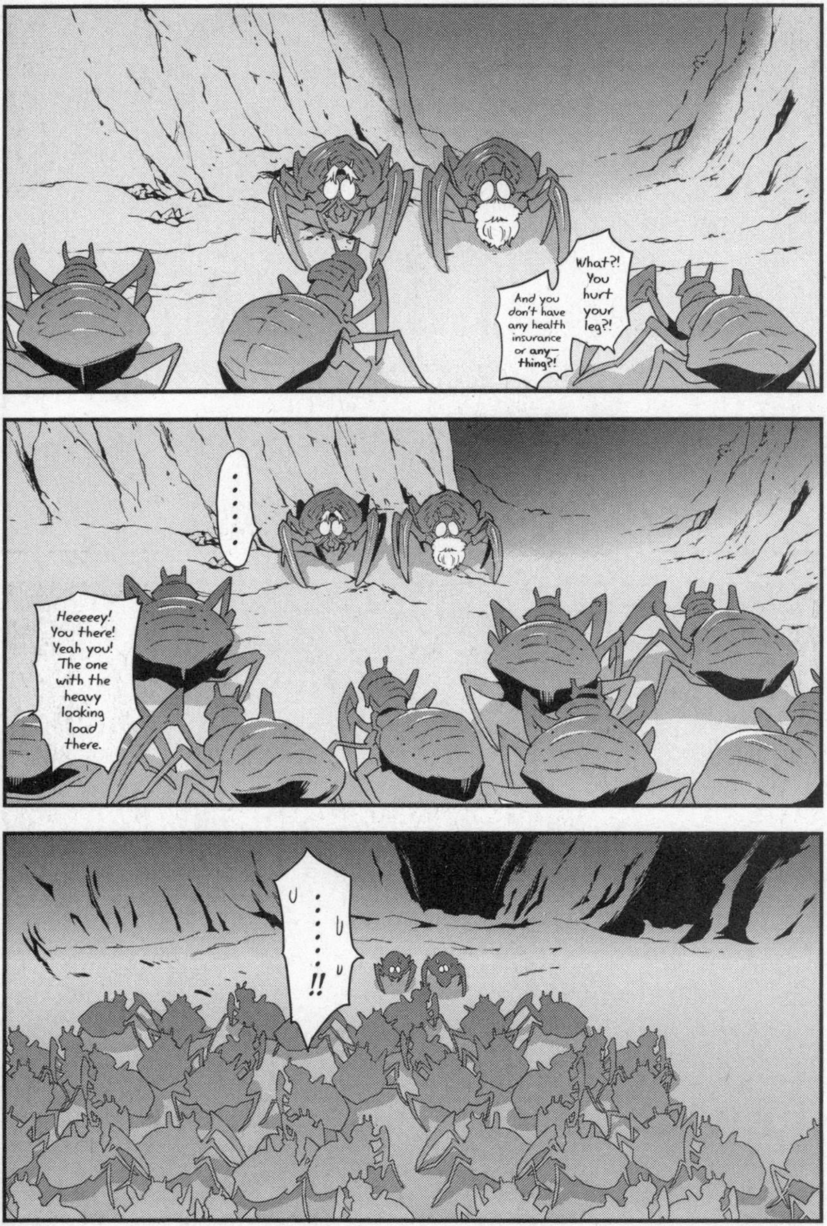
What?! You hurt your leg?!
And you don't have any health insurance or any-thing?!
......
Heeeeey! You there! Yeah you! The one with the heavy looking load there.
......!!

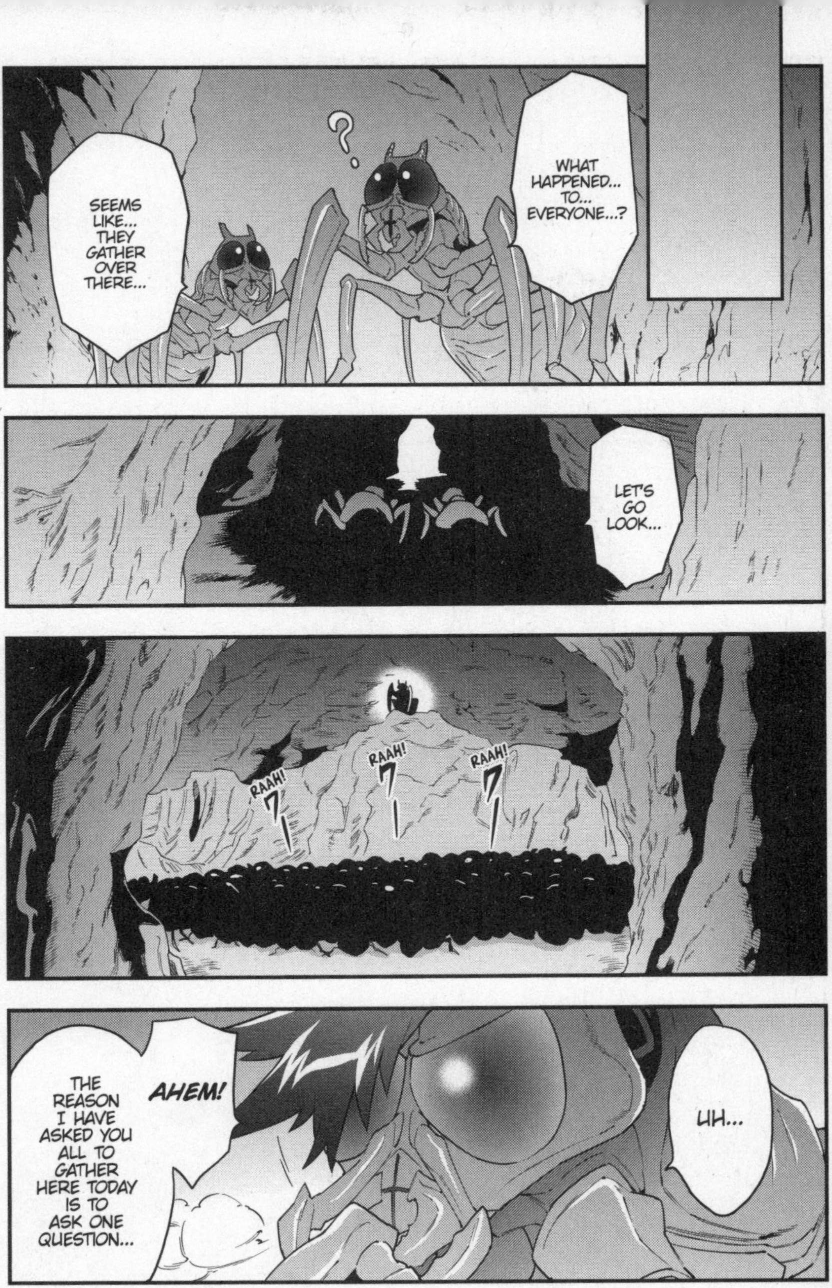
WHAT HAPPENED... TO... EVERYONE...?
SEEMS LIKE... THEY GATHER OVER THERE...
LET'S GO LOOK...
RAAH!
RAAH!
RAAH!
UH...
AHEM!
THE REASON I HAVE ASKED YOU ALL TO GATHER HERE TODAY IS TO ASK ONE QUESTION...

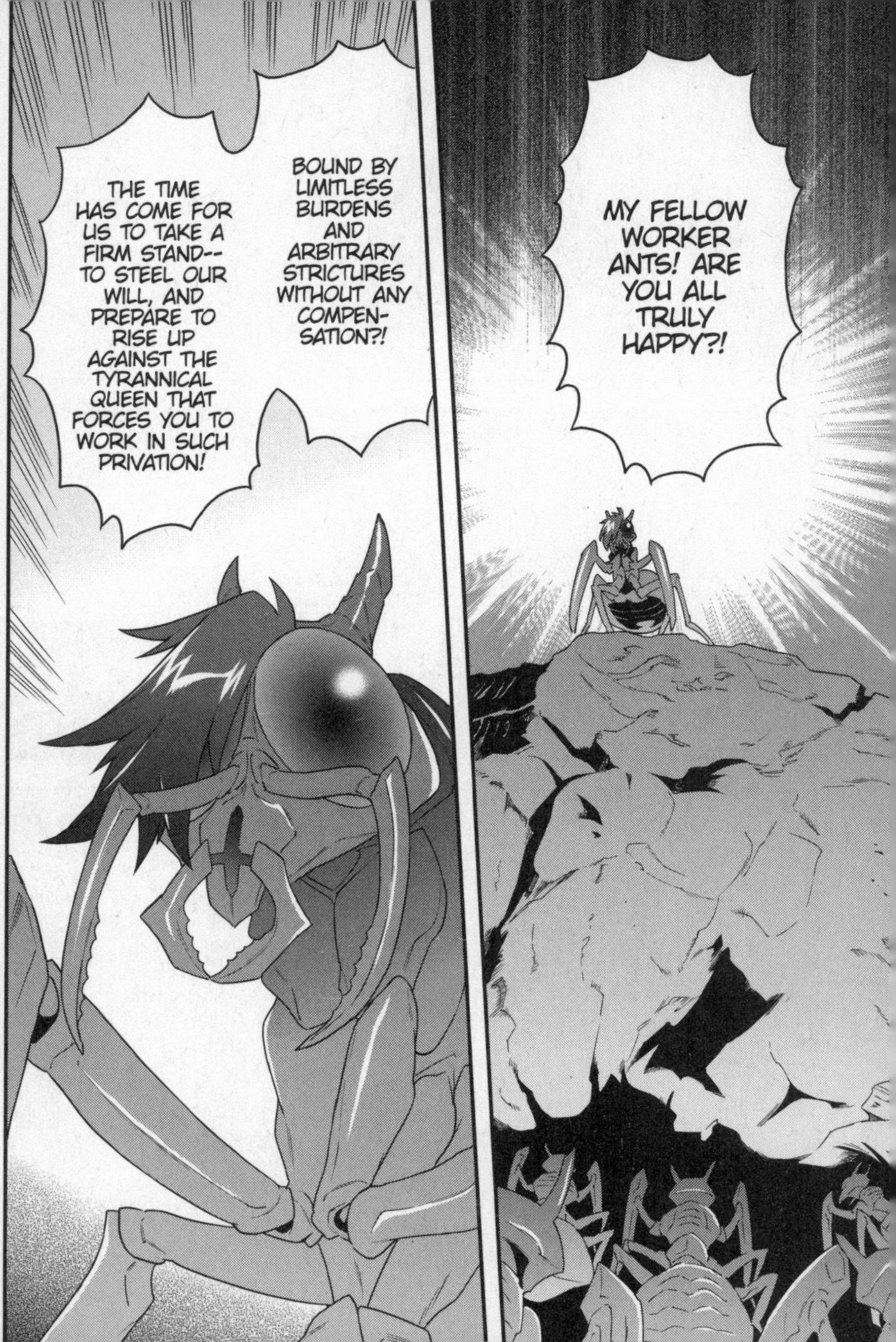
MY FELLOW WORKER ANTS! ARE YOU ALL TRULY HAPPY?!
BOUND BY LIMITLESS BURDENS AND ARBITRARY STRICTURES WITHOUT ANY COMPEN-SATION?!
THE TIME HAS COME FOR US TO TAKE A FIRM STAND-- TO STEEL OUR WILL, AND PREPARE TO RISE UP AGAINST THE TYRANNICAL QUEEN THAT FORCES YOU TO WORK IN SUCH PRIVATION!

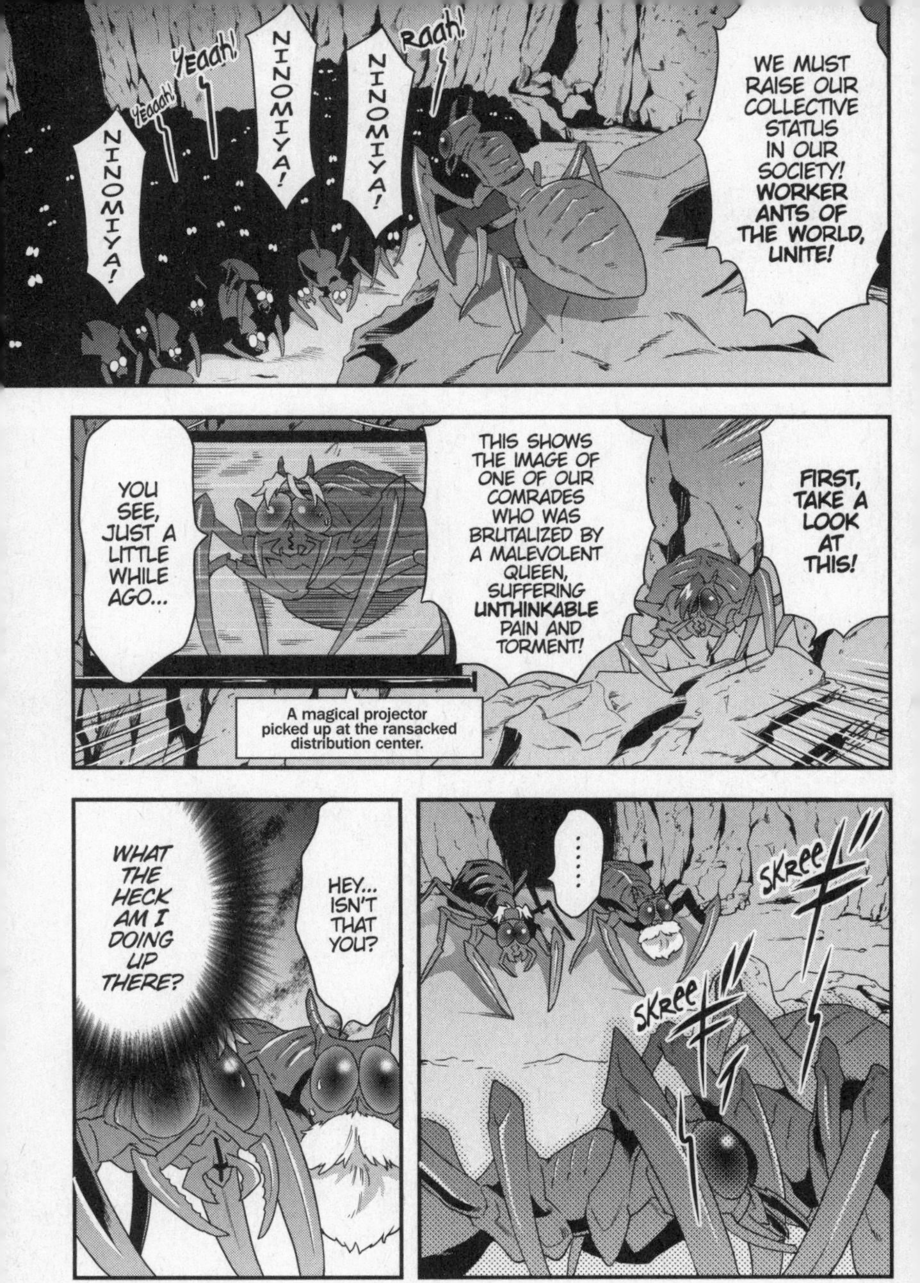
WE MUST RAISE OUR COLLECTIVE STATUS IN OUR SOCIETY! WORKER ANTS OF THE WORLD, UNITE!
Raah!
NINOMIYA!
NINOMIYA!
Yeaah!
Yeaaah!
NINOMIYA!
FIRST, TAKE A LOOK AT THIS!
THIS SHOWS THE IMAGE OF ONE OF OUR COMRADES WHO WAS BRUTALIZED BY A MALEVOLENT QUEEN, SUFFERING **UNTHINKABLE** PAIN AND TORMENT!
YOU SEE, JUST A LITTLE WHILE AGO...
A magical projector picked up at the ransacked distribution center.
......
SKREE!!
SKREE!!
HEY... ISN'T THAT YOU?
WHAT THE HECK AM I DOING UP THERE?

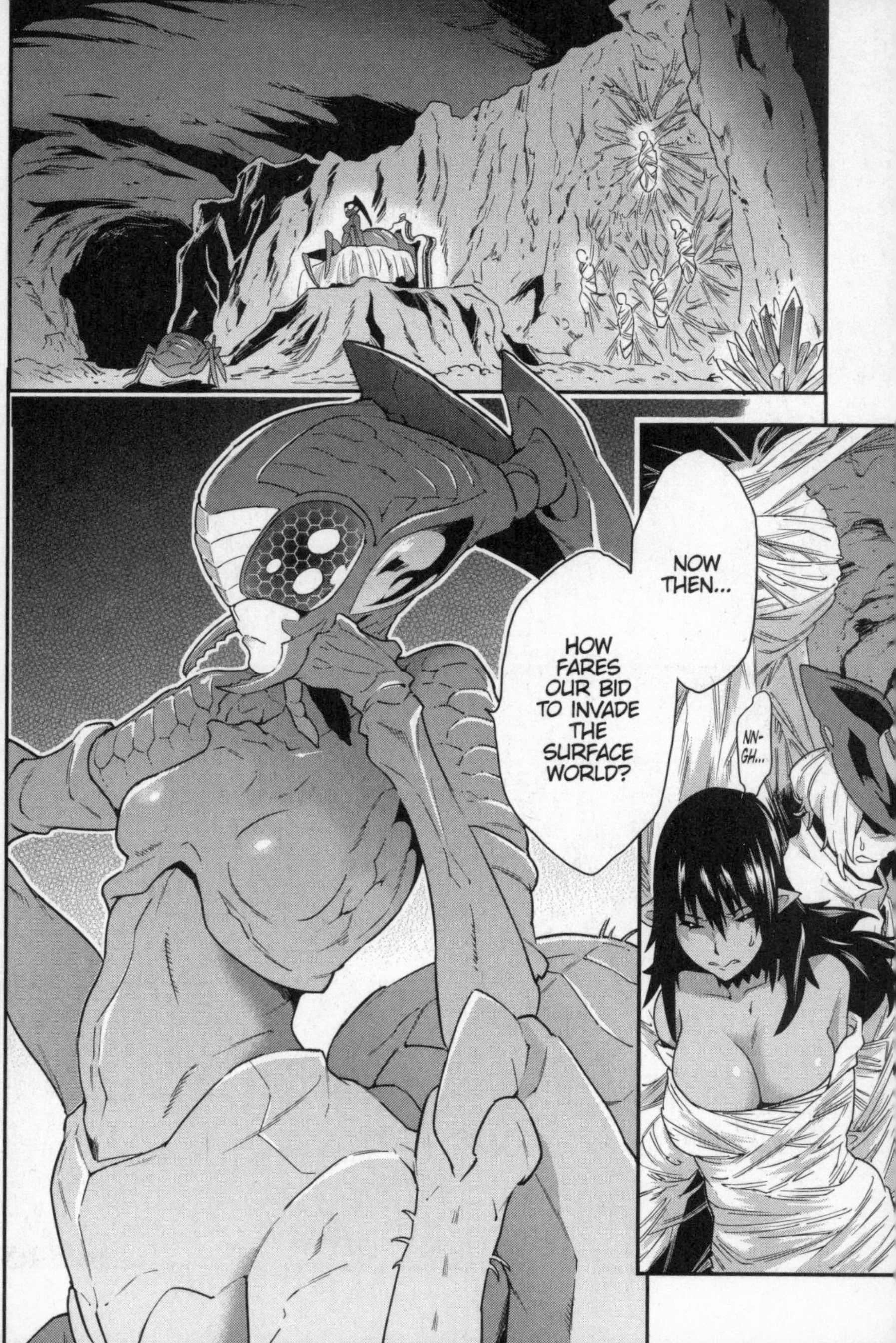
NOW THEN...
HOW FARES OUR BID TO INVADE THE SURFACE WORLD?
NN-GH...

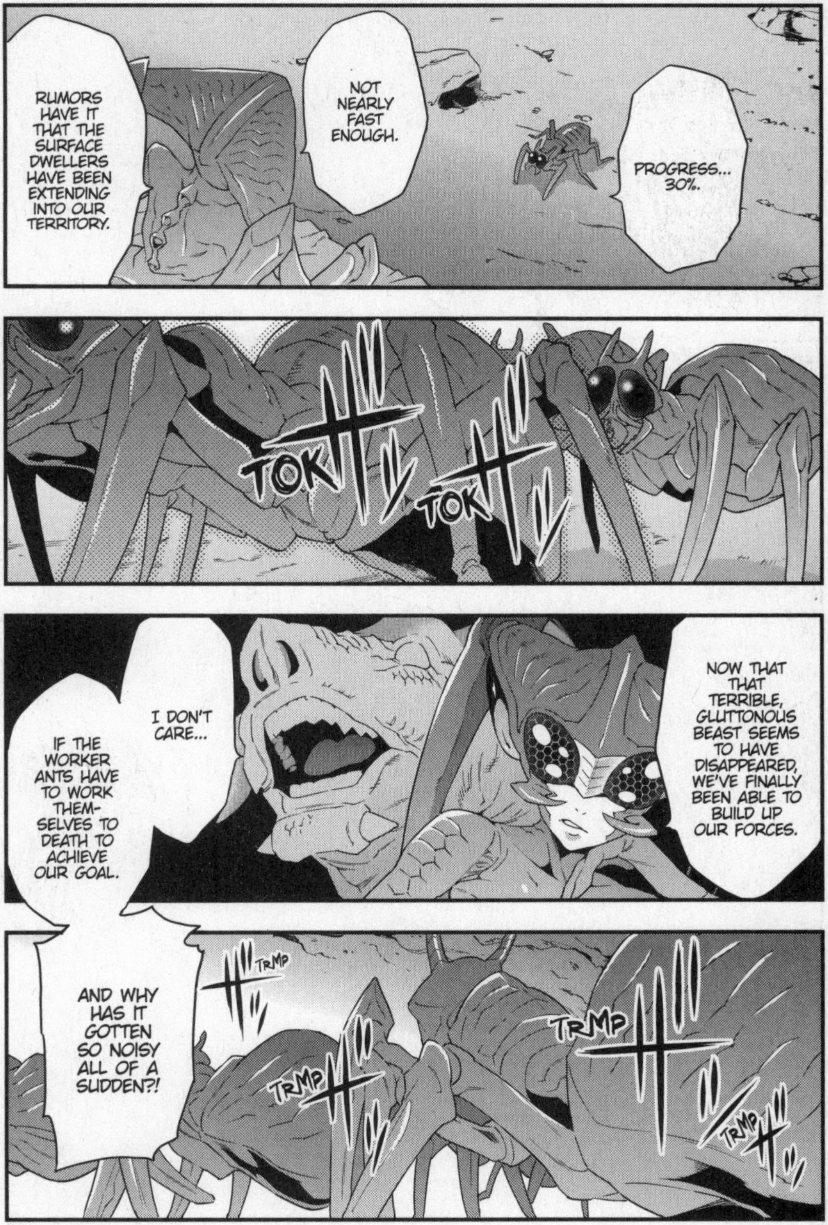
PROGRESS... 30%.
NOT NEARLY FAST ENOUGH.
RUMORS HAVE IT THAT THE SURFACE DWELLERS HAVE BEEN EXTENDING INTO OUR TERRITORY.
TOK
TOK
NOW THAT THAT TERRIBLE, GLUTTONOUS BEAST SEEMS TO HAVE DISAPPEARED, WE'VE FINALLY BEEN ABLE TO BUILD UP OUR FORCES.
I DON'T CARE...
IF THE WORKER ANTS HAVE TO WORK THEMSELVES TO DEATH TO ACHIEVE OUR GOAL.
TRMP
TRMP
TRMP
TRMP
AND WHY HAS IT GOTTEN SO NOISY ALL OF A SUDDEN?!

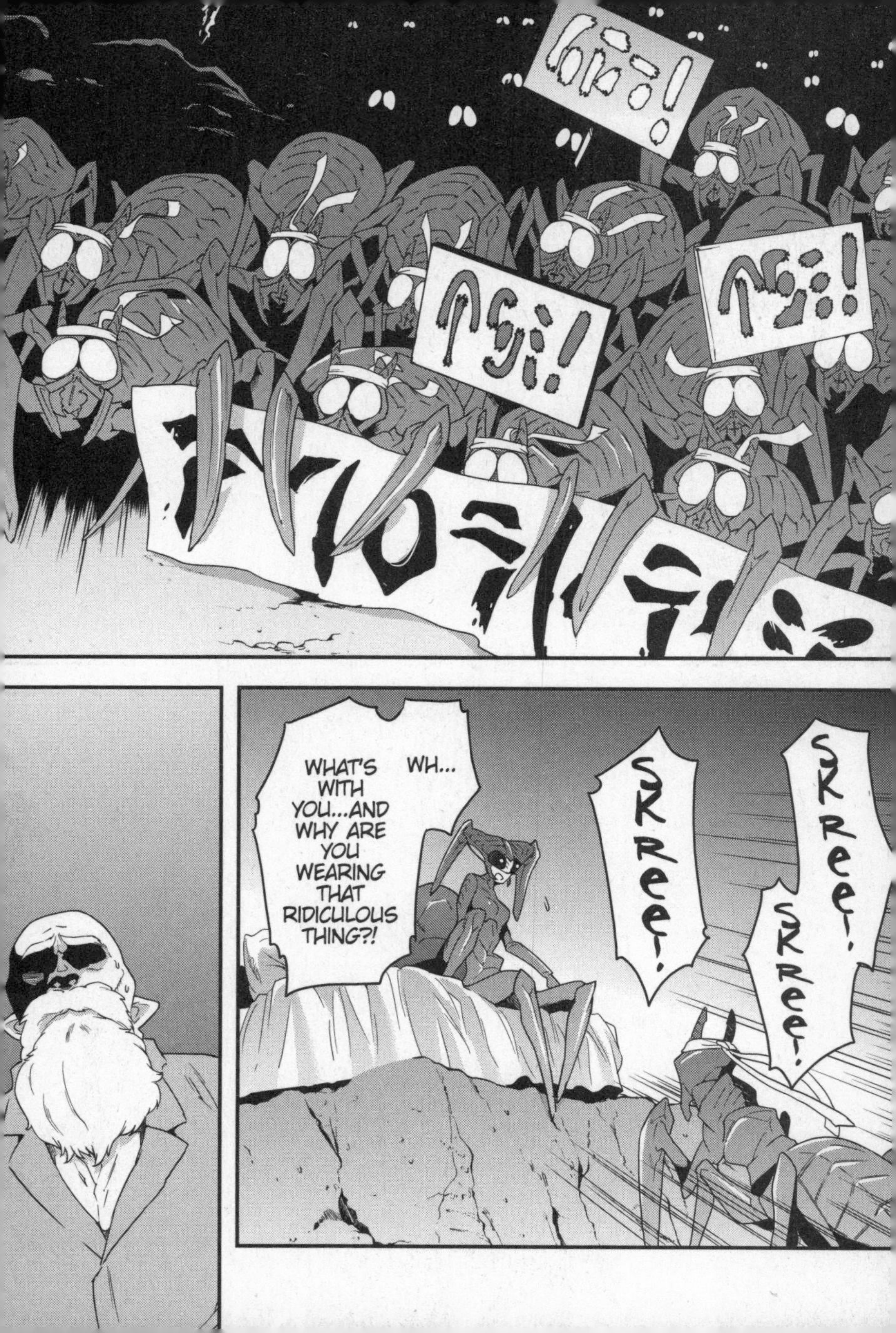
SKREE!
SKREE!
SKREE!
WH... WHAT'S WITH YOU...AND WHY ARE YOU WEARING THAT RIDICULOUS THING?!

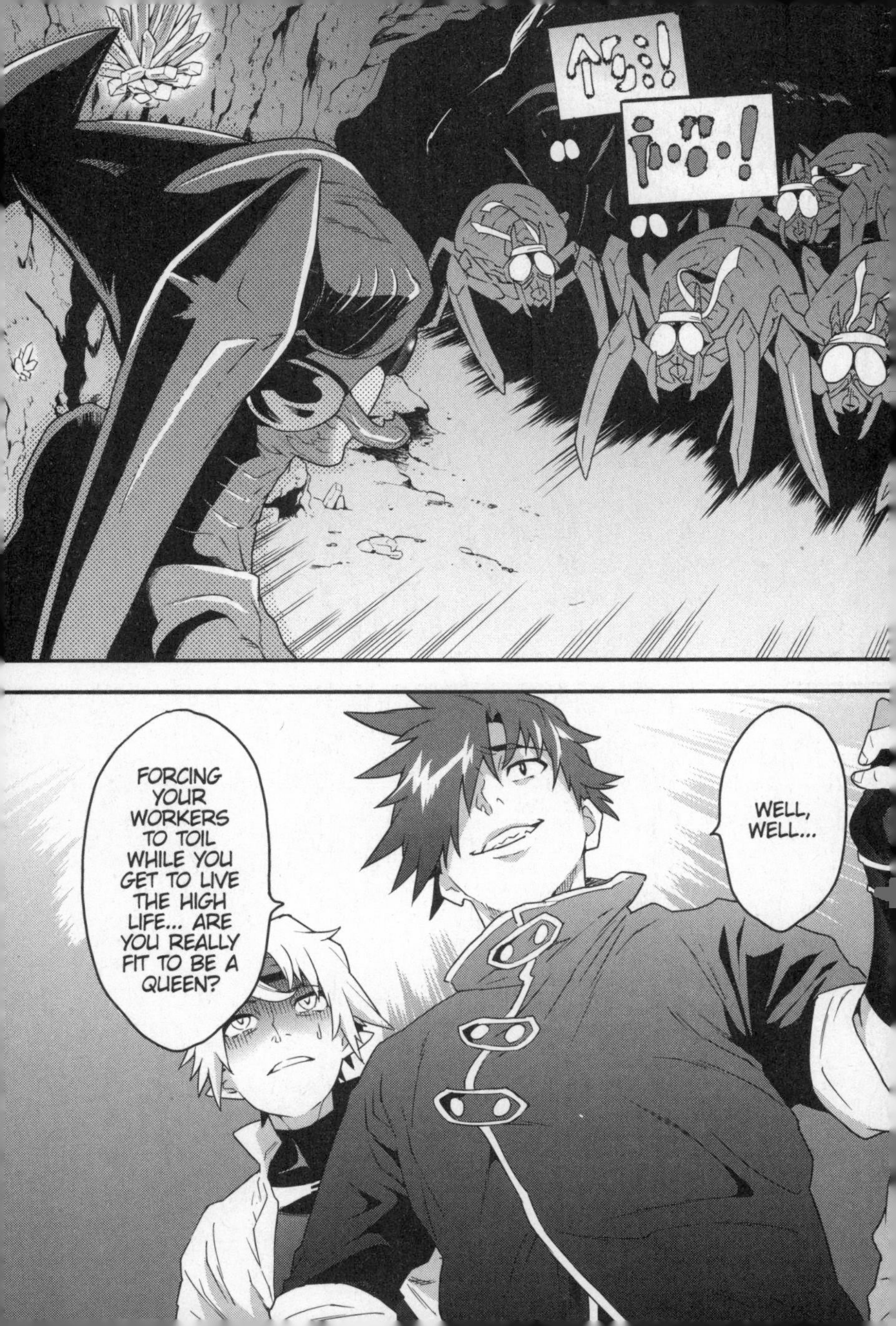
WELL, WELL...
FORCING YOUR WORKERS TO TOIL WHILE YOU GET TO LIVE THE HIGH LIFE... ARE YOU REALLY FIT TO BE A QUEEN?

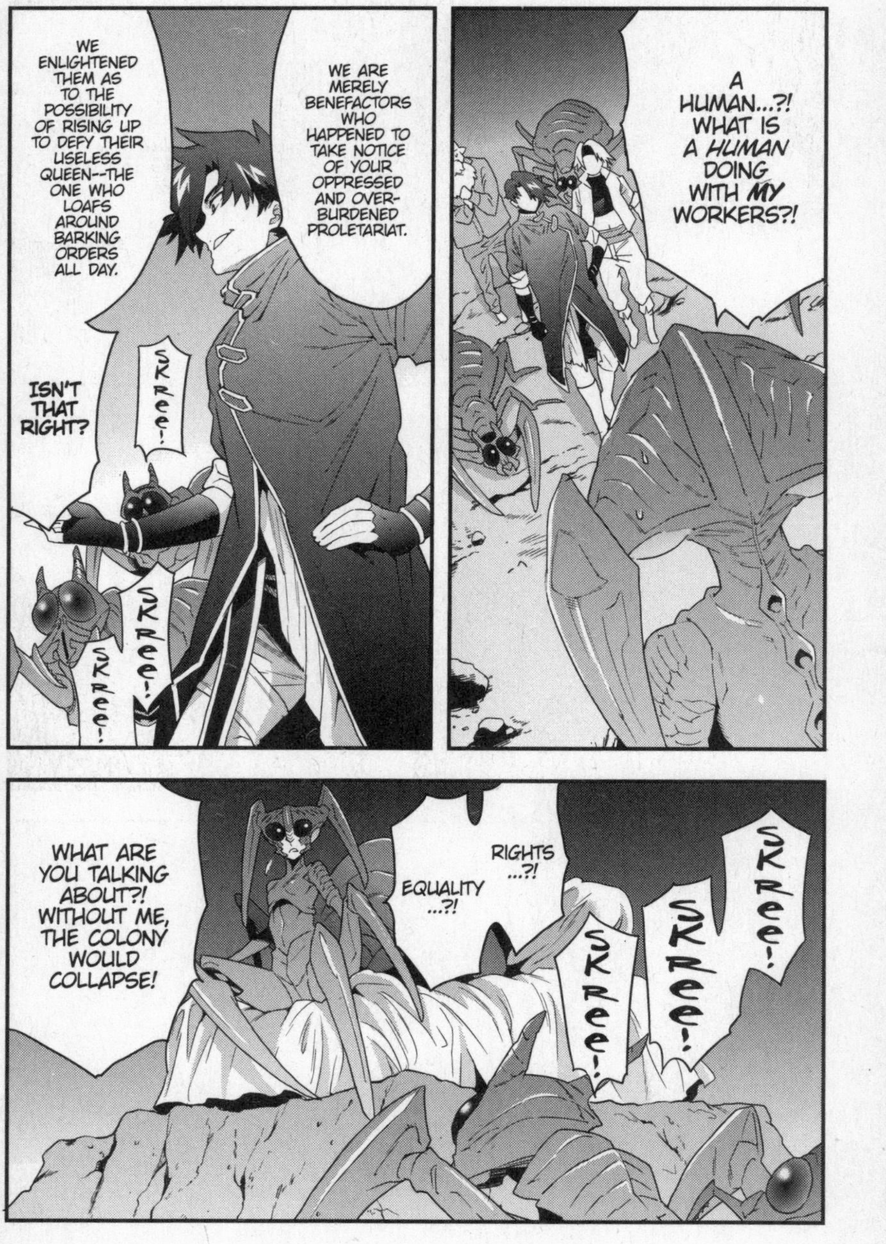
A HUMAN...?! WHAT IS A *HUMAN* DOING WITH **MY** WORKERS?!
WE ARE MERELY BENEFACTORS WHO HAPPENED TO TAKE NOTICE OF YOUR OPPRESSED AND OVER-BURDENED PROLETARIAT.
WE ENLIGHTENED THEM AS TO THE POSSIBILITY OF RISING UP TO DEFY THEIR USELESS QUEEN--THE ONE WHO LOAFS AROUND BARKING ORDERS ALL DAY.
SKree!
ISN'T THAT RIGHT?
SKree!
SKree!
SKree!
SKree!
SKree!
RIGHTS ...?!
EQUALITY ...?!
WHAT ARE YOU TALKING ABOUT?! WITHOUT ME, THE COLONY WOULD COLLAPSE!

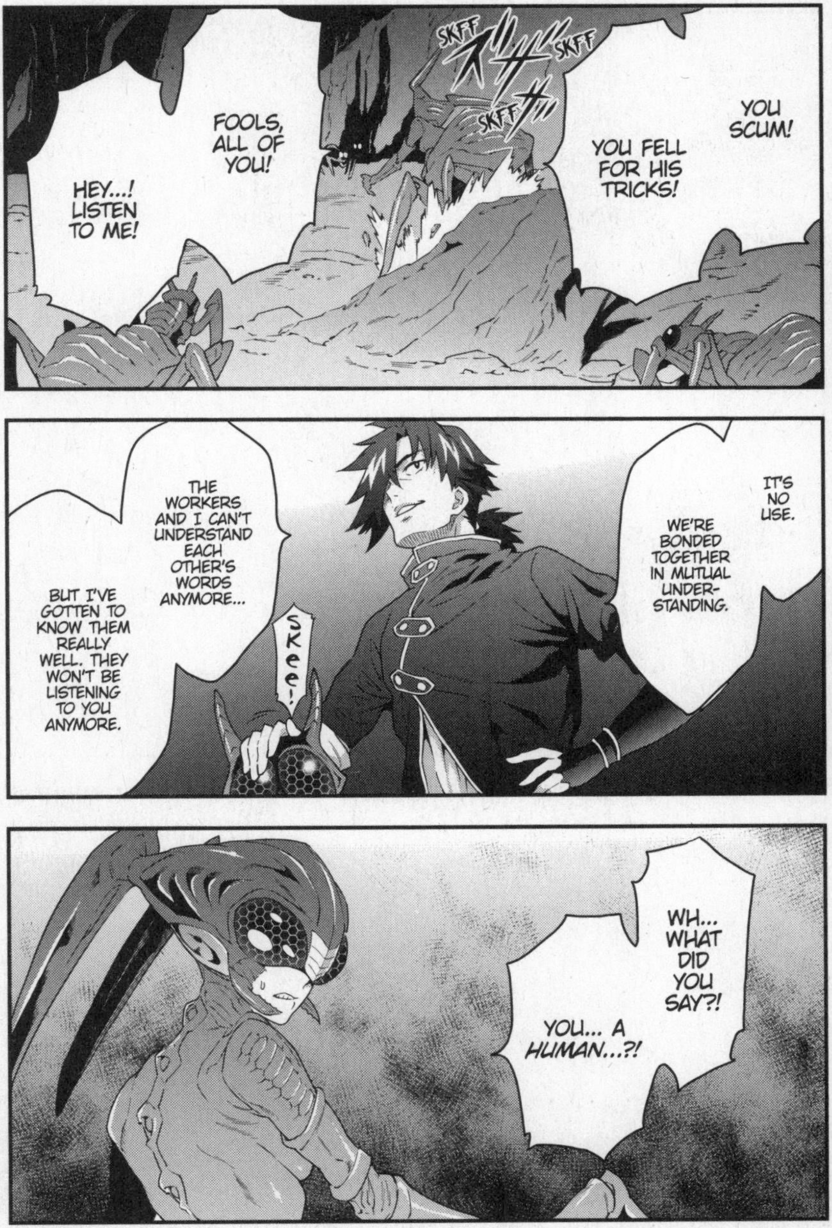
YOU SCUM!
YOU FELL FOR HIS TRICKS!
SKFF
SKFF
SKFF
FOOLS, ALL OF YOU!
HEY...! LISTEN TO ME!
IT'S NO USE.
WE'RE BONDED TOGETHER IN MUTUAL UNDER-STANDING.
Skee!
THE WORKERS AND I CAN'T UNDERSTAND EACH OTHER'S WORDS ANYMORE...
BUT I'VE GOTTEN TO KNOW THEM REALLY WELL. THEY WON'T BE LISTENING TO YOU ANYMORE.
WH... WHAT DID YOU SAY?!
YOU... A HUMAN...?!

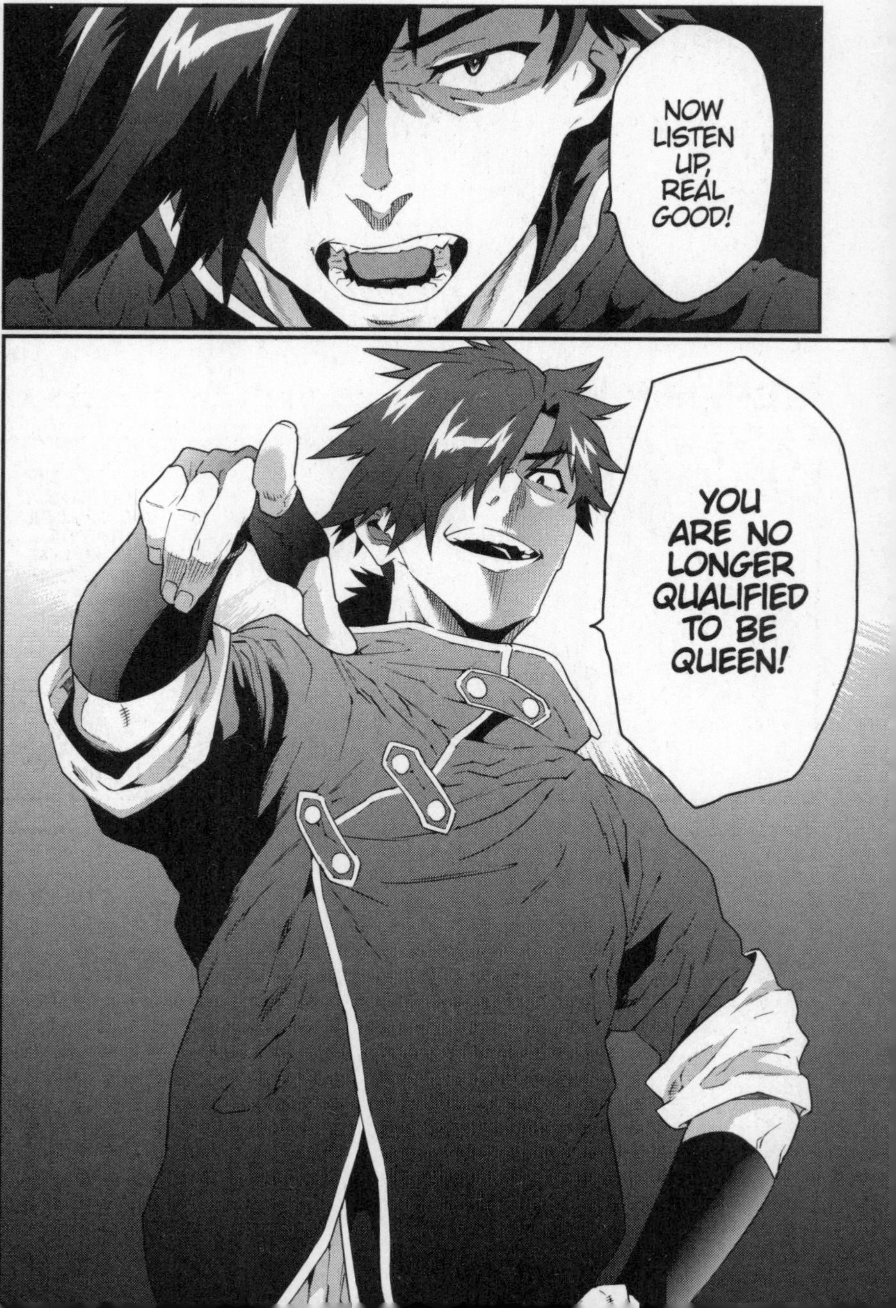
NOW LISTEN UP, REAL GOOD!
YOU ARE NO LONGER QUALIFIED TO BE QUEEN!

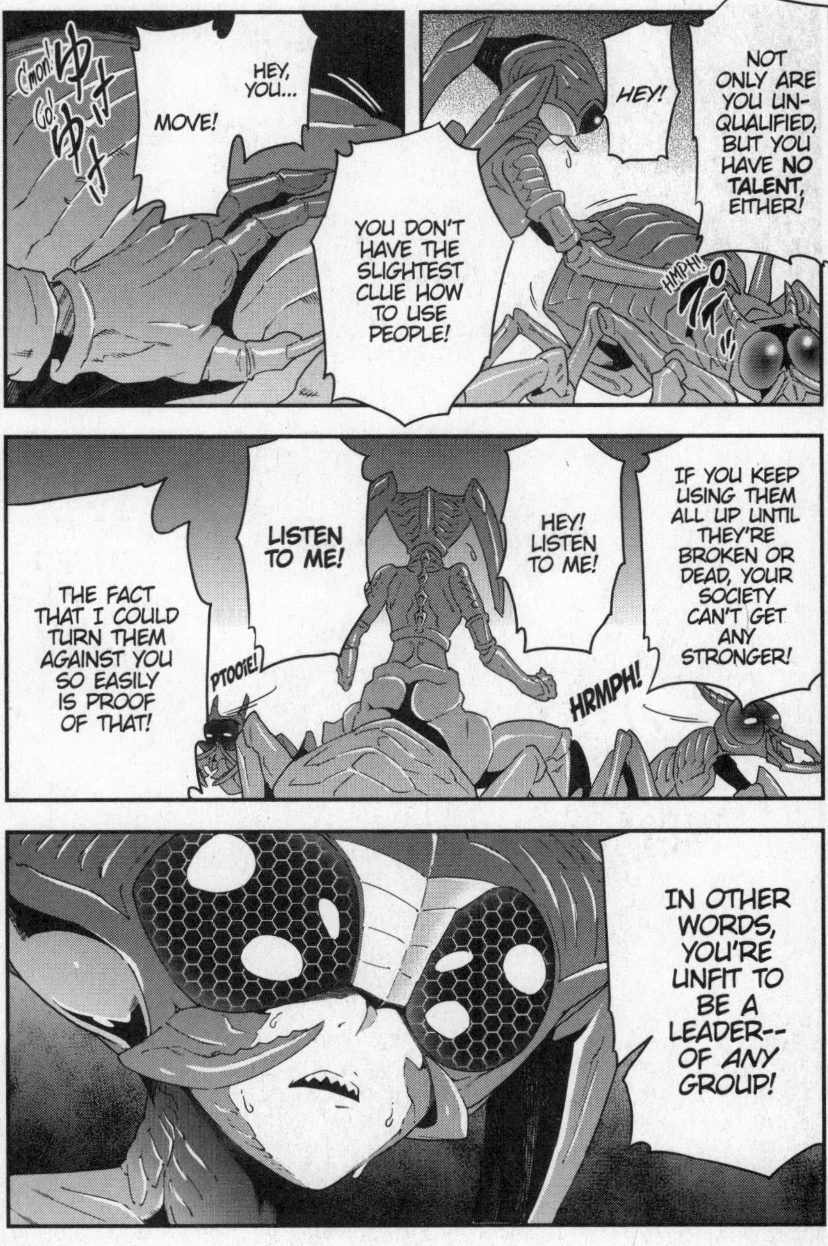
NOT ONLY ARE YOU UN-QUALIFIED, BUT YOU HAVE NO TALENT, EITHER!
HEY!
HMPH!
HEY, YOU...
MOVE!
C'mon! Go! ゆけゆけ
YOU DON'T HAVE THE SLIGHTEST CLUE HOW TO USE PEOPLE!
IF YOU KEEP USING THEM ALL UP UNTIL THEY'RE BROKEN OR DEAD, YOUR SOCIETY CAN'T GET ANY STRONGER!
HEY! LISTEN TO ME!
LISTEN TO ME!
HRMPH!
THE FACT THAT I COULD TURN THEM AGAINST YOU SO EASILY IS PROOF OF THAT!
PTOOIE!
IN OTHER WORDS, YOU'RE UNFIT TO BE A LEADER-- OF ANY GROUP!

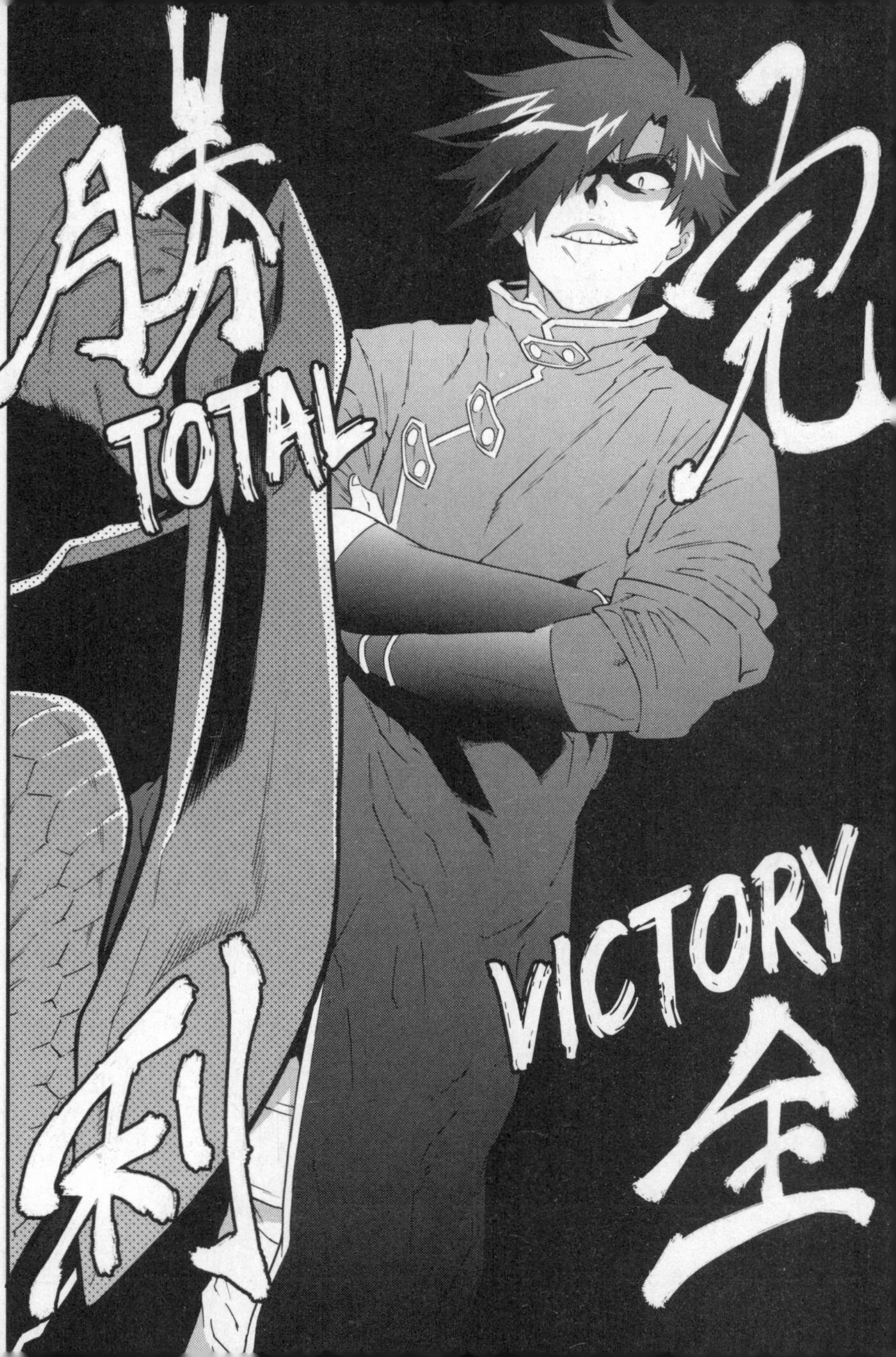
完
全
勝
利
TOTAL
VICTORY

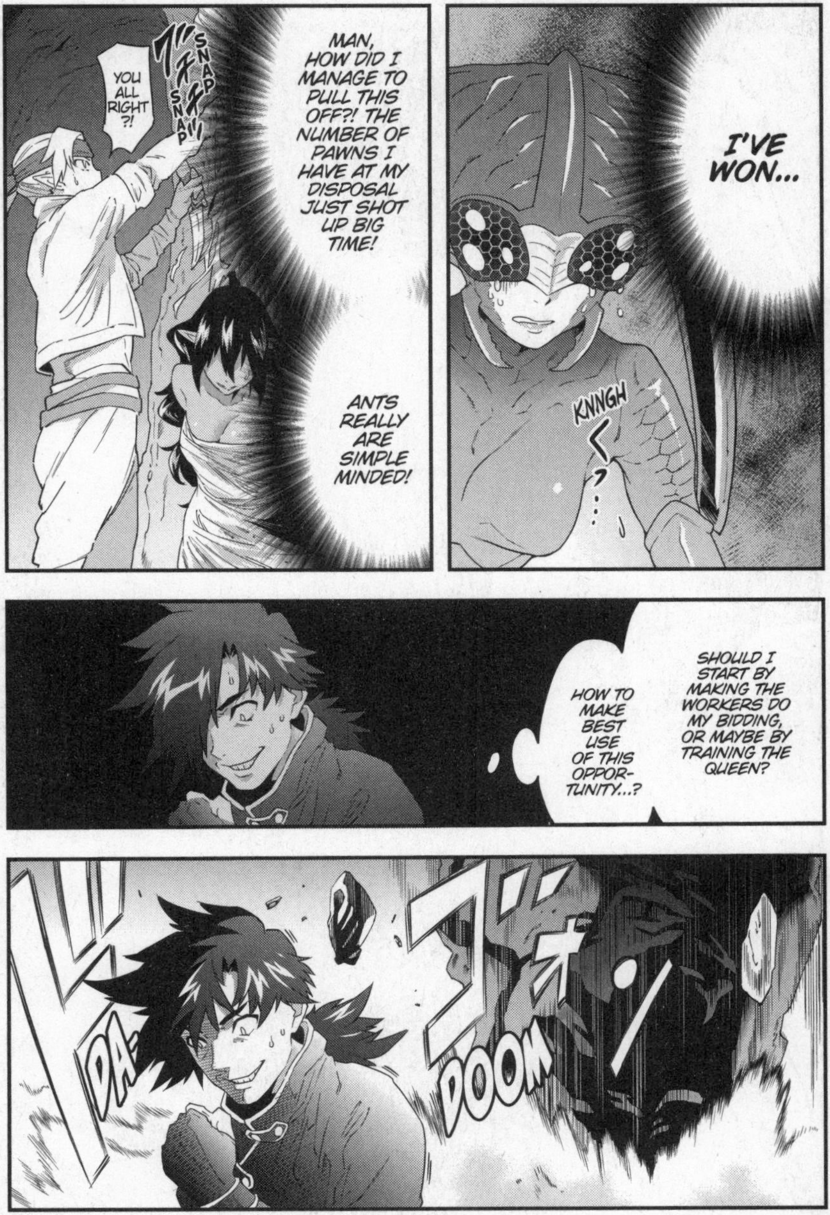
I'VE WON...
KNNGH
MAN, HOW DID I MANAGE TO PULL THIS OFF?! THE NUMBER OF PAWNS I HAVE AT MY DISPOSAL JUST SHOT UP BIG TIME!
SNAP SNAP
YOU ALL RIGHT?!
ANTS REALLY ARE SIMPLE MINDED!
SHOULD I START BY MAKING THE WORKERS DO MY BIDDING, OR MAYBE BY TRAINING THE QUEEN?
HOW TO MAKE BEST USE OF THIS OPPOR-TUNITY...?
DOOM
DA-

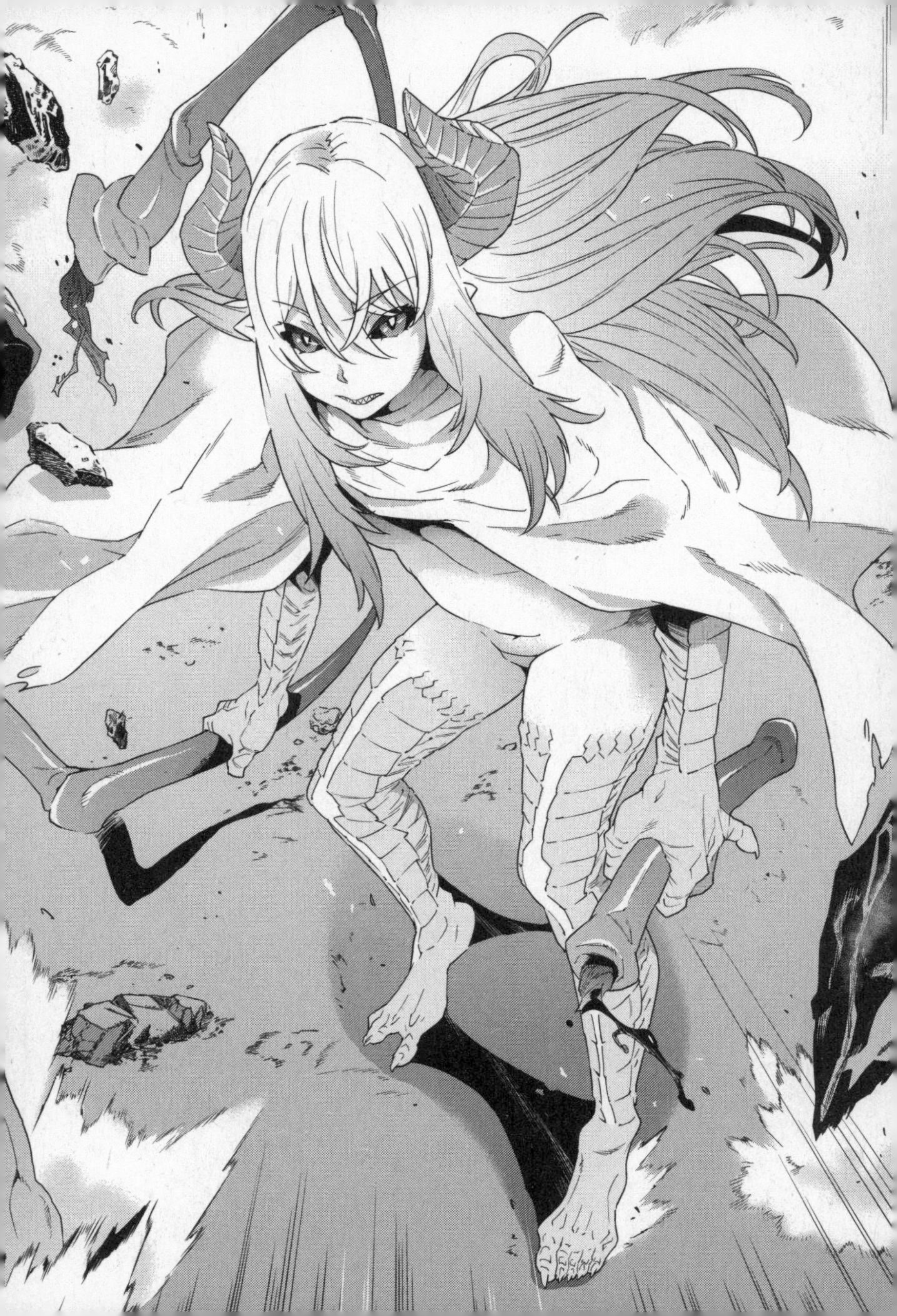

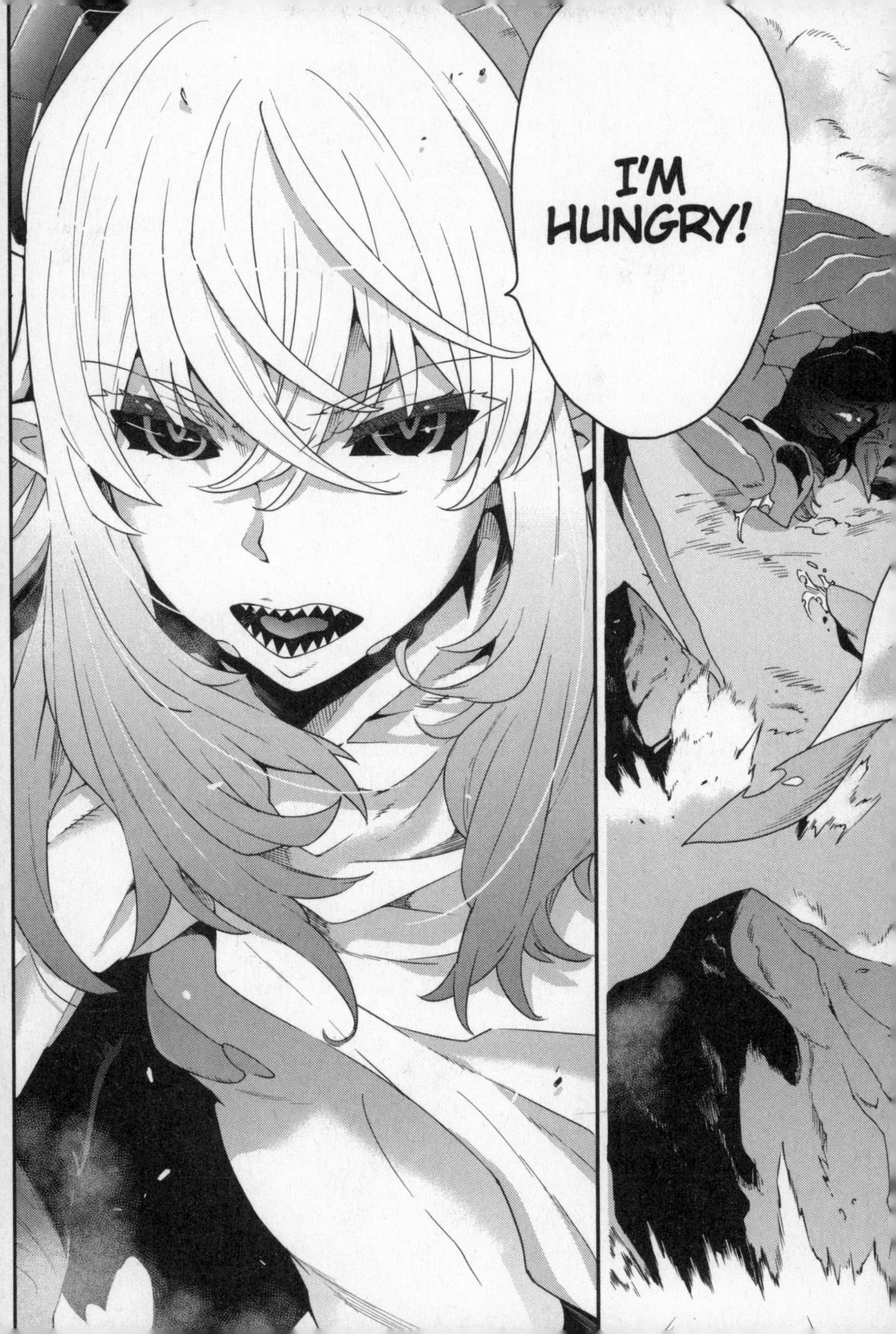
I'M HUNGRY!

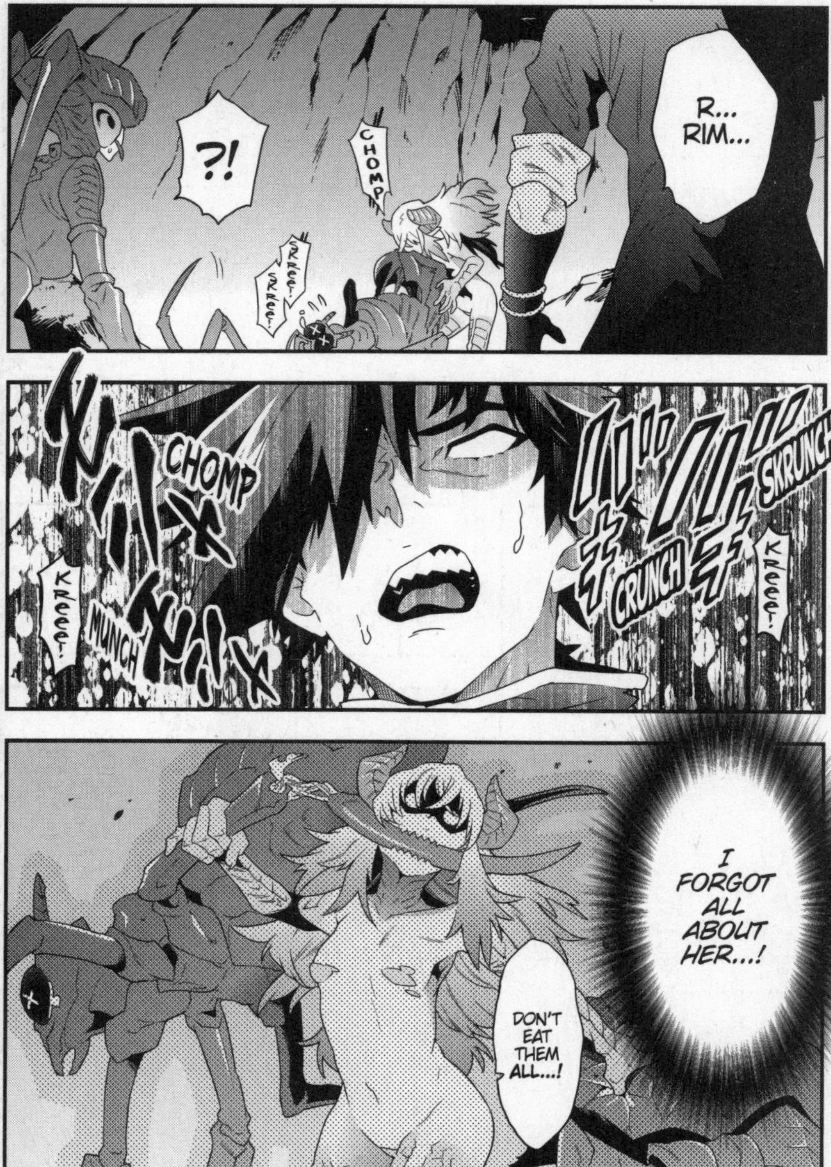
R... RIM...
CHOMP
Skree! Skree!
?!
SKRUNCH
Kreee!
CRUNCH
CHOMP
MUNCH
Kreee!
I FORGOT ALL ABOUT HER...!
DON'T EAT THEM ALL...!

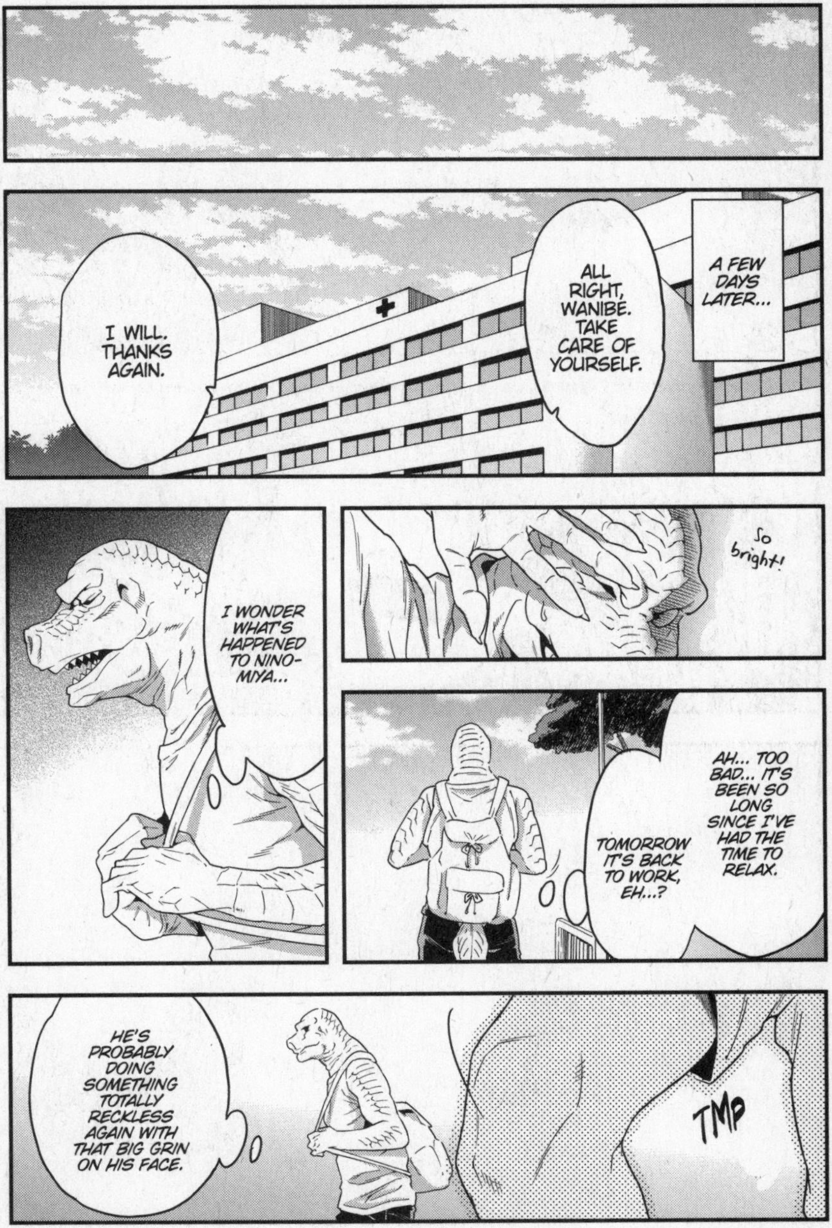
A FEW DAYS LATER...
ALL RIGHT, WANIBE. TAKE CARE OF YOURSELF.
I WILL. THANKS AGAIN.
So bright!
AH... TOO BAD... IT'S BEEN SO LONG SINCE I'VE HAD THE TIME TO RELAX.
TOMORROW IT'S BACK TO WORK, EH...?
I WONDER WHAT'S HAPPENED TO NINO-MIYA...
TMP
HE'S PROBABLY DOING SOMETHING TOTALLY RECKLESS AGAIN WITH THAT BIG GRIN ON HIS FACE.

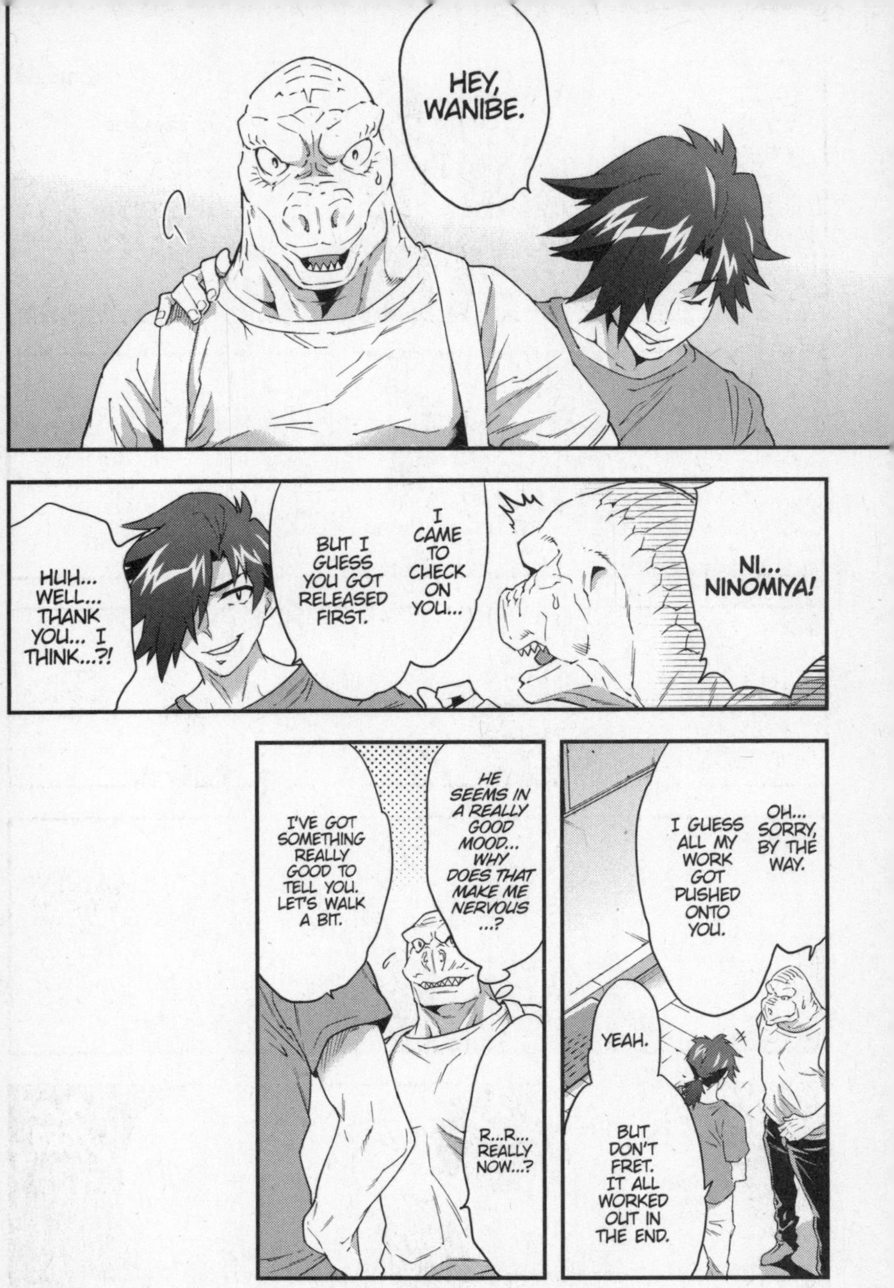
HEY, WANIBE.
NI... NINOMIYA!
I CAME TO CHECK ON YOU...
BUT I GUESS YOU GOT RELEASED FIRST.
HUH... WELL... THANK YOU... I THINK...?!
OH... SORRY, BY THE WAY.
I GUESS ALL MY WORK GOT PUSHED ONTO YOU.
YEAH.
BUT DON'T FRET. IT ALL WORKED OUT IN THE END.
HE SEEMS IN A REALLY GOOD MOOD... WHY DOES THAT MAKE ME NERVOUS ...?
I'VE GOT SOMETHING REALLY GOOD TO TELL YOU. LET'S WALK A BIT.
R...R... REALLY NOW...?

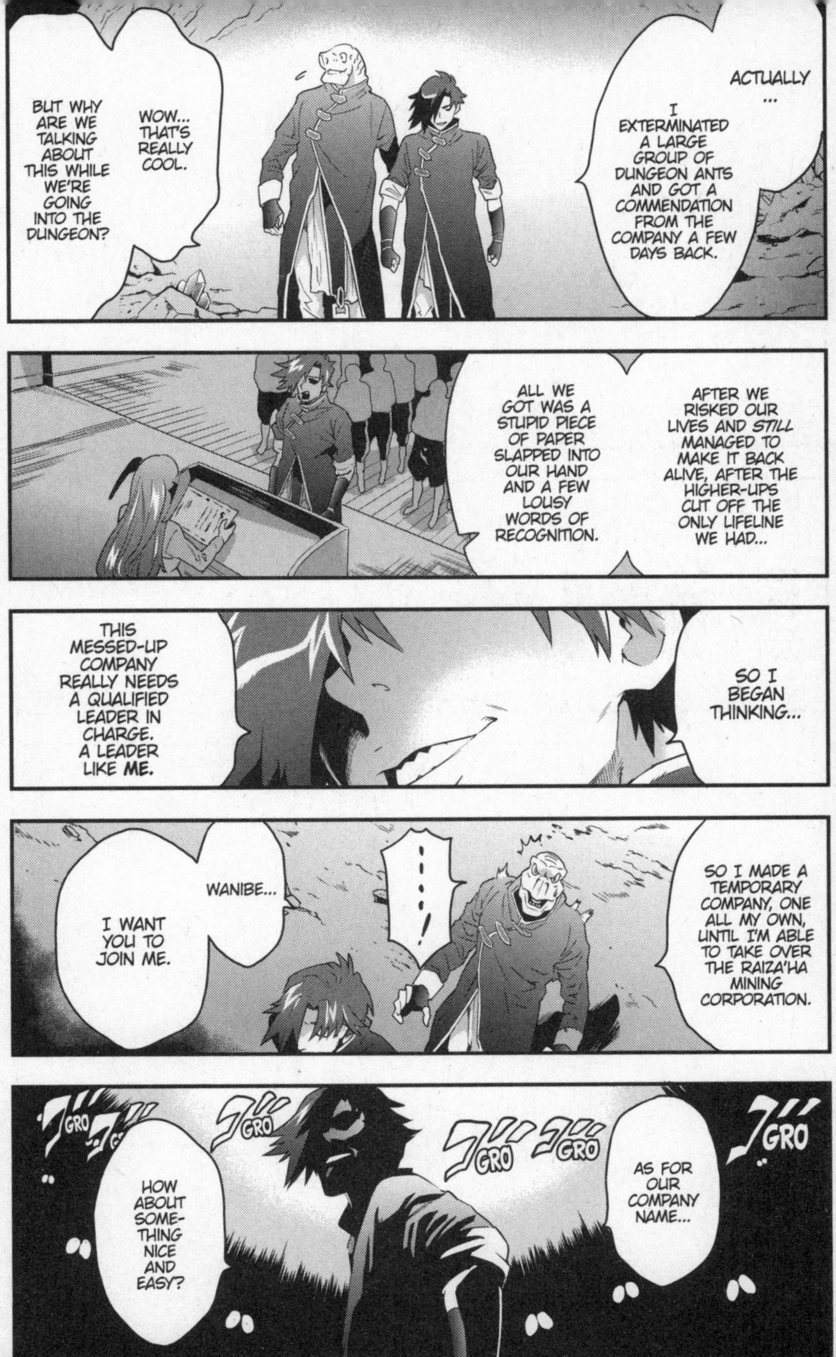
ACTUALLY...
I EXTERMINATED A LARGE GROUP OF DUNGEON ANTS AND GOT A COMMENDATION FROM THE COMPANY A FEW DAYS BACK.
WOW... THAT'S REALLY COOL.
BUT WHY ARE WE TALKING ABOUT THIS WHILE WE'RE GOING INTO THE DUNGEON?
AFTER WE RISKED OUR LIVES AND STILL MANAGED TO MAKE IT BACK ALIVE, AFTER THE HIGHER-UPS CUT OFF THE ONLY LIFELINE WE HAD...
ALL WE GOT WAS A STUPID PIECE OF PAPER SLAPPED INTO OUR HAND AND A FEW LOUSY WORDS OF RECOGNITION.
SO I BEGAN THINKING...
THIS MESSED-UP COMPANY REALLY NEEDS A QUALIFIED LEADER IN CHARGE. A LEADER LIKE ME.
SO I MADE A TEMPORARY COMPANY, ONE ALL MY OWN, UNTIL I'M ABLE TO TAKE OVER THE RAIZA'HA MINING CORPORATION.
...!
WANIBE...
I WANT YOU TO JOIN ME.
GRO
GRO
GRO
GRO
GRO
AS FOR OUR COMPANY NAME...
HOW ABOUT SOMETHING NICE AND EASY?

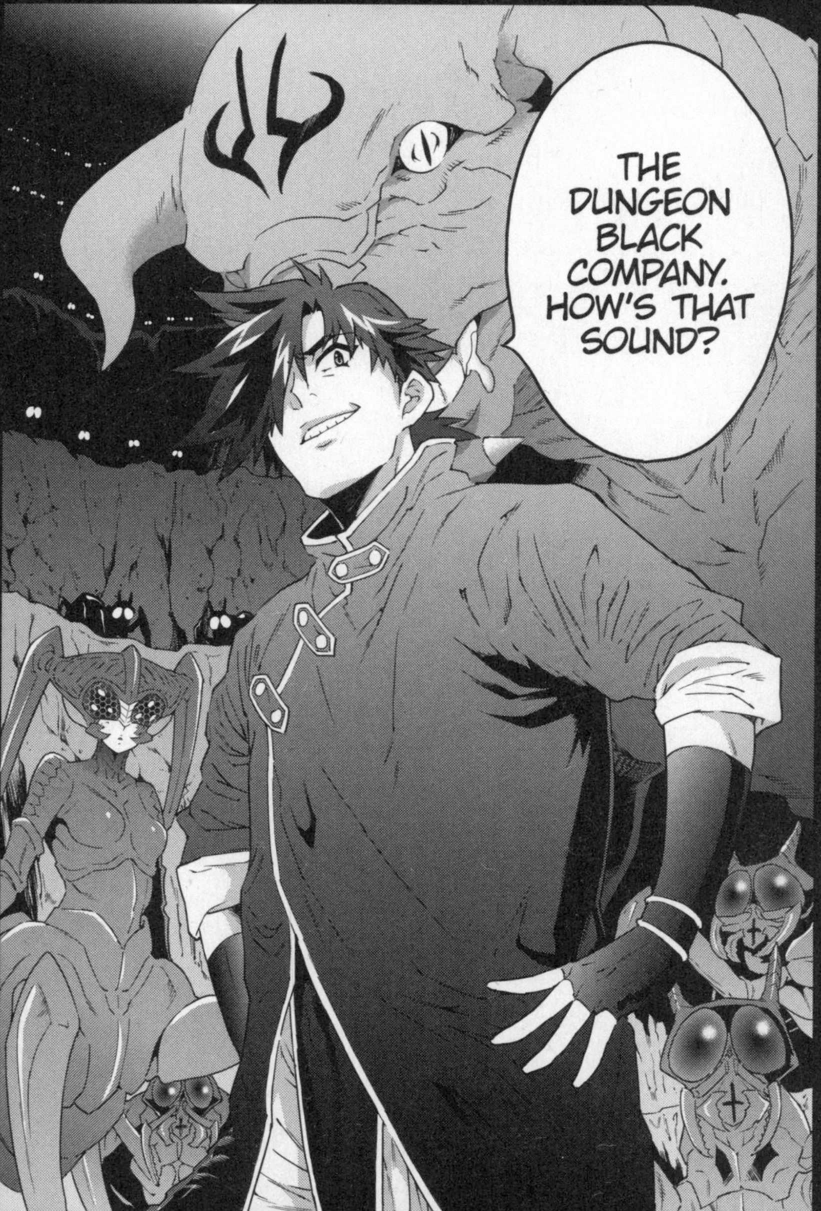
THE DUNGEON BLACK COMPANY. HOW'S THAT SOUND?

The Dungeon of Black Company Vol. 1 – END

THE DUNGEON OF
BLACK COMPANY

SEVEN SEAS ENTERTAINMENT PRESENTS

THE DUNGEON OF
BLACK COMPANY Vol. 1

story and art by YOUHEI YASUMURA

TRANSLATION
Wesley Bridges

LETTERING AND RETOUCH
Meaghan Tucker

COVER DESIGN
KC Fabellon

PROOFREADER
Tom Speelman
Stephanie Cohen

EDITOR
J.P. Sullivan

PRODUCTION ASSISTANT
CK Russell

PRODUCTION MANAGER
Lissa Pattillo

EDITOR-IN-CHIEF
Adam Arnold

PUBLISHER
Jason DeAngelis

ISBN: 978-1-626927-98-8

Printed in Canada

First Printing: May 2018

10 9 8 7 6 5 4 3 2 1

FOLLOW US ONLINE: *www.sevenseasentertainment.com*

READING DIRECTIONS

This book reads from ***right to left***, Japanese style.
If this is your first time reading manga, you start
reading from the top right panel on each page and
take it from there. If you get lost, just follow the
numbered diagram here. It may seem backwards at
first, but you'll get the hang of it! Have fun!!

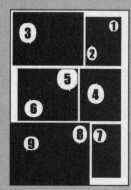